THE CREATION OF THE MODERN GERMAN ARMY

Monographs in German History

CONTENTS

LIST OF ABBREVIATIONS

Archives

BA-K: Bundesarchiv, Koblenz
BA-MA: Bundesarchiv-Militärchiv, Freiburg
BArch: Bundesarchiv, Lichterfelde
BHStA: Bayerisches Hauptstaatsarchiv
BKA: Bayerisches Kriegsarchiv
GLAK: Generallandesarchiv, Karlsruhe
HStASt: Hauptstaatsarchiv, Stuttgart
MAE: Ministère des affaires étrangères, Paris
PA-AA: Politisches Archiv, Auswärtiges Amt

Journals

CEH: *Central European History*
HJ: *Historical Journal*
HZ: *Historische Zeitschrift*
GG: *Geschichte und Gesellschaft*
GH: *German History*
JCH: *Journal of Contemporary History*
JMH: *Journal of Modern History*
LBIYB: *Leo Baeck International Yearbook*
MgM: *Militärgeschichtliche Mitteilungen*
VfZ: *Vierteljahrshefte für Zeitgeschichte*

Political terms

DDP: German Democratic Party
DNVP: German Nationalist People's Party
DVP: German People's Party
KPD: Communist Party
IMCC: Inter-Allied Military Control Commission
SPD: Socialist Party

Acknowledgements

Since starting this project as a postgraduate thesis I have received help from many quarters. Grants from the British Humanities Research Board, the German Academic Exchange Service, the Robert Gardiner Scholarship, the Sir John Plumb Fund for young historians, the Cambridge European Trust and University College, Dublin have made possible trips to numerous archives and libraries in Germany. I would like to thank the archivists at Bundesarchiv, Koblenz; Bundesarchiv-Militärarchiv, Freiburg; Bundesarchiv, Lichterfelde; Bayerisches Hauptstaatsarchiv; Bayerisches Kriegsarchiv; Generallandesarchiv, Karlsruhe; Hauptstaatsarchiv, Stuttgart; Ministère des affaires étrangères, Paris; and Politisches Archiv, Auswärtiges Amt.

On my trips to Germany, I was fortunate to stay with friends who turned otherwise lonely research trips into enjoyable visits. I would like to thank Danny Dolan (Frankfurt), Hugh Eakin and Alisa Roth (Berlin), and Guy Russ (Regensburg) for their hospitality and good humour. For a number of years I have been able to present and test my research at various seminars and I wish to express my gratitude to Professor Chris Andrew, Professor T. C. W. Blanning, Professor David Reynolds and Dr Robert Tombs (University of Cambridge); Mr Anthony Nicholls and Professor Hartmut Pogge von Strandmann (University of Oxford); Professor John Horne and Dr Alan Kramer (Trinity College, Dublin). I have also benefitted from the advice and criticisms of Professor Richard Bessel, Dr Chris Clarke and Professor Jay Winter. Dr Brendan Simms, who supervised my doctoral thesis, has been extremely generous in his advice long after his official duties were over. Without his comments, this book would have been far poorer. I cannot hold anyone other than myself responsible for the remaining errors.

For the past three years, I have lectured at University College, Dublin, and I am grateful for the encouragement of staff and students, without which the writing of this book would have been a far more difficult task.

My deepest debt of gratitude is to my parents, Deirdre and Herbert Mulligan, who have supported me in many different ways over the years. This book is dedicated to them.

William Mulligan, Dublin, August 2003.

Chapter 1

INTRODUCTION

*I*n general surveys of the Weimar Republic, the figure of General Walther Reinhardt appears at two points – as the quixotic opponent of the treaty of Versailles, who advocated continuing the war on German territory in order to save the honour of a nation, and as the one honourable general who sought to rally the *Reichswehr* behind the government during the Kapp Putsch in March 1920.[1] He is then ushered off the stage. Yet Reinhardt is a significant figure in the history of the *Reichswehr*, and – as this study will argue – the most significant figure between November 1918 and March 1920. After resigning in the aftermath of the Kapp Putsch, he continued to serve in the army until 1927, and after he left the army he lectured on military affairs to young officers in Berlin. He has been overshadowed by his successor as head of the army command (*Chef der Heeresleitung*), Hans von Seeckt, by his fellow Württemberger, Wilhelm Groener, and by the *éminence grise* of the Weimar republic, Kurt von Schleicher, all of whom have rightly received substantial attention from historians of the period.[2]

This study is concerned principally with the period between November 1918 and March 1920, when Reinhardt was the officer responsible for the transition to the peacetime army. During this period as head of the Demobilization Department in November and December 1918, as Prussian Minister of War from January 1919 until October 1919, and finally as *Chef der Heeresleitung* from October 1919 until the Kapp Putsch

---

1. See for example, Detlev Peukert, *The Weimar Republic. The Crisis of Classical Modernity*, London, 1991, 69; Heinrich August Winkler, *Weimar, 1918-1933. Die Geschichte der ersten deutschen Demokratie*, Munich, 1993.

2. Gerhard Rakenius, *Wilhelm Groener als erster Generalquartiermeister. Die Politik der Obersten Heeresleitung*, Boppard am Rhein, 1977; Hans Meier-Welcker, *Seeckt*, Frankfurt, 1967; Johannes Hürter, *Wilhelm Groener. Reichswehrminister am Ende der Weimarer Republik*, Munich, 1993; Claus Guske, *Das politische Denken von des Generals von Seeckt. Ein Beitrag zur Diskussion des Verhältnisses Seeckt-Reichswehr-Republik*, Lübeck, Hamburg, 1971; Friedrich-Karl von Plehwe, *Reichskanzler Kurt von Schleicher. Weimars letzte Chance gegen Hitler*, Esslingen, 1983.

in March 1920, Reinhardt established the institutional framework for the new *Reichswehr*. He undermined the soldiers' councils, he established the regulations on service within the *Reichswehr*, he centralised the military ministries of the individual states, and he set up the structures of the *Reichswehrministerium*. He was also a central figure in the two major dramas of the period, the debate over the Versailles treaty and the Kapp Putsch. After resigning as *Chef der Heeresleitung* in March 1920 he became commander of *Wehrkreis V* in Stuttgart. In this capacity he exercised plenipotentiary powers in the state of emergency in 1923 and sent the *Reichswehr* into Thuringia, effectively overthrowing the KPD-SPD coalition. Before his death in 1930 he was involved in important national debates on military policy and he gave courses on military thought to young officers in the late 1920s. He had as varied a career as any of his peers, and he left an important legacy in terms of ideas and institutions.

Even contemporaries who recognised his contribution to the establishment of the *Reichswehr* after 1918 acknowledged that he did not figure in the public's pantheon of famous generals. In February 1934 General Werner von Fritsch, newly appointed *Chef der Heeresleitung*, recalled his predecessors, Generals Kurt von Hammerstein, Wilhelm Heye and Hans von Seeckt, names familiar to the public. He continued: 'One name is missing, that of an exceptional man who was there at the beginning, of whose work the public does not know all that much, but whose imperishable service will always remain, the founder of the post-war German army: General Reinhardt.'[3] In 1936, Reinhardt's successor as commander of 5th Division, General Hahn wrote 'that the contributions of General Reinhardt to the creation of the army are not even known, much less even acknowledged.'[4] Georg Wetzell, the editor of *Das Militärwochenblatt*, agreed that while 'within the army [his achievements] may be known', his name had passed the public by.[5]

Reinhardt, in fact, was regarded by those who knew him as one of the central figures during the revolutionary period. Hermann Metz, who sat on the Preliminary Commission for the Peacetime Army (*Vorkommission für das Friedensheer*) which drew up the regulations on service for the *Reichswehr*, wrote after the Second World War:

> It fell to the then Minister of War, General Reinhardt, to lay the basis for the new army. He is the creator of the army, not General von Seeckt, as people now believe. The latter was its designer and trainer. Rabenau's books on Seeckt have too much influence on the historiography of this period. Reinhardt gets too little attention. Reinhardt was not much liked by Seeckt, Groener or Loßberg, but he had great prestige within the officer corps.[6]

3. HStASt M 660/034, Bü 54, newspaper cutting, dated 1 February 1934.
4. HStASt M 660/014 Heft 54, Hahn to Wetzell, 6 February 1936.
5. HStASt M 660/011 Heft 51, Wetzell to Hahn, 12 February 1936.
6. BA-MA RW 1/13, Hermann Metz to the *Bundesarchiv*, 4 September 1955.

His adjutant, Fleck, credited him with finding the 'right path' for military policy in 1919.[7] Wilhelm Heye, who had been *Chef der Heeresleitung* between 1926 and 1930, claimed in a draft biography written in 1942 that Reinhardt 'laid the groundwork for Seeckt and Hitler', though he later returned to this passage and crossed out 'Hitler'.[8] Wolfram Wette, in his biography of Gustav Noske, the SPD *Reichswehrminister* during Reinhardt's period as Prussian Minister of War and *Chef der Heeresleitung*, partly concurred with these judgements and called him 'the spiritual father of the temporary *Reichswehr* law', which laid the basis for the establishment of the post-war army.[9]

Heye's amendment is symptomatic of a wider confusion about the nature of Reinhardt's contribution to the history of the Weimar Republic and the German military.[10] In the January 1936 issue of *Wehrfront*, a Nazi-backed military magazine with a circulation of 150,000, one Johannes Häußler argued that Germany had been defeated in 1918 because of a Jewish-Bolshevist plot, which aided their materialistic western allies. Moreover:

> the mutineers' government, but above all General Reinhardt (who is not to be confused with the *Freikorps* leader Colonel Reinhard, now leader of the *Kyffhäuser* League), were completely under the influence of the Central Soldiers' Council. With his decrees and regulations he hastened the collapse of the demobilized army; among other things he decreed the destruction of the imperial badges of rank and the political surveillance of the officers of the old army.

In the face of 'persecution and treachery' German nationalist groups had to set up volunteer units to fight further left-wing uprisings. It was these *Freikorps* groups which kept alive the spirit of national liberation from Jewish Bolshevism, while men like Reinhardt sacrificed principles in order to further their careers.[11] Häußler's condemnation of Reinhardt repeated many of the arguments that officers who refused to come to terms with the political reality of the Weimar Republic used against him in early 1919. In some respects it was a negative interpretation of Reinhardt as the general who supported the Republic. Within the context of military policy in the 1930s it was also a forlorn attempt to claim the military tradition for the *Freikorps* over the professional officer corps whom Hitler had flattered as 'the second pillar of the state.'

7. Cited in Fritz Ernst, 'Aus dem Nachlaß des Generals Walther Reinhardt', *Die Welt als Geschichte*, 18, 1958, 95.
8. BA-MA N 18/4, 'Lebenserrinerungen des Generaloberst Wilhelm Heye. Teil II, Wie ich den Weltkrieg erlebte, 1914–1942', fos. 221–22; Heye's phrase was 'Vorarbeiter Seeckts und Hitlers'.
9. Wolfram Wette, *Gustav Noske. Eine politische Biographie*, Düsseldorf, 1988, 358.
10. On views of the *Reichswehr* in the Third Reich see Markus Pöhlmann, *Kriegsgeschichte und Geschichtspolitik: der Erste Weltkrieg. Die amtliche deutsche Militärgeschichtsschreibung 1914–1956*, Paderborn, 2002, 220–27.
11. Johannes Häußler, 'Wie die Freikorps entstanden', *Wehrfront*, 1 January 1936.

Hahn was quick to counter Häußler's view of Reinhardt. Reinhardt, he claimed, was not an opportunist but a realist who dealt effectively with a difficult situation after the war. Reinhardt had the 'capacity for work and skill' necessary for the task of demobilization which was his first post after the war. As Prussian Minister of War he 'carried out the duties and tasks given to him in the [revolutionary] political environment, in order to rescue what was possible in the interests of the army. ... His straightforward manner and his great expert knowledge gained him general respect.' Hahn concluded that Reinhardt had laid the basis for Seeckt's later work, and therefore he stood 'at the beginning of the history of our young army.'[12] However Hahn's piece was not published by either *Wehrfront* or *Das Militärwochenblatt*. Instead the Commander of the Wehrmacht, Werner von Blomberg, who had been a close colleague of Reinhardt in Stuttgart in the first half of the 1920s, promised to write an article countering Häußler's accusations. In 1942, on the seventieth anniversary of Reinhardt's birth, one Colonel Scherff republished one of Reinhardt's essays, 'Führer- und Feldherrntum'. Scherff prefaced the article by claiming that Reinhardt's views on leadership in war were 'confirmed by today's events and the military leadership personality of the Führer, Adolf Hitler.'[13] Rather than betraying the German military tradition, Scherff argued that Reinhardt had preserved it until it could flourish in the Third Reich.

Some on the left of the political spectrum might have agreed with this assessment of Reinhardt, although views were divided. In an early biography of Schleicher, two socialist writers, Kurt Caro and Walter Oehme, described Reinhardt as a 'thoroughly loyal officer' whose 'heart belonged to the new state'.[14] Reinhardt's arguments in favour of resisting the military units involved in the Kapp Putsch consecrated his reputation as a loyal supporter of the Republic, and has continued to influence historical assessments of his character.[15] But during the 1920s this reputation was undermined. Reinhardt played an important role in forcing the collapse of the Thuringian KPD-SPD coalition government in 1923, he attacked the DDP and SPD for their military policies, and a series of rumours linked him to right-wing paramilitary groups. In early September 1930, just weeks before the election, which saw the Nazis become the second largest party in the *Reichstag*, the German pacifist Carl von Ossietzky lamented the generals' lack of loyalty to the Republic, but he argued that it was not unsurprising since the case of Reinhardt had shown that loyalty

---

12. HStASt M 660/014 Heft 54, unpublished manuscript by Hahn, entitled 'General der Infanterie Walther Reinhardt. Eine Richtigstellung.'
13. Colonel Scherff, 'General der Infanterie Walther Reinhardt zum Gedächtnis', *Militärwissen-schaftliche Rundschau*, 1942, 90.
14. Kurt Caro, Walter Oehme, *Schleichers Aufstieg. Ein Beitrag zur Geschichte der Gegenrevolution*, Berlin, 1933, 58, 96.
15. Peukert, *Weimar*, 69.

was repaid with dismissal and relative obscurity. He concluded that 'in his anger [Reinhardt] went to the other side; he died as a convinced supporter of the radical right. That is how one demonstrates to the young lieutenant that loyalty does not pay. So one shows those with good will that they have no prospects.'[16]

After the war, Theodor Heuss, the first President of the Federal Republic, invoked Reinhardt as part of a positive German military tradition during a speech at the *Führungsakademie* in 1959. He had known Reinhardt in the late 1920s when they had both taught at the *Hochschule für Politik*, and Heuss admired his teaching style and his historical knowledge. However, he still felt that he had to explain Reinhardt's rôle during the German revolution. In his view, Reinhardt became Prussian Minister of War 'not because he was a revolutionary, but because there had to be somebody, who would risk his life and his reputation, who had courage and understanding.'[17] This was similar to Hahn's characterisation of Reinhardt as a selfless and pragmatic officer and patriot. On the other hand it shifted Reinhardt to a new liberal democratic context, instead of placing him in a tradition that led to Hitler's *Wehrmacht*. In short contemporary politics have shaped Reinhardt's historical reputation.

In the two years before Heuss's appearance at the *Führungsakademie* the Heidelberg historian, Fritz Ernst, had rescued Reinhardt from his almost total post-war oblivion. In 1957 he published an article-length biography, and the following year a collection of documents from Reinhardt's *Nachlaß*.[18] It is possible that these publications were intended as precursors to a full-scale biography of Reinhardt, but Ernst died in 1963. Based almost solely on papers in Reinhardt's *Nachlaß*, the two pieces presented a heroic picture of a conservative officer who took up the reins of military policy at a critical moment. Ernst asked pointedly whether any of the officers in the Supreme Command who took Reinhardt to task for a variety of concessions to the new regime could have done any better.[19] Reinhardt was naïve, compared to Groener who displayed a 'mistrust', and therefore could not understand 'what Reinhardt really wanted and what the motives of his actions were.'[20] Ernst accepted Reinhardt's view that the post of Prussian Minster of War was a 'crown of thorns'.[21] In this preliminary work on Reinhardt, Ernst made two important points. First, he argued that Reinhardt was not 'left-leaning', as Groener and other critics in the officer corps asserted, but shared the conservative ethos of

16. *Carl von Ossietzky. Sämtliche Schriften*, eds Barbel Boldt, Ute Maack, Gunther Nickell, 8 vols, Munich, 1994, vol. 5, 438.
17. Theodor Heuss, *Soldatentum in unserer Zeit*, Tübingen, 1959, 27.
18. Ernst, 'Aus dem Nachlaß'; Fritz Ernst, 'Walther Reinhardt (1872–1930)', *Zeitschrift für württembergische Landesgeschichte*, 16, 1957, 331–64.
19. Ibid., 339.
20. Ibid., 345.
21. Ibid., 339.

the officer corps.[22] Second, he recognised the central rôle of the Prussian Ministry of War in the establishment of the new army, an argument which other historians have ignored, as they still concentrate on the activities of the Supreme Command and the *Freikorps*. Ernst's argument presents a more balanced picture of the relationship between the Ministry of War and Supreme Command in 1919.[23]

When Ernst was writing his pieces on Reinhardt, the historiography of the Weimar Republic and the *Reichswehr* was still in its infancy, and it is worth reviewing the development of this historiography before outlining the argument of this book.[24] The earliest historical writings on the *Reichswehr* focused on its loyalty, or lack of it, to the Republic to which it had pledged allegiance. After the Second World War the German army was discredited due to its association with the National Socialist regime. This, combined with the fact that the historiography on the Weimar Republic was primarily concerned with how Hitler came to power in January 1933,[25] prompted historians to look at the rôle of the *Reichswehr*. In an influential study in 1955 by the American historian, Gordon Craig, the German army during the nineteenth and twentieth centuries was portrayed as one of the most effective 'opponents of constitutional reform, liberalism and democracy.'[26] The introduction of parliamentary liberal democracy in 1918, he argued, made little difference to the position of the army in the 'real constitution', and by 1920 it was becoming a 'state within a state.'[27] It is significant that one of the earliest German historians of the *Reichswehr*, Wolfgang Sauer, also tended to see 1920, and the replacement of Reinhardt by Seeckt as *Chef der Heeresleitung*, as a significant turning point in Weimar's civil-military relationship. He argued that the officer corps was broadly split into three groups – a monarchical one under General Walther von Lüttwitz, one willing to accept the new state, represented by Wilhelm Groener and Reinhardt, and one under Seeckt, which followed a policy of *attentisme*, of preserving the army intact until a more "positive" political situation came about. The Kapp Putsch brought the Seeckt group to the fore, and since he moulded *Reichswehr* policy, this non-committal attitude towards the republic prevailed.[28]

22. Ibid., 359–60.
23. Ibid., passim.
24. Eberhard Kolb, *The Weimar Republic*, London, 1988, 154–56; Michael Geyer, 'Die Wehrmacht der deutschen Republik ist die Reichswehr. Bemerkungen zur neueren Literatur', *MgM*, 14, 1973, 152–99.
25. Karl Dietrich Erdmann, 'Die Geschichte der Weimarer Republik als Problem der Wissenschaft', *VfZ*, 3, 1955, 5.
26. Gordon A. Craig, *The Politics of the Prussian Army, 1640–1945*, New York, 1964 edn, xiv.
27. Ibid., 342–43; id, *Germany, 1866–1945*, Oxford, 1978, 396.
28. For an overview of Sauer's work, see his essay in Karl Dietrich Bracher's *Die Auflösung der Weimarer Republik. Eine Studie des Machtverfalls in einer Demokratie*, Düsseldorf, 1984 edn, 205–53.

Since the appearance of Craig's and Sauer's pioneering work in the 1950s the question of the room for manoeuvre (*Handlungsspielraum*) of the period 1918 to 1920 has been scrutinised.[29] Many historians have written pessimistically about the chances of establishing a more quintessentially liberal *Reichswehr*. Francis Carsten, in the only overview of the *Reichswehr*'s history to date, argued that 'The officer corps was bound to consider the revolution and its consequences as an attack upon Itself and its whole world. It could only react to the revolution and the new order with strong opposition. That the officers, in spite of this, put themselves at the disposal of the new government was an event which had far-reaching consequences.'[30] Both Eberhard Kolb and Ulrich Kluge, in their monographs on the workers' and soldiers' councils movement, argued that the SPD-led Council of People's Commissars, which replaced the imperial regime until the election of the National Assembly, failed to rid Germany of the imperial élites. Kluge concluded that already in early 1919:

> Germany had a military system, whose leaders had sworn formal loyalty to the new order, but were far from ready to defend the substance of this order. The influence which the army re-established shortly after 9 November 1918 was too great to be accommodated by the republican constitution. The one chance to create a military system in Germany, which corresponded to the demands for inner consolidation and the intentions of wide sectors of the population, had been missed.[31]

On this reading, the German army is seen as one of those elements of continuity which contributed to the instability of the Republic.[32] The persistence of military Influence In German politics, despite its shattering defeat in 1918, is commonly attributed to the weakness of the SPD, and its lack of political courage in excluding the old imperial ruling classes.[33]

29. Reinhard Rürup, 'Friedrich Ebert und das Problem der Handlungsspielräume in der deutschen Revolution 1918/9', in *Friedrich Ebert und seine Zeit. Bilanz und Perspektiven der Forschung*, eds Rudolf König, Hartmut Soell, Hermann Weber, Munich, 1990, 69–87; Wolfgang J. Mommsen, *Imperial Germany, 1867–1918. Politics, Culture and Society in an Authoritarian State*, London, 1995, 233–53.

30. F. L. Carsten, *The Reichswehr and Politics, 1918 to 1933*, Oxford, 1966, 398.

31. Ulrich Kluge, *Soldatenräte und Revolution. Studien zur Militärpolitik in Deutschland 1918/9*, Göttingen, 1975, 356; Eberhard Kolb, *Die Arbeiterräte in der deutschen Innenpolitik, 1918–1919* Frankfurt, 1978.

32. Wolfgang Elben, *Das Problem der Kontinuität in der deutschen Revolution. Die Politik des Staatssekretäre und der militärischen Führung vom November 1918 bis Februar 1919*, Düsseldorf, 1966, 126–46; Fritz Fischer, *From Kaiserreich to Third Reich. Elements of Continuity in German History, 1871–1945*, London, 1986.

33. The last major contribution to this debate was Wette's, *Noske*, Düsseldorf, 1988; see also the review article, Leo Haupts, *Historische Zeitschrift*, 249, 1989, 448-9, and Rainer Butenschön, Eckart Spoo (eds), *Wozu muss einer der Bluthund sein? Der Mehrheitssozialdemokrat Gustav Noske und der deutsche Militarismus des 20. Jahrhunderts*, Heilbronn, 1997.

Others have argued that the social origins of the officer corps inclined against support for liberal democracy.[34]

Ranged against this critique of the *Reichswehr* as a destabilizing influence in the polity is a body of work that argues that the *Reichswehr* saved the Weimar Republic in 1919 from left-wing radicals, and held Germany together in 1923. This idea of the *Reichswehr* as a pillar of the German state was not just popular with interwar writers in Germany, but also found favour with the first historian of the *Reichswehr*, and subsequent Vichyite, Jean Bénoist-Méchin:

> It was [the army] which prevented Germany from collapse and helped overcome a succession of crises. It eliminated little by little all the men whom it judged were damaging to the nation. Invisible but active, in the shadows in periods of détente, but always intervening at the critical moment, the *Reichswehr* never ceased to arbitrate the situation. It was the cover, thrown over the crevasse that linked the Second to the Third Reich.

Bénoist-Méchin identified three factors which allowed the *Reichswehr* to exercise influence in German politics and society. First, the *Reichswehr* was a relatively homogenous group in a deeply divided society. Second, generals spent long periods in office, compared to the swift change of governments. Finally the *Reichswehr* was certain of its political goals when other groups were uncertain of theirs.[35] One of the interesting characteristics of Bénoist-Méchin's thesis is that he praised the *Reichswehr*'s record for the very reasons for which post-Second World War historians lamented its rôle in the Weimar republic, such as its political influence and as an element of continuity between the Kaiser and Hitler.

However the positive contribution of the *Reichswehr* to the Weimar republic has been noted by a number of historians, who either avoid seeing 1933 as a logical culmination of the republic's history, or else argue that the officer corps, and, in particular, Schleicher, offered the last hurdle to Hitler's *Machtergreifung*. Heinz Hürten argues that '[I]f a teleological view of German history with 1933 as its endpoint is avoided, then the policy of co-operation between the Council of the People's Commissars, its successor governments and the military, cannot be simply regarded as an early step towards ruin, but must be interpreted as successful.'[36] In defence of the *Reichswehr* he suggests that political realities are not based upon laws, as socialist and liberal critics of militarism might suggest, but upon force. The *Reichswehr* was the guarantor of the

34. Detlef Bald, *Der deutsche Offizier. Sozial- und Bildungsgeschichte des deutschen Offizierkorps im 20. Jahrhundert*, Munich, 1982, 14–15, 22–23.
35. Jean Bénoist-Méchin, *Histoire de l'armée allemande depuis l'armistice*, 2 vols, Paris, 1936, vol. 1, 11–18.
36. Heinz Hürten, *Der Kapp Putsch als Wende. Über Rahmenbedingungen der Weimarer Republik seit dem Frühjahr 1920*, Düsseldorf, 1989, 19.

legal order in the Weimar Republic.[37] The establishment of the new state required co-operation between the military and civilian institutions. Co-operation was sustained by a basic consensus on the need for the reestablishment of order, German unity and defence against Bolshevism.[38] Harold Gordon, a former officer in the American army, also defended the record of the *Reichswehr*. He inverted the question of responsibility, and argued that the government was in fact a hindrance to the 'law and order' policies of the army.[39] Government vacillation, the treaty of Versailles, and the impending dissolution of *Freikorps* units damaged the morale of the *Reichswehr*. The Kapp Putsch is presented as a revolt of the 'disinherited', and he suggestively writes that the disenchanted *Freikorps* soldiers were 'raw material to be moulded by bold and daring revolutionaries.'[40]

Both Hürten's and Gordon's work stress the rôle of the *Reichswehr* as the *ultima ratio* of the state, and that this rôle was underpinned by its monopoly of 'legitimate force'. Recently, this line of argument has been applied to the rôle of the *Reichswehr* leadership in the crisis of the early 1930s. As the major power factor in Germany, the *Reichswehr* had the potential to decide the outcome of events. Eberhard Kolb and Wolfram Pyta concluded that 'a presidential dictatorship supported by the *Reichswehr*' offered the best chance for the Weimar Republic to overcome the crisis, and to return later to a parliamentary system of government.[41] Whereas viewing the history of the *Reichswehr* through the lens of the National Socialist regime led to the castigation of the political activities of the officer corps by Carsten, Wette and others, Pyta presents Schleicher and his allies in the *Reichswehrministerium* as the last barrier to Hitler's *Machtergreifung*.[42]

Beyond the question of whether the officer corps supported or destabilized the Weimar republic, lies the matrix of rearmament, foreign policy, domestic political stability and the nature of modern industrial warfare. It is from this perspective that the most fruitful insights into civil-military relations have emerged. For example, Pyta argues that Schleicher measured

---

37. Heinz Hürten, *Reichswehr und Ausnahmezustand. Ein Beitrag zur Verfassungsproblematik der Weimarer Republik in ihrem ersten Jahrfünft*, Düsseldorf, 1977; id, *Rahmenbedingungen*, 5–7.
38. Ibid., 11–12; see also Winkler, *Weimar*, 33–67, although he argues that more could and should have been done to establish a democratic social and political order; Rakenius, *Groener*, 125–27.
39. Harold Gordon, *The Reichswehr and the German Republic, 1919–1926*, Princeton, 1957, 73–74, 81–89.
40. Ibid., 90, 94.
41. Eberhard Kolb, Wolfram Pyta, 'Die Notstandsplanung unter den Regierungen Papen und Schleicher', in *Die deutsche Staatskrise 1930–1933. Handlungsspielräume und Alternativen*, ed. Heinrich August Winkler, Munich, 1992, 155–81.
42. Wolfram Pyta, 'Vorbereitungen für den militärischen Ausnahmezustand unter Papen/Schleicher', *MgM*, 51, 2, 1992, 385–428; id, 'Konstitutionelle Demokratie statt monarchische Restauration. Die verfassungspolitische Konzeption Schleichers in der Weimarer Staatskrise', *VfZ*, 47, 3, 1999, 417–41.

'the capability of a political system by whether it was in a position to guarantee the central matter of concern to the military: namely rearming Germany and pursuing power politics, backed by military force.'[43] Historians have exploited new ideas about civil-military relations to investigate the reactions of the German officer corps to modern industrial warfare.[44] Michael Geyer, who has made the most significant contributions to research in this area, criticised the inadequacy of sources used in previous studies, and pointed out that the liberal or even the eighteenth-century absolutist conception of civil-military relations was misleading in examinations of interwar military history.[45] He argued 'that the decisive element of industrialised warfare is the socialisation (*Vergesellschaftung*) of the military and the means of waging war. The conduct of war can no longer be limited to the military instrument, as is the traditional view of absolutist and liberal thought but becomes part of national defence, which encompasses the whole of society.'[46] The strict division of the civil and military sphere collapsed with the onset of modern industrial warfare. Geyer drew on theorists such as Morris Janowitz and Samuel Huntington, while Ernst Willi Hansen, who wrote about the relations between the *Reichswehr* and industry, used various models of the 'military-industrial complex'.[47]

At the root of the debate on the Reichswehr's reaction to future war lie three questions: what would characterise the war of the future, how did the officer corps prepare for it, and how did the spectre of it impact upon the civil-military relationship in the Weimar years?[48] Of course, at the centre of this debate stood the experience of the First World War, which did much to shape the expectations of the next war.[49] Recent research has suggested that

43. Ibid, 419–20.
44. Gerald D. Feldman, *Army, Industry and Labor in Germany, 1914–1918*, Providence, Oxford, 1992 edn.; it was first published in 1966; Michael Salewski, 'Reichswehr, Staat und Republik', *Geschichte in Wissenschaft und Unterricht*, 5, 1980, 271–88. The notion of total war is contentious; see the various contributions, *Great War, Total War. Mobilisation and Combat on the Western Front, 1914–1918*, eds Roger Chickering, Stig Förster, Cambridge, 2000; *An der Schwelle zum totalen Krieg. Die militärische Debatte über den Krieg der Zukunft 1919–1939*, ed. Stig Förster, Paderborn, 2002.
45. Michael Geyer, 'Der zur Organisation erhobene Burgfrieden', in *Militär und Militarismus in der Weimarer Republik*, eds Klaus-Jürgen Müller, Eckardt Opitz, Düsseldorf, 1978, 15–27.
46. Michael Geyer, *Aufrüstung oder Sicherheit. Die Reichswehr in die Krise der Machtpolitik, 1924–1936*, Wiesbaden, 1980, 3–6.
47. Michael Geyer, 'The past as future: the German officer corps as profession', in *German professions, 1800–1950*, eds Geoffrey Cocks, Konrad Jarausch, Oxford, New York, 1990; Ernst Willi Hansen, 'Zum "Militärischen-Industriellen Komplex" in der Weimarer Republik', in *Militär und Militarismus*, eds Müller, Opitz, 101–40.
48. For recent debates on visions of future war in the interwar period, see the contributions in Förster, ed., *An der Schwelle*, and *The Shadows of Total War. Europe, East Asia and the United States, 1919–1939*, eds, Roger Chickering, Stig Förster, Cambridge, 2003.
49. Chickering, Förster, eds, *Great War, Total War*; John Horne, ed., *State, Society and Mobilization in Europe during the First World War*, Cambridge, 1997, 1–17.

the First World War was not a total war, and that the concept of total war would be better thought of in terms of a Weberian ideal type which enables analysis of broad issues in the history of warfare in the first half of the twentieth century.[50] For contemporaries, the military debate started and ended with total war. Chickering and Förster comment: '"Total war" became a popular topos during the period between the two world wars of the twentieth century. It was coined during the first of them, and it subsequently played an important role in deliberations everywhere about the future of war.'[51] This does not necessarily mean that soldiers wanted total war. As Markus Pöhlmann, who has examined the German military journals of the interwar period, writes: '"To avoid or to prepare [for total war]?" – the central metadiscourse of the German military élite in the interwar period can be framed in this formula.'[52] There was no escape from the next war, which German soldiers assumed was inevitable.[53] The major divisions within the German officer corps concerned the nature of the war.

For many historians it has made more sense to classify the Weimar officer corps on the basis of their theories of war, rather than on their attitude to the Republic.[54] Thus Wilhelm Deist argues that the group around Colonel Joachim von Stülpnagel, who advocated a theory of Volkskrieg, or the participation of the whole populace in some war-related activity, 'was not held together by a single political conviction or strategy, but by the common goal of maintaining and increasing the military efficiency of the Reichswehr.'[55] Stülpnagel's ideas had superseded those of Seeckt, who had stressed the viability of a small army, in the wake of the Reichswehr's inability to resist the French occupation of the Ruhr in 1923.[56] Yet the Volkskrieg theory was replaced by a complex new security policy, drafted by Wilhelm Groener after he became Reichswehrminister in 1928. The dispute between the political officers headed by Schleicher and Groener, and the militarist officers, led by General Werner von Blomberg, previously Reinhardt's chief of staff in Wehrkreis V, has been well-documented.[57] Groener set clear guidelines for the use of the Reichswehr that recognised the weaknesses of the 100,000 men army. He accepted the primacy of political control over the military forces of the state. Johannes Hürter, author of a monograph on Groener as Reichswehrminister, concluded that 'Groener's sense of reality and his conceptual

50. Roger Chickering, Stig Förster, 'Introduction', in *Shadows*, 7.
51. Ibid., 3.
52. Markus Pöhlmann, 'Von Versailles nach Armageddon. Totalisierungserfahrung und Kriegserwartung in deutschen Militärzeitschriften', in Förster, ed., *An der Schwelle*, 351.
53. Ibid., 323–4.
54. Ernst-Willi Hansen, 'The Military and the Military Political Breakdown in Germany, 1918 and France, 1940', in *The Military in Politics and Society in France and Germany in the Twentieth Century*, ed Klaus-Jürgen Müller, Oxford, 1995, 92.
55. Wilhelm Deist, *The Wehrmacht and German rearmament*, London, 1986 edn, 5.
56. Wilhelm Deist, 'Die Reichswehr und der Krieg der Zukunft', *MgM*, 49, 1, 1989, 85–6.
57. Deist, *Wehrmacht and German Rearmament*, 4–20; Hürter, *Groener*, 73–98.

ability appeared tailor-made to place the work in Bendlerstraße [Reichs-swehrministerium] on a planning basis that was at once pragmatic and ori-entated towards the future.'[58] However Groener's cautious policy was swept aside by the political and economic crisis of the early 1930s, which brought Hitler to power. Hitler appointed Blomberg as Reichswehrminister, and he reversed Groener's gradualist approach. Pragmatism was cast aside, and a dynamic but ultimately flawed rearmament plan was pursued in order to prepare Germany for the next war.[59] In general, historians have identified four different responses to the challenge of future war in the Weimar era: Seeckt's small but highly trained and mobile force[60], Stülpnagel's Volkskrieg theory, Groener's realistic concept of German security, and Blomberg's dynamic rearmament programme.

Historians have also identified these different approaches to the ques-tion of war with different attitudes towards the republic. Corum argues that 'von Seeckt's decision to retain a disproportionately high percentage of General Staff affairs was right for the army and nation. It was less democratic than Reinhardt's vision, but von Seeckt was correct in recog-nising the organisational and technical abilities of the General Staff as having first priority.'[61] Groener accepted the primacy of political control, not out of a liberal conviction about civil-military relations, but because it served his purpose. Under Groener the *Reichswehr* began the process of 'moving into the executive', of acknowledging the political framework within which military policy had to be formulated and seeking to utilise that framework for its own ends.[62] Like Groener, both Stülpnagel and Blomberg sought to bring the *Reichswehr* closer to the state and society. Yet their more radical views on modern warfare had different conse-quences. Geyer argues that in the 1920s the *Reichswehr* 'set out to organise society for the purpose of war according to its efficiency-oriented maxims in a national scheme for converting civil into military society in case of war. This made the *Reichswehr* into an exceedingly dangerous organisation.' The military mission of the *Reichswehr*, which ultimately aimed at the revision of the treaty of Versailles, led it to desta-bilize both internal and external politics.[63]

It is within the context of the primacy of foreign policy and the chang-ing relationship between war, the state, and society that Reinhardt must

58. Ibid, 91; on the debate within the *Reichswehr* see also, Geyer, *Aufrüstung oder Sicherheit*, 201–17.
59. Deist, *Wehrmacht and German Rearmament*, 21–3.
60. James Corum, *The Roots of Blitzkrieg. Hans von Seeckt and German Military Reform*, Kansas, 1992; Williamson Murray, 'Armored Warfare: the British, French and German Experi-ences', in *Military Innovation in the Interwar Period*, eds Williamson Murray, Alan Millett, Cambridge, 1996.
61. Corum, *Roots of Blitzkrieg*, 34; Murray, 'Armored Warfare', 36.
62. Hürter, *Groener*, 37 8; Geyer, *Aufrüstung oder Sicherheit*, 234.
63. Geyer, 'The Past as Future', 197–9.

be seen.[64] He was not a conservative, as Ernst argued, but a radical militarist who was close to Stülpnagel in terms of his view of future war. Like all officers he saw Germany's main goal after the war as the restoration of Germany as a Great Power. This was only possible with the use or threat of military force. He shared the pessimistic belief that international relations could not be regulated by laws, customs or institutions like the League of Nations. Ultimately each state had to protect itself with military force from the predatory designs of its neighbours.[65] The rapid establishment of a reliable military force in early 1919 was essential to the continued existence of Germany. It was not just the Weimar Republic that faced internal unrest, it was also Germany that faced the threat of Polish and Bolshevist invasion and Allied occupation. Only military force, in his view, could prevent the worst consequences of defeat.

If this was a common, and indeed necessary belief, for a professional officer, Reinhardt's view of the future of warfare made him one of the most radical militarists of the interwar period. Reinhardt, drawing on the experience of the First World War, believed that societies, and not simply armies, waged war.[66] The militarization of society had to be total, down to the use of women at the fighting front, and old men on the home front. His views were presented in a rational and logical manner, but there is no doubt about the radical nature of what he proposed. The institutions of the state were assessed on their ability to function in war, and society was to be militarized in peacetime. Even in 1919 the rationalisation of the *Kaiserreich*'s military institutions was implemented with one eye firmly on the conduct of a future war. The military and national interests were conflated. This marked him out from Seeckt, who advocated a professional army, instead of the *Millionenheeren* of the pre-war period, and Groener, who subordinated the military agenda to the broader interests of national security.

Reinhardt's advocacy of the militarization of German society led him to a peculiarly inclusive vision of the *Volksgemeinschaft* or national community.[67] The creation of a *Volksgemeinschaft* was a central issue in Weimar politics, and there were a variety of competing visions, based on different principles. Reinhardt's aim was to maximize German military

64. Brendan Simms, 'The Return of the Primacy of Foreign Policy'; William Mulligan, 'The *Reichswehr*, the Republic and the Primacy of Foreign Policy, 1918-23' both in *German History*, 21, 3, 2003: special issue: The Primacy of Foreign Policy in German History, eds William Mulligan, Brendan Simms, 275–91, 347–68.
65. See Seeckt's dismissal of hopes for 'eternal peace' in Guske, *Das politische Denken*, 173.
66. Dennis E. Showalter, ''Plans, Weapons, Doctrines. The Strategic Culture of Interwar Europe', in Chickering, Förster, eds, *Shadows*, 66.
67. Gunther Mai, '''Verteidigungskrieg'' und Volksgemeinschaft''. Stattliche Selbstbehauptung, nationale Sicherheit und soziale Befreiung in Deutschland in der Zeit des Ersten Weltkrieges', in *Der erste Weltkrieg. Wirkung, Wahrnehmung, Analyse*, ed. Wolfgang Michalka, Munich, 1994.

strength, and therefore anyone within Germany who could contribute to it, Catholic, Jewish or Protestant, working-class or nobility, man or woman, was a potential member. On the other hand, pacifists and internationalists (including communists) were excluded from this community, the latter because they rejected the principle of the nation-state. If the army was the representative of military values within society then it could not afford to alienate or exclude any social groups from its ranks. It was this principle which led Reinhardt to promote the recruitment of working-class soldiers, and most notably to oppose the Kapp Putsch because it would damage the *Reichswehr*'s image with republicans. This inclusive vision marked a departure from the conservative military thought of the *Kaiserreich* era when working-class recruits were distrusted as SPD supporters.[68]

If the primacy of foreign policy informed Reinhardt's principles, then the implementation of those ideas was dependent on the political constellations of the day – within the officer corps, within the government, and within Weimar Germany's society. Between November 1918 and March 1920 there was a bitter dispute between the Ministry of War and the Supreme Command (and the General Staff, after the latter's dissolution). This was in many respects the inevitable consequence of having two major bureaucracies dealing with military policy. During the *Kaiserreich* era the relationship between the Ministry and the General Staff had been fraught as they clashed over military budgets and recruitment policy.[69] After the war it became clear that there would be a restructuring of military institutions, and the struggle began to dominate the *Reichswehrministerium*. Proposals and counter-proposals were heavily influenced by bureaucratic self-interest. The sense of conflict was sharpened by the personal rivalry between Reinhardt, the Minister for War, and Groener, the leading officer of the Supreme Command. While Groener has rightly been seen as a politically astute character, Reinhardt was not naïve, and in the personal and bureaucratic rivalry it appeared as though he had triumphed against Groener and then Seeckt until the Kapp Putsch led to Reinhardt's fall and Seeckt's succession.

Reinhardt's power in 1919 was mainly due to his strong relationship with Ebert and Noske. Within the officer corps Reinhardt was a weak figure, who only enjoyed the support of his closest advisers. He was unable to exert his authority over more recalcitrant and even rebellious elements. Therefore his relationship with the cabinet was fundamental to his achievements in 1919. They trusted his professional expertise, and with their political support he was able to outmanoeuvre his rivals within the officer corps, as well as reform the military administration and

---

68. Stig Förster, *Der doppelte Militarismus. Die deutsche Heeresrüstungspolitik zwischen Status-Quo-Sicherung und Aggression, 1890–1913*, Stuttgart, 1985, 94–7.
69. See generally Förster, *Doppelte Militarismus*.

command structures. Whereas Seeckt's tenure as *Chef der Heeresleitung* ended due to his deteriorating relationship with Otto Gessler, the *Reichswehrminister*, it is notable that Reinhardt resigned because of a Putsch from within the officer corps. This was a massive blow to the principle of civilian control of the military, although whether Reinhardt would have co-operated with the Republic in the longer term was dependent on whether it would enable the restoration of German military power.

There were other political factors which Reinhardt had to take into account. Military policy was not formulated in isolation from the rest of German politics, and Reinhardt had to compete for scarce resources. The composition of the National Assembly enabled Reinhardt to push through his programme of centralising the states' war ministries. However Reinhardt was less successful at promoting the military agenda in the discussions about the treaty of Versailles. Military defeat meant that German foreign policy was reliant upon business and financial weight, rather than military power.[70] The government was less willing to 'go to the wall' for concessions on military aspects of the treaty than it was to retain threatened territories. The Reich Finance Ministry was unhappy at the amount of money it spent on the army, and tried to force Reinhardt to speed up the pace of demobilization. The constellation of political power within which Reinhardt operated in 1919 offered opportunities and risks. The revolution meant that the structures of the state would be changed, but in early 1919 it was not clear what changes these forms would take. What Reinhardt had to do, was to make sure these changes favoured the military as much as was possible. To that extent he was a supreme pragmatist.

While his actions in 1919 showed the possibilities for co-operation between the Republic and the officer corps, there were clear limits. The primacy of foreign policy prescribed two aims in Weimar Germany. First, the Reich had to be preserved. The survival of Germany as a potential actor in the continental struggle for supremacy was the first test for the Republic. The officer corps had to co-operate with the Republic to ensure this. Open conflict between the Republic and the army would have led to civil war and the collapse of Germany. By the end of 1923 the test of survival had been passed. But Reinhardt's ultimate goal was the restoration of German military power and the reversal of the outcome of the First World War. Could such an expansionary policy be achieved within the context of the Republic?[71] This remains an open counterfactual question, precluded by the dynamic assertion of German power by the Nazis.

It can be considered at the levels of foreign and domestic policy. By the time of Reinhardt's death, in September 1930, Stresemann's co-operative

---

70. Peter Krüger, *Deustchland und die Reparationen 1918/9. Die Genesis des Reparationsproblems in Deutschland zwischen Waffenstillstand und Friedensschluß*, Stuttgart, 1973.

71. Henry Ashby Turner, 'Continuity in German foreign policy? The case of Stresemann', *International History Review*, 1, 4, 1979, 519–20.

western orientated policy had been replaced by the more unilateralist approach of the Brüning government, which successfully revised the reparations issues and opened the disarmament conference, which had to lead to either change in the military status quo, or else unilateral German rearmament. Against that Germany stood isolated, having failed embarrassingly to forge a Customs Union with Austria and alienated French good will through its unilateralist approach. Nonetheless Stresemann's multilateral approach was unlikely to allay French nervousness about German rearmament, so from the perspective of military policy, the approach of the early 1930s, combined with the secret programme of rearmament, showed the opportunities for an assertive Germany. The quiet support for rearmament by the SPD cabinet members was a startling contrast to the official military policy of the party, which focused on disarmament, arbitration and institutional guarantees of the international order. The domestic political balance of power, despite the pessimism of officers in the early 1930s, had clearly shifted to the right and support for military values. Yet there was no way in which the governments of the early 1930s had sufficient power to implement the militarization of society on the scale desired by Reinhardt. When he died in 1930, Reinhardt was definitely less enamoured with the Republic than he had been in 1919, but he still did not oppose it.

A biography of Reinhardt is an account of civil-military relations in the Weimar Republic, and thus it goes to the heart of one of the most important issues of Weimar historiography. Reinhardt, even more so than Groener in 1919, realised the opportunities provided by the Republic. Yet not only was he a pragmatist, but he was also a radical militarist, with an almost utopian vision of a militarised national community. Like all military planners, he was future-orientated. This was not simply a matter of rational professionalism, but also of messianic hope in Germany's future as a Great Power. His relationship with the Republic depended on the potential for the fulfilment of this mission. Reinhardt, both a pragmatist and a radical militarist, stood simultaneously at opposite ends of the spectrum of the officer corps. For example, Stülpnagel was a radical militarist, opposed to the Republic from a very early stage; Groener accepted the subordinate place of military power in national strategy and generally supported the Republic. Reinhardt embodied the tension of these positions, and tried to resolve it by pushing for a militarized state and society *within* the framework of the Republic, if possible, but *outside* it, if necessary.

This study is based on a wide range of primary source material, some of which has already been published. If Ernst's collection was the most obvious source for this study, then the collections in the series *Quellen zur Geschichte des Parlamentarismus* and *Akten der Reichskanzlei* have also been invaluable. There are also a number of published diaries, most notably those of Colonel Albrecht von Thaer, an officer in the OHL

(German Supreme Command during and just after the First World War), Gustav Böhm and Ernst van den Bergh, both officers in the Prussian Ministry of War.[72] There are a number of documents which have been published in leading journals, such as Heinz Hürten's collection, which deals with the initial reaction of Württemberg to the centralisation of German military ministries.[73] Apologetic memoirs of varying quality also exist.[74]

The chief source for this study is Reinhardt's *Nachlaß*, which is held in the *Hauptstaatsarchiv*, Stuttgart, and in microfilm form at the *Militärarchiv* in Freiburg.[75] It contains letters to leading officers and politicians of the day, memoranda on military policy, the texts of lectures and articles by Reinhardt, and press cuttings. The *Nachlaß* was held by Reinhardt's daughter, Lotte, a teacher in Stuttgart, after her father's death in August 1930. On 7 September 1939 she gave some papers to the *Heeresarchiv* in Stuttgart.[76] A year later an archivist wrote to her: 'Noticeably little is available on service and personal presentations, which would have been made during the war.'[77] Lotte Reinhardt gave the archive some more material, mainly press cuttings and photos.[78] It is probable that she retained some of her father's papers, because Ernst, who had contacted her, was able to publish extracts from letters between Reinhardt and his wife, Luise, which dealt with Reinhardt's views of the end of the First World War. However these letters are not in the *Nachlaß*, and so an important source of information for Reinhardt's personal views has been lost. Ernst also believed that the letters for the whole of 1919 were lost. This is unfortunate because one must assume that the correspondence between them was copious. Reinhardt had spent four years at war, and then on his return spent much of his time in either Berlin or Weimar, while the family home was in Stuttgart.[79]

72. *General Major a. D. Albrecht von Thaer. Generalstabdienst an der Front und in der OHL. Aus Briefen und Tagebuchaufzeichnungen 1915–1919*, ed. Siegfried Kaehler, Göttingen, 1958; *Adjutant im Preussischen Kriegsministerium, Juni 1918 bis Oktober 1919. Aufzeichnungen des Hauptmanns Gustav Böhm*, eds Heinz Hürten, Georg Meyer, Stuttgart, 1977; *Aus den Geburtsstunden der Weimarer Republik. Das Tagebuch des Obersten Ernst van den Bergh*, ed. Wolfram Wette, Düsseldorf, 1991.

73. Heinz Hürten, 'Heeresverfassung und Länderrecht. Württemberg in den Auseinandersetzungen der Weimarer Nationalversammlung um die Bildung einer einheitlichen Reichswehr', *MgM*, 23, 1978, 147–82.

74. See for example, Rüdiger von der Goltz, *Meine Sendung in Finnland und im Baltikum*, Leipzig, 1920; Gustav Noske, *Von Kiel bis Kapp. Zur Geschichte der deutschen Revolution*, Berlin, 1920.

75. The *Signaturen* (references) are HStASt, M 660/034, and BA-MA, N 86.

76. HStASt, M 660/034, Bü 55, Lotte Reinhardt to the Heeresarchiv, 7 September 1939.

77. HStASt, M 660/034, Bü 55, Heeresarchivrat to Lotte Reinhardt, 2 August 1940.

78. HStASt, M 660/034, Bü 55, Lotte Reinhardt to the Heeresarchiv, 11 September 1940.

79. Ernst, 'Aus dem Nachlaß', 39–40; efforts to locate papers in private hands have been unsuccessful, but I would like to thank the *Militärgeschichtliches Forschungsamt* for their help in this search.

Unlike many of his contemporaries, Reinhardt did not leave any memoirs, either published or unpublished. On several occasions he was asked to write a major work. When Reinhardt was promoted to commander of *Reichswehrgruppe II* in December 1924, Dr Otto Berger of Bergers Literärisches Büro, took the opportunity, not only to send him a letter of congratulations, but also to inquire whether he was interested in publishing his memoirs, with particular reference to the period 1918 to 1920.[80] Three years later Berger renewed the offer, and reminded Reinhardt that the firm was also publishing the memoirs of such eminent people as Wilhelm Blos, the former state president of Württemberg.[81] Verlag Deutsche Wille also expressed an interest in publishing Reinhardt's account of his time as Prussian *Kriegsminister* as part of a collection.[82] However the persistent attempts of publishers to get Reinhardt to put pen to paper failed. Nonetheless, after his death, his elder brother Ernst was concerned to rescue his sibling from obscurity. He edited a series of lectures which Reinhardt had given in 1928 and 1929, and published them with Ernst Mittler und Sohn.[83] Ernst Reinhardt had also contacted many of his brother's former colleagues, and used their most eloquent tributes in the biographical sketch at the beginning of the book.[84]

Together the *Nachlaß* and Ernst Reinhardt's edition of his brother's lectures constitute the core sources for any study of Walther Reinhardt. However the *Findbuch* (catalogue) also contains a word of warning from Major General Sieglin for the biographer: 'The papers cannot give a complete picture of this soldier, who in the first place was a man of action and decision, and made much more of an impact with the spoken than with the written word.'[85] The normal difficulties of evaluating sources is compounded for the student of German military history due to the bombing of the army ministry building in April 1945. While some material which was believed to have been destroyed in the bombing has been discovered in archives in eastern Europe and the former Soviet Union, much material has been lost permanently.[86]

To supplement the material in Reinhardt's *Nachlaß* this study has drawn on material from a wide variety of archives. The starting point for

80. HStASt, M 660/034, Bü 30, Otto Berger to Reinhardt, 16 December 1924.
81. HStASt, M 660/034, Bü 30, Otto Berger to Reinhardt, 29 September 1927.
82. HStASt, M 660/034, Bü 37, K. Franke to Reinhardt, 19 August 1927.
83. *Walther Reinhardt. Wehrkraft und Wehrwille. Aus seinem Nachlaß mit einer Lebensbeschrei-bung*, ed. Ernst Reinhardt, Berlin, 1932.
84. BA-MA, N 247/185, Ernst Reinhardt to Hans von Seeckt, Ulm, 16 September 1930; *Wehrkraft und Wehrwille*, 20–1.
85. Findbuch to BA-MA, Nachlaß Reinhardt, N 86.
86. Uwe Löbel, 'Neue Forschungsmöglichkeit zur preußisch-deutschen Heeresgeschichte. Zur Rückgabe von Akten des Potsdamer Heeresarchiv durch die Sowjetunion', *MgM*, 51, 1,1992, 143–49; Helmut Otto, 'Der Bestand Kriegsgeschicht-liche Forschungsanstalt des Heeres im Bundesarchiv-, Militärisches Zwischenarchiv Potsdam, *MgM*, 51, 2, 1992, 429–41.

any study of German military history is the *Militärarchiv* in Freiburg, which holds many of the private papers of leading officers from the period, as well as the *Armeeverordnungsblatt* and *Heeresverordnungsblatt*, which provide much information on the topics such as troop welfare, and the rôle of *Vertrauensleute*, which have received little attention in the historical literature on the *Reichswehr*. The federal archives in Koblenz and Berlin also yielded a significant amount of material, including a set of files on the development of the crisis in 1923 in Thuringia, where Reinhardt had plenipotentiary executive powers during the state of emergency.[87] The political archive of the Foreign Office, Bonn, provided material on Reinhardt's role in formulating foreign policy in 1919. The documents in Reinhardt's *Nachlaß* give the impression that he was only involved in foreign affairs in May and June 1919, when the debate over the treaty of Versailles was at its height. The Foreign Office files demonstrate that he also cast an eye towards events in eastern Europe, and was negotiating with the German-Austrians about the implications of an *Anschluß* for military policy.

The loss of files in April 1945 has been ameliorated to a certain extent by the federal structure of the German state which meant that the Prussian *Kriegsministerium* often sent out directives to other military ministries in Bavaria, Saxony, Württemberg and Baden. Together with the reports of envoys from these states, these documents reveal hitherto obscure policy debates within the Prussian *Kriegsministerium*. For example the *Reichswehr* committee, set up in early 1919 to formulate policy for the new army, has often been passed over in the literature, despite its important role. Files from the *Hauptstaatsarchiv*, Stuttgart and the *Generallandesarchiv*, Karlsruhe, contain reports on important meetings that underline the important rôle the Prussian Ministry of War, and by extension Reinhardt, played in establishing the new army. Other files found in the state archives in Munich, Stuttgart and Karlsruhe illuminated issues such as the centralisation of the war ministries in October 1919, the establishment of the *Reichswehrministerium* and the development of local civil-military relations in *Wehrkreis V* during the 1920s, issues which have received only cursory attention from historians.[88] Finally, the Prussian cabinet minutes, held at the *Geheimes Staatsarchiv*, Dahlem, proved a useful source since Reinhardt was a Prussian minister until late September 1919.

87. Most of the historiography on 1923 has been devoted to the crises in Saxony and Bavaria, and there is no monograph on Thüringia, although there is a study on socialist policies in that state between 1918 and 1923, Beate Häupel, *Die Gründung des Landes Thüringens. Staatsbildung und Reformpolitik, 1918-1923*, Cologne, Vienna, 1995, 160–73.
88. Hürten, 'Heeresverfassung und Länderrecht', is the only investigation of the process of military centralisation, and it focuses on the position of Württemberg during the initial negotiations in early March.

REINHARDT IN PEACE AND WAR, 1872–1918

Walther Reinhardt was born in Stuttgart on 24 March 1872 to Emilia and Karl Heinrich August von Reinhardt. The family background was one of service to the Württemberg state which had became part of the German *Reich* in 1871. His father fought in the wars of German unification, his paternal grandfather had been a municipal administrator and his maternal grandfather a professor of forestry at the university of Tübingen.[1] Just before Reinhardt's birth his father had been promoted to the general staff of the newly created 27th (2nd Royal Württemberg) Division in Ulm, an indication that the family had a steady position in Württemberg life. Reinhardt's own identity acknowledged his Württemberg roots, but was dominated by the new Reich. His own description of his father as a 'Württemberger, faithful to the *Heimat*, who developed into a convinced Reich-German', could equally describe his own affinities.[2] The Reich which Bismarck had founded and for which millions had fought and died in the First World War had primacy in his identity.[3]

To that extent Reinhardt reflected the experience of somebody born in the *Gründerzeit* generation. His close identification with the Reich was coupled with a deep admiration, bordering on veneration, for Prussia and her achievements, particularly in the military sphere. In 1885 he entered the cadet school at Oranienstein, apparently with the grudging approval of his father who was wary of choosing a career at such an

---

1. His early life is described in *Walther Reinhardt. Wehrkraft und Wehrwille. Aus seinem Nachlaß mit einer Lebensbeschreibung*, ed. Ernst Reinhardt, Berlin, 1932, 1–4; Fritz Ernst, 'Walther Reinhardt (1872–1930)', *Zeitschrift für Württembergische Landesgeschichte*, 1957, 331–32; the personal file on his father is available in the HStASt, M 430/1, 2155.

2. Ernst, 'Reinhardt', 332, from his *Abschiedsansprache*, 12 January 1928.

3. HStASt, M 660/034, Bü 26, *Wehrkreis Verordnungsblatt*, 18 January 1924, contains a announcement by Reinhardt celebrating the foundation of the *Kaiserreich*.

early stage.[4] Reinhardt acknowledged the formative impact which the Prussian cadet system on him. In the frugal lifestyle of the cadets, he saw the virtues which had led Prussia to unify Germany.[5] One of his duties as *Chef der Heeresleitung* (head of army command) was to speak at the closure of the Berlin Cadet School in March 1920: 'the spirit of the cadet corps was the spirit of the army. Its aim was the formation of a sprightly race, healthy in body and mind, trusting in God, faithful, comradely and honourable and above all, enthusiastic, because without enthusiasm nothing great can be achieved.'[6] Reinhardt saw these characteristics, embodied in the Prussian and then the German army, as the motor of German history. Belief in the historical mission of Prussia, as creator and protector of Germany, and his own experience of the Prussian military, promoted the development of a close identification with the new Reich.[7] It was as a German, rather than as a Württemberger, that Reinhardt imagined himself.

Reinhardt spent much of his early career between Württemberg and Berlin. After completing his basic military education in Berlin, Reinhardt entered the prestigious Olga Regiment in Württemberg, as *Portepée-Fähnrich* (cadet officer) on 9 February 1891. He was soon back in the classroom, this time at the new war school at Hersfeld. The aim of the war school was to educate the best cadets to a higher level. This course continued until the autumn when he took an officers' examintion, in which he showed 'exceptional knowledge'.[8] Reinhardt advanced his career through merit, rather than connections or background, and can be seen as one of the emerging type of bourgeois officer, like his fellow Württemberger, Wilhelm Groener, or Erich Ludendorff, later Quartermaster General and the most influential officer during the last two years of the war.[9]

He returned to Olga Regiment and was promoted to the rank of lieutenant, with a patent dated 8 February 1891. There are indications that he had many interests outside of military affairs. For example, he met Albrecht von Thaer, later an officer with the Supreme Command, at the War Academy in Berlin. After Reinhardt's death Thaer wrote to Ernst Reinhardt, 'I often came into contact with your brother. The friendship

4. *Wehrkraft und Wehrwille*, 2; John Moncure, *Forging the King's Sword. Military Education between Tradition and Modernization – the Case of the Royal Prussian Cadet Corps, 1871–1914*, New York, 1993, 79–86; Steven Clemente, *For King and Kaiser! The Making of the Prussian Army Officer, 1860–1914*, New York, 1992, 81.
5. Ernst, 'Reinhardt', 2.
6. HStASt, M 600/034, Bü 24, newspaper clipping on Reinhardt's speech, 9 March 1920.
7. One of the newspaper cuttings in Reinhardt's *Nachlaß*, celebrating the 200th birthday of Prussia in 1901, stressed the historical mission, HStASt, M 660/034, Bü 6, *Tägliche Rundschau*, 18 January 1901, 'Zweihundert Jahre preussischer Geschichte.'
8. BA-MA, N 86/1, Belobigung für Portepée-Fähnrich W. Reinhardt, 13 November 1891.
9. Arden Bucholz, *Moltke, Schlieffen and Prussian war planning*, New York, 1991, 2–4; Wolfgang Venohr, *Ludendorff. Legende und Wirklichkeit*, Frankfurt, 1993.

was based on mutual respect. We discussed (and corresponded on) many questions that lay close to our hearts, not only military or political questions, but ones about humanity, also religious ones.'[10] During a stay in Berlin at the *Militär-Turn-Anstalt* in 1895 and 1896 he met Luise Fürbringer, daughter of Professor Paul Fürbringer, one of the leading doctors at Friedrichshain hospital in Berlin. On 7 April 1900 the couple married. The marriage was a happy one, and they had three daughters, Lotte, Hedwig and Ursula.[11] The choice of marriage partner is significant. First, the Fürbringer family were of Jewish extraction, and Reinhardt would have needed the permission of his superior officer to marry her.[12] Later Reinhardt won a reputation as one of the few philosemitic officers in the German army and this is an early indication of the courage with which he opposed the prevalent anti-Semitic prejudice amongst the German officer corps.[13] Second, Luise Fürbringer came from a *Bildungsbürgertum* (professional-middle class) background and this is another demonstration of the fact that Reinhardt was at ease in a wide range of social company. It could be argued that they represented an emerging and self-confident professional class.[14]

Not only do Reinhardt's social connections indicate that he was at ease with the world outside the officers' mess, but his political views also indicate some divergence from the stereotypical officer.[15] There are indications that Groener's antagonism to Reinhardt, which came to the fore in 1919, dated from their days in the Württemberg army, when Groener formed the erroneous impression that Reinhardt was a 'leftist'.[16]

10. HStASt, M 660/034, Bü 1, Reinhardt to Schlieffen, 16 June 1903; *Wehrkraft und Wehrwille*, 4–5 Thaer kept in close touch with Reinhardt, see *General Major a. D. Albrecht von Thaer. Generalstabdienst an der Front und in der OHL. Aus Briefen und Tagebuchaufzeichnungen 1915–1919*, ed. Siegfried Kaehler, Göttingen, 1958, 75–6, 283–4.

11. *Wehrkraft und Wehrwille*, 5; *Deutsche Allgemeine Zeitung*, 10 August 1930, carries Reinhardt's death notice along with some family details.

12. Friedrich Wilhelm Euler, 'Die deutsche Generalität und Admiralität bis 1918', in *Das deutsche Offizierkorps 1860–1960*, ed. Hans Hubert Hoffmann, Boppard am Rhein, 1980, 204.

13. Werner Angress, 'Prussia's Army and the Jewish Reserve Officer Controversy before World War I', *Leo Baeck Institute Yearbook*, 17, 1972, 19–42; id, 'Das deutsche Militär und die Juden im Ersten Weltkrieg, *MgM*, 19, 1, 1976, 77–146. Werner Jochmann, 'Die Ausbreitung des Antisemitismus', in *Deutsches Judentum im Krieg und Revolution*, ed. Werner Mosse, Tübingen, 1971.

14. *German professions, 1800–1950*, eds Geoffrey Cocks, Konrad Jarausch, New York, Oxford, 1990; David Blackbourn, 'The German Bourgeoisie: An Introduction' in *The German Bourgeoisie*, eds David Blackbourn, Richard Evans, London, 1991; for a different view see Jürgen Kocka, 'The European pattern and the German case' in *Bourgeois Society in Nineteenth Century Europe*, eds Jürgen Kocka, Allan Mitchell, Oxford, Providence, 1993, 3–39.

15. On the Württemberg officer corps in general see, Joachim Fischer, 'Das württembergische Offizierkorps 1866–1918', in Hoffmann, ed., *Das deutsche Offizierkorps*, 99–138.

16. Johannes Hürter, *Wilhlem Groener. Reichswehrminister am Ende der Weimarer Republik*, Munich, 1993, 5–6; Groener joined the Infantry Regiment 121 at Ludwigsburg in 1884, where Reinhardt later served. However in the relatively small Württemberg military community, rumours of Reinhardt's political predilections would presumably have spread rapidly.

When Reinhardt was serving with the Olga Regiment he proposed a scheme whereby all officers would contribute to a fund, which would then be used to distribute money to the less well off officers in the regiment.[17] In the Reinhardt-*Nachlaß* was a newspaper account of the SPD party conference in November 1892. The reports come from *Die Tägliche Rund-schau*, and were factual in nature; Reinhardt was probably interested in the debate on military policy.[18] In 1890 William II had instructed that bourgeois officers with an aristocratic mentality were to be recruited to fill the swelling ranks.[19] Reinhardt's interest in SPD policy hardly conformed to type. It is uncertain whether anyone knew Reinhardt was reading reports on SPD conferences, but it is worth noting that his rather leftist reputation did not damage his prospects of promotion. Apart from a collection of articles on matters of military interest, his allegiance to the monarchy is evident from the collection of articles on the accession and death of Frederick III, the untested model of a liberal monarch.[20]

In 1901 Reinhardt was seconded to the Great General Staff for a two-year stint in the French department. His then immediate superior, General von Kuhl noted, as others would later, that despite 'his unusual capability for work, he always remained fresh and cheerful.'[21] Reinhardt spent a considerable amount of time both in France and studying the French army from this point onwards. In the summer of 1903 he visited France for three months.[22] By 1917 it is clear that Reinhardt had developed a deep antipathy to the French, but it is impossible to say whether this antipathy had existed before the war. From his collection of newspaper cuttings it is evident that Reinhardt took a general interest in French affairs.[23]

Hence before the outbreak of the war Reinhardt had established himself amongst the élite of the German officer corps. At the end of 1912 Reinhardt was asked to organise a course in military affairs for Crown Prince Philipp Albrecht, son of the Catholic Archduke Albrecht, heir to the Württemberg throne.[24] While the course covered the standard topics of military

17. Ernst, 'Reinhardt', 336; Kaehler, ed., *Thaer*, 281. Some of the anti-Semitism of the officer corps was apparently due to their indebtedness to money-lenders, many of whom were Jewish. See Clemente, *For King or Kaiser*, 163.

18. HStASt, M 660/034, Bü 6, *Die Tägliche Rundschau*, selections from 16 and 18 November 1892; Wolfgang Treue, *Deutsche Parteiprogramme, 1861–1954*, Göttingen, 1954, 72–74, which gives details of the SPD military programme decided upon in 1891 at Erfurt; Nicholas Stargardt, *The German Idea of Militarism. Radical and Socialist critics, 1866–1914*, Cambridge, 1994.

19. Stig Förster, *Der doppelte Militarismus. Die deutsche Heeresrüstungspolitik zwischen Status-Quo-Sicherung und Aggression, 1890–1913*, Stuttgart, 1985, 20–24.

20. HStASt, M 660/034, Bü 6, *Tägliche Rundschau*, 15 and 16 June 1888.

21. Cited in *Wehrkraft und Wehrwille*, 6.

22. HStASt, M 660/034, Bü 1, Reinhardt to Schlieffen, 16 June 1903.

23. HStASt, M 660/034, Bü 6 contains a series of cuttings; on German views of France before 1914, see Mark Hewitson, *National Identity and Political Thought in Germany. Wilhelmine Depictions of the Third French Republic, 1890–1914*, Oxford, 2000.

24. HStASt, M 660/034, Bü 4, Reinhardt to the Crown Prince, Stuttgart, 28 December 1912

education, such as geography and history, the introduction to the course gives an insight into how Reinhardt viewed the military profession on the eve of the war. He stressed that the 'soldiering profession, conceived as a life-long task, claims the whole man.' He pointed to the organisational and leadership qualities which were necessary, and argued that it was an ideal preparation for those who sought to move into positions of leadership, in a typical association of political and military leadership skills. His list of models included Moltke, Blücher, William I and Francis Joseph, but not William II. The introduction suggested the confidence of an officer in late Wilhelmine Germany, who saw the soldiering profession as the most worthy pursuit. On the other hand his interest in SPD military policy and his philosemitic attitude must have brought to his attention the fissures in German society.[25]

It is doubtful however that Reinhardt would have risen to prominence without the onset of war, and indeed the defeat and the departure of a generation of German generals. The war undoubtedly accelerated his career. There is no contemporary evidence to reveal his reactions to the outbreak of war in August 1914, and utterances after the war may have been distorted by memory and political necessity. The image of civil peace, or the *Burgfrieden*, which purported to end the era of social and political division within Germany between the classes, and concentrate energy on the external foe, was a central motif during the war years and then in the Weimar Republic. It represented an idealised view of German society.[26] In a lecture in the late 1920s he remarked: 'The loss of the individual's military capability was often talked about, particularly before the war. The war brought a pleasant surprise. The generation of 1914 proved itself well.'[27] Certainly before the war there was a current in German thought that was critical of the materialism of Wilhelmine society, and it was feared that this would affect the quality of the ordinary soldier. In this context Reinhardt's image of 1914 and the *Burgfrieden* was standard fare in military circles in Weimar Germany.

Like many other Germans he saw the war as defensive. In a draft official history of the Württemberg army, written while Reinhardt was commander of *Wehrkreis V*, France was portrayed as the aggressor. From 1904 (possibly a reference to the Anglo-French Entente) and the first Moroccan crisis to the introduction of a three year military service law in 1913, Germany had been suspicious of French intentions, according to Reinhardt.[28] The alleged threat to Germany, presumably due to the sense

25. HStASt, M 660/034, Bü 4, 'Einführung'; see also Bü 6 for newspaper cuttings from the *Schwarzwalder Bote*, 29 January 1909, and 3 February 1909 on the lack of Württemberg officers in the Württemberg army.

26. Jeffrey Verhey, *The Spirit of 1914. Militarism, Myth and Mobilization in Germany*, Cambridge, 2000, 206–30.

27. *Wehrkraft und Wehrwille*, 69.

28. HStASt, M 660/034, Bü 49, Das Generalkommando des XIII (Kgl. Württ.) Armee, fos. 1–2.

of encirclement, justified the attack: 'If the forces of the aggressor are similar to ours, then the best defence is to attack and defeat him. We tried this in 1914.'[29] Unlike many other generals and politicians, who either tried to portray Russia as the aggressor, or Britain as the main enemy, Reinhardt laid both charges at the feet of the French. Reinhardt's willingness after the war to publish German records to repudiate war guilt charges can be seen as further evidence that he believed that Germany was fighting a defensive war.[30]

Reinhardt spent the whole war on the fighting front, and mostly on the western front. This experience was different from that of his two major rivals after the war, Wilhelm Groener, who had to grapple with labour issues and the war economy at the War Office, and Hans von Seeckt, who spent most of the war on the Eastern front, where the fronts could shift rapidly. At the start of the war Reinhardt was serving in the General Staff of 13th Army Corps, part of 5th Army. The Chief of Staff, Fritz von Loßberg, had been given three weeks leave on 20 July, and was only warned in the early afternoon of 30 July of a 'imminent danger of war'.[31] On 8 August the trains rolled out of Stuttgart, and in Reinhardt's words 'now, what had been planned for over forty years for the defence of the Fatherland, would come to be realised.'[32] This was a further indication of the sense of encirclement, engendered by Germany's geopolitical position between France and Russia. Efficient mobilisation was the first pre-condition of the success of the risky Schlieffen plan which left little room for delay or the frictions of warfare.[33] Loßberg's memory of the march into France was that while the Luxembourgeois were friendly to the Germans, German troops were fired upon by French civilians, whom, he admits, were executed.[34] On 22 August 13th Army Corps encountered the French 5th Army Corps, whose morale Reinhardt described as good. Throughout the war he emphasised the risk of underestimating the French, who, as he pointed out, were defending their homeland. However the Württemberg forces pushed them back: 'impact, artillery battle, the succumbing of the French, their retreat, our pursuit, the clear work of a glorious day.'[35] Reinhardt made neither reference to *franc-tireurs* nor to the atrocities committed by soldiers of 13th Army Corps.[36]

29. *Wehrkraft und Wehrwille*, 101.
30. *Akten der Reichskanzlei. Kabinett Scheidemann, 13. Februar bis 20. Juni 1919*, ed. Hagen Schulze, Boppard am Rhein, 1971, 155.
31. Fritz von Loßberg, *Meine Tätigkeit im Weltkriege, 1914–1918*, Berlin, 1939, 2.
32. HStASt, M 660/034, Bü 49, Das Generalkommando des XIII (Kgl. Württ.) Armee, fo. 2.
33. Stig Förster, 'Der deutsche Generalstab und die Illusionen des kurzen Krieges, 1871–1914. Metakritik eines Mythos', *MgM*, 40, 1, 1995, 61–95.
34. Loßberg, *Tätigkeit*, 13.
35. HStASt, M 660/034, Bü 49, Das Generalkommando des XIII (Kgl. Württ.) Armee, fo. 7.
36. John Horne and Alan Kramer, *German Atrocities, 1914. A History of Denial*, New Haven, 2001, 60–2

He noted the transition from the mobile war at the end of August to the war of position at the battle of the Marne which took place in the second week of September, and ended any German hopes for a speedy victory. After the war the Schlieffen plan became the subject of debate.[37] Reinhardt accepted the principle that if one took the offensive then it was necessary to attack the core (*Lebenszentren*) of the enemy state. However while he recognised that the Schlieffen doctrine of envelopment had worked at Tannenberg in Eastern Prussia in September 1914 when Hindenburg and Ludendorff had surrounded and defeated a larger Russian force, he concluded that 'enough ink has flowed [on the Schlieffen plan], in which the question of the march through Belgium plays no small role.' Less tentatively he regretted that 'we missed the co-operation of the statesman and the army leader, which is already necessary at the stage of the war plan.'[38] Yet he did not offer any alternatives to the Schlieffen plan, unless his comments that it was easier to fight in one's homeland than on enemy soil, can be taken to mean that Germany should have adopted a defensive, long-war strategy in 1914. Instead Reinhardt would immerse himself in the tactical demands of the war of position. This manner of thinking led to a war of attrition.[39] By 8 September 13th Army Corps had been held up. Five days later it retreated for the first time, marking the beginning of Reinhardt's experience of the *Stellungskrieg*: 'in short the onset of the *Stellungskrieg* changed the face of service in the General Command – now there was permanent equipment in the offices, a growth of written work, an increasing need for technical and artillery material, and better personal care, offset by work late into the night.'[40]

Stellungskrieg became a central point of post-war debate about military doctrine as military planners sought to restore decisiveness to operations.[41] Reinhardt did not endorse it; nor did he offer as radical an alternative as Seeckt's doctrine of mobile warfare. For Reinhardt the war of attrition demonstrated that Germany had not maximized its resources. He pointed to French levels of recruitment which were far higher than German ones before 1914. The reliance on the superiority of German troops had been an error. While they proved themselves in the early battles, he also noted that 'it was not sufficient.'[42] According to Reinhardt's

37. Annika Mombauer, *Helmuth von Moltke and the Origins of the First World War*, Cambridge, 2001.
38. *Wehrkraft und Wehrwille*, 169–70.
39. Hew Strachan, 'From Cabinet War to Total War: The Perspective of Military Strategy, 1861–1918', in *Great War, Total War. Mobilisation and Combat on the Western Front, 1914–1918*, Cambridge, 2000, eds Roger Chickering, Stig Förster, 27.
40. HStASt, M 660/034, Bü 49, Das Generalkommando des XIII (Kgl. Württ.) Armee, fo. 11.
41. Hew Strachan, 'War and Society in the 1920s and 1930s'; Dennis E. Showalter, 'Plans, Weapons, Doctrines. The Strategic Culture of Interwar Europe', both in Roger Chickering, Stig Förster, eds, *The Shadows of Total War. Europe, East Asia and the United States*, Cambridge, 2003, 35–81.
42. *Wehrkraft und Wehrwille*, 101.

analysis, Germany had enough resources and therefore presumably could have won the war in the early months, rather than lacking resources from the very outset. The First World War did not lead him to conclude that mass armies were flawed military instruments, but rather to call for even more mobilization. To this extent his argument is similar to Ludendorff's, which claimed that it was the failure to mobilize sufficiently which led to German defeat. If Seeckt inclined towards limited warfare, Reinhardt looked towards total warfare.

At the end of November, 13th Army Corps was transferred to the Eastern front to form part of the left wing of 9th Army at the Bzura. Once again Reinhardt experienced *Stellungskrieg*. By the autumn of 1915, 13th Army Corps was back in the west and Reinhardt had been promoted to Lieutenant Colonel. His time in the east made a deep impression on him. After the war he articulated the stereotype that the inhabitants east of the Elbe made the best soldiers, and that this part of Germany was the 'mother soil' for the German people.[43] Yet for Reinhardt, France remained the *Erbfeind*, the hereditary enemy of Germany. For his final posting of the war, Reinhardt became the Chief of Staff of 7th Army, headed by General von Boehn, in February 1917. He believed that German resources should be concentrated against France, rather than against the British and Imperial forces. Whereas France and Germany were locked in an existential struggle, the British did not face a similar calamity. It was after a successful defensive battle in the spring of 1917 that Reinhardt appeared to come to this conclusion.[44] He picked up an article, from the newspaper of 7th Army, which pointed out that without British help, the French would have lost the war.[45] The political logic of the Anglo-French alliance escaped Reinhardt who considered the impact of an attack on French morale, morale being a highly important element of military strength.[46]

After the war, in a rather distorted view of the events of 1918, Reinhardt wrote:

> The spring offensive of 1918 was mainly directed at the English whom we liked to see as the main enemy. ... The question of whether equal losses would inflict the same moral impression on the French and the English was, in my view, hardly considered at the time. However it is certain that a far smaller part of the English people's strength (*Volkskraft*) was fighting in France, than that of the French. In my opinion only the latter could have been defeated.[47]

43. HStASt, M660/034, Bü 30, Reinhardt published an article in *Ostland*, 28 January 1928; and in general see, Michael Burleigh, *Germany Turns Eastward. A Study of* Ostforschung *in the Third Reich*, Cambridge, 1988, 18-22.
44. HStASt, M 660/034, Bü 14, Reinhardt to Groener, 15 July 1917.
45. HStASt, M 660/034, Bü 14, Lieutenant Joho, 'Mass für Mass', *Kriegszeitung der 7. Armee*.
46. Christian Müller, 'Anmerkungen zur Entwicklung von Kriegsbild und operativ-strategischem Szenario im preußisch-deutschen Heer vor dem Ersten Weltkrieg', *MgM*, 57, 2, 1998, 385-442.
47. *Wehrkraft und Wehrwille*, 167.

For Reinhardt and other leading generals in the Weimar period, the moral element of warfare remained fundamental. Although there was a recognition that materiel was essential, the stress on morale led Reinhardt to call for the spiritual militarization of the individual. The struggle between nations was not reduced to the respective strengths of their economies, but became a conflict between cultures. The onset of modern industrialized warfare had meant that the issue of morale became transplanted from the army to the whole nation.[48]

1917 was the year of the defensive on the western front, and the performance of 7th Army earned Reinhardt the decoration of *Pour le mérite*. He became known as 'the defensive lion of Laon.'[49] The following year, the German Supreme Command, dominated by Ludendorff, decided to go on the offensive, before the arrival of American troops swung the war in the Allies' favour.[50] Although 7th Army pushed the French back over the river Marne in May 1918, the German lines were overstretched. On 15 July, 7th Army began to attack once more, but its forces were too weak. On 18 July, the French commander of the Allied forces, Ferdinand Foch launched a carefully prepared counter-attack against 7th Army. The use of tanks, which emerged from the woods around Villers-Cotterets, surprised the German forces. Although Ludendorff later commented that the defeat at the hands of British forces on 2 August was the 'blackest day' in German history, the defeat of 7th Army marked the end of the series of German offensives.[51] The initiative now lay with the Allies. Occasionally, after the war, opponents of Reinhardt associated him with the defeat of 7th Army, and indeed a number of myths were deployed to apportion or to deflect blame.

The retreat of 7th Army was portrayed as a successful defensive battle, but the account given by Loßberg, the liaison officer from the German Supreme Command to 7th Army, shows that Ludendorff had lost his nerve, and that valuable time was lost in organising a retreat. Ludendorff had overestimated the powers of resistance of 7th Army, and when his hopes were disappointed he blamed others: '[T]o my regret', Loßberg recalled, 'he raised unjustified accusations against the head of the Operations Department (Colonel Wetzell) and his colleagues who had failed in their assessment of the fighting abilities of 7th Army.'[52] Loßberg, who had hurried to the front, suggested an organised retreat to the defensive Siegfried line. Ludendorff, fearing the impression such a retreat would make on the rest of the army and the home front, refused to sanction a withdrawal. Meanwhile Boehn and Reinhardt, 'robust people with good nerves', in the words of Loßberg, tried to defend the position of 7th Army

48. Ibid., 166.
49. BA-MA, N 86/14, Telegram, May 1917; *Wehrkraft und Wehrwille*, 15.
50. Holger Herwig, *The First World War. Germany and Austria, 1914–1918*, London, 1997, 392–95.
51. Erich Ludendorff, *Meine Kriegserinnerungen 1914–1918*, Berlin, 1919, 535–47.
52. Loßberg, *Tätigkeit*, 344.

as best they could.[53] It was only on 26 July 1918 that the Supreme Command issued an order to retreat. The famed system of decentralising command, and allowing local commanders to make decisions based on an accurate assessment of the situation, no longer existed.

There were deeper problems. Even before the 1918 offensives, and especially in June when the German Supreme Command ordered the next major operation, 7th Army had pointed to the exhaustion of the soldiers and the lack of resources. On 24 June, the artillery commander of 241 Infantry Division warned that 'the general situation of 7th Army demands a temporary pause in the fighting at the moment.'[54] In January 1918 Reinhardt was asking the (Army Group) Crown Prince for more infantry to maintain fighting capability: 'the current infantry forces are insufficient for a deep attack over a width of two kilometres; the troops would exhaust themselves on the first day, the commanders would be forced to use divisions from the second wave of the attack on that first day, and therefore on the second and third days there would not be enough to continue the battle.'[55] By the time of the July offensive, the manpower situation of 7th Army had deteriorated. On 19 June the (Army Group) Crown Prince decided to postpone the start of the attack for five days until 15 July, an indication of the difficulties in getting materiel and men to the front.[56] Hence before the July offensive there were clear indications and warnings that the German armies were exhausted. Nonetheless these voices were dismissed by the German Supreme Command which cheerily claimed on 5 June 1918: 'Neither the English nor the French armies are capable of a major offensive at this time. We will continue our offensive and impose our initiative on the enemy.'[57] The optimism, based on a flawed assessment of relative strengths, prevented Ludendorff from recognising the weakness of 7th Army, and therefore delayed its retreat after Foch's counter-attack.

The options for German military strategy once the United States entered the war were extremely limited. After the war Reinhardt argued that American entry into the war at the same time as the Nivelle offensive and French mutiny in 1917 had saved the Allies.[58] In 1918, as the early offensives foundered, the pressure of time increased: 'In the place of one attack pursued to victory, several attacks were planned. Each one needed intensive preparation, which cost time. Each one demanded

53. Ibid., 348.
54. BA-MA, PH 5 II 482, Report of Artillery Commander, Infantry Division, 241, No 871/I geh., 24 June 1918.
55. BA-MA, PH 5/I, 32, AOK 7, Reinhardt to (Army Group) Crown Prince, Ia Nr 102/Jan 18 geh. II. Ang, 29 January 1918, fos. 15–16.
56. Reichsarchiv, *Der Weltkrieg*, vol. 14, Berlin, 424.
57. Ibid., 414.
58. HStASt, M 660/034, Bü 51, manuscript entitled 'Die Frühjahrskämpfe 1918 in Frankreich und das Eingreifen der Amerikaner'.

massive sacrifices of costly human life on the German side, which were replaced increasingly unsatisfactorily and with great difficulty. From week to week, from attack to attack, the danger grew that neither time nor resources would suffice to break out of the ring, before the masses of American troops made it impossible.'[59] He contrasted the arrival of fresh American troops with the 'draining impact of constant tension for the German troops.'[60] It was the entry of the United States into the war which saved the Allies and robbed the Germans of any hope for victory.

Reinhardt's version of defeat borrowed some elements of the stab-in-the-back myth, but it did not embrace the usual vitriolic denunciations of socialists, Jews and Sparticists. Nor did he single out specific politicians. This less virulent form of the stab-in-the-back myth has been lost in the concentration on more extreme explanations. On 12 October 1918 he wrote to his wife: 'The affairs of the Reich government are making me worried. We are not capable of creating a united Fatherland, that is a great weakness. All are guilty of this, I believe the right no less than the left.'[61] Instead defeat was the result of exhaustion. His resignation letter to the General Staff, after his transfer to the Demobilization Department of the Prussian Ministry of War, is especially revealing: 'The German army has been forced off the glorious path of victories of the first four years of the war onto the thorny way of bitter defence by the overbearing power of the enemy, the collapse of its allies, some decisive tactical defeats and our own errors.'[62] At this moment of defeat Reinhardt admitted that the responsibility for the defeat lay with the army. In one of his lectures at the end of the 1920s he pointed to the style of war as a cause of defeat:

> In the west between 1914 and 1918 ever more bloody frontal battles developed, initially lasting several days, then several weeks, which our former leaders disparagingly equated with ordinary victories, if they should lead to such. Ultimately Germany was crushed without encirclement or other operational skills by such continual fighting and forced into a shameful capitulation.[63]

Yet if Reinhardt had blamed the style of war for German defeat, he failed to mention any alternatives, nor did he develop any in the 1920s as Seeckt did.[64] Instead he resorted to the argument that Germany's defeat was due

---

59. Ibid., 11.
60. Ibid., 19–20.
61. Ernst, 'Aus dem Nachlaß', 42; unfortunately the letters published by Ernst could not be found in Reinhardt's papers, and as Ernst pointed out there were relatively few letters in the first place.
62. BA-MA, N 86/14, Reinhardt to the General Staff of 7th Army and the Quartermaster General of the Army, 6 November 1918; reprinted in Ernst, 'Aus seinem Nachlaß, 43–44, footnote 5.
63. *Wehrkraft und Wehrwille*, 171.
64. See Chapter 9.

to the material superiority of the enemy, though again he continued to stress the moral dimension of war.

The idea of the *Übermacht* (superiority in terms of power, but not moral superiority) found resonance in Weimar Germany. When Friedrich Ebert, then the leading member of the provisional government, the Council of People's Commissars, welcomed the troops back, he resorted to this argument.[65] It ennobled the failure of the German army in the First World War, and it also avoided the excesses of more virulent stab-in-the-back legends. It fused the army and the home front into one, and although never properly utilised, it provided a basis for the reconstruction of a *Volksgemeinschaft* as a new period of suffering began. Reinhardt's assessment of defeat in 1918 fits into this tradition. In an open letter to old soldiers in 1924 Reinhardt used the phrase 'undefeated but overcome'.[66] In his manuscript on the battle of July 1918 he asked rhetorically: 'What decided the war? That, which decides all wars, not a single military success, but that the will of the German people to continue the war, was broken.'[67] He concluded by assessing the significance of the battle in July 1918: 'The great expenditure of effort to which the German people were being roused once again after four years of war, could only be borne if it led to victory. If that did not happen, then a counter-reaction was bound to set in. That began shortly after the retreat of 7th Army behind the Aisne and the Vesle. Therefore the events of the events of the second half of July are of so much significance.'[68]

Defeat in 1918, rather than the treaty of Versailles, became the starting point for the revisionist agenda of the Weimar era. France replaced Britain as Germany's main enemy, something which Reinhardt had advocated during the war. After the war France returned to its position as the *Erbfeind*, or hereditary enemy, for many Germans, a position which limited the opportunities for a genuine rapprochement between the two states. Reinhardt fully subscribed to the view that France was Germany's main enemy *during the war*. On 17 October 1918 he complained to his wife that the SPD did not understand 'the spirit and hatred of our enemies.' On 11 November 1918, the day the war ended, he wrote: 'The external position is really bad. The French are extracting the last drop of blood in order to maintain the position that the unity of enemies created rather than [French] power and skill, for as long as possible.'[69] It was not the treaty

65. Friedrich Hiller von Gaertringen, '"Dolchstoss"-Diskussion und "Dolchstoss-Legende" im Wandel von vier Jahrzehnten', in *Geschichte und Gegenwartsbewußtsein*, Göttingen, 1963, 132.

66. HStASt, M 660/034, Bü 27, 'An die Kameraden der Regimenten der alten Armee, deren Überlieferungen von den Truppenteilen der 5. Division gepflegt wird.'

67. HStASt, M 600/034, Bü 51, 'Die Frühjahrskämpfe 1918 in Frankreich und das Eingreifen der Amerikaner', fo. 24.

68. Ibid., fo. 68.

69. Fritz Ernst, 'Aus dem Nachlaß des Generals Walther Reinhardt', *Die Welt als Geschichte*, 18, 1958, 42, 49.

of Versailles that Reinhardt sought to reverse, but the result of the First World War. The loss of Germany's semi-hegemonial position in Europe was the starting point for revision, and revisionist claims were strengthened by the reception of the treaty.

By 1918 Reinhardt also clearly recognised the internal dimensions of the primacy of foreign policy, most importantly the cohesion of society and the unity of leadership. This, he suggested, marked a major break from the pre-1914 mode of military thought.[70] However there is no evidence of his views on the major domestic political issues such as the relationship between trade unions and employers, the Prussian electoral reform, propaganda, the military state of emergency and the growing fractures within Wilhelmine society.[71] Indeed Reinhardt, even in the 1920s, had no specific suggestions for the establishment of social cohesion. This probably resulted from his experience of the war. As a commander at the front he had no dealings with these issues. He realised that excluded and disenfranchised groups had to be integrated, but he never pointed to reforms of the legal system or the welfare state. Rather he tended to focus on the external enemy and call for domestic social and political harmony during national crises. He simply assumed that all Germans had a stake in the defence of the Fatherland. The lack of detail on these matters is striking, showing the limits of Reinhardt's imagination and horizons. When he engaged with domestic political issues, he followed a pragmatic, not a programmatic, path.

Reinhardt fully expected Germany to recover from defeat. His assessments of the causes of defeat were therefore no mere melancholy musings, but influenced his thought and policies in the Weimar Republic. By not singling out various groups (perhaps with the exception of pacifists) responsible for defeat Reinhardt was able to co-operate with the new regime. While he was no republican, he did not believe that he was working for traitors. Moreover his image of the *Volksgemeinschaft* could remain intact – neither socialists nor democrats were automatically excluded. Reinhardt's sole criterion for membership was the willingness to defend the Fatherland. Finally, and contradictorily, while he ascribed the Allied victory to superior economic resources, he ascribed German defeat to war weariness and a lack of will to continue to prosecute the war. This meant that he continued to focus on the remobilization of the German mind in the Weimar period.

70. *Wehrkraft und Wehrwille*, 39.
71. On social upheaval, see Jürgen Kocka, *Klassengesellschaft im Krieg. Deutsche Sozialgeschichte 1914–1918*, 2nd edn, Göttingen, 1978.

Chapter 3

COMING TO TERMS WITH THE NEW REGIME

On 9 November 1918 Kaiser William II abdicated and the German Republic was declared. On the same day the provisional government, known as the Council of People's Commissars, and composed of the two socialist parties, the USPD and the larger and more moderate SPD, was established. Crucially, for their relationship with the officer corps, the SPD was most concerned about social stability and the maintenance of the Reich's unity.[1] Two days later, on 11 November 1918, a German delegation signed the armistice. Between then and 19 January 1919 when decrees on the relationship between officers and troops were issued – it was also the day elections to the National Assembly took place – important decisions in military policy were taken. The limitations on policy were severe. Demobilization, the restoration of order within Germany and the beginning of border defence in the east shaped the possibilities for the new military policy. Within these limits there was a struggle, principally between the officer corps and the soldiers' councils, which had emerged at the end of the war in order to represent the interests of the ordinary soldier. Winning the support of the provisional government was essential to the outcome of this struggle. Yet there was also change and debate within the officer corps as the nascent conflict between the Prussian Ministry of War and the Supreme Command began. In these conditions Reinhardt came to terms with the new regime. If he appeared to profit by rising to the position of Minister of War, he also incurred damage to his reputation within the officer corps, due to the compromises which he felt necessary for the sake of military reform.

On 3 November 1918 Reinhardt was appointed to head the Demobilization Department of the Prussian Ministry of War, one of the most important positions in the German military in late 1918. According to his brother, the Ministry of War, unaware of the condition of soldiers at the

---

1. Dieter Groh, Peter Brandt, *"Vaterlandslose Gesellen". Sozialdemokratie und Nation 1860–1990*, Munich, 1992, 175–78.

front, wanted a senior officer from the front to fill the post.[2] In October, as the situation worsened, the Ministry of War asked the Supreme Command to send an officer 'who knew the conditions at the front' to head the Demobilization Department.[3] The transfer from the General Staff to the Ministry of War came at a crucial moment in Reinhardt's career. His presence in Berlin during the revolutionary period brought him to the attention of senior SPD politicians. If the war had promoted his military career, then his immediate post-war appointment propelled him into the ranks of the most senior officers.

Reinhardt's initial impressions of events behind the front were formed on his journey to Berlin where he arrived on 8 November. His account illustrates the relative separation of the battle front from pressing concerns on the home front. At the headquarters at Spa on 7 November he was taken aback by 'a dark, stormy atmosphere' which he contrasted to the stable conditions at 7th Army headquarters.[4] Had he known that the same day a meeting of front officers with General Wilhelm Heye had concluded that the army would not support the Kaiser, he might have been less surprised.[5] His train journey to Berlin involved a series of stops, due to disorder. Reinhardt believed that the crowds were not 'malicious', but simply 'wild soldiers on leave'. In Berlin Reinhardt was surprised by appearance of officers in civilian clothes. He had clearly underestimated the revolutionary atmosphere in Germany, much of which was directed against the military pillar of the *Kaiserreich*'s regime.

It is in this context that Reinhardt's later claim that he momentarily thought of resistance when he heard of the *Kaiser*'s abdication must be assessed:

> Naturally we reacted in a fairly excited manner, and considered as far as possible the means of resistance. However due to the authority of Hindenburg and Scheüch, as well as the critical situation of our comrades at the front, there appeared to be no positive side [to resistance], so we decided unanimously to follow the Minister, who, like all the other specialist Reich Secretaries of State, was staying in office for the moment.[6]

Reinhardt saw the unrest as the social disorder of an exhausted society, when, in fact, the nature of the revolt had changed from the social to the

---

2. BA-MA, N 86/15, Abschrift, note from Prussian Minister of War, Scheüch to Reinhardt, 3 November 1918; *Walther Reinhardt. Wehrkraft und Wehrwille. Aus seinem Nachlaß mit einer Lebensbeschreibung*, ed. Ernst Reinhardt, Berlin, 1932, 16.
3. BA-MA, N 86/59, 'Demobilmachung'; most of this document, which was written by Major Fleck, one of Reinhardt's subordinates at the Ministry of War, has been reprinted in Fritz Ernst, 'Aus dem Nachlaß des Generals Walther Reinhardt', *Die Welt als Geschichte*, 1958.
4. Ibid., 44–47.
5. Ekkehart P. Guth, *Der Loyalitätskonflikt des deutschen Ofizierkorps, 1918-1920*, Frankfurt, 1983, 15.
6. Ernst, 'Aus seinem Nachlaß', 45.

political in early November. As Reinhardt later told the provisional government, the Council of People's Commissars, on the day of his appointment as Prussian Minister of War, he was a 'convinced monarchist.'[7] He had broken down in tears when he first heard of the abdication.[8] He was no natural adherent to the republican cause but he was realist enough to recognise the political significance of Scheüch's and Hindenburg's pledge to remain in office. It is also significant that, even after the event, he reproduced Scheüch's justification for staying in office, namely 'in the interests of the welfare of the armies at the front.'[9] Loyalty to comrades would lead to service with the new regime. As yet there was no alliance with the Council of People's Commissars, which contained the two socialist parties, the SPD and the USPD, but military support for the *Kaiser* was clearly futile.

By the following day a *de facto* alliance between the Ministry of War, which was in command of troops within Germany and the Council of People's Commissars existed and this marked yet another stage in Reinhardt's ascent. On the evening of 9 November, Scheüch ordered Reinhardt to the Chancellery. Attired in civilian clothes, Reinhardt took down the conditions of the ceasefire, an experience which he likened to that which 'a medieval delinquent must have had, as his body was broken bone by bone.'[10] The severity of the conditions and the continuing unrest in the city led Otto Wels, a moderate SPD leader, to suggest the formation of an armed unit to protect the provisional government.[11] On 10 November Friedrich Ebert, leader of the provisional government, and Scheüch appointed Reinhardt to head the so-called *Ordnungsdienst*.[12] This guard cleared the governmental area, around Wilhelmstraße, of allegedly menacing crowds and the Council of People's Commissars was liberated momentarily from the pressures of street politics. In his account of the first days of the revolution Reinhardt attached considerable significance to this episode: 'I had, without knowing it, or aiming at it, gained the trust of the People's Commissars who for the first time recognised the importance of military support.'[13] However Scheüch's adjutant, Gustav Böhm, claimed that Reinhardt 'did not have much' to do with the

---

7. *Die Regierung der Volksbeauftragten 1918-19*, eds Susanne Miller, Erich Matthias, 2 vols, Düsseldorf, 1969, vol. 1, 148; Ernst-Heinrich Schmidt, *Heimatheer und Revoltuion 1918. Die militärischen Gewalten im Heimatgebiet zwischen Oktoberreform und Novemberrevolution*, Stuttgart, 1981, 361.
8. Ernst, 'Aus seinem Nachlaß', 52.
9. *Adjutant im preussischen Kriegsministerium Juni 1918 bis Oktober 1919. Aufzeichnungen des Hauptmanns Gustav Böhm*, ed. Heinz Hürten, Stuttgart, 1977, 61.
10. Ernst, 'Aus seinem Nachlaß', 45.
11. Ibid., 45.
12. Ibid., 45; BA-MA, N 86/15, Abschrift, 'Vollmacht', 10 November 1918, signed Ebert, Scheüch.
13. Ernst, 'Aus dem Nachlaß', 47.

impromptu guard. It is more likely that this was just one of a succession of events which brought the Württemberger to the attention of the new leaders.[14]

While Reinhardt overstated the impact of the events of 10 December the relationship between the Council of People's Commissars and the Ministry of War helped stabilise the revolution. It was a domestic equivalent to the Ebert-Groener pact. This arrangement between the leading officer within the Supreme Command, Wilhelm Groener, and the leading figure of the Council of People's Commissars, Ebert, involved the subordination of the army to the Council in return for the Council's support for the officers' right of command (*Befehlsgewalt*) and the maintenance of law and order. All this was designed to facilitate demobilization, one of the most pressing social and political problems facing the new regime. It was the first of a series of informal arrangements which shaped the civil-military relationship. It also confirmed the dominance of the officers in the sphere of military policy, due to their presumed professional expertise. Although the links between Ebert and Groener were crucial to the maintenance of order, the strong position of the Ministry of War during this period has often gone unnoticed.[15] Its officers were at the heart of the decision-making process in Berlin and would use this to considerable effect in the months to come.

Within days of the revolution, Reinhardt had adjusted to the new environment. This involved assessments of the political actors in Berlin, and of the future prospects for Germany, assessments which were essential in shaping his policy choices. He had already identified the danger of further social disorder and political radicalism, a common theme for senior officers and moderate socialists who dominated the political decision making process in Berlin. In November 1918 the officer corps' sense of *raison d'état* dictated that they would support the SPD members of the provisional government. On 11 November he wrote to his wife: 'So much is turning on the question of whether the "orderly" socialists or the "wild" socialists get the upper hand, that it does not occur to one to think about what has collapsed.'[16] Two days later he was more specific:

> We are still in flux, the old socialist party has not yet got control, but at the moment only it offers a guarantee of order. Therefore we have to support it. It seems as though Ebert is succeeding in maintaining his leading position. I have got to know all these men over the past few days. He [Ebert] makes a really good impression. Almost all the elements of order are supporting him.[17]

14. *Adjutant im preussischen Ministerium*, 65–6.
15. Schmidt, *Heimatheer*, 410; on the Ebert-Groener relationship see Gerhard Rakenius, *Wilhelm Groener als erster Generalquartiermeister. Die Politik der Obersten Heeresleitung*, Boppard am Rhein, 1977.
16. Ernst, 'Aus seinem Nachlaß', 48.
17. Ibid., 48.

Under the pressure of radical change and the search for an anchor, new perceptions could arise quickly.[18]

While immediate circumstances dictated the choice of political partners, there was also an element of optimism amongst many officers that the wheels of history would turn in Germany's favour once more. When leaving the General Staff Reinhardt wrote: 'The heavy storms of the present must find us as men who will calm them, as men who are not overwhelmed by problems, but who mature in spite of the ever-increasing difficulties.'[19] Looking towards a better future also meant looking at the rôle of German youth, a topic in which Reinhardt was interested without having any detailed views. While dismayed by the anti-militarist sentiments prevalent in Berlin, Reinhardt believed that 'our youth are growing up, they are worth our work, our life, and that is our connection with the hope of a better future, which I will not allow to disappear.'[20] Youth, recovery and the inculcation of German (military) values provided him with a vision for the future. Historical analogies, and the belief in the rhythms of history, were also an important part of an optimistic discourse which persuaded many natural opponents of the Weimar Republic to support it initially.[21] Reinhardt spoke of the inspiration which the Prussian military reformers and their achievements after the disaster at the battle of Jena, offered to him in 1919 when he was establishing the *Reichswehr*.[22]

The immediate task at hand was the demobilization of the returning troops, sufficient to test the most optimistic spirit. Even his department was chaotic: 'At the moment we are lacking the right organisation, we have too many groups working alongside one another.'[23] According to one of his closest colleagues during these months, Major Fleck, Reinhardt's method of work 'was to get to know personally those with whom he had to deal. Due to his lack of prejudice and his sense of reality he saw and judged the power relationships more accurately than many other personalities at the time.'[24] Demobilization had been planned in the firm conviction of a German victory. The evidence from the summer of 1918 onwards that this hope was not going to be fulfilled was studiously

---

18. Michael Epkenhans, '"Wir als deutsches Volk sind doch nicht klein zu kriegen." Aus den Tagebüchern des Fregattenkapitäns Bogistav von Selchow, 1918/19', MgM, 55, 1 , 1996, 212–13.

19. Ernst 'Aus dem Nachlaß', 44, footnote 5.

20. Ibid., 49.

21. William Mulligan, 'Historical stereotypes and the Franco-German relationship after the First World War', paper given at Conference of the Historical Society, 17 May 2002, Atlanta, Georgia.

22. *Wehrkraft und Wehrwille*, 117–19.

23. Ernst, 'Aus dem Nachlaß', 48.

24. Ibid., 52.

ignored by the Ministry of War.[25] Now rule of thumb, improvisation and a *laissez-faire* approach dominated demobilization. Or as the Ministry of War's guidelines, presumably heavily influenced by Reinhardt, but signed by Scheüch and Göhre, obfuscated: 'Demobilization will take place in a different way than planned, owing to the end of the war.'[26]

These guidelines set out initial policy. Demobilization policy was a belated attempt to impose some control over a chaotic process which had already begun: 'The internal and external situation, and especially the ceasefire conditions render the numerous anticipated measures necessary, which are already in process.'[27] They stressed that the army was to return to its peacetime status, and they did not intend to pre-empt any decision on the future form of the army. However there was a possible contradiction in this policy, since if the army returned to its peacetime status, it would put itself in a formidable position when it came to structure the new army. The main consideration was to fulfil the terms of the armistice. However, within these parameters, questions of domestic order and external defence were raised. The guidelines declared it an aim 'to defend those areas which we still possess', a policy which the military leaders continued to advocate in 1919 for territories which were disputed by Poland. When this requirement had been fulfilled, troops could demobilize, although the cohorts from 1898 and 1899 were to remain in the army indefinitely, while those of 1896 and 1897 were to remain for a transitional period.[28] On 15 November Reinhardt had written a memorandum, which was similar to the guidelines, and perhaps influenced them. While noting the different difficulties of space and time facing the German armies in the east and west, respectively, he underlined the security role of the army. He considered the Czechs, Poles and Bolshevists to be a threat to Germany, and he even maintained that 'if we dissolve the army immediately we will no longer have a counterweight in the peace negotiations.'[29] The myth of the 'unbeaten army' led generals to continue to think in terms of *Machtpolitik*[30], and it was only with the debate over the treaty of Versailles that the officer corps was forced to recognise the extent of their military weakness.

The maintenance of an army pre-supposed control which the officer corps simply could not wield in 1918. There was little difficulty for the Supreme Command in persuading soldiers that it was in their best interests to obey their officers and follow them over the river Rhine, to avoid

25. For an analysis of demobilization see Richard Bessel, *Germany after the First World War* (Oxford, 1993).
26. BA-MA, N 86/15, Richtlinien für den Demobilmachung', 15 November 1918.
27. Ibid.
28. Ibid.
29. BA-MA, N 86/15, 'Zur Aufklärung über Fragen der Zurückführung des deutschen Heeres'.
30. *Zwischen Revolution und Kapp-Putsch: Militär und Innenpolitk, 1918-1920*, ed. Heinz Hürten, Düsseldorf, 1977, 30-31.

internment by the Allies. However, once the troops had reached the demarcation line set by the armistice, they no longer needed to obey their superiors. Many simply wandered off home at the earliest opportunity, rather than travel to the point of demobilization of their unit. Reinhardt told his colleagues on 21 November: 'Our army is streaming back to the homeland in an unbroken movement.' While he acknowledged that a continuation of hostilities was unlikely on the western front, he reiterated his concerns about the situation on Germany's eastern borders. Further he noted that there was a public order risk if the troops simply demobilized themselves since they would keep their weapons.[31]

In response to the progress of demobilization on the ground Reinhardt amended the demobilization decrees at the end of November. He remained adamant that 'under all circumstances security and work duty, order, the guarding of prisoners and the protection of the border, as well as the implementation of demobilization must be guaranteed.'[32] After getting the agreement of the states' war ministries, the Ministry of War issued a compilation of the decrees issued to date with the relevant amendments. Giving primacy to public order and border defence, it warned: 'The fulfilment of these tasks must be guaranteed in the first place. Otherwise the most serious dangers will emerge for the country.' No soldier was to demobilize of his own accord, and the cohorts of 1896 to 1899 were retained. It also co-opted the workers' and soldiers' councils, instructing them to dissuade demobilized soldiers from rushing to Berlin where employment and housing opportunities were limited.[33] While the officers were generally suspicious of the soldiers' councils, they were prepared to co-operate with them, especially in the case of welfare and demobilization.[34]

Yet the flurry of decrees, the co-operation of the soldiers' councils and the promise of demobilization money did little to control the self-demobilization of the troops. In one of the more sarcastic decrees, Reinhardt suggested: 'Many of the delays, accommodation and welfare difficulties, particularly at railway nodal points have arisen because neither the field unit nor the post responsible for the return of the army are aware of the point of demobilization. To avoid these difficulties ... field and reserve troops and posts must find out the point of demobilization before their

31. HStASt, M 660/034, Überblick über die Lage der Demobilmachung und der Entlassungen am 21. November'; *Adjutant im preussischen Kriegsministerium*, 87.

32. HStASt, M 1/4, Bü 1067, Circular from Prussian Ministry of War to the Reich Ministry of the Interior, the War Ministries of Bavaria, Saxony and Württemberg, 27 November 1918, with appendix, fo. 340–41.

33. Richard Bessel, 'Unemployment and Demobilisation in Germany after the First World War', in *The German Unemployed*, eds Richard Evans, Dick Geary, New York, 1987.

34. *Dokumente zur deutschen Verfassunsgsgecshichte. Dokumente der Novemberrevolution und der Weimarer Republik, 1918-1933*, 3 vols, ed. E. R. Huber, Stuttgart, 1966, vol. 3, 9–13; Kluge, *Soldatenräte*, 99–101.

departure.'[35] Up to half a million men left their units of their own accord in the weeks following the Armistice. Reinhardt, in a meeting of the Economic Demobilization Office on 18 and 19 December 1918 pointed to the collapse of discipline due to 'domestic upheaval', and 'raw urge to return home', once units had crossed the Rhine.[36] In a private conversation with Lieutenant Knoerzer, adjutant of the Württemberg military plenipotentiary in Berlin, Reinhardt not only criticised the 'debilitating influence of Berlin', but he also admitted: 'One should not have any illusions about the state of the front army. In general people have maintained discipline, but only because they are going home and they know that without order a great many will fall into [Allied] captivity.' The actual course of demobilization marked a setback for those officers who had hoped to use the core of the old army to maintain public order and border defence. Reinhardt lamented the problem of trying to 'form twenty divisions from the 180 divisions of the western army, which are absolutely necessary for border defence east of the neutral zone.'[37] By the end of 1918 the German army was therefore considerably weaker than officers had expected.

In the midst of the demobilization process, on 15 December, Scheüch resigned, claiming that the 'work of the Ministry of War on demobilization is, as far as one can say in the current circumstances, on the right path.' Angered by the anti-militarist spirit abroad in Berlin, he believed it impossible to continue as Minister of War. However he also agreed to stay on until a successor had been found.[38] The process of choosing Scheüch's successor is highly significant because it was the first major military appointment made by the Council of People's Commissars. There were five main candidates. Groener, Reinhardt, Colonel Hans von Feldmann who worked with the Supreme Command, Gustav Noske, the SPD's military expert who had been sent to Kiel at the outset of the revolution, and Captain Wilhelm Boelke who was the favourite of the USPD. Personal ambition, bureaucratic infighting and political differences characterised the politics of the appointment.

Scheüch's resignation may have been prompted by disputes with the Supreme Command, as well as by anti-military sentiment. On 9 December the Supreme Command had ordered the General Command not to accept instructions from the Ministry of War.[39] A group of officers based in the Supreme Command had developed a plan to bring reliable troop units to Berlin, and under the guise of a celebratory return to launch a

---

35. HStASt, M 1/4, 1067, Prussian Ministry of War circular, D Nr 5936/18 AM, 6 December 1918.
36. Bessel, *Germany*, 75.
37. *Zwischen Revolution und Kapp*, 24–25.
38. BA-MA, N 23/1, Abschrift, Scheüch to the Council of People's Commissars, the Prussian Cabinet, 15 December 1918; the text is also in Huber, ed., *Dokumente*, 36.
39. Rakenius, *Groener*, 151–52.

coup which would install Ebert as an effective dictator and then dissolve the workers' and soldiers' councils.[40] The leading officers in this affair, Hans von Haeften, Bodo von Harbou and Arnold Lequis, sought the support of the Ministry of War. According to Böhm, Scheüch 'had nothing against the plan', but would not participate. Haeften, who met both Reinhardt and Scheüch, also noted that neither wanted to be involved, but mainly for political reasons.[41] Harbou was more openly critical and complained to Kurt von Schleicher, Groener's chief adviser, that Scheüch was unwilling to stand up to the soldiers' councils.[42] The Ministry of War had been discredited in the eyes of the Supreme Command, and it may have been this internal military politics which caused the resignation of Scheüch. The episode also marked a return of the bureaucratic struggle for control of military policy between the Ministry of War and the Supreme Command which lasted until the summer of 1919.

Scheüch would not have recognised Groener's hand behind these manoeuvres in December 1918, because when Groener approved of the plan, he also suggested that another 'politically skilled general' should be in charge.[43] Doubtless like Reinhardt and Scheüch, he recognised the political dangers, and was hedging his bets. Ebert's refusal to support the plot to make him dictator scuppered the plan. News of the upcoming vacancy at Bendlerstrasse had seeped out before Scheüch sent in his letter of resignation on 15 December. The previous day he had forewarned the Supreme Command by telling the Ministry of War's representative with the Supreme Command, Major von Heydekamp, of his impending resignation. Scheüch's preference as successor was Groener, a choice which 'did not find a particularly warm reception' with the Council of People's Commissars, despite Ebert's approval.[44] Reinhardt was not the first choice amongst the officer corps. On 13 December Reinhardt's friend Albrecht von Thaer, an officer in the Supreme Command, was suddenly asked by Groener if he would like to be the next Minister of War. Thaer replied that he thought Groener had already pencilled Reinhardt's name in for that position. Groener, while acknowledging that 'it could be him', remarked that 'he stands too far to the left.'[45] After Thaer's refusal, Groener persisted in the tactic of trying to foist an officer from the

40. Ibid., 137–52; Kluge, *Soldatenräte*, 222–39.
41. BA-MA, N 35/9, Haeften's account in 'Erlebnisse 1918', vol. 2, fo. 129; Rakenius, *Groener*, 141.
42. BA-MA, N 42/11, Bericht des Majors von Harbou über die Tätigkeit des Generalkommandos Lequis, fos 25–27; Rakenius, *Groener*, 144–46.
43. BA-MA, N 35/9, 'Erlebnisse 1918', vol. 2, fos. 129–30.
44. BA-MA, N 23/1, Scheüch note on his resignation, fo. 20; *Adjutant im preussischen Kriegsministerium*, 106–107.
45. *Generalmajor Albrecht von Thaer. Generalstabsdienst an der Front und in der Obersten Heeresleitung. Aus Briefen und Tagebuchaufzeichnungen 1915–1919*, ed. Siegfried Kaehler, Göttingen, 1958, 281.

Supreme Command into the Ministry of War. He must have recognised that the position was a poisoned chalice, and that it was preferable to control the rival bureaucracy from a distance.

Scheüch later claimed that Groener would have accepted the position had the provisional government approached him directly.[46] However Groener was not shy about proposing his own candidates. After a dinner on 20 December, Scheüch reported: 'Gr[oener] does not want to be my successor, even if the government offer it to him, because he believes, as he has often said, that he can do better service later and because he does not want to waste himself now. I think he is thinking very selfishly indeed, and therefore not correctly. Now is not the time for a seat warmer.' Scheüch was even more taken aback by Groener's suggestion of Feldmann, 'even though he did not know him very well.'[47] According to Böhm, Scheüch 'talked a lot that evening about what could bring Groener to propose Feldmann.'[48] The vacillation of the senior officers allowed the Council of People's Commissars to take the initiative. At a meeting on 17 December 'there was a strong disposition to appoint a civilian, because they thought he would be freer in his treatment of the officer question.' However, Scheüch, who played a rôle in the choice of his successor, had already warned the provisional government that a civilian would find it 'impossible to control the officers of the Ministry of War.'[49]

At this stage yet a further complication entered into the equation, namely the so-called Hamburg points. On 9 December some officers in Hamburg had attempted a coup against the new order. This failed, but stoked the fears of many on the left that the officer corps was a hotbed of counterrevolutionary activity. In order to control the military a number of suggestions were put forward which ultimately were codified in a speech by the Hamburg SPD member, Walther Lamp'l to the Congress of Workers' and Soldiers' Councils on 18 December.[50] The Hamburg points made seven demands, which amounted to a radical challenge to existing military structures. The Council of People's Commissars would exercise the right of command; in the garrisons the soldiers' councils would have right of command, not the officers; officers would be elected by their soldiers, while discipline was to be maintained by the soldiers' councils. Finally as a 'symbol of the break up and abolition of unthinking obedience' all badges of rank would be

46. BA-MA, N 23/1, Scheüch note on his resignation, fo. 21.

47. BA-MA, N 23/1, Scheüch note on his resignation, fo. 21.

48. *Adjutant im preussischen Kriegsministerium*, 113.

49. BA-MA, N 23/1, Scheüch note on his resignation, fo. 21; *Adjutant im preussischen Kriegsministerium*, 110.

50. Eberhard Kolb, *Die Arbeiterräte in der deutschen Innenpolitik, 1918-1919*, Frankfurt, 1978, 199-202.

removed.[51] An army based on the Hamburg points would have been a militia force.[52]

The officer corps was alarmed by the potential impact of the Hamburg points, and reacted immediately. Fortunately for them, an eighth point, which would have given the Hamburg points immediate legal effect, was not accepted by the Congress. This meant that the details would have to be worked out, giving the officer corps an opportunity to blunt the impact of the Congress's challenge.[53] Scheüch was first into the ring to defend the position of the officer corps. In a letter to leading officers he summed up the principal argument against the Hamburg points: 'Altogether these decisions are not compatible with any type of functioning army, no matter what the political background is.'[54] The motivation behind the military's opposition to the Hamburg points was not primarily political; rather it was based on an ideal of military efficiency. That the maxim of military efficiency might ultimately have a political consequence was clear, but of secondary importance to the officer corps.

As experts in military affairs the officer corps believed they had the right to give advice to their new political masters, and the SPD felt that it was necessary to listen to the opinions of the experts. The most direct intervention against the Hamburg points was made by the Supreme Command. Although Groener and Hindenburg initially supported the soldiers' councils, they turned against them after a meeting of the soldiers' councils of the field army at Bad Ems on 1 and 2 December failed to fulfil their hopes.[55] When the Supreme Command heard of the Congress proposals, Hindenburg drafted a telegram which stated that the army remained loyal to Ebert and the Council of Peoples' Commissars. He asked for Ebert's support for the guidelines that had been issued just after the revolution. They encouraged co-operation between soldiers' councils and officers, so that the retreat and demobilization could proceed as smoothly as possible. He also objected to the fact that the Hamburg points would pre-empt any decision on the future of the army, a decision that should be made by a national assembly.[56] At a meeting with the Council of People's Commissars on 20 December, Groener rejected the Hamburg points for four reasons. First, the points were impractical for the organisation of an army. Second, in the climate of disorder and demobilization it was unwise to undertake experiments in military policy. Third, the officers would resign, undermining the Allies' trust in the Council as

---

51. *Der Zentralrat der deutschen sozialistischen Republik, 19.12.18 – 8.4.19. Vom ersten zum zweiten Rätekongress*, eds Eberhard Kolb, Reinhard Rürup, Leiden, 1968, 2–4.
52. Ibid, 4; William Mulligan, 'Restoring Trust within the *Reichswehr*: The Case of the *Vertrauensleute*', *War & Society* 20, 2, 2002, 75.
53. Kluge, *Soldatenräte*, 252–54.
54. BA-MA, N 23/1, Scheüch to senior officers, 19 December 1918.
55. Rakenius, *Groener*, 131–32.
56. BA-MA, N 46/30, Hindenburg telegram, no date, fo. 23.

a stable negotiating partner. Finally, the badges were of rank were not mere superficialities (*Äußerlichkeiten*) but 'a good part of my life', an emotional argument, and one which found resonance amongst the officer corps.[57] Ebert agreed to treat the Hamburg points as guidelines, not as writ.[58] Groener, who blithely proposed Feldmann as Scheüch's successor that evening, must have known that the next Minister of War would have to compromise on the Hamburg points, hence damaging that officer's prestige.

The Council of People's Commissars faced a dilemma, since they were dependent on the officer corps who had rejected the Hamburg points, but had recognised the Congress who had passed the resolution as an interim legislature. On 18 December, after the passage of the decrees, the Council of People's Commissars met, and it was at this stage that Reinhardt first emerged as a potential replacement.[59] Efforts to get Scheüch to rescind his resignation failed while the USPD's candidate, Boelke, was unacceptable to both the officers and the SPD, a sign of the rapidly declining influence of the USPD over military policy.[60] On 23 December, Böhm made an interesting entry into his diary: 'Ebert has lost some of his faith in Scheüch after a conversation at the Ministry of War in which [Scheüch] stood up for the officers' badges of rank in a hot-tempered manner. Ebert regards this issue as a "silly button affair" of subordinate importance to the other issues.'[61] Reinhardt had come to a similar conclusion, although independently of Ebert, and this marked him out from the ranks of senior officers. On the same day that Ebert quarrelled with Scheüch, Baake spoke positively of Reinhardt 'who appeared to the Reich government to be particularly competent and reliable.'[62]

Although the Council of People's Commissars came back once again to the idea of appointing Noske, and making Reinhardt his Under Secretary of State (a situation which one could argue emerged after Noske's appointment as *Reichswehrminister*), the politics now favoured Reinhardt's appointment. On 29 December Scheüch gave his stamp of approval.[63] Reinhardt appears to have been unaware that his name was circulating as a potential Minister of War, and many of his assumptions about the process were incorrect. In a letter to his wife, who was suffering from tuberculosis, on 30 December:

57. Rakenius, *Groener*, 114–16.
58. Mulligan, 'Restoring trust within the *Reichswehr*', 76
59. Rakenius, *Groener*, 160.
60. *Adjutant im preussischen Kriegsministerium*, 112.
61. Ibid., 116.
62. Ibid., 116.
63. Ibid., 120–6; BA-MA, N 23/1, Scheüch's note on his resignation, fo. 22.

You remember that Scheüch's resignation was still up in the air. Now it turns out that he has actually recommended me as his successor, and the People's Commissars have agreed to this. On first hearing this I was not exactly thunderstruck, but I was taken aback by how quickly and suddenly it should all happen. I asked for time to consider it until tomorrow and will declare myself ready if they want me. In current times it is a crown of thorns. ... The question of [my] suitability is quite another thing. It is a massive task and I am no Hercules. But I will do my best as before and take the wheel, if it is passed to me, after mature consideration.[64]

He tried to console his wife that he expected to be replaced after the elections to the National Assembly.

Reinhardt was cautious about accepting the post, and he recognised the political difficulties that he would face. He told the officers in the Ministry of War just before he accepted the position:

I already know the difficulties that will arise since I, as a Württemberger colonel, will be superior to Prussian generals. I also know that I am putting my good reputation as a soldier, and my good name on the line; that my comrades and friends will not understand me. But, gentlemen, I want you in this hour to hear that no ambition, no vanity has moved me to take this step, only the clear recognition that it is my duty.[65]

The sense of foreboding is striking. To shore up his political position he had tried to ensure that the Supreme Command approved of his appointment: 'I saw how awkward the position of the office of the Minister of War could be if the Supreme Command started causing difficulties. Therefore I expressly made my appointment dependent on Hindenburg's approval, which duly arrived. I took it for granted that Groener had given up on Feldmann's candidature.'[66] This was written in 1921, and throughout 1919 he experienced a series of disputes with the Supreme Command and Groener, in particular. Unaware that he was not Scheüch's recommendation, and mistakenly believing that the Supreme Command's approval of his appointment meant co-operation on military policy, he accepted the post of Minister of War, a post in which he would have only one solid political base, and that was the support of the Council of People's Commissars, and later Noske, the SPD *Reichswehrminister*.

This base of support was ensured by the withdrawal of the USPD from the Council of People's Commissars on 30 December in protest at the military policy and therefore the appointment of Reinhardt, and by the support of Ebert and Noske for his candidacy at the joint meeting of Council of People's Commissars and the Central Council, which represented the workers' and soldiers' councils. Although Reinhardt had not

64. Ernst, 'Aus dem Nachlaß', 50.
65. Ibid., 53.
66. Ibid., 51.

been the first choice of either the leading officers or the SPD, he fulfilled the requisite conditions, namely he was an officer, and he was trusted by the SPD. Ebert was impressed by Reinhardt's strong work ethic, and also believed that he would be acceptable to the public.[67] On 30 December, at a meeting of the Council of People's Commissars, Noske reported on his talks with Reinhardt. Although Reinhardt had admitted that he was 'a convinced monarchist', he had also pledged that he would not use troops against the civilian authorities.[68] In the light of this and Reinhardt's performance at the meeting on 31 December, Kluge's conclusion that he offered a 'programme of lies' seems unnecessarily harsh.[69]

At the meeting on 31 December, discussions centred on a letter from Reinhardt to the Council of People's Commissars, which laid out the conditions under which he would accept the post of Minister of War.[70] He would be responsible to the Council of People's Commissars, and would exercise the *Kommandogewalt* (right of supreme command)[71] on its behalf. Then Reinhardt outlined his opinion of the Hamburg points. He was willing to change the form of badges and other military markings, although the need for order, and the instant visual recognition of authority, meant that badges of rank could not be abolished altogether. He also conceded that wearing weapons off duty was unnecessary, but insisted that military honours and medals won in time of war could be worn. The future form of the army was an issue for the National Assembly, due to be elected on 19 January 1919. Until then the size of the army would be reduced. Neither administrative nor front officers would be discriminated against during the process of reducing the army to its peace-time levels. The election of officers by troops would be forbidden, since it would lead to 'unsustainable conditions'. However the soldiers' councils could make complaints against officers, and if these were proved to be true then the officer would be removed. Ultimately the choice of officer would be made by the Minister of War. Finally, all remaining officers 'must make a commitment to serve the current government loyally, and not to plot against it.'[72] Reinhardt's approach to the issues raised by the Hamburg points demonstrated a greater willingness to compromise than Groener. While he agreed with Groener that officers could not be elected and also stressed the importance of the National Assembly, he was prepared to make concessions, such as the replacement of imperial badges of rank and the right of soldiers to lodge complaints against officers.

---

67. Gustav Noske, *Erlebtes aus Aufstieg und Niedergang einer Demokratie*, Offenbach, 1947, 178.
68. *Regierung der Volksbeauftragten 1918-19*, vol. 1, 148.
69. Kluge, *Soldatenräte*, 72–3.
70. *Zentralrat*, 115–137, reproduces the minutes of the meeting and the letter.
71. *Kommandogewalt* translates as power of command, while *Befehlsgewalt* translates as power of order. To avoid these awkward translations I have retained the German expressions. *Kommandogewalt* is the right of the head of state to issue commands, whereas *Befehlsgewalt* refers to the right of officers to issue orders.
72. *Zentralrat*, 117.

In a discussion between Reinhardt and the members of the Central Council and Council of People's Commissars ensued, the new Minister of War wanted to make clear to them the tasks he held to be essential. While he was not a stereotypical officer, he had served for thirty years, and now his primary concern was to help Germany recover from the post-war crisis. 'We must move forward … I want to be a faithful office-holder, but also beyond that, a man filled with warm feelings for the German people. I am motivated by the certain hope that we will emerge from this difficult period. That is only possible however if the distrust disappears, if the great splits in our *Volk* can be mended and if we can come together as brothers.'[73] After describing himself as a loyal servant, he outlined his view of how Germany could re-establish her power. Progress could only be achieved by a united society, a vision which had echoes of the *Burgfrieden* of July 1914. The hopeful image of fraternal peace must have come easily to a man who before 1914 had tended to identify Germans as Germans, rather than dividing them into class, or race, with all the confrontational implications which such a division implied.

However benign this vision, and however accurate his critique of the Hamburg points were, his appointment had political implications. Reinhardt gave the civilian leadership an opportunity to reject him and search for another candidate. Just as Groener had intervened with advice on 20 December, so did Reinhardt on 31 December. He was able to use the structures of government, and the difficult situation of Germany, to persuade the Council of People's Commissars and the Central Council to adopt his military policy. His letter with its preconditions marks a change in his view of the political situation. Whereas at the beginning of December he felt it would be counterproductive to offer advice to the civilian authorities on military policy, because he would lose the trust of the USPD, he was now ready to step forward and outline military policy. The political constellation had become more favourable to the military in the seven weeks since defeat. The departure of the USPD from government was an indicator that the future of German politics would be established by an alliance of the SPD and centre parties.

Reinhardt's appointment as Minister of War also illustrates the nature of the SPD's relationship to the officer corps. At the meeting on 31 December Ebert argued that the officer corps had demonstrated its expertise during the process of demobilization. Ebert claimed that Reinhardt had proved himself as a 'competent organiser … For the establishment of the new army we need intense work and great organisational skill. Colonel Reinhardt is the man for this job.'[74] Ebert accepted the advice offered by the officer corps time and again, and this was fundamental to the influence exercised by them. Ebert admired qualities such as competence and

73. Ibid., 118.
74. Ibid., 119.

efficiency, and in the field of military policy the officer corps was able to lay a monopoly claim to these qualities. Yet the officer corps was not a monolithic block. The different reactions of Reinhardt and Groener to the Hamburg points were merely an early indication of divergent approaches to military policy. If the advice proffered was almost invariably accepted, then the *choice* of adviser became highly significant. While Reinhardt was not prepared to sacrifice the principles of military efficiency to satisfy all radical demands, his conception of military efficiency differed sufficiently from that of many of his fellow officers to allow compromises on several issues. The significance of Reinhardt's period in the highest military positions is that he demonstrated the possibilities for developing military policy within the framework of the new state.

Before Reinhardt was accepted as the new Minister of War, members of the Central Council questioned him further on his attitude to the election of officers and the *Befehlsgewalt*. Reinhardt's answers indicate the way in which some of the ideas behind the Hamburg points could be integrated into an efficient military organisation. While not accepting the election of officers, he was prepared to entertain complaints about officers which would be lodged by the soldiers' councils. He pointed out that it was imperative that an officer enjoy the trust of his unit if he wished to be able to command them effectively. Hence it was important to restore the trust between officers and men which had been lost during the war.[75] 'I see in the soldiers' councils the right means for this. I believe that we cannot do without them, that we simply have to find the right place for them', he concluded.[76] The officer corps had been attempting to utilise the soldiers' councils for practical tasks since the early days of the revolution. Co-operation would allow a swifter retreat. However these attempts were isolated and focused on a specific task.[77] Reinhardt's conception was more permanent. Rather than seeing the soldiers' councils as an opponent, he was trying to enlist them in his own project of restoring trust within the German army.

Groener's view that the post of Minister of War would be a poisoned chalice received early confirmation when Reinhardt met with leading Supreme Command officers on 5 January 1919. He travelled to Wilhelmshöhe on 2 January, and stayed with his close friend Thaer, who commented in his diary that Reinhardt 'is a noble man, a courageous well-meaning character, actually too good for this world.'[78] The agenda for the meeting was wide-ranging, including the treaty negotiations, the

---

75. *Wehrkraft und Wehrwille*, 40; Wolfgang Kruse, 'Krieg und Klassenheer. Zur Revolutionierung der deutschen Armee im ersten Weltkrieg', *GG*, 22, 1996, 530–61; Wilhelm Deist, 'Verdeckter Militärstreik im Kriegjahr 1918?', in *Der Krieg des kleinen Mannes. Eine Militärgeschichte von unten* ed. Wolfram Wette, Munich, 1992.

76. *Zentralrat*, 122.

77. Huber, ed., *Dokumente*, 11–12.

78. Kaehler, ed., *Thaer*, 283.

soldiers' councils, demobilization and the role of the Ministry of War during the revolution, which must have continued to aggrieve the Supreme Command.[79] Reinhardt had divided the various issues facing the officer corps into trivial and important ones. However his categorisation of badges of rank as trivial shocked many of the Supreme Command officers. Major Joachim von Stülpnagel, an officer of the Supreme Command, argued that the badges were a symbol of the officer's honour, and that their abolition would be a surrender to a socialist government, which would lose the officer corps the respect of 'the right-thinking populace.'[80] Stülpnagel's approach received support from many of the officers present at the meeting, a clear sign of the argument's powerful emotional resonance. Reinhardt, whose position was only supported by Heye, took a more calculated approach to the future. He argued that the officer corps would have to work hard to rebuild the army and the nation. In order to achieve this prime goal, sacrifices and compromises would have to be made, and *Äußerlichkeiten* (superficialities) came low on his list of essential factors for military efficiency.[81] Fleck, who travelled with Reinhardt, concurred with this view: 'The actual circumstances were such that in order to achieve the important points it was necessary to give in on other points.'[82]

In the longer term Reinhardt shared the broad policy aims of the Supreme Command. In private conversation with Thaer, he outlined his military mission, which was 'a free Germany, if at all possible in her old borders, with a strong, modern army, with the newest weaponry.'[83] Although he did not leave behind a programmatic statement of his aims his views are clear from the combination of statements and actions. He believed that it would take Germany fifteen years to recover from the effects of the First World War. In his opinion the new regime was the most stable form of the German state in the current situation, which would allow the pursuit of this mission, and this made concessions on what he felt were superficialities, necessary and ultimately beneficial. While he recognised the limitations placed by political and social factors on the development of military policy, he did not share the same military policy goals as either the provisional government or the Weimar coalitions. Yet as long as it was possible, and perhaps more to the point, necessary, to co-operate with these governments and the new interest groups in German politics, this difference in policy aims would remain immaterial. Pragmatism dictated momentary compromises, whilst maintaining the possibility of achieving the ultimate mission. Nonetheless he

79. BA-MA, N 42/11, Programm für die Besprechung mit dem Herrn Kriegsminister, 5 January 1919, fo. 39.
80. BA-MA, N 5/17, Stülpnagel memorandum of the meeting on 5 January 1919, fo. 11.
81. Ibid., fo. 11.
82. Ernst, 'Aus seinem Nachlaß', 53.
83. Kaehler, ed., *Thaer*, 283–84.

failed to persuade many of his fellow-officers of his point of view, and this would lead to widespread opposition to the decrees on 19 January 1919 which regulated discipline, the *Kommandogewalt*, the *Befehlsgewalt*, salutes and uniforms.

Reinhardt's insistence on the officers' sole right to the *Kommandogewalt* can only have been strengthened by the Sparticist uprising in Berlin which began on 5 January. Although it was quickly quashed, and then used as an excuse for terroristic outrages by *Freikorps* soldiers, among the SPD leaders and military the events reinforced the sense of threat and the reliance on units that were not hostage to the whims of the soldiers' councils.[84] Fleck described it as the 'highpoint of the struggle for the state.'[85] Ernst van den Bergh, a moderate officer at the Ministry of War, asserted that 'the Bolshevist, or rather Russian danger [through the return of troops predisposed to Bolshevism from the East] is greater than the Polish danger.'[86] In an interview on 12 January Reinhardt expressed his delight that 'the criminal trouble' had been suppressed. He promised that future disturbances would be dealt with in a similar fashion: 'We owe that not just to the German *Volk*, which longs for order, calm and peace, but we also must bear in mind our reputation abroad, to have forces for the defence of our border and the protection of the right to self-determination of the German *Volk*.'[87] The SPD, now the sole party in the provisional government, shared many of the assumptions of the officers about the threat of further revolts in Germany and the necessity of a strong military force. So between Reinhardt's appointment and the start of negotiations on the decrees, the political balance had continued to move towards the officer corps.

These decrees were formulated during negotiations between the Minister of War and the Central Council. The two representatives of the Minister of War were Paul Göhre, the under-secretary and member of the SPD, and Major Höfer, who had been on Reinhardt's staff since November. Reinhardt appears to have exercised careful control over Höfer and Göhre. Reinhardt's key role in these negotiations was a consequence of both the SPD's lack of confidence in formulating their own military policy and the opportunities of an authoritative adviser to shape policy. The negotiations were based on three documents drafted by the Minister of War, which dealt with the *Kommandogewalt*, uniforms and the salute. These drafts were themselves a response to the Hamburg points. Thus the negotiations can be seen as a dialogue between the radical military demands of the revolution and the traditional conception of military principles. Max Cohen,

---

84. Peter Lösche, *Der Bolschewismus im Urteil der Deutschen Sozialdemokratie 1903–1920*, Berlin, 1967, 170–71.
85. Ernst, 'Aus seinem Nachlaß', 53.
86. *Aus den Geburtsstunden der Weimarer Republik. Das Tagebuch des Obersten Ernst van den Bergh*, ed. Wolfram Wette, Düsseldorf, 1991, 78-79.
87. HStASt, M660/034, Bü 19, *Berliner Lokal-Anzeiger*, 13 January 1919.

who chaired the first meeting on 13 January noted 'that these regulations from the Ministry of War are not the final ones, but are rather a basis. The Ministry of War wants to listen to the suggestions of the Central Council and the Council of People's Commissars.'[88] This spirit of compromise was also helped by the state of disorder and general lack of stability, which was afflicting German society. Both sides recognised that January 1919 was not the time to make an unequivocal stand on their ideals.

The first four points dealt with the issues of *Kommandogewalt* and *Befehlsgewalt*. The Minister of War's draft sought to combine military efficiency with guarantees that military power would not be used against the 'Republic'. There was to be a clear chain of command, with the Council of People's Commissars having the *Kommandogewalt*, which would be exercised by the Minister of War. Lower down the chain of command the officers would retain their *Befehlsgewalt*. This structure of command was accompanied by a series of guarantees. The Minister of War would be aided by an under-secretary. This position was filled by Göhre, and was designed to allow supervision of the Ministry of War's activities. It underlined the principle of civilian control which had been established by giving the Council of People's Commissars the *Kommandogewalt*. Officers were responsible to their superiors and ultimately the government in their exercise of the *Befehlsgewalt*. Soldiers' councils were also to supervise the activities of officers, and ensure that they did not abuse their *Befehlsgewalt*. The structures outlined in this draft were hierarchical in the traditional military sense but also provided the civilian authorities with opportunities to discover and prevent disloyalty at an early stage.[89]

The Central Council accepted the structures of the *Kommandogewalt* without much opposition. However they argued that the guarantees offered against abuse of the *Befehlsgewalt* were too ambiguous. Officers were supposed to inform soldiers' councils of orders, but this was insufficient. It was decided that the soldiers' councils would have to countersign an order before it became valid. Hermann Wäger, who had been a member of a soldiers' council in Lithuania, argued that a countersigned order would allow a speedier execution of orders, since soldiers would have more trust in the order, than one simply dispatched by an officer, who might be plotting against the Republic.[90] On 14 January Göhre reopened this issue. Reinhardt had told him that the Central Council's decision would cause endless conflict between soldiers' councils and officers, and damage the fabric of the army. The Ministry of War's arguments were based on the reality of battle. Göhre pointed out that in some of the street battles which had taken place around Berlin since Christmas, it would have been impossible to get a countersignature for each order. He

88. *Zentralrat*, 339.
89. Ibid., 340–45.
90. Ibid., 345–46.

also argued that soldiers' councils in western Germany were preventing recruitment drives for volunteers to fight in the East, as well as holding up other routine military business. Göhre pointed to the urgency of the situation: 'At this moment when the Bolshevists, on the basis of their experiences, are reintroducing the old form of discipline, we would destroy the last remnants of discipline, and make any military action impossible. That means collapse, and the break-up is already proceeding in our army, our army is simply falling apart. There would be no longer be any army.'[91] The officer's exclusive *Befehlsgewalt* could not be infringed upon, and other means would have to be found as a guarantee of their political loyalty. Göhre suggested that the confirmation of officers in their posts by soldiers' councils would be the most effective means of ensuring loyalty, particularly when combined with the role of the soldiers' council as a general political watchdog.[92]

The debate on the *Befehlsgewalt* exposed the problem of force in a revolutionary situation. The political and constitutional structures of Germany in early 1919 were very fluid. The use of force was an essential element of political life. The Hamburg points were born out of the fear of counterrevolution. The Sparticist revolt in Berlin in the first days of January 1919 had illustrated the threat from the left. The excesses of the military units in putting down the revolt and murdering Rosa Luxembourg and Karl Liebknecht was evidence that the officers' *Befehlsgewalt* needed to be under strict supervision. It became a question of from whom the revolution was being protected. Whereas the Central Council were fearful of reactionary threats, the officers feared a further revolt from the radical left. This did not mean a repudiation of the revolution, but rather its stabilisation and even termination with the election of the National Assembly, one of the central demands of officers since November. In an interview with the *Berliner Lokal Anzeiger*, Reinhardt had mentioned the use of troops to allow the elections to proceed on 19 January.[93] In a letter to his wife on 30 December, he depicted the election of the National Assembly as the end of the transition period.[94] Reinhardt's support for the sole right of the officers to the *Kommandogewalt* was not motivated by reactionary designs, but by a belief that an efficient military force was necessary to defend the Republic from further lurches to the left.

By 16 January Reinhardt had prepared a new draft for negotiations that day. The structure of the chain of command remained virtually unchanged from the first draft, although it was made explicit that the constitution could determine the Minister of War's exercise of the *Kommandogewalt*. The officers' *Befehlsgewalt* in military matters was preserved, and the

---

91. Ibid., 357.
92. Ibid., 357–62.
93. HStASt, M 660/034, Bü 19, *Berliner Lokal Anzeiger*, 13 January 1919.
94. Ernst, 'Aus seinem Nachlaß', 50.

soldiers' councils were given the role of political supervision. However, in areas such as troop welfare, pay and holidays, the soldiers' councils had a right to countersign standing orders. There was also a provision for *Vertrauensleute*, or soldiers' representatives, at company level. Likewise they were to look after troop welfare. The rôles assigned to the soldiers' councils and the *Vertrauensleute* were a recognition of the importance of establishing trust between the officers and troops, trust being a vital pre-condition for discipline.[95] Reinhardt's concept, which he first outlined on 31 December 1918, of using the soldiers' councils to create an efficient military organisation, had effectively blunted the more radical demands of the Hamburg points and the Central Council.

On the afternoon of 17 January Reinhardt made his only personal appearance at the negotiations. The main topic on the agenda was the salute. Reinhardt's approach to this issue is indicative of his attempt to create a new ethos within the post-war army. According to his draft 'The military salute should not be an obligation, but rather the expression of comradeship. For this reason both (soldiers and officers) have the duty to salute each other.'[96] In many respects Reinhardt's vision of an army without cleavages between officer and soldier, of an army focusing on the goal of re-establishing German power, was a reflection of his aspirations for a united German society. It is also an early indication of a new conception of the soldier, which emerged in 1919. He was seen as a volunteer, and the army had to make a positive appeal to his ideals and aspirations, rather than instil fear into him. This marked a move away from the imperial norms of *Kadavergehorsam* ('corpse-like obedience') and conscription.

The discussions with the Central Council concluded on 17 January. Two days later, three decrees were jointly issued by the Central Council, the Ministry of War, and the Council of People's Commissars. In short, they contained the results of the negotiations between 13 and 17 January. The Council of People's Commissars had the *Kommandogewalt*, which was exercised by the Minister of War. The officers retained their *Befehlsgewalt*. This established a model of civilian control of the military that would characterise the *Reichswehr*. Rather than having several layers of control, by enabling the soldiers' councils to choose the officers, the government relied on the hierarchical chain of command, of which it formed the pinnacle. This was due to the unwillingness to disrupt military organisations during a revolutionary period, faith in constitutional structures and processes, a lack of broad political support for radical changes and a good relationship with the senior officers. These factors continued to shape policy regarding civilian control of the military up to the Kapp Putsch.

95. *Zentralrat*, 422–25.
96. Ibid., 439.

Officers lost their badges and the form and ethos of the salute were changed to restore trust. The soldiers' councils could lodge complaints against officers and could also operate as political supervisors – although such a role never really materialised. However the decrees did not apply to mobile units, which were fighting within Germany and on the borders in the east.[97] This clause was crucial because these units were the backbone of German military power in 1919, and hence these units were under a similar disciplinary regime as had existed in the First World War: an illiberal one, opposed by many in government. Finally it should be noted that these decrees applied to an army that was soon to be replaced by the temporary *Reichswehr*. Therefore the decrees can be interpreted partly as an experiment, the results of which would influence the structures of the temporary *Reichswehr*.

Reinhardt was prepared for a storm of abuse.[98] He had already experienced the hostility of Supreme Command officers at Wilhelmshöhe, and, perhaps as a pre-emptive strike against his critics within the officer corps, he attached an appeal to the decrees which appeared in the *Armeeverordnungsblatt*. It was a mixture of soothing rhetoric for the battered ego of the army, and a statement of his policy aims. He praised the German army for withstanding four years of war, while insinuating that the home front had collapsed under the pressure, ultimately leading to the November revolution. In this moment of need Germany's leaders remained united to save the Fatherland:

> Following the appeal of their leaders the officers and soldiers put themselves at the disposal of the new powers in the state. The great divide was avoided. There were, however, many obstacles on the way to the creation of a new trust between leaders and soldiers. Naturally great difficulties have to be overcome in a time of transition. ... Today's orders on *Kommandogewalt*, appointments to posts, uniforms and salutes are such measures (to overcome mistrust). They open new ways of co-operation, which must be successfully entered into by the officers in a spirit of co-operation with the soldiers' councils.[99]

Reinhardt was appealing for a spirit of co-operation, which he felt was a key to the state's progress. The restoration of German military power could not be achieved against the will of the civilian authorities. At the end of January in response to a query about the decree from the Württemberg Ministry of War, Reinhardt claimed: '[T]he sacrifices which are made now, are not at the expense of one party or the government party, but they are for the good of the *Volk* and the Fatherland.'[100]

---

97. Ibid., 441–48.
98. Ibid., 434–35.
99. Ibid., 441–42.
100. HStASt, M 1/4, 1712, Reinhardt, Göhre to the Württemberg Ministry of War, 31 January 1919.

The reaction to the decrees was a barometer of Reinhardt's authority as Minister of War and the reading was not favourable. Much noise and bombast was generated by the opponents of the decrees within the officer corps, both in private letters and public excoriation of Reinhardt. Groener wrote to Ebert on 27 January and condemned the decrees 'as a terrible mistake.' The soldiers' councils were causing havoc in the east, and rather than limiting the power of the soldiers' councils, the decrees had only fuelled their ambitions. In blunt fashion, he advised that the National Assembly should legislate the soldiers' councils out of existence.[101] The two representatives of officers' interests, the *Deutscher Offizierbund* (German Officers' League) and the *Nationalverband deutscher Offiziere* (National Federation of German Officers), competed with each other in attacking the decrees.[102] Major Wentzel, writing in *Das Militärwochenblatt*, saw the decrees 'as nothing other than a conscious and also successful attempt at humiliating the officer corps in front of the whole people.'[103] The criticisms were a mixture of polemic and substantive points. If the polemic represented the frustration of many in the officer corps at their loss of status in society, which was symbolised by the loss of their badges, the substantive criticism pointed out many of the difficulties which were caused by trying to run an army by consensus. These included cases of wilful disobedience by the soldiers' councils, disruption of troop transport to the east and attacks on officers. Other officers recognised the difficulties of Reinhardt's position. Just over a month after the decrees were issued Reinhardt met a number of Prussian generals to discuss military affairs, one of whom, General Bockmann, told him 'that in the opinion of the *Gardekorps* the Prussian army and *Heimat* could find no better representative than the person of the current Minister of War.'[104] However this was a minority opinion.

Despite the comforting letters and the defensive speech Reinhardt's position within the army had been weakened. First, he had a number of disadvantages to overcome. He was a Württemberger in the Prussian Ministry of War. Groener, also a Württemberger of course, and the most powerful officer in the army, was hostile towards him, partly because of his leftist reputation and partly because he was blamed for key defeats in October 1917 and July 1918. Second, he had underestimated the emotional significance of badges for the mass of the officers. What he saw as a clever concession which would save the *Befehlsgewalt* was interpreted by many officers as an assault on their honour. Third, the decrees of 19 January were discredited by the behaviour of local officers and soldiers' councils. The spirit of compromise which had characterised the

101. *Zwischen Revolution und Kapp-Putsch*, 51–53; Wette, *Noske*, 341–43.
102. BA-MA, N 23/1, *Die Post*, 30 January 1919, fo. 106.
103. *Das Militärwochenblatt*, 6 February 1919, 1699–1700.
104. BA-MA, N 86/16, General Bockmann to Reinhardt, 27 February 1919.

negotiations between the Central Council and the Ministry of War was almost wholly absent at a local level. While Reinhardt's ideas were reasonable in theory, they proved unworkable in practice. Since they failed to reinforce discipline or satisfy demands for political control of the officer corps, there was little incentive to support them.

Whether officers or soldiers' councils were to blame for the failure of the decrees is perhaps immaterial.[105] The officer corps blamed the soldiers' councils and convinced Noske and Ebert that the indiscipline in the army was leaving Germany vulnerable to left-wing radicals, and the Poles and Bolshevists.[106] Another model of military organisation had emerged, the *Freikorps*, and they proved to be more effective fighting units than battalions with soldiers' councils. Reinhardt recognised the trend of opinion within the officer corps and the leadership of the SPD was against the soldiers' councils, and although he still maintained that a close relationship between officer and soldier was essential to efficiency, he lost faith in the ability of the soldiers' councils to carry out this task. He began to undermine them with various measures. Reinhardt, the pragmatist, was quick to learn from previous experience.

This process could not have taken place without the support of Noske. His growing opposition to the soldiers' councils deprived them of an authority to which they could appeal. The destruction of the soldiers' councils was the consequence of a community of interests between the officer corps and the civilian government for the restoration of public order. It should also be remembered that the more centrist elements within the SPD had been strengthened by the formation of a coalition of the Catholic Centre party, the liberal Democratic Party and the SPD after the elections to the National Assembly in January 1919. In a speech to the National Assembly on 17 February, on occasion on which *Der Tag* described him as 'being inconspicuous despite having a not uninteresting face', Reinhardt argued that the decrees of 19 January were only temporary.[107] He had already accepted that 'it must be up to the National Assembly to regulate the peace-time army.'[108] Given the likely decision of the National Assembly on soldiers' councils, this was an astute political tactic. Yet it was one which Reinhardt arrived at after the failure of the decrees of 19 January became evident. The institution of the *Vertrauensleute* which was established in the *Reichswehr* marked Reinhardt's second attempt to restore trust in the officer-troop relationship, and it showed a continuity of thought with the January decrees.

---

105. For the view from the perspective of the soldiers' councils, see Kluge, *Soldatenräte*, 278–83.
106. *Zwischen Revolution und Kapp-Putsch*, 52.
107. *Der Tag*, 20 February 1919; *Norddeutsche Allgemeine Zeitung*, 20 February 1919; *Verhandlungen der deutschen Nationalversammlung*, vol. 326, Berlin, 1920, 177.
108. HStASt, M 1/4, 1712, Reinhardt and Göhre to the Württemberg Ministry of War, 31 January 1919.

The first priority in 1919 was an army that could keep order. Once the soldiers' councils were seen as a hindrance rather than an aid there was no possibility that they would find a role in the temporary *Reichswehr*, which the National Assembly established on 6 March 1919. Noske found it 'absolutely intolerable, that numerous soldiers' councils should prevent the applications of volunteers for border protection in the East and the home-based units, and should also try to prevent the arming and transport of the volunteers.'[109] The Centre and Democratic parties' spokesmen echoed the need for order, and made no mention, let alone defence, of soldiers' councils in the military policy debates in the National Assembly.[110]

The soldiers' councils were simply dissolved along with their units in the old imperial army. When the temporary *Reichswehr* was established there was no place for the soldiers' councils.[111] This was not the result of a long-term plan to ease the soldiers' councils out through the back door of a dissolving army, as Fleck suggested after the event.[112] Instead Reinhardt initially supported them as a means of restoring trust between the ranks. When these hopes were proved illusory, not alone did he prevent their establishment in the temporary *Reichswehr*, but he also undermined their position in the old army.[113] The continuing process of demobilization also enabled the removal of members of the soldiers' councils from the army.[114] By June 1919 the soldiers' councils had disappeared.

Four general features of Reinhardt's military policy emerged in early 1919. First, he promoted the subordination of the military to civilian authorities. He recognised that the Council of People's Commissars would have the *Kommandogewalt*. Second, the goal of military efficiency was the key to his military policy. This was the basic principle of his thought and led him to insist that the officers retain their *Befehlsgewalt*. However it also led him to encourage the creation of an ethos of trust and comradeship within the army, as a means of making it a more effective military organisation. Military efficiency was part of a larger goal of restoring Germany's position in Europe. Third, he was prepared to move with the changing political situation, and adapt his policies to needs of the moment. This meant that he sought co-operation with the soldiers' councils as a means of rebuilding trust. Once they had proved ineffective, and as he came to believe, damaging, he changed his policy and undermined them. He was able to do this because the political landscape had been

109. Gustav Noske, *Von Kiel bis Kapp. Zur Geschichte der deutschen Revolution*, Berlin, 1920, 94.
110. See the speeches of Siehr and Gröber on 25 February 1919, *Die deutsche Nationalversammlung im Jahre 1919 in ihrer Arbeit für den Aufbau des neuen deutschen Volkstaates*, 6 vols, ed. Eduard Heilfron, Berlin, 1920, vol. 2, 739–44.
111. The establishment of the temporary *Reichswehr* is the subject of chapter 4.
112. BA-MA, N 86/59, memorandum by unknown author (possibly Fleck), fo. 5.
113. *Armeeverordnungsblatt*, 1919, 213.
114. *Armeeverordnungsblatt*, 1919, 246.

changed by the establishment of a bourgeois-SPD coalition government after the elections to the National Assembly in January 1919. Finally, he proved remarkably effective at getting military policy accepted at the higher levels of government. Although he had the title of minister, he was more of a military adviser, who sat in the cabinet. By co-operating with the new civilian regime, Reinhardt demonstrated the constitutional and political possibilities that existed for the pursuit of military goals. The new state had not proved incompatible with the furtherance of military goals.

Chapter 4

SETTING THE AGENDA ON MILITARY POLICY, JANUARY–JUNE 1919*

*R*einhardt's first attempt to forge military policy had received a mixed welcome. During the first half of 1919 his policy initiatives began to show the benefits of co-operating with the new regime. While previous studies have concentrated on the rôle of Seeckt and Groener in the establishment of the *Reichswehr*, a close examination of the temporary *Reichswehr* law, the establishment of new disciplinary structures, and the amalgamation of the war ministries of Prussia, Bavaria, Saxony, Württemberg and Baden, shows that Reinhardt was at the heart of the creation of the modern German army. He continued the policy of pragmatic co-operation and showed that the new state could be shaped on terms favourable to the military. The success of the moderate left (the SPD) and centre (the DDP and the Catholic Centre Party) in the elections of January 1919 and the violent suppression of radical left-wing movements, such as the Sparticists in January and the Munich Soviet Republic in May, showed that the drift to the left, feared by officers, had halted. The first half of 1919 was one of the most harmonious in civil-military relations in the Weimar Republic (which was not simply a narrative of unrelieved antagonism).

Reinhardt had not intended the decrees of 19 January to be the final solution to the structures of the new regime's army. They only applied to the non-mobile forces within Germany, and therefore not to the *Freikorps* units which were to constitute a large part of the new army. The attempt of the soldiers' councils to establish a dominant position in the new army had failed by the beginning of February. Reinhardt had prevented the

*Parts of this chapter have appeared in William Mulligan, 'Restoring Trust Within the *Reichswehr*: The Case of the *Vertrauensleute*', *War & Society*, 20, 2, 2002, 71–90, and William Mulligan, 'Civil-military Relations in the Early Weimar Republic', *Historical Journal*, 45, 4, 2002, 819–41. I would like to thank the publishers, University of New South Wales and Cambridge University Press, for permission to reproduce parts of these articles.

institution of the soldiers' councils establishing a strong position with the German military forces. Units from the demobilized army, which became part of the *Reichswehr*, shed their soldiers' councils at the point of transition. This, combined with the integration of *Freikorps* units and the establishment of new units, meant the disappearance of the soldiers' councils.

Military policy for the new army, the *Reichswehr*, was formulated between late January 1919 and 31 March 1919 when the decrees governing discipline, recruitment, pay and other issues of internal regulation were issued. Negotiations with the federal states on the unification of the states' war ministries began in early February, after the publication of the draft constitution. Reinhardt was at the centre of this process which laid the basis for the *Reichswehr* in the Weimar Republic. The political environment had become more favourable to the officer corps since the beginning of the year. The elections to the National Assembly had not resulted in a socialist majority, and therefore the SPD went into the so-called Weimar coalition with the Democratic Party and the Centre Party, both of whom were favourable to the officer corps, or at least the moderate element of it. Reinhardt also remained in control of military policy, particularly as leading generals such as Groener and Seeckt became more occupied with border defence in the east, than with the details of military policy in Berlin. Although they presented their views, it was a group within the Ministry of War known as the *Reichswehr* committee which formulated the *Reichswehr* law, passed on 6 March 1919, and the decrees of 31 March, which 'contained the embryo of all the regulations which later shaped the face of the *Reichswehr*.'[1] The work of this committee has largely passed unnoticed in the historiography.[2]

The initial impetus to set up a special committee to deal with military policy came from Groener in a cabinet meeting on 21 January.[3] The main issue on the agenda was the formation of a new army. Each member agreed that it was necessary to form a stable military force as soon as possible – even food supplies were threatened in the absence of a military force.[4] For Noske, it would allow the government 'to create some sort of order. Earlier the soldiers' councils were the power factor; now we have become the power factor.'[5] For others like Eugen Schiffer there could be

---

1. Fritz Ernst, 'Aus dem Nachlaß des Generals Walther Reinhardt', *Die Welt als Geschichte*, 1958, 58.
2. It receives no specific mention in either F. C. L. Carsten, *The Reichswehr and Politics, 1918-1933*, Oxford, 1966, or Harold Gordon, *The Reichswehr and the German Republic 1919-1926*, Princeton, 1957; Wolfram Wette drew attention to its role briefly in *Gustav Noske. Eine politische Biographie*, Düsseldorf, 1988, 361.
3. *Die Regierung der Volksbeauftragten 1918-19*, eds Susanne Miller, Erich Matthias, 2 vols, Düsseldorf, 1969, vol. 1, 285-91.
4. William Carl Matthews, 'The Economic Origins of the *Noskepolitik*', CEH, 27, 1, 1994, 80.
5. *Regierung der Volksbeauftragten*, vol. 1, 287.

'no financial credit without moral credit, without military credit.'[6] While Reinhardt recognised the need for a strong army to combat Polish and Czech threats to the German border, and Bolshevist threats internally, he stressed that the police should bear responsibility for upholding domestic order. He was aware that if the army became involved in bloody internal battles as a matter of course then it would lose its prestige. The reaction of many of the working class to the suppression of the Sparticist revolt was a clear indication of this danger. But for the moment military force was to be used to suppress economic and social protest, as Ebert made clear on 31 January: 'if one has sufficient means of force, then governing is easy; it has been very difficult to create a military force; finally we have succeeded. The government will do everything necessary to bring our economy into operation again and to eliminate the transportation difficulties.'[7] Social disorder offered an opportunity to the officer corps by making them indispensable to the government. However it also threatened long-term damage to the reputation of the military, as Reinhardt warned. The most practical suggestion of the meeting on 21 January was tabled by Groener, who recommended that a committee be set up 'for the establishment of a people's army'.[8] The idea was accepted by the cabinet, but discussion of the details were postponed until a future meeting. Soon afterwards the *Reichswehr* committee was convened.

By 3 February the Saxon Ministry of War had informed its counterpart in Stuttgart of the existence of the *Reichswehr* committee in the Prussian Ministry of War, which was chaired by Colonel Richard von Pawelsz, a friend of Reinhardt's since they had attended the cadet school together at Oranienstein.[9] The composition of the *Reichswehr* committee was unclear, but it was dominated by the Ministry of War and there were no representatives from the civilian government.[10] Reinhardt later mentioned that nearly all the heads of departments within the Ministry of War took part in the discussions.[11] The absence of government representatives was emblematic of the approach of politicians to the details of military policy issues. The cabinet sanctioned the committee, allowed it to go about its business, and accepted the recommendations, decrees and laws drafted by the committee. No coercion was involved – the President had to agree to issue the decrees and the National Assembly had to pass the temporary *Reichswehr* law. Arguably the policies developed

6. Ibid., 288.
7. Gerald Feldman, *The Great Disorder. Politics, Economics and Society in the German Inflation, 1914–1924*, Oxford, 1993, 123.
8. *Regierung der Volksbeauftragten*, 290.
9. HStASt, M 1/4, Bd 1612, Württemberg Ministry of War to Renner, 6 February 1919, fos. 20–21.
10. HStASt, M 1/4, Bd 1612, Nachrichtenblatt, Ministry of War, nr 26, 4 February 1919, fo. 22.
11. Ernst, 'Aus dem Nachlaß', 57.

within the *Reichswehr* committee represented a consensus from the moderate left to the moderate right. Whether this was the result of momentary terror of further revolutionary threats from the left, or the German politician once again mesmerised by the professional expertise of the officer, it should not diminish the scale of support for the *Reichswehr* law in March 1919.[12] Reinhardt was aware that he had to balance traditional military principles and contemporary political demands: 'We were looking for a legal basis which would be militarily acceptable to the old officers and politically acceptable to the new rulers.'[13]

Within the military the Prussian Ministry of War was in the dominant position. Policy which would have a long term impact on the *Reichswehr* was being formulated in the *Reichswehr* committee, the Ministry of War's sphere of influence. The Supreme Command tried to exert some influence on policy, by formulating draft plans. On 12 February, Groener asked Seeckt for his views on the future of the army. Five days later Seeckt produced a draft plan for a transitional and permanent army, which Groener passed on to Reinhardt.[14] Seeckt also wrote to Reinhardt on 1 March, detailing his views on military policy, but by this stage the agenda had been set by the memorandum of 5 February, written by Reinhardt and Pawelsz. None of Seeckt's ideas were evident in either the *Reichswehr* law or the decrees at the end of March. Groener had refused to take the post of Minister of War but in doing so he allowed Reinhardt to step into that position and exercise the decisive influence over German military policy in 1919. The Ministry of War's history in 1919 might not compare to the eventful history of the *Freikorps*, but both have a place in an assessment of the creation of the *Reichswehr*.

The nature of the remaining sources makes it difficult to explore Reinhardt's thoughts on the creation of the *Reichswehr*. His *Nachlaß* contains a paper, entitled 'Memorandum on the establishment of the *Reichswehr*'.[15] In the Bavarian *Hauptstaatsarchiv* there are a number of supplements to a memorandum bearing the same title, to which Pawelsz signed his name and which appears to be related to the Reinhardt memorandum.[16] These supplements were sent out to the various participants on the *Reichswehr* committee, and it appears as if they were written at the same time. The memorandum was a summary of preliminary discussions within the Ministry of War on the future of the army. Considering Reinhardt's position as Minister of War, his appointment of Pawelsz and their friendship,

---

12. Wette, *Noske*, 358-68.
13. *Deutsche Allgemeine Zeitung*, 'Der Geburtstag der Reichswehr', by Walther Reinhardt, 6 March 1929.
14. BA-MA, N 247/77, Entwurf, Seeckt to Groener, 17 February 1919, fos 8-10; Hans Meier-Welcker, *Seeckt*, Frankfurt, 1967, 203-204.
15. BA-MA, N 86/16, Denkschrift über die Aufstellung der Reichswehr.
16. BHStA, Gesandtschaft Berlin, 1352, Denkschrift über die Aufstellung der Reichswehr, RA, 100/2.19, geh. RA, signed von Pawelsz.

it can be assumed that he had a decisive input into the memoranda.[17] It is unclear which other officers in the Ministry of War had a rôle in drawing up the document, or if Noske or Göhre contributed.[18]

Reinhardt and Pawelsz started by noting that Germany's geopolitical position and the unstable internal situation 'needs a sufficient, functioning army.'[19] They clearly saw the *Reichswehr* as an instrument of the National Assembly, which was in line with the views of all the leading officers. The *Reichswehr* would protect the Assembly, and also implement its decisions, if called upon. After all, the moderate majority and the officers shared the same aim of suppressing any further left-wing revolts and holding the Reich together. The officers were not republicans by conviction, but by political necessity. Reinhardt, therefore, was a *Vernunftrepublikaner*, or a pragmatic republican.[20] The *Vernunftrepublikaner* were not a homogenous grouping, but covered a range of the political spectrum which accepted that the Weimar Republic was the only viable form of the German state after the war, but who invested little or no emotional energy in the promotion of republican values. For soldiers, who accorded primacy to the military mission and the re-establishment of Germany as a Great Power, the Republic was acceptable if first, there were no alternatives, and if, second, it allowed the achievement of military policy goals. When it failed on both accounts in the early 1930s, officers were quick to distance themselves from the Republic.

The establishment of a military force in a short space of time presented Reinhardt with a problem. The quickest way to form an army was 'by using the military institutions and bureaucracy at hand.'[21] But, as Reinhardt recognised in November 1918, the prestige of these institutions had suffered. Hence they had to adopt a new ethos and make concessions to the changed political situation. The memorandum argued that 'much value is placed in strict discipline, which alone guarantees the military worth of the troops; however old or mistaken institutions, which arouse distrust or aversion in the present domestic political climate, must definitely be thrown overboard.'[22] The assumptions are clear. Military efficiency demanded disciplined troops but those military institutions that did not reach the necessary standard had no place in the new army. Yet widespread political and social distrust of the military would prevent the

17. Friedrich Rau, *Personalpolitik in der 200 000 Mann Reichswehr*, Inaugural Dissertation zur Erlangung des Doktorgrades der philosophischen Fakultät, Munich, 1970, 92–96, discusses the memoramda and has a number of long extracts, but only mentions Pawelsz's name.
18. Wette, *Noske*, Düsseldorf, 1988, 361–68, 532–33, is critical of Noske's failure to get more involved in the detail and formulation of policy.
19. BA-MA, N 86/16, Denkschrift über die Aufstellung der Reichswehr.
20. Hürter, *Groener*, 28.
21. BA-MA, N 86/16, Denkschrift über die Aufstellung der Reichswehr.
22. Ibid.

regeneration of German military power, so changes would have to be made. The acknowledgement that the officer corps was seen as 'a shield of reaction' by many groups is an indication of the Ministry of War's real-istic view of the political situation in 1919. While the officer corps believed that the ideal solution was to give 'the young republic a young republican army', they were aware that this was not possible, because there were no explicitly republican military institutions, which had the same levels of expertise as the officer corps. In Germany's situation the creation of an inexperienced army would have weakened the state. It was from this matrix of factors that the *Reichswehr* emerged, an army which combined elements of the *Kaiserreich* army, with certain elements of the republican ideal.[23]

After outlining the framework of military policy, they then discussed the organisation of the army. It was hoped to establish an army of 350,000 men. Although conscription was 'the reliable and democratic basis of every army', Reinhardt and Pawelsz noted that many people were tired of military service, and would resent conscription. They wanted volunteers to make up the bulk of the army, which would be picked from the old army, the *Volkswehr* units set up by the law of 12 December 1918 and the *Freikorps* fighting in the east. In this way 'the German state will in the foreseeable future be in control of a unified, organised army, which although newly created, will have sufficient connections with our old battle-tested army, and retain its rich military experiences and high values.'[24] This reference to the military virtues of the old imperial army reflects the tensions within the Ministry of War's military policy. Since those concerned with policy-making did not believe that a fully republi-can army could be established, owing to Germany's situation, they had to resort to the qualities of the imperial army, qualities which Reinhardt admired. The framework within which they made policy decisions was constrained, as the memorandum pointed out, by the low prestige of the army in society at large, and by the threats to the state that forced Rein-hardt and his colleagues to look for quick solutions.

To build up the army as quickly as possible, they believed that it was necessary to convince society at large of the need for a military force. It was suggested that the government and the press embark on a propa-ganda campaign, which would 'raise the comprehension of, and keep alive among all groups, the threats facing us.'[25] An important aspect of the proposed campaign was that they hoped to target all sectors of society. The aim behind the recruitment system put forward by Reinhardt and his colleagues at the Ministry of War cannot be seen as an attempt to freeze the working class and other groups traditionally ignored or

23. Ibid.
24. Ibid.
25. Ibid.

distrusted by the officer corps out of the army. Reinhardt would have seen such a policy as counter-productive, because it would have reduced the social base that the *Reichswehr* needed in order to achieve its military missions, both internally and externally. That the *Reichswehr* ultimately discriminated against various groups in German society went against his policy. The memorandum concluded that 'all the love and trust that was and is given to the old army, must in this moment be transferred to the *Reichswehr*. The quicker and more suddenly it is created, the more it will be given the unanimous support of the people, and this will improve its political value abroad and at home.'[26] Social cohesion was an indispensable pre-condition for the revival of Germany's Great Power position, although Reinhardt's idealisation of the pre-1914 relationship between the military and society was misleading.

Necessity meant the *Reichswehr* had little choice but to use officers and NCOs brought up in the military traditions of the *Kaiserreich*. Reinhardt and Pawelsz argued that 'the quicker these (officers and NCOs) manage to successfully integrate into the new structures of the republican army, the quicker and more completely will they win back the old respect of the people and the troops. We must differentiate what we can sacrifice of the old in order to get rid of mistrust and ill will, and what we must retain in order to forge a useful weapon out of the *Reichswehr*.'[27] The memorandum started by arguing that a republican army would be the most appropriate military force for the new regime, but ended by arguing that the military virtues of the imperial army would be the basis of the *Reichswehr*. This movement from the ideal of a republican army to the reality that would be the *Reichswehr* was the result of the narrow range of options open to him. It represented his genuine attempt to fulfil the conditions of military efficiency while also taking the new political order into account.

At the end of the memorandum in the Reinhardt papers there was a reference to a second part which would discuss issues relating to the internal structures of the *Reichswehr*, such as wages, disciplinary codes and *Vertrauensleute*. The second part was signed by Pawelsz, but was almost certainly written in conjunction with Reinhardt. The opening sentence reaffirms the compatibility between elements of the old army and the new regime: 'It is proper to take the new situation into account in the form and structure of the army, and use the good things from the old army as a base.'[28] The rest of the memorandum outlined some innovative structures which would be introduced into the *Reichswehr*, and which were based on a new conception of the soldier. The soldier was no longer a conscript to be drilled into submission, but was now a

26. Ibid.
27. Ibid.
28. BHStA, Gesandtschaft Berlin, 1352, Denkschrift über die Aufstellung der Reichswehr.

volunteer, whose rights were to be protected, and who was to be rewarded for his service.

Perhaps the most necessary task in establishing an army is to recruit the soldiers. The recruitment system in Germany in 1919 was chaotic, a time when officers went around the country forming volunteer units. It was reminiscent of Wallenstein's heyday, a comparison which Reinhardt, an admirer of Schiller's plays, might have appreciated.[29] The rationalization of the recruitment system was fundamental to any effort to regain control of the wide variety of military forces emerging in Germany after the First World War. The lack of an alternative military infrastructure to the imperial army led the Ministry of War to suggest that recruitment should be organised by the officers of the brigades and regiments of the imperial army. It was necessary 'to get rid of the damaging and wild system of recruiting, and put the establishment of new units on a solid basis. At the same time as the creation of the *Reichswehr* the remaining units of the old army are to be formed into base units.'[30]

Changing attitudes to the rank and file were clearly reflected in the proposed wage structure, which was based 'on the view to entice applicants for the *Reichswehr* and to remunerate highly those who have the greatest claim.'[31] To encourage well-trained troops to stay on there was a bonus, which was raised for each three years of service. The wage policy was part of the project of professionalizing the army. It would allow applicants to view the *Reichswehr* as a career. Previously the only careers in the army had been for the NCOs and the officers. By extending the principles of promotion and wage rises to all levels of the army the Ministry of War was trying to reshape the traditional conception of the soldier-conscript which had emerged during the nineteenth century. In 1919 several hundred NCOs were promoted to the rank of officer.[32] The soldier was now a volunteer, and therefore the army had to compete in the same labour pool with other industries.

An oft-repeated complaint by critics of the imperial army was that the soldiers were subjected to *Kadavergehorsam* (corpse-like obedience), an accusation which took on a gruesome resonance during the First World War.[33] An institution, the *Vertrauensleute*, which was favoured by officers,

29. *Walther Reinhardt. Wehrkraft und Wehrwille. Aus seinem Nachlaß mit einer Lebensbeschreibung*, ed. Ernst Reinhardt, Berlin, 1932, 97–98; *Adjutant im preußischen Kriegsministerium Juni 1918 bis Oktober 1919. Aufzeichnungen des Hauptmanns Gustav Böhm*, eds Heinz Hürten, Georg Meyer, Stuttgart, 1977, 138-39.
30. BHStA, Gesandtschaft Berlin, 1352, Denkschrift über die Aufstellung der Reichswehr.
31. Ibid.
32. Hans Meier-Welcker, 'Der Weg zum Offizier in Reichsheer der Weimarer Republik', *MgM*, 19, 1976, 147.
33. Nicholas Stargardt, *The German Idea of Militarism. Radical and Socialist Critics, 1868-1914*, Cambridge, 1994, 39-40.

had emerged in the imperial army at the end of the war.[34] The decrees of 19 January gave the *Vertrauensleute* a rôle in smaller units. The failure of the decrees made the *Vertrauensleute* an even more attractive solution to disciplinary policy. The Ministry of War's memorandum referred to the Supreme Command decree of 10 November 1918[35]: 'For the *Reichswehr* the formation of soldiers' councils will not be recommended. As the Supreme Command decreed for the field army at the time, the *Reichswehr* will limit itself to the election of *Vertrauensleute*.'[36] However the Ministry of War's policy on *Vertrauensleute* was more comprehensive than the Supreme Command's, and the Ministry of War recommended that the *Vertrauensleute* should be involved in disciplinary matters as well as the social and economic concerns of the troops.

The instructions for *Vertrauensleute*, drafted in the memorandum, demonstrate both the disenchantment with the soldiers' councils, and certain elements of continuity with the thinking behind the decrees of 19 January.[37] The *Vertrauensleute* were to act as a 'link' between the rank and file and the officers, and promote the virtues of 'joy of service and subordination, comradeship and honour, devotion to duty and self-discipline'.[38] The *Vertrauensleute* also took over the rôle of the soldiers' councils in disciplinary affairs. The motivation behind the policy was to improve discipline by giving the soldiers a right of complaint, and hence deterring officers from bullying volunteers. The legitimacy of the *Vertrauensleute* as mediator between the officers and troops was to be grounded in the electoral process for the post.[39]

The aims of the policies outlined in the two memoranda by Reinhardt and Pawelsz were twofold, to form an efficient military force in as short a time as possible, and to fit this force into the new political and social framework created by the November revolution. These memoranda now became the basis of discussions in the *Reichswehr* committee. The committee appears to have worked in a number of stages. On 25 February 1919 Noske brought the temporary *Reichswehr* bill before the National Assembly. The bill had been drafted by the *Reichswehr* committee and jurists within the Ministry of War. The aim of the bill was to legalise the volunteer units by creating a new army, which the units of the old army could also join.[40] It allowed for elected representatives to deal with social and disciplinary issues.[41] Due to the lack of sources on cabinet meetings in

34. William Mulligan, 'Restoring Trust Within the *Reichswehr*: The Case of the *Vertrauensleute*', *War & Society*, 20, 2, 2002, 80.
35. Ibid., 80.
36. BHStA, Gesandtschaft Berlin, 1352, Denkschrift über die Aufstellung der Reichswehr.
37. Mulligan, 'Restoring Trust Within the *Reichswehr*', 81–82.
38. BHStA, Gesandtschaft Berlin, 1352, Denkschrift über die Aufstellung der Reichswehr.
39. Ibid.
40. Ernst, 'Aus dem Nachlaß', 58; Wette, *Noske*, 358-62.
41. *Armeeverordnungsblatt*, 1919, nr. 25.

February it is not possible to say whether the cabinet made changes to the draft bill for the establishment of the temporary *Reichswehr*.[42] Before discussing the debate it is important to note that the bill was only supposed to be valid for one year, but that it would be renewed by the National Assembly the following year, and that this quirk gave the structures of the temporary *Reichswehr* a permanency they might otherwise not have had.

The bill was subjected to the rigours of democratic control in a debate in the National Assembly on 25 and 27 February. The bill was well received by the people's representatives. In the speeches a number of themes appear constantly. First, there was a sense of urgency. The SPD deputy, Schöpflin, kept his speech short, arguing that 'long speeches have no use, now it is necessary to act quickly and energetically. The emergency situation and the welfare of the German people demands it.'[43] Gröber, the spokesman for the Centre party, also argued that the current position of Germany called for the quick formation of the *Reichswehr*, as did Julius Atzmann, a Protestant pastor and People's Party deputy.[44] The deputies from the Weimar coalition parties, the SPD, Democratic, and Centre Parties, all noted the importance of 'strict discipline', although they sought to avoid a return to the '*Kadavergehorsam*' of the imperial army. Siehr, a Democratic deputy from East Prussia, argued that good discipline should not prevent 'the replacement of certain flaws of the old system in a democratic spirit', and saw the election of *Vertrauensleute* as a means to achieve an inner democratisation of the army.[45] While the parties of the Weimar coalition saw promotion from the ranks and the election of *Vertrauensleute* as a sign of a changed military policy they were wary of the recruitment system. Schöpflin hoped 'that enough volunteers would be found, also from the socialist working class, so that these do not simply leave volunteering to other social groups.'[46] The bill establishing the temporary *Reichswehr* was accepted by 348 out of the 421 deputies. The most significant opposition came from the ranks of the USPD, who urged the adoption of a recruitment system which would attract working-class applicants, and also objected to the articles on promotion and the replacement of the soldiers' councils with *Vertrauensleute*.[47]

---

42. *Das Kabinett Scheidemann. 13. Februar bis 20. Juni 1919*, ed. Hagen Schulze, Boppard am Rhein, 1971, xix–xxiii.
43. Eduard Heilfron, *Die deutsche Nationalversammlung im Jahre 1919 in ihrer Arbeit für den Aufbau des neuen deutschen Volkstaates*, 6 vols, Berlin, 1920, vol. 1, 739.
44. Ibid., 739–40, 769–76.
45. Ibid., 742.
46. Ibid., 738.
47. Wette, *Noske*, 362–68.

The fact that they accepted the policy initiatives set forth in the Ministry of War's memoranda indicates that the majority of the populace shared the view of Reinhardt and his colleagues that a military force had to be formed urgently, and therefore they had to make do with the raw materials at hand. No one deluded themselves that it was a perfect solution, hence the title 'temporary *Reichswehr*', just as it was that no one could know of the chaotic political situation of March 1920 which would force an extension of the law for another year. The DDP and the Centre Party spoke of military policy in terms of an effective, not a republican, army.[48] Within the limits set by the political situation of February and March 1919 the deputies of the National Assembly felt that the internal structures of the temporary *Reichswehr* were the best solution to the problem of forming an army in the new state. The debate was a further illustration of the nature of the relationship between the military and the civilian structures of government. The law, drafted by the Ministry of War, had to be accepted by the National Assembly before it could be implemented. If Reinhardt had taken a lead in policy formulation, he also had to ensure that the draft law would be passed by the Assembly. 92 deputies out of 421 voted against the law, and that included some DNVP deputies who thought the law too radical![49] It is only with the wisdom imparted by hindsight that it is possible to criticise the members of the National Assembly for not attempting to fashion a more quintessentially republican army.[50]

The law established the basis for the creation of the *Reichswehr*, but some details had to be worked out, and would be issued as decrees on 31 March 1919, signed by Reinhardt, Noske and Ebert. On 22 February Pawelsz sent out a list of topics to be discussed in meetings between 25 February and 1 March, which included the role of *Vertrauensleute*, discipline, wages and uniforms.[51] These discussions led to the amendment of some of the policies suggested in the memoranda of the Ministry of War. The amended drafts were then discussed at a second series of meetings between 8 and 14 March.[52] There were three significant changes to the policies outlined in the memoranda. First, officers who did not enjoy the

48. Hartmut Schustereit, 'Unpolitisch-Überparteilichkeit-Staatstreu; Wehrfragen aus der Sicht der Deutschen Demokratischen Partei, 1919–1930', *MgM*, 16, (1974), 131–33; Werner Schneider, *Die Deutsche Demokratische Partei in der Weimarer Republik*, Munich, 1978, 117–18; Wilhelm Zimmermann, in his study, *Die Wehrpolitik des Zentrums in der Weimarer Republik*, Frankfurt, 1994, 29–40

49. Jürgen Schmädeke, *Militärische Kommandogewalt und parlamentarische Demokratie. Zum Problem der Verantwortlichkeit des Reichswehrministers in der Weimarer Republik*, Lübeck, Hamburg, 1966, 35–36.

50. The debates in the National Assembly on military policy have not been comprehensively studied, but critics of the process include Schmädeke, *Militärische Kommandogewalt und parlamentarische Demokratie*, 31–37; Wette, *Noske*, 532–33.

51. HStASt, M 10, Bd. 3, Sitzungen des weiteren und engeren Beratungskreis des RA, 22 February 1919, fo. 22.

52. HStASt, M 77/1, Bü 82, Pawelsz memo, 4 March 1919.

trust of their troops were not necessarily removed automatically from their post, a change which strengthened the position of the officers vis-à-vis the troops. Second, the old system for calculating officers' wages, based on the length of time served, was retained instead of the more differentiated system proposed in the memorandum. This had the consequence of favouring longevity over promotion. It would also mean that if an officer from the old army found himself at a lower rank in the *Reichswehr* he would not suffer from a loss of income. Third, it was decided to retain elements of the old uniform, such as the caps, and the coats. However the old 'shoulder pieces' (*Achselstücke*) were to be abolished.[53]

The issue which dominated the discussions between 8 and 13 March was recruitment. On 5 March 1919 Göhre and Pawelsz pointed out that the most important task for the new *Reichswehr* was recruitment. This could only begin when applicants knew what the terms of service would be, namely wages, discipline, holidays and general welfare.[54] The impact of the wage level on recruitment had already been discussed during the first set of meetings in February. Then the representative of the *Reichsschatzamt* argued that the wage bill outlined in the memoranda would cost 1 billion Marks for wages, and 2 to 3 billion Marks in supplementary expenses on food, accommodation and equipment, compared to an equivalent cost in 1914 of 1.2 billion Marks.[55] Cuts in the wage bill had been provisionally accepted in the memoranda, but now were opposed by both Reinhardt and the Supreme Command. The Supreme Command argued that lower wages would deter recruits, while Reinhardt demanded that money must be raised because 'the Reich is still at war, and that this means that a regulation of the budget according to peace-time guidelines is not yet possible.'[56] The cost of the army was defended by the Ministry of War against the Reich Finance Ministry, which sought to reduce expenditure, and exercise some control over the level of inflation. The Ministry of War argued consistently up to the Kapp Putsch that the state had to pay soldiers a sufficient wage to maintain public order, and that the German people owed soldiers who had risked their life at the front, and then in the suppression of left-wing revolts, a moral debt.

When the committee met again the recruitment system was on the agenda.[57] Reinhardt appears to have attended these meetings, and one

53. HStASt, M 77/1, Bü 82, Sitzungsberichte über die Sitzung des Reichswehrausschusses, 8-13 March 1919.
54. BHStA, Gesandtschaft Berlin, 1352, Prussian Ministry of War, 5 March 1919, Nr. 258.3.19 A1.
55. BHStA, Gesandtschaft Berlin, 1352, Captain von Pechmann to Sperr, 28 February 1919.
56. BHStA, Gesandtschaft Berlin, 1352, Captain von Pechmann to Sperr, 1 March 1919.
57. The exact dates when discussions on recruitment took place are uncertain, and they may have been spread over a number of days; BHStA, Gesandtschaft Berlin, 1352, Bavarian plenipotentiary to Bavarian Ministry for Military Affairs, 8 March 1919; HStASt, M 1/4, Bd. 1612, memorandum entitled 'Werbungen für die Reichswehr', 11 March 1919.

report noted that the Minister of War stressed the urgency of beginning recruitment. To speed up the process the General Commands, which were the command headquarters of the various corps of the imperial army, were put in charge of recruitment.[58] The continuity of personnel between the imperial army and the *Reichswehr* was also promoted by giving preferences to those soldiers who had served before 1918. These soldiers would form the core regiments of the *Reichswehr*.[59]

The series of meetings of the *Reichswehr* committee on the internal structures and terms of service in the *Reichswehr* appears to have ended in mid-March. The process of consultation between Noske and Ebert on the one hand and Reinhardt on the other in the period between the conclusion of the *Reichswehr* committee's business and the publication of the decrees in the *Armeeverordnungsblatt* on 31 March 1919 cannot be uncovered. Given the significance of the decrees it must be assumed that Noske and Ebert gave them a more than a passing glance. The decrees owe their structure to the memoranda drafted in February. For instance the *Vertrauensleute* were seen as a 'link' between officers and troops, and were responsible for the morale and performance of their units.[60] The *Vertrauensleute* represented a change in the disciplinary culture of the German army, although one that was maintained unevenly throughout the 1920s.[61]

The decrees on promotion and recruitment were a more detailed version of the policy outlined in the memos. *Feldwebel* (sergeants), who had served six months at the front and distinguished themselves, could apply to become officers. To aid them and other NCOs achieve the required results in the officers' examinations the Ministry of War had established a six-weeks course.[62] Recruiting was carried out by the *Generalkommando*. The decree warned against 'unreliable elements', but failed to define the criteria of reliability.[63] The criteria for the choice of officers was clearer, and favoured those 'who during the war had proved themselves skilled and successful in the handling of troops, and who had served longer and more successfully at the front than other applicants.'[64] Owing to the scarcity of places in the officer corps, this clause would become the subject of a debate between those who favoured front officers, and those who favoured general staff officers. Despite having got most of his policies from the committee stage to the statute book, Reinhardt still had to implement the decrees in the political and social context of 1919.[65]

58. BHStA, Gesandtschaft Berlin, 1352, Bavarian plenipotentiary to Bavarian Ministry for Military Affairs, 8 March 1919.
59. HStASt, M 1/4, Bd. 1612, memo entitled 'Werbungen für die Reichswehr', 11 March 1919.
60. *Armeeverordnungsblatt*, nr. 30, 1919, 272.
61. Mulligan, 'Restoring Trust Within the *Reichswehr*', 83–90.
62. *Armeeverordnungsblatt*, nr. 30, 1919, 278-80.
63. *Armeeverordnungsblatt*, nr. 30, 1919, 266–67.
64. *Armeeverordnungsblatt*, nr. 30, 1919, 266.
65. See Chapter 7 on the Kapp Putsch.

The second area in which Reinhardt dominated policy-making in the first half of 1919 was the centralisation of the states' war ministries.[66] There was opposition from the states, mainly Bavaria, Wurttemberg and Baden. Yet Reinhardt had the backing of his political superiors and the support of the National Assembly, just as he had over the temporary *Reichswehr* law. He also had the support of most officers. From early 1919 Reinhardt planned to replace the polycratic and ineffective military structures of the *Kaiserreich* with a centralised bureaucracy.[67] By radically restructuring German military bureaucracy, Reinhardt encroached on several vested and personal interests. Between February and June 1919 he was engaged in negotiations with Bavaria, Saxony, Württemberg and Baden, which wanted to avoid excessive control from Berlin. He used the political constellation to his advantage by allying with the centralising ministers in the Weimar coalition and using the majority in the National Assembly who wanted a more centralised Reich as a threat against the federal states. While co-operation was a political necessity in planning the *Reichswehr* law, it became a political advantage in his negotiations with the states.

In the *Kaiserreich* four states – Prussia, Bavaria, Saxony and Württemberg – retained independent ministries of war. Military unity was provided by the General Staff and the Kaiser.[68] The post-war form of military unity was by no means a foregone conclusion. After all the German revolution had occurred at state level, before it occurred at Reich level. There were also some separatist movements in the east and the Rhineland.[69] As was the case with the council movement, it was the election of the National Assembly that proved decisive. It moved the momentum away from the states and towards the Reich. By the end of 1919 financial and military structures were more centralised than in the *Kaiserreich*, although Reich-state relations would continue to be a massive issue in Weimar politics.[70] The issue cut across traditional political divisions that enabled Reinhardt to marry political necessity with

66. For a more detailed account of the unification of the states' war ministries see William Mulligan, 'Civil-military Relations in the Early Weimar Republic', *Historical Journal*, 45, 4, 2002, 819–41; generally see Gerhard Schulz, *Zwischen Krieg und Diktatur. Verfassungspolitik und Reichsreform in der Weimarer Republik*, 2 vols, Berlin, 1987, vol. 1, 21–320.

67. John Wheeler-Bennett, *The Nemesis of Power. The German Army in Politics, 1918-1945*, London, 1961 edn, 41.

68. Thomas Nipperdey, *Deutsche Geschichte, 1866-1918: Machtstaat vor der Demokratie* (Munich, 1992), 202; Lothar Gall, *Bismarck. The White Revolutionary, 1815-1871*, 2 vols, London, 1990, vol. 1, 371–72.

69. K. Reimer, *Rheinlandfrage und Rheinlandbewegung (1918-1933)*, Frankfurt, 1979; Ralph Schattkowsky, 'Separation in the Eastern Provinces of the German Reich at the End of the First World War', *JCH*, 29, 1994, 305–24.

70. Feldman, *Great Disorder*, 161; Reginald Phelps, 'Aus den Groener-Dokumenten', *Deutsche Rundschau*, 1957-58, 735–38; Jane Caplan, *Government Without Administration. State and Civil Service in Weimar and Nazi Germany*, Oxford, 1988, 26–28.

professional principles. It also demonstrated the potential for the institutions of the new state to be shaped according to the principles of military efficiency.[71] Politicians and officials at Reich level tended to stress the importance of centralised power, while those at state level sought to retain their powers; there was a mixture of genuine belief and hard-headed self-interest on both sides.

The most important figure in the early stages of the debate was Hugo Preuß, a liberal lawyer, appointed to the Interior Ministry's committee to draw up a constitution. On 3 January 1919 he produced a draft and an accompanying essay. His principal concern was to ensure that the will of the whole German people was democratically expressed in the *Reichstag*. He wanted to break up the Prussian state which he saw as an obstacle to a centralised Reich. In Preuß's system the centralised Reich would have the vast majority of the power, including control over external affairs, economic policy, the railways and the postal system. The same principle would apply to military affairs, although he recognised that the Allies would have some say in the final composition of Germany's military forces.[72] He argued that centralised control would facilitate democratic control.[73] The nature of sovereignty in Germany had changed; it emanated from the people, not the Kaiser. As the highest representative body, the *Reichstag* and the national government had to be in charge of the army, hence the centralised control. States would become administrative units, bereft of real power.[74]

This radical conception of a centralised German Reich found little support among the political parties in the National Assembly, and there was no possibility that Prussia was going to be replaced by a number of smaller administrative units.[75] Although the National Assembly was not prepared to accept the more radical ideas of Preuß, the majority of its members were in favour of a more centralised state, including the largest party, the SPD. They supported one of the most important reforms, the centralisation of the tax system.[76] Matthias Erzberger of the Centre Party, despised by officers for his role in the Peace Resolutions of July 1917, had carried out financial reforms that could only be approved of from the military point of view. In the late 1920s Reinhardt commented that 'the

71. Heinz Hürten, 'Heeresverfassung und Länderrecht: Württemberg in den Auseinandersetzungen der Weimarer Nationalversammlung um die Bildung einer einheitlichen Reichswehr', *MgM*, 23, 1978, 147–82.

72. Hugo Preuß, *Staat, Recht und Freiheit. Aus 40 Jahren deutscher Politik und Geschichte*, Hildesheim, 1964, 370–84.

73. Wette, *Noske*, 532.

74. Mulligan, 'Civil-military relations', 822.

75. Dietrich Orlow, *Weimar Prussia, 1918-1925. The Unlikely Rock of Democracy*, Pittsburgh, 1986, 89–91; Heinrich August Winkler, *Weimar 1918-1933. Die Geschichte der ersten deustchen Demokratie*, Munich, 1993, 99–100.

76. Feldman, *Great Disorder*, 161–66.

transfer of direct income tax to the financial administration of the Reich solved the basic question, seen simply from the point of military effectiveness, better than ever before in German history.'[77]

The revolution opened up the possibility of creating an *improved* state, as the military saw it. Pragmatic officers sensed an opportunity for co-operation with the Republic on this basis. In a letter to President Friedrich Ebert (SPD), Groener argued that the opportunity presented by the revolution 'must be exploited under all circumstances in order to make the German dream of a powerful state, encompassing the whole German race, and based on a strong central power, reality.'[78] Clearly the officers corps and the SPD had different ultimate goals, but for a moment their intermediate aim of a centralised state overlapped, producing a powerful reforming alliance. The development towards the unitary state in 1919 was an indication that the Weimar Republic was not necessarily antithetical to the officer corps' view of an ideal state.[79] Remaking the state represented a much more positive element of co-operation between the military and the Republic than the defensive preservation of the *Befehlsgewalt*.

While Groener was advising Ebert to press for the most unitary state possible, Reinhardt had a crucial role in unifying the states' ministries. He conducted the negotiations with the various states, and at the end of his career he saw the creation of the *Reichswehrministerium* as his most significant achievement.[80] First and foremost, it was a question of efficiency and practicality.[81] The *Kaiser* had been the unifying focal point of the military constitution of the *Kaiserreich*.[82] Once he abdicated, German military unity was fragile. In order to replace both the symbolic and actual unity provided by the Kaiser, it was necessary to establish a more unified administrative and command structure. As Reinhardt made clear, in the course of negotiations with the states, the unwieldy structures of German military administration had hampered the war effort.[83] The centralisation of military administration appeared even more important after the experiences of the First World War. Second, Reinhardt's sense of allegiance was to Germany rather than to his native state, Württemberg. In January 1924 he wrote to 5th Division, commemorating the anniversary of the

77. *Wehrkraft und Wehrwille*, 84; Niall Ferguson, 'Public Finance and National Security: The Domestic Origins of the First World War Revisited', *Past and Present*, 142, 1994, 144, 155–58.
78. *Zwischen Revolution und Kapp-Putsch: Militär und Innenpolitk, 1918-1920*, ed. Heinz Hürten, Düsseldorf, 1977, 53.
79. Mulligan, 'Civil-military relations', 823.
80. *Wehrkraft und Wehrwille*, 51.
81. Michael Geyer, 'The Past as Future: the German Officer Corps as Profession', in *German Professions, 1800-1950*, eds Geoffrey Cocks, Konrad Jarausch, Oxford, 1990, 197–200.
82. *Wehrkraft und Wehrwille*, 83–84.
83. BArch R 43 I/1863, Niederschrift über die Verhandlung der Staatenvertreter in Weimar, 5–8 February 1919, fo. 248.

founding of the Bismarckian Reich. Bismarck had been able to unify all the parts of Germany, and millions had died trying to defend that creation, strengthening the bonds of unity by their sacrifice.[84]

Yet he was opposed to the dissolution of Prussia. Reinhardt argued that the collapse of Prussia would defeat the aim of centralisation by making Germany weaker. On 14 January 1919 at a meeting of the Council of People's Commissars, Reinhardt was the first to speak in favour of Prussia's position within Germany, after Preuß had called for its dissolution:

> Prussia has become great through its state-building powers, which have not yet disappeared. German unity has been achieved through the unity of ever bigger states; not for nothing does Berlin lie on the edge between the industrial west and the agrarian east. The question is whether, without a strong Prussia, the many different parts of Germany would possess the centripetal power, in order to resist the attempts to amalgamate with non-German neighbouring states.[85]

Reinhardt accepted the principles of centralisation, but not Preuß's means of achieving this goal. For Reinhardt the process of centralisation could be part of the organic development of the *Reich* rather than a mechanistic and unhistorical imposition. His interpretation of the mission of Prussia was a combination of the practicalities of power politics with historical idealism.

Although Reinhardt opposed the break up of Prussia, Preuß's draft plan of the constitution opened the way for the unity of the states' war ministries. Article 3 of the first draft stated: 'Reich affairs, which are exclusively the legislative and administrative prerogative of the Reich, include the defence of the Reich on land, sea and in the air.'[86] As early as 10 January, there were vague suggestions of a unified Ministry.[87] Various decrees and the *Reichswehr* law also pointed to increased centralisation. The decrees of 19 January 1919 were formulated in negotiations between the Prussian Ministry of War and the Central Council, representative of the soldiers' councils. This was a *de facto* centralisation of military policy in Berlin.[88] At a cabinet meeting on 21 February it was formally agreed that the unification of the states' ministries could proceed. All administrative and command functions would become the prerogatives of the Reich.[89] While ministers helped in the initial negotiating process, the detail of policy was left to the officers.

84. HStASt, M 660/034, Bü 26, *Wehrkreis Verordnungsblatt*, 18 January 1924.
85. *Die Regierung der Volksbeauftragten 1918-19*, 2 vols, eds Susanne Miller, Erich Matthias, Düsseldorf, 1969, vol. 2, 240–44.
86. Ibid., 249.
87. *Aus den Geburtsstunden der Weimarer Republik: das Tagebuch des Obersten Ernst van den Bergh*, ed. Wolfram Wette, Düsseldorf, 1991, 79–82.
88. *Der Zentralrat der deutschen sozialistischen Republik, 19.12.18-8.4.19*, eds Eberhard Kolb, Reinhard Rürup, Leiden, 1968, 441–48.
89. BA-MA, N 86/16, Abschrift, memorandum of cabinet meeting, 21 February 1919.

Negotiations were complicated by the opposition of the states to the loss of their war ministries and military rights.[90] This opposition was based on regional identity, fear of 'Borussification', hatred of Prussia, and regional political interest.[91] Seeckt also tried to exploit the states' aims to prevent the centralisation of the military structure, which he feared would lead to the General Staff's loss of independence and Reinhardt's dominance in military policy formulation:

> There could be no more certain bond [of unity] than the blood which has flowed in numerous battles, and yet all our hopes of the realisation of a Reich army have come to nought. The particularist efforts of the federal states have come to the fore so strongly during the revolution that it does not seem worthwhile to introduce the desired form of the Reich army with physical force. Such a structure would have no permanency. The only thing which we can rescue is the tradition of the army, be it in Prussia, Bavaria, Saxony or Württemberg. This gives us the hope to build on this basis of tradition.[92]

Unity would be provided by the General Staff's planning functions as it was in the *Kaiserreich*. Seeckt's trump card was the particularist sentiment in the south German states. Reinhardt's success in centralising the ministries contributed in no small way to strengthening his position for the struggles with Seeckt and Groener during the summer of 1919 for control of military policy.

At a meeting of the states and Reich on 25 January, Preuß put the case for a united military organisation, which would allow 'the security of national existence against foreign threats and the maintenance of peace and order at home.'[93] However his calls for a unitary state, be they couched in terms of democracy, or of national existence, held little appeal for the states. Georg Gradnauer, the Saxon Minister President, suggested that only limited constitutional decisions should be taken in the current situation, while Eisner warned that the states must be included in any constitutional debates. Finally Ebert agreed to establish a committee for the states that would deal with constitutional issues, a move which opened the way for negotiations.[94] To co-ordinate their position on Reich military policy the Württemberg government organised a meeting of Baden, Bavarian, Saxon and Württemberg military ministers

---

90. These ministries went under various names after November 1918; in Baden, where a new ministry was established, it was called "Ministerium für militärische Angelegenheiten" (Ministry for Military Affairs); Bavaria used the same term; in Prussia, Saxony and Württemberg the name "Kriegsministerium" (Ministry of War) was retained.

91. Mulligan, 'Civil-military relations', 825–27.

92. BA-MA, N 247/66, Abschrift, Seeckt to Reinhardt, 1 March 1919, 'Vorschlag zur Gestaltung des künftigen Heeres', fos. 29–30.

93. BArch, R 43 I/1863, Memorandum of meeting on the Constitution on 25 January 1919, fos. 70–71.

94. Ibid., fo. 99.

and advisers in Stuttgart on 3 February 1919.[95] The result of the meeting was a vague agreement that the states would maintain a broad front against plans to sweep aside their rights. The defence of their rights was their main argument. Immanuel Hermann, the SPD Württemberg Minister of War, suggested that they adopt the standpoint, 'that the status quo cannot be changed without the approval of the states.'[96] It was difficult for the states to agree on any detailed plan because first, they were uncertain of what Reinhardt intended to do, and second they had divergent interests themselves. Therefore they ended up reacting to the initiatives taken by the Prussian Ministry of War.

The united front of Baden, Bavaria and Württemberg, which had shown most interest in opposing a centralised military organisation, was tested at a meeting of the states with Reinhardt, and two aides, at the Fürstenhaus in Weimar between 5 and 8 February. Franz Sperr, the Bavarian military envoy, was adamant that the states' rights should be preserved. He was supported by the Baden and Württemberg representatives. However, Preuß insisted on a united army, within whose framework some concessions could be made to the states.[97] Reinhardt pointed out that practical considerations suggested the unification of the war ministries:

> While recognising the wartime performance of each contingent, one must still say that too many variations existed in the army. ... At the moment we can simplify and make (the army) cheaper; the details are the concern of the *Reichswehr* law. The states' wishes should be accommodated as far as possible. Beneath the *Reichswehrministerium* will be the Austrian, Prussian, etcetera, high commands. These can be given some administrative functions (housing troops, and similar functions). Training and education must be under the control of the Reich, since they are central to the spirit of the army. That the Reich general staff must be united is self-explanatory, as well as justice and conscription. In the future we will not be able to maintain a large army. Therefore I suggest: 'The defence of the Reich is exclusively the affair of the Reich. The necessary institutions will be administered according to the *Reichswehr* law'.[98]

Reinhardt's position vis-à-vis the states was strong. He had more positive suggestions and significant political backing. However neither Reinhardt nor Preuß were able to get Bavaria and its dogged military envoy, Sperr, to agree to the changes in the draft constitution.[99]

Two days after the end of the meeting at the Fürstenhaus in Weimar, Konrad von Preger, the Bavarian envoy to the Reich, reminded Ebert that he had promised not to sideline the states by using the vast majority in

95. Hürten, 'Heeresverfassung und Länderrecht', 154–64.
96. Ibid., 160.
97. BArch, R 43 I/1863, Niederschrift über die Verhandlung der Staatenvertreter in Weimar, 5–8 February 1919, fos. 241–48.
98. Ibid., fos. 248.
99. Ibid., fos. 248–49.

the National Assembly in favour of a centralised Reich.[100] This letter was prompted by the removal of the fourth clause of Article 5 of the Constitution, which dealt with military affairs. Article 5 was a confusing mix, promising a united administrative organisation, whilst also explicitly guaranteeing Bavaria's *Sonderrechte*. The removal of the fourth clause clarified the situation, but to the detriment of Bavaria, by excluding the guarantee.[101] The removal of the fourth clause was the subject of a further Reich-states meeting between 18 and 20 February. Preuß explained that members of the Centre Party had been behind the change. Preger felt 'surprised and disconcerted', whilst Sperr stated categorically that a united army was not a possibility at the moment.[102] Reinhardt replied that the other clauses gave guarantees that the states' wishes would be considered in the framework of a united army. He urged the states to take 'a step forwards towards unity'.[103]

Reinhardt's early conception of a united army had a number of features. First, the Ministry would be integrated into the Weimar constitution. The President and the *Reichswehrminister* would have the power to appoint senior officers and issue orders. These were similar to the powers of the Kaiser. Second, Reinhardt was not prepared to allow the continued existence of the states' war ministries. Third, he was prepared to give the larger states, and here he included Hessen and Baden, *Kommandostellen* (command centres). By this he meant that the larger states could have their own units, and that the command structure would be based on the Reich's federal structure. Hence the chain of command would run from the *Reichswehrminister* in Berlin to commanders in Munich, Karlsruhe and Dresden and so on. Since the *Reichswehrminister* would exercise central control this chain of command would not damage the unified structure of the army, and it would also go some way towards appeasing the states.

The political momentum was shifting in favour of a unitary *Reichswehrministerium*, and there was general support within the officer corps for the policy.[104] It was clear that the National Assembly desired a more centralised Reich, and this had enabled the government to remove the fourth clause guaranteeing previous agreements. Having made his general position clear to the states' representatives Reinhardt was now able to concentrate on negotiating an accord with them. Initially this took the form of pressurising individual states, particularly Baden and Württemberg. The two south-western German states occupied a key position. As the smallest states that could support an independent military bureaucracy, it was

100. BArch, R 43 I/1863, Preger to Ebert, Weimar, 10 February 1919, fo. 57.
101. BArch, R 43 I/1863, Zusammenfassung des Entwurfs einer Verfassung des deutschen Reiches, Beschlüsse des 8. Ausschusses, fo. 433.
102. BArch, R 43 I/1863, Memorandum on meeting of *Staatenausschuss*, Weimar, 18-20 February 1919, fo. 299.
103. Ibid., fos. 300–02.
104. Mulligan, 'Civil-military relations', 829.

imperative to persuade them to accept a unitary solution to the issue of military organisation. Since Saxony had shown less enthusiasm for preserving their rights, and preferred to position itself as a mediator between Prussia and southern Germany, this would leave Bavaria isolated.

The first major steps towards the final resolution of the Reich-states military relationship were taken at a series of meetings between Reinhardt, Erzberger and Otto Landsberg, the Reich Justice Minister, and representatives from Württemberg on 5 and 6 March.[105] On 5 March a preliminary agreement was concluded under which Württemberg would constitute a self-contained military area, known as a *Wehrbezirk*. The commander of the *Wehrbezirk* would be appointed by the Reich President, from a list submitted by the Württemberg government. Officers in the *Wehrbezirk* would be named by the Reich President, in conjunction with the commander. The commander would be responsible for the distribution of troops and army manoeuvres within Württemberg. Hence, as the Württemberg military adviser, Horn, commented the only real concession was the position of the *Wehrbezirk*'s commander. The possibility of retaining the Württemberg Ministry of War was not even on the agenda.[106] That evening Erzberger rejected the counterproposals drawn up by Renner and Horn. He favoured a unified *Reichswehrministerium* for three reasons. First, it coincided with the aims of his plan for a more unified budgetary and financial system in the Reich. Second, the Reich needed control of the military to shore up the position of the Reich government. Finally, it was in the interest of the states 'if everything were organised by the Reich, because then the predominance of Prussia would be replaced by the power-base of the Reich.'[107] Reinhardt also used this argument to impress the states with the need for a unified ministry. He pointed out that Prussia could only be expected to make the same concessions as other states:

> In the Prussian army, as well as in the Prussian government, and I believe the hearts of the Prussian people, the will is present to join the army to the Reich. As a Württemberg colonel, I have the permission of the senior officers of the Prussian army. However it would not be understood in Prussia if the other states were not willing to make the same concessions as they demand from Prussia.[108]

Both Reinhardt and Erzberger were able to manipulate fear of Prussia to force Württemberg into a unified *Reichswehrministerium*. Reinhardt was able to force an agreement on Württemberg by getting support from like-minded (on this issue) ministers and pointing to the unitary tendencies of the National Assembly.[109]

105. Ibid., 830.
106. Hürten, 'Heeresverfassung und Länderrecht', 165.
107. Ibid., 165–66.
108. Ibid., 151–52.
109. Mulligan, 'Civil-military relations', 831–32.

Bavaria seemed set to continue its opposition, claiming that treaty rights from 1870 were being infringed and that Bavarian public opinion would not countenance a unitary state. Meetings between 8 and 12 March ended without agreement.[110] But on 14 March the major breakthrough was achieved when the so-called 'Weimar Agreement' was concluded. Reinhardt's 'southern German stubbornness' had paid dividends.[111] This agreement was apparently the result of similar pressure that was applied to Württemberg. A Baden envoy noted the pressure which the impending defeat of a motion in the National Assembly to preserve the states' special rights added to the situation: 'This produces a situation that, in view of the unitary tendencies of the overwhelming majority of the National Assembly, makes it imperative that the larger states, no matter if, and to what extent they had their own military administration up to this point, reach an agreement with the Reich, which takes into account their interests in the *Reichswehr* law.'[112] The states aimed to secure certain guarantees which would be enshrined in the *Reichswehr* law, which was due to be drafted later in 1919, instead of having guarantees written into the constitution. Whereas the special rights of 1870 took the form of treaties between Bavaria, Württemberg and the North German Confederation, the rights accorded to the states in 1919 were based on a much less binding agreement.

The preamble to the Weimar agreement stated that it aimed to ensure the unity of the *Reichswehr*, and in so far as was compatible with this aim, the states would have certain rights, but no ministries. Each of the named states, Baden, Bavaria, Prussia, Saxony and Württemberg, would form 'an enclosed area, each with a high commander', who would be named by the Reich President on the suggestion of the state, and could be removed by the latter.[113] Units based in these states would be composed of citizens from that state, or region. The high commander would have to take the state's economic interests into account when he was planning exercises, while arms contracts would also have to be equitably distributed between the states. The states would also have military representatives in the *Reichsrat*, which was the upper house in the German parliament and composed of states' representatives, as well as in the *Reichswehrministerium*, allowing the states to play a role in the formulation of military policy. The states could use troops at times when their police forces were unable to control unrest. Since symbols played as important a role in the German revolution as any other, troops would also wear a badge to denote from which region they came.

---

110. Ibid., 832–34.
111. *Aus den Geburtsstunden der Weimarer Republik*, 111.
112. GLAK, Abt. 233/12441, Baden envoy to the Baden cabinet, 18 March 1919.
113. GLAK, Abt. 233/12441, Baden envoy to the Baden cabinet, 18 March 1919, contains a copy of the agreement.

Most of the states' rights were consultative, and they had no active way of influencing military policy, except through their representatives on the *Reichsrat* and in the *Reichswehrministerium*. One adviser to the Baden government, believed that the right of a state to remove a high commander was 'the main basis for the states' government to influence military affairs'.[114] This was the only significant right that the states had to influence military policy. Yet these representatives would only have a limited influence on military policy and would find it difficult to protect any particular interests of the states. Other concessions were symbolic, and although important for preserving regional military traditions, would have little impact on the formulation of military policy. The Weimar agreement was significant for more than its terms, which in any case were to be the subject of a further three months of debate between Reinhardt and the states. The existence of the agreement prevented an open conflict between the states and the Reich. The Reich government may have used intense political pressure to force an agreement, but ultimately it did not unilaterally abandon the special rights of 1870. By signing up to the agreement, all the states recognised that the military constitution of the *Kaiserreich* with its special privileges for certain states was no longer tenable in the post-1918 Germany. Preger and other leading officials were worried by the surrender of so much control to the Reich, and on 22 March he lamented that Bavaria was no longer 'a sovereign federal state, but simply a constituent state under the Reich.'[115] For Reinhardt and other Reich officials this situation was ideal.

Captain Gustav Böhm, Scheüch's former adjutant, who had accompanied Reinhardt to the negotiations in Weimar, saw the abolition of the states' ministries as evidence of Reinhardt's readiness to sacrifice his own position for the good of the German military, 'a glowing witness to his selfless, purely objective judgement of the situation.' This contrasted with the Württemberg Minister of War, Hermann, whom Böhm lampooned for trying to maintain his ministry, which could only command one brigade.[116] While the abolition of the states' war ministries would end Reinhardt's current position, he was also going to be one of the leading contenders for the senior posts in the *Reichswehrministerium*. By placing himself at the centre of bureaucratic politics and reorganisation Reinhardt had increased his chances for influence within the future army. Had the Prussian Ministry of War not taken a leading role in the centralisation project, it could have found itself marginalised when the debate on other structures, such as the relationship between the General Staff and the ministries, came to pass.

---

114. GLAK, Abt. 233/12441, Baden envoy to the Baden cabinet, 18 March 1919.
115. Diethard Hennig, *Johannes Hoffmann: Sozialdemokrat und Bayerischer Ministerpräsident*, Munich, 1990, 248.
116. *Adjutant im Preussischen Kriegsministerium*, 141.

The Weimar agreement was sent back to the states' governments for approval. The three south German states were all opposed to some of the terms. Württemberg, while willing to abolish its war ministry, now wanted the high commander to be subordinate to the state government in accordance with the old rights, which would have effectively negated the impact of setting up a unified *Reichswehrministerium*.[117] On the initiative of Bavaria the south German states tried to restore unity amongst themselves at a meeting on 29 March in Stuttgart. A wide range of topics were on the agenda and the meeting can be seen as a counterpoint to the centralising project of the Reich government.[118] Yet the momentum was with Reinhardt. While the south German states were trying to pull together, the Prussian Ministry of War planned some changes to the Weimar agreement. On 2 April the five largest states met again. Colonel Waitz, the Prussian Ministry of War's representative at this meeting and almost certainly instructed by Reinhardt, argued that the right of states to remove the high commander infringed the right of the Reich president. This led to a change in the Weimar agreement, and the power of the states was further diminished.[119] The right of the state government to remove the high commander had been the most effective means of influencing regional military policy, since the high commander was in charge of issues such as manoeuvres, recruitment and the distribution of troops. Now the high commander was totally dependent on the Reich government, and hence less liable to pressure from the states.

The negotiations dragged on as Bavaria held out for a slower move towards a unitary army.[120] To overcome this opposition Reinhardt was prepared to use the vast majority in the National Assembly in favour of centralising the army to force the states to accept an agreement over which they had some influence. The SPD Minister President of Baden, Adam Remmele, was also disappointed with the revised accord, since now that the states' government could not remove a high commander they had no significant means of influencing military policy. However Remmele decided that in view of Prussian, Saxon and Württemberg support for the agreement, Baden would be unwise to make a stand with Bavaria.[121]

Bavaria's position had been further weakened by the establishment of a Councils' Republic in Munich in April 1919. At first the Bavarian government, led by Johannes Hoffmann (SPD) and based temporarily at Bamberg, tried to suppress the revolt without outside help, but a defeat at Dachau, just outside Munich, forced them to ask Philipp Scheidemann,

117. GLAK, Abt. 233/12441, Württemberg Ministry of War to Baden cabinet, 15 Mar. 1919.

118. Wolfgang Benz, *Süddeutschland in der Weimarer Republik: ein Beitrag zur deutschen Innenpolitik, 1918-1923*, Berlin, 1970, 133–39.

119. HStASt, E 130 b, Bü 3728, Hildenbrand to the Württemberg cabinet, 3 April 1919.

120. GLAK, Abt. 233/12441, Baden envoy to Baden Minister of the Exterior, 8 April 1919.

121. GLAK, Abt. 233/12441, Remmele to Baden Minister of the Exterior, 10 April 1919.

the SPD chancellor, for military aid.[122] Reinhardt contacted Hoffman and told him that the Reich would take charge of the operation, a statement which did not soothe injured Bavarian egos.[123] The plan to defeat the revolt was drawn up in the Prussian Ministry of War by Generals Walther von Lüttwitz and Burghard von Oven. On 2 May a mixture of Bavarian and Reich troops marched into Munich. It was a clear demonstration that Bavaria was dependent on the Reich in a moment of crisis, though the Bavarians chose not to draw this lesson from this episode.[124] Instead Sperr had written to the other states on 30 April, criticising the amended Weimar agreement, particularly the lack of the states' control over appointments.[125]

A meeting followed on 7 May, which represented the most significant changes to the Weimar agreement of March. Both Prussia, also representing the Reich, and Bavaria wanted to change the term high commander to state commander, which better signified the role of the commander in the Reich-state relationship. However their conceptions of the position of the state commander differed radically. The Prussian Ministry of War opposed giving the state commander any special powers of command, whereas Bavaria wanted him to have the right to inspect troops. Prussia's conception secured the position of the state commander as a representative of the Reich to the various states, whereas the Bavarian plan conceived of the state commander as a representative of the state, a conception linked to the suggestion that the state could have a veto over the appointment of commanders. In the new agreement the Prussian conception of the state commander was adopted, but there were other concessions to the states. The economic interest of the state in military matters was stressed, and arms contracts were no longer to be fixed according to capability but by a board (*Ausgleichsstelle*) composed of representatives for the various states. Finally several officers, not just one per state, could be appointed to the *Reichsrat*.[126]

The agreement of 7 May was then sent back to the states' governments, and five weeks later Reinhardt presented the draft to the Reich cabinet. The main terms had been present in the Weimar agreement. The new terms included the creation of the post of state commander, named on the suggestion of the state government and supposed to look after the state's interests, and the establishment of the *Ausgleichsstelle*. The state commander would also be consulted by the *Reichswehrministerium* on proposed laws, and ministry officials would be recruited from all areas

122. Hennig, *Hoffmann*, 293–98.
123. Ibid., 299.
124. Ibid., 293–328; Allan Mitchell, *Revolution in Bavaria, 1918-1919: The Eisner Regime and the Soviet Republic*, Princeton, 1965, 304–30.
125. GLAK, Abt. 233/12441, Sperr circular to Prussia, Baden, Saxony, Württemberg, 30 April 1919.
126. GLAK, Abt. 233/12441, Baden envoy to the Baden Minister of the Exterior, 7 May 1919.

of the Reich.[127] The agreement gave the states' governments no concrete opportunity to intervene in the formulation of military policy, but did allow the states the formal voice of the state commander to complain about any damage done to the state's interests by military policy. Agreement had been reached, and the various war ministries of the states would be united. Reinhardt had rationalised the regional military structures of the *Kaiserreich* with the full support of the civilian government. On 16 June the cabinet confirmed the agreement which was now the basis for the Reich-state relationship in *Reichswehr* law, eventually passed in March 1921. Neither did the cabinet accept any of the reservations which the states had entered in the protocol with the agreement.[128] The unification of the various states' war ministries is an example of how the cabinet could delegate authority to negotiate to an officer, and retain the final right of approval. Rather than being seen as a possible military influence in civilian government the procedure adopted by the Reich must be interpreted as rational cabinet-style government.

The cabinet approved the agreement with the states on 16 June, but twelve days later Germany signed the treaty of Versailles. Reinhardt believed that in a 200,000 man army Baden, Saxony and Württemberg could have their own enclosed divisions, the commander of which would double as the state commander. However the 100,000 man army meant that Baden and Württemberg would have to share the 5th division, whilst Saxony would share the 4th division with Prussia.[129] It was only on 30 July that the states and Reinhardt met, and agreed on a solution, whereby Baden, Saxony and Württemberg would each have an enclosed brigade, and the senior commander from this brigade would act as the state commander.[130] Reinhardt attempted to pin this further centralisation of German military structures on Versailles, in a speech to the National Assembly on 30 July, but the treaty had merely reinforced a tendency for which he had negotiated.[131]

On 1 October the states' war ministries were dissolved. The internal form of the *Reichswehrministerium* which took over their duties was the focus of bureaucratic wrangling between the Supreme Command and the Ministry of War throughout the summer of 1919. It marked the end of the independent Prussian army, and as Ute Frevert pointed out in a recent study, the creation of 'a national institution'.[132] For some, like the melodramatic Ernst van den Bergh, this was a cause of momentary lament:

127. *Kabinett Scheidemann*, 439–43.
128. *Kabinett Scheidemann*, 468.
129. GLAK, Abt. 233/12441, Reinhardt to Baden envoy to the Reich, 8 July 1919.
130. GLAK, Abt. 233/12441, Baden envoy to the Reich to the Baden Ministry of the Exterior, 30 July 1919.
131. *Verhandlungen der deutschen Nationalversammlung*, vol. 328, 2116.
132. Ute Frevert, *Die kasernierte Nation. Militärdienst und Zivilgesellschaft in Deutschland*, Munich, 2001, 308.

'after the collapse of the people in arms the good, old form of the Prussian army is caving in. There is no longer a Prussian army, no longer a
Prussian Ministry of War!'[133] Reinhardt, in a more positive manner,
sought to invoke its tradition for the future: '[W]e would not be worthy
of such a proud tradition if we mourned idly. The great German Fatherland needs every man, every ounce of strength, it needs the spirit of duty
and the willingness to sacrifice. We see the holy legacy of the Prussian
army in the fostering of these traditions. We will maintain them faithfully
and from this source draw the power for the work of rebuilding the
beloved Fatherland.'[134] The language of war was clearly still a part of
Reinhardt's vocabulary. The *Deustches Offizierblatt* also considered it a
moment of rebirth producing a 'unifying power that would help us over
the difficult moral and physical dangers of the present.'[135]

At the end of March Reinhardt met with the liaison officers from the
Generalkommandos and spoke openly about the general ideas which
informed his pragmatic politics. He noted that Germany was still 'in the
middle of organising the state and the army.'[136] The aim was to create 'a
functioning *Reichswehr*' for the period of transition, which was a reference
to the temporary status of the *Reichswehr*. Yet even if the *Reichswehr* was
only supposed to be a temporary solution to German military policy, he
reiterated the principle that the *Reichswehr* must take account of changed
political circumstances. 'We do our beloved Germany no favours', he
argued, 'if we do not move with the times.'[137] Hence it was in the interests of the army to co-operate with the new regime. Reinhardt believed
that this regime would stabilise around the parties of the centre. By
allying with them the *Reichswehr* would prevent the political situation from
lurching to either extreme, a principle that was to guide Reinhardt's opposition to the Kapp Putsch, as well as to the left-wing radicalism. The
location of German politics at the centre of the political spectrum would
offer an opportunity for internal unity. This was subordinated to the
primacy of foreign policy, both in the short and long term: 'It is our task
to resist the violations of the Entente as much as possible so that we
remain a viable state and simultaneously defeat the Bolsheviks at our
border. If we solve these colossal tasks, then we will rise once more.'[138]
The political constellation of the first half of 1919 had suited the pragmatic, reformist Reinhardt.

133. *Aus den Geburtsstunden der Weimarer Republik,* 121.
134. Ernst, 'Aus dem Nachlaß', 93.
135. *Deutsches Offizierblatt,* 7 August 1919, 751.
136. BA-MA, N 86/16, Besprechung mit den Verbindungsoffizieren, 31 March 1919.
137. Ibid.
138. Ibid.

Chapter 5

REINHARDT AND THE TREATY OF VERSAILLES

*T*he treaty of Versailles undermined Reinhardt's hopes of 'rebuilding the beloved Fatherland' and Germany's military power and completely changed the dynamics of military policy formulation in 1919. The reduction of the army to 100,000 and the abolition of the General Staff had an immediate impact. Both caused massive demoralization in the *Reichswehr*. This, allied to a reawakening of the latent distrust which many officers felt towards the Republic, led along a tortuous path to the Kapp Putsch. It added to the domestic political restrictions on Reinhardt's freedom of manoeuvre. For him, as for many others, the weeks between the first news of the terms on 8 May and the signing of Versailles on 28 June, were a moment of political trauma. His realistic appraisal of domestic politics was replaced by a mystical faith in the powers of East Prussia to provide the birthplace for a new war of liberation. Reinhardt, the radical militarist, took the place of Reinhardt, the pragmatist, and had he been successful, the Republic and Germany would both have been destroyed. Yet it is just as significant that he stayed in office after June 1919. He realised that the officer corps could not realise its foreign policy programme in opposition to the Republic and the wishes of the people. His continued acceptance of the Republic contrasted with the attitude of the officers who moved towards mutiny after Versailles. Pragmatic support of the Republic remained a guiding principle of his military policy. Reinhardt's failure to win the argument in June 1919 was fortunate, but it was also symptomatic of the inability of the officer corps to impose their views on the foreign policy agenda. In contrast to the domestic policy arena where the government relied on the military to preserve order, in the foreign policy sphere industrialists and bankers were favoured. During the Weimar Republic they possessed the economic power with which Weimar governments hoped to restore Germany's Great Power position.[1]

---

1. For a different view see Peter Grupp, *Deutsche Außenpolitik im Schatten von Versailles, 1918-1920. Zur Politik des Auswärtigen Amts vom Ende des Ersten Weltkrieges und der Novemberrevolution bis zum Inkrafttreten des Versailler Vertrages*, Paderborn, 1988, 33–36; also Klaus-Jürgen Muller, 'Military and Diplomacy in France and Germany in the Interwar Period', in Klaus-Jürgen Müller, ed., *The Military in Politics and Society in France and Germany in the Twentieth Century*, Oxford, 1995, 111–14.

Aside from the preparations for the peace talks (which, it was assumed, would follow the deliberations of the Allies) Reinhardt's input into foreign policy issues in the first half of 1919 was limited. It involved either consultations with the Foreign Office or organisational issues, as in the case of the proposed *Anschluss* with Austria, one of the Habsburg Empire's successor states. The idea enjoyed a brief moment of popularity before the treaty of Versailles forbid such a union.[2] On 23 March the German-Austrian envoy to Germany suggested that a commission should be set up to negotiate on the two states' financial and currency systems. He hoped that Germany would sent six delegates to Vienna by the end of the month.[3] The following day Reinhardt wrote to Graf Ulrich Brockdorff-Rantzau, the German Foreign Minister. He wanted two German-Austrian delegates to come to Berlin to negotiate on the military issues of unity.[4] The reply came almost a month later, and Rantzau agreed that while military issues were not of prime concern in the negotiations at this stage, contacts between the two states should continue.[5]

Contacts had been established between the two armies before Rantzau's reply. General August von Cramon, the German military plenipotentiary in Vienna, urged the Ministry of War to discuss major bills, such as the forthcoming German-Austrian bill on military welfare, and ensure that both armies would be as compatible as possible before the *Anschluss*.[6] Reinhardt told Rantzau that Austria wanted 'to form the army so that their integration into the future Reich army can be completed without particular hindrance.'[7] Rantzau replied that 'from a political point of view I can only warmly welcome closer contacts with the German-Austrians.'[8] He was content to let the Ministry of War's representatives deal with the details of policy at this stage. Ultimately the *Anschluss* never came to pass. On 15 March André Tardieu, the French Foreign Minister, convinced the American representative on the territorial committee to insert a passage in his final report against the *Anschluss*.[9] There is little evidence beyond well-meaning intentions that any serious steps towards unity had been taken. However the episode is significant in that it reveals some of the assumptions which Reinhardt held before May 1919. The *Anschluss* would have

2. Hugo Preuß, *Staat, Recht und Freiheit. Aus 40 Jahren deustcher Politik und Geschichte*, Hildesheim, 1964, 378-79; Klaus Schwabe, *Woodrow Wilson, Revolutionary Germany and Peacemaking, 1918-1919. Missionary Diplomacy and the Realities of Power*, Chapel Hill, 1985, 241-43.
3. PA-AA, Ost. Nr 95, 9010, Envoy of the German-Austrian Republic, Verbal note to the Foreign Office, 23 March 1919.
4. PA-AA, Ost. Nr 95, 9010, Prussian Ministry of War to the Foreign Office, 24 March 1919.
5. PA-AA, Ost. Nr 95, 9010, Foreign Office to the Prussian Ministry of War, 17 April 1919.
6. PA-AA, Ost. Nr 95, 9010, Cramon to the Prussian Ministry of War, 31 March 1919.
7. PA-AA, Ost. Nr 95, 9010, Prussian Ministry of War to the Foreign Office, 5 April 1919.
8. PA-AA, Ost. Nr 95, 9010, Foreign Office to the Prussian Ministry of War, 24 April 1919.
9. Schwabe, *Wilson*, 242.

effectively compensated Germany for the territory she would surrender in the east and west. From a geopolitical point of view it would have strengthened the Republic, giving it access to the Balkans area.

Reinhardt concerned himself only sporadically with military policy in the east where the Supreme Command was in charge of border defence.[10] The Baltic and eastern Europe was a highly complex area after the First World War, with new states, ethnic minorities, competing ideologies and Great Power politics mixed into the plot. The central aim of the German military was to preserve Germany's position in the east, by weakening Poland and forging links with the Baltic states, Lithuania, Latvia and Estonia, which felt threatened by both Poland and Bolshevism. However if Germany weakened Poland, then it would strengthen Bolshevism which Reinhardt tended to see as the greater danger in 1919.[11] Britain and France brought their weight to bear on the region by supporting the Baltic and Polish states respectively. They also demanded that Germany send troops to Lithuania to help the struggle with the Bolshevists. This stored up problems for the second half of 1919. Events in the east, where Germany was a relatively strong military power, showed that the defeat in 1918 had broken the army so decisively that, even here, it failed to exert influence over policy.

In the last months of the war, Reinhardt's superior, General Eberhardt, commander of the 7th Army, had told the rank and file that they must continue to fight in order to force the Allies to grant tolerable terms.[12] To many Germans, President Woodrow Wilson's Fourteen Points appeared to the basis for a tolerable peace, with neither 'victor nor vanquished'.[13] The hopes for a national revival which helped hold Germany together in the early part of 1919 were to a large extent based on the expectation of a 'fair' peace.[14] In view of his reputation for sober assessments of political situations it is surprising that Wilhelm Groener was the optimist *par excellence*.[15] Groener believed that United States would dominate the peace negotiations and hinder the more extreme demands of the French government. Reinhardt kept himself informed about the French view of the negotiations, and had a copy of President Raymond Poincaré's speech at the opening of the peace conference in January 1919, which had stressed the French blood spilt in defence of *la patrie*.[16] Yet his knowledge of French

---

10. Gerhard Rakenius, *Wilhelm Groener als erster Generalquartiermeister. Die Politik der Obersten Heeresleitung*, Boppard am Rhein, 1977, 165.
11. BArch R 43 I/117, Reinhardt to Scheidemann, 11 March 1919, fo. 5.
12. See Chapter 2.
13. Marshall M. Lee, Wolfgang Michalka, *German Foreign Policy, 1917–1933. Continuity or Break?*, Leamington Spa, 1987, 20–22.
14. Fritz Klein, 'Between Compiègne and Versailles: the Germans on the Way from a Misunderstood Defeat to an Unwanted Peace', in *Treaty of Versailles. A Reassessment after 75 Years*, eds. Manfred F. Boemeke, Gerald D. Feldman, Elisabeth Glaser, Washington DC, 1999, 203–05.
15. Rakenius, *Groener*, 168-72.
16. HStASt, M 660/034, Bü 21, extract from *Le Temps*, 19 January 1919.

attitudes to the peace negotiations was probably cancelled out by his lack of sympathy for them and his own *Wunschgedanken*, so that he was also shocked by the terms.

One of the common assumptions of German diplomats, politicians and soldiers in 1919 was that the peace terms would be settled after some type of negotiations. With this in mind, Reinhardt contacted the Foreign Office. On 12 February he sent proposals for negotiations on arms limitations. The German guidelines for the peace negotiations would allow the delegates to press for 'a thorough disarmament and the removal of legal conscription by international regulation.'[17] Due to the economic and political position of Germany, Reinhardt argued that such an international limitation would be of great benefit. While Britain and United States would not be overly affected by a ban on conscription, Reinhardt believed that France would find it difficult to retain a strong army based on volunteers. However the disadvantage for Germany of a volunteer army would be its prohibitive cost. Reinhardt was clearly seeking a balance of power, a concept which he understood in military terms. For him the bottom line was that all states would reduce their armaments to German levels.[18] This would in fact give Germany a preponderance of power on the continent because of its economic and human resources, and the goal of reducing armaments to the German level was pursued again by the *Reichswehr* in the 1920s for this very reason. Reinhardt asked the Foreign Office to establish a commission, and on 18 February Rödiger of the Foreign Office replied that a discussion of the issues would take place in Berlin among all the concerned departments.[19]

However it is not clear whether discussions actually took place, and if they did, they had little impact, because the cabinet and senior officers were still debating military terms for the negotiations, when the delegation set off for Versailles in April. The German delegation to the Ceasefire Commission had already expressed its annoyance at a lack of clear directions from the Ministry of War.[20] The plethora of military institutions, which existed in the first half of 1919, hindered the development of an adequate policy. However it was not simply an organisational failure. Reinhardt, after all, was a member of the cabinet, but made little attempt to establish the priority of the army for the negotiations. This contributed to the relegation of military affairs behind financial and territorial

17. PA-AA, Weltkrieg 540/3, Prussian Ministry of War to the Foreign Office, 12 February 1919; in the memorandum of 5 February, which dealt with the establishment of the *Reichswehr*, conscription was rejected because of the opposition it would arouse from the war-weary.
18. PA-AA, Weltkrieg 540/3, Prussian Ministry of War to the Foreign Office, 12 February 1919.
19. PA-AA, Weltkrieg 540/3, Foreign Office to Prussian Ministry of War, 18 February 1919; the results of these discussions could not be found.
20. BA-MA, N 46/130, Denkschrift, 11 March 1919 to the Prussian Ministry of War.

concerns. While the generals were able to discuss future military planning amongst themselves at great length as Groener showed at Kolberg on 22 March, and Reinhardt showed nine days later in Berlin, they did not recognise the importance of making their plans clear to the Foreign Office at an early stage. This allowed the agenda to be set by other interest groups, who had a different conception of the new regime's foreign policy needs.[21]

The next opportunity for the officer corps to influence policy was in the formation of the peace delegation being sent to Versailles, for what the government hoped would be negotiations. Hans von Seeckt was appointed to the delegation by the cabinet on 16 April. [22] Whether the delegation had been well briefed on military affairs is unclear. Since Reinhardt's contact with the Foreign Office in February no clear guidelines had been issued. At a cabinet meeting on 22 March Reinhardt had rejected a limitation on arms that applied only to Germany. He continued 'Our needs must be set by us. The delegation has to know what the minimum is.'[23] Numbers had been bandied about in military circles. Seeckt believed that 200,000 men would be sufficient in the circumstances of 1919.[24] In a set of guidelines given to Seeckt by the Supreme Command, the minimum number of 300,000 appeared. The Supreme Command also argued that Germany had to retain a conscript army for financial reasons.[25]

However at a cabinet meeting on 21 April it was decided to agree to the mutual abolition of conscription. [26] Reinhardt, who was not present at the meeting on 21 April, objected to this at the next meeting three days later, but was overruled.[27] Why Reinhardt was now prepared to support a conscript army is not clear. The temporary *Reichswehr* law had already been passed, and the decrees of 31 March were issued. Reinhardt recognised the difficulties of a conscript army. But in principle he favoured the idea, and perhaps he felt that prohibitions on a conscript army, which might suit Germany in 1919, would limit room for manoeuvre in years to come. It should also be remembered that the *Reichswehr* was formed as a temporary army, and the fact that conscription was rejected at this stage would not necessarily preclude its introduction at a later date. Nonetheless the cabinet meeting on 21 April was a clear signal that the civilian

---

21. Peter Krüger, *Die Aussenpolitik der Republik von Weimar*, Darmstadt, 1985, 42, argues that the foreign policy of the Weimar republic was determined by a liberal conception of international relations and German economic power.
22. *Kabinett Scheidemann*, 175–78.
23. Ibid, 88.
24. BA-MA, N 247/77, Entwurf, 17 February 1919.
25. Hans Meier-Welcker, *Seeckt*, Frankfurt, 1967, 218-19; BA-MA, N 247/67, Supreme Command to Seeckt, fo. 2.
26. *Kabinett Scheidemann*, 202.
27. Ibid, 227.

government was the dominant force in foreign policy, even in the military aspects. It was a further sign that the military needs of Germany were to be relegated below her economic and territorial needs, even against the advice of military advisers who had dominated domestic military policy issues.

Despite the importance of the army to the internal stability of Germany, the officer corps were unable to exploit their domestic political weight to shape the foreign policy agenda, in which they ultimately had more interest. This was an early sign of the tension at the heart of the relationship between the *Reichswehr* and the Republic. They had to compete with influential advisers from the Foreign Ministry, who did not necessarily share the same conception of international relations as their military counterparts. A meeting between Groener and Rantzau on 4 April was indicative of the problems both the Ministry of War and the Supreme Command faced in prioritising their suggestions for the negotiations.[28] Groener talked generally about German policy for the forthcoming negotiations.[29] Yet apart from opposing the League of Nations if Germany was not part of it, Groener made no firm points. Eventually Rantzau even asked him what the point of the monologue was.[30] Just as Reinhardt had begun to engage the Foreign Office in a debate on the future of German military policy in February, so now did Groener. Yet neither of them descended from the realm of generalities. This may be partly due to the fluidity of military policy in 1919 since the army would be shaped, as many officers recognised, by the peace treaty. Senior officers failed to focus on issues such as the number of men, the organisation of the army and the weaponry. The most concrete guidelines in the instructions for the German delegation were mutual disarmament to a level compatible with security and a demilitarized zone in both France and Germany.[31] In a series of cabinet meetings after 21 March on the guidelines for the peace delegation Reinhardt failed to mention any of these topics.

On 7 May the German peace delegation was handed the peace terms. Reinhardt was dismayed, and his emotional response to the crisis is best seen through a number of newspaper articles which he wrote anonymously in May.[32] The articles appeared in a variety of papers, the *Norddeutsche Allgemeine Zeitung*, the *Tag*, the *Kölner Volkszeitung*, but they do not appear to have excited much attention in the general outrage at the time. The articles were the first indication of Reinhardt's position in June 1919 when he argued that rejection of the treaty and the maintenance of national honour

28. *Akten zur deutschen auswärtigen Politik. November 1918 bis Mai 1919*, Serie A, 1918-1925, vol. 1, Göttingen, 1982, 394–99, hereafter *ADAP*; Rakenius, *Groener*, 200–202.
29. *ADAP*, 397.
30. Ibid., 397.
31. BA-MA N 247/66, Richtlinien für die deutschen Friedenshändler, 23 April 1919, fo. 12.
32. Fritz Ernst, 'Aus dem Nachlaß des Generals Walther Reinhardt', *Die Welt als Geschichte*, 1958, 67–68.

were more important to the revival of Germany than the preservation of the Reich. The logic of this position was an Allied invasion and a far more severe peace than the treaty of Versailles. What would be a national catastrophe would sow the seeds for regeneration, in the view of Reinhardt and other advocates of this position. 'Catastrophic nationalism' would emerge in the summer of 1919, linked just as in October 1918 and 1923 with the military doctrine of *Volkskrieg*.[33] The summer of 1919 was the only occasion on which Reinhardt advocated 'catastrophic nationalism' as a political solution, although it had an important place in his military theories in the late 1920s.

Why? First, if national honour was conceived of as an important part of national power, as a means of mobilizing the populace, then it was under far more significant threat in 1919 (and later during the crisis over extradition), then it was in 1918 when the myth of an honourable defeat, or the more virulent stab-in-the-back legend, was adopted. In 1923 the occupation of the Ruhr was portrayed as a brutal act of French oppression which could stimulate a national revival. It was the 'shame paragraphs', which generated the most outrage in 1919 because they threatened, in the eyes of the officers, national rebirth in a way which defeat had not. Second, on the assumption that the *Volkskrieg* was a feasible military solution, the chances of it succeeding must have seemed higher in the summer of 1919 than on the other two occasions. Six months earlier Germany was on the crest of revolution. By 2 May the Soviet Republic in Munich had been crushed. In 1923 inflation and growing political radicalism made any *Volkskrieg* a difficult proposition. But in 1919 Germany seemed united in its condemnation of Versailles. Reinhardt and others hoped to exploit this to counter the other option of acceptance. The primacy of foreign policy was Reinhardt's guide, and to that extent his shift from *Vernunftrepublikaner* to a radical militarist, did not so much represent a bizarre interlude in his career, but an adaptation to the circumstances.

Reinhardt was numbed by the terms, which he saw as a 'act of force' and 'a crime'.[34] In an article entitled 'The plan for military strangulation', Reinhardt railed against the inequality of the terms. 'If we submit to the current terms of the Diktat, not only will the mute accusations of our fallen afflict our conscience, but the howls of our children and grandchildren will burden our death-sleep with a curse.'[35] For Reinhardt Versailles was a blow to hopes for a national revival. The terms would perpetuate the results of the First World War. He continued, 'the worst articles are not the most noticeable, like loss of land and the reparations,

33. Michael Geyer, 'Insurrectionary Warfare: The German Debate about a *levée en masse* in October 1918', *JMH*, 73, 2001, 459–527.
34. HStASt, M 660/034, Bü 21, memorandum, dated 10 May 1919; this also appears to be the draft of an article.
35. HStASt, M 660/034, Bü 21, 'Der militärische Erdrosselungsplan', *Der Tag*, 11 May 1919.

but the hidden articles, destroying German freedom and self-determination.'[36] Reinhardt feared that the treaty would forever hang over Germany like the sword of Damocles. By condemning Germany to an existence of perpetual bondage to the Allies, the terms represented the collapse of international law. Clemenceau was seen as the architect of this 'crime', and Wilson as his sidekick, 'in spite of all his pretty speeches'.[37]

Naturally Reinhardt was most concerned about the military terms. He believed that the 100,000 men army was too small to defend borders and to keep internal peace. He argued that the Allies had entered into a vicious circle of repressing German strength. 'The more one tortures his victim, the more one robs him, then the more sternly and coldly one must continue to rob him, in order to guard against the rising of despair. The military conditions have been framed from this point of view.'[38] Perhaps the one firm guideline that the officer corps had given to the delegation was that the military terms imposed on Germany should also apply to their neighbours. Reinhardt lamented the lack of 'reciprocity'.[39] The military terms were the guarantee of French political dominance on the continent, and in May 1919 Reinhardt could see little possibility for a German national revival. Reinhardt listed the weakness of Germany's military position. In the east they had to surrender their forts to the Poles, while in the west Germany was 'totally defortified'. Germany was prohibited from creating a defensive system against air attack. Reinhardt believed that these restrictions on defensive weapons signified the aggressive nature of the terms.[40]

Reinhardt was also active in the cabinet, using his position at the heart of government to put forward the army's case. On 8 May the first cabinet meeting took place since the terms had been handed over. The cabinet clearly felt that the terms were unacceptable. Reinhardt believed that these terms could be negotiated, although he underlined that 'our negotiators can only have a basis, if they can explain definitively and in full agreement with the Reich government, that a change in the terms is necessary and is the reason for the negotiations.'[41] He was not only determined to renegotiate the terms but he was also worried about the impact that their publication would have on the army. He argued that minimum terms should include both East and West Prussia and Upper Silesia staying in Germany in the hope that this would appease the army. 'In my opinion the behaviour of the troops is of the greatest significance for

36. Ibid.
37. HStASt, M 660/034, Bü 21, 'Die Verhängung des Zustandes der Rechtslosigkeit', Entwurf, 12 May 1919, appeared in *Kölner Volkszeitung*, 13 May 1919.
38. HStASt, M 660/034, Bü 21, memorandum, dated 10 May 1919.
39. HStASt, M 660/034, Bü 21, 'Die Verhängung des Zustandes der Rechtslosigkeit', Entwurf, 12 May 1919.
40. HStASt, M 660/034, Bü 21, 'Der militärische Erdrosselungsplan', *Der Tag*, 11 May 1919.
41. HStASt, M 660/034, Bü 21, memorandum on cabinet meeting of 8 May 1919.

everything else, and I ask the Reich government in their actions to take into account morale of the volunteers as well as the *Reichswehr* troops. In the coming days of tension and turbulence we definitely need the strong support of the forces of order.'[42] Reinhardt was exploiting the position of the army as the *ultimo ratio* of the republic in setting out his demands for negotiations with the Allies. This was a common tactic of the officer corps when they presented advice to the government. Yet Reinhardt was not merely scare-mongering. He genuinely believed, and with good reason, that army would fall apart under the pressure of the terms. This would be fatal and would lead to the collapse of the state.

He was kept well informed of the arguments within the peace delegation, which were discouraging from the military's point of view. According to Seeckt the suggestions of the peace delegation which were being sent to Berlin had been drawn up without the participation of the army and navy representatives.[43] At a meeting on 8 May Seeckt had admitted that military questions would not enjoy the same priority as economic ones, but he argued that a strong military was necessary to protect German economic interests. His conclusions were bleak: 'We are defenceless, our neighbours are not. I do not know if the League of Nations is feasible. History tells me the opposite, but in spite of this it may be possible.'[44]

In response to Seeckt's fears that the military were being sidelined in the discussions, Reinhardt circulated a memorandum of 10 May to the most senior officers including Groener, Ernst Wrisberg, and Arnold Möhl, entitled 'Minimum demands at the peace conference.'[45] It was an attempt to achieve a coherent view from the officer corps. The counter-proposals would be based on the League of Nations and Wilson's Fourteen Points. The memorandum asked the senior officers to consider some questions when formulating their proposals. These included what number of troops were necessary to keep order, which institutions could be demilitarized, what the relationship between the people and the army would be, what type of police force Germany would have, and how the 'recruitment' would be organised.[46] At this stage Reinhardt's ideas on how to approach the terms had not crystallised. On the one hand he hoped that some elements could be renegotiated. However his interest in the dual use of civilian institutions for military purposes also indicates that he saw possibilities for evading the terms.

42. HStASt, M 660/034, Bü 21, memorandum on cabinet meeting of 8 May 1919.
43. BA-MA, N 247/66, Seeckt to Reinhardt, 9 May 1919.
44. BA-MA, N 247/66, Sitzung der Bevollmächtigen Behörden, Versailles, 8 May 1919, fos 81–9.
45. HStASt, M 660/034, Bü 21, Mindestforderungen bei der Friedenskonferenz, 10 May 1919.
46. HStASt, M 660/034, Bü 21, Mindestforderungen bei der Friedenskonferenz, 10 May 1919.

There was a third option which Reinhardt would finally settle on once the Allies agreed on final terms in June. The full extent of Reinhardt's opposition to the terms was revealed at a meeting 14 and 15 May in Berlin with Groener, who has written the only account of this meeting, and other officers. Reinhardt, according to Groener, 'for the first time advocated in all seriousness, the idea to temporarily surrender German unity, and to resist the enemy from an independent east. I had no empathy for this plan which was played out in many Prussian heads. The maintenance of Reich unity was the *conditio sine qua non*, for which I was ready to make any sacrifice'.[47] However Groener's minutes of the meeting merely outline his conditions for accepting the peace which were an end to the blockade, and to the interminable conflict between France and Germany. He also pointed to the threat from Poland, but did not mention Reinhardt's 'East Prussian policy'.[48] Yet even if Reinhardt had not mentioned the idea of an East Prussian state at this meeting, it was clear from his initial reaction that he would not accept the Allied terms. However the implications of that refusal had to be worked out, and indeed Reinhardt may have hoped that the German counter-proposals would make the peace more tolerable. The officer corps was splitting into two camps on the terms. Groener represented those officers who were not willing to risk German unity, while Reinhardt represented those who rejected the terms. A rejection of the terms would probably lead to an invasion and the subsequent break-up of the Reich. This debate would be resolved over the five weeks, but at this stage both Reinhardt and Groener were hoping to renegotiate the terms. Previously Groener was prepared to accept a 300,000 men army, but now he demanded a 350,000 men army, an incredible demand in the light of the terms which had been presented to the German government.[49] There was little chance that this would be accepted, and perhaps Groener was demanding a relatively large army so as to force the cabinet to adopt a strong position on the military counter-proposals.

Two officers worked on the counter-proposals. Colonel Xylander, a member of the peace delegation at Versailles, produced a memorandum on 16 May entitled 'Basic arguments against the peace conditions'.[50] General Ernst von Wrisberg of the Ministry of War also drafted some counterproposals.[51] Whereas Xylander was concerned to expose the flaws in the terms, such as the dangers of a volunteer, as opposed to a

47. Wilhelm Groener, *Lebenserinnerungen. Jugend, Generalstab, Weltkrieg*, Göttingen, 1957, 492–93.
48. BA-MA N 46/130, Meeting at the Prussian Ministry of War, 15 May 1919.
49. Groener, *Lebenserinnerungen*, 493.
50. PA-AA, Deutsche Friedensdelegation, Versailles, R 22671, 'Grundsätzliche Bedenken gegen die militärische Friedensbedingungen', Colonel Xylander, 16 May 1919.
51. PA-AA, Deutsche Friedensdelegation, Versailles, R 22671, 'Die Militärische Friedensver-tragsent-wurfs der Gegner Deutschland', General Wrisberg, 18 May 1919.

conscript, army, Wrisberg argued that all states should disarm. For each state, 0.5% of the population should be under arms, and there should be no restrictions on officers or conscription.[52] On 17 May the cabinet agreed that the counter-proposals would press for a 200,000 men army. At a further meeting on the morning of 20 May there was an inconclusive discussion about the counter-proposals and concessions. The military terms were not raised; instead the focus was on territorial and financial matters, so Reinhardt must have assumed that the demand for a 200,000 men army remained.[53] However, unbeknown to Reinhardt, the position of the army was being undermined. On 19 May Rantzau and five other members of the delegation, but no officers, had written to the Foreign Office because they were unhappy with the demands for a 200,000 men army, which Seeckt was making. Rantzau believed that it would be better to concede on the military issues in the hope of winning territorial or financial concessions, and therefore would agree to a 100,000 men army.[54] At a second cabinet meeting on 21 May, from which Reinhardt was absent, it was agreed to accept a 100,000 men army.[55]

However Reinhardt was not informed of this change of plans through normal cabinet channels, but by Seeckt in a letter on 25 May. Seeckt was angry that his demands had been changed without his knowledge and felt that political considerations were making Germany defenceless.[56] Seeckt did not hold Reinhardt responsible for the changes, but the cabinet, where he mistakenly believed that Reinhardt had been outvoted.[57] Groener joined in the protest, noting that 'the military question has been given up in order to gain more in other questions.' He feared that the volunteer forces would be embittered by the small army.[58] Reinhardt also lodged his objections at a cabinet meeting on 26 May, and he won a small concession. Now the delegation would seek a stronger army, although for a limited period of time.[59] This did not deal with the fundamental fear of the officer corps that Germany would be left defenceless in the future. The cabinet's amendment to the guidelines was directed against the insecurities of the revolutionary period, more than at long-term military security. Reinhardt recognised this, and wrote back to Seeckt, instructing him that 'pressure must be applied to achieve a corresponding strength and consolidation of the *gendarmerie*.'[60] This was a poor substitute for an extra 100,000 men in the *Reichswehr*.

52. Ibid.
53. *Kabinett Scheidemann*, 336, 353–56.
54. PA-AA, Deutsche Friedensdelegation, Versailles, R 22671, Rantzau to the Auswärtiges Amt, 19 May 1919, Abschrift.
55. *Kabinett Scheidemann*, 358.
56. HStASt, M 660/034, Bü 21, Seeckt to Reinhardt, 25 May 1919.
57. BA-MA, N 247/66, Besprechung, 25 May 1919, fos 149–53.
58. HStASt, M 660/034, Bü 21, Groener to Scheidemann, Harbou, 27 May 1919.
59. HStASt, M 660/034, Bü 21, Protocol Auszug, 26 May 1919.
60. HStASt, M 660/034, Bü 21, Reinhardt to Seeckt, 26 May 1919.

The whole episode of drafting the counter-proposals illustrates the limits of the officer corps' influence in German politics. The officers' fears that Germany would be defenceless against external attack seemed hollow. If the treaty was passed in anything approximating to the terms of 7 May, none of Germany's neighbours would have had sufficient reason to launch a war of aggression. Of equal importance many officers associated the end of German military power with the end of any hopes for national regeneration. Seeckt, disclaiming any responsibility for the terms, told Rantzau: 'I feel myself duty-bound and justified in expressing that Germany, by freely accepting the demilitarization due to political considerations of the day, has sacrificed its last and highest possession, its national honour. Such a step must and will have the most disastrous consequences for the internal and external future of our Fatherland.'[61] Seeckt's argument, based on the relationship between honour, military power and national regeneration was similar to those put forward by Reinhardt and others in June. This was Seeckt's final intervention in the debate, and he kept his counsel when Reinhardt and Groener clashed at Weimar. This enabled him to maintain his reputation within the officer corps and his alliance with Groener against Reinhardt. When Seeckt was asked by Stülpnagel if he and Hindenburg would put themselves at the head of a resistance movement in June 1919, Seeckt refused, due to the lack of popular support. As Meier-Welcker pointed out, he effectively accepted the conditions, but was wise enough not to say so.[62]

If Germany rejected the final settlement, then an invasion was widely expected. On 18 May Reinhardt visited his adjutant, Gustav Böhm, in hospital, and told him that the cabinet would not sign agree to the Allied terms.[63] Invasion scares were not just the stuff of bed-side gossip. On 19 May Noske and Reinhardt issued a secret decree to the *Reichswehr* commanders and the Bavarian and Württemberg governments with instructions on what to do in case of an attack.[64] Air attacks were expected. The main aim of the plan was to prevent panic among the populace. The nature of the defence was to be as passive as possible, and the use of aeroplanes was not foreseen.[65] The existence of detailed plans for an air attack indicates that the *Reichswehrministerium*, at least, believed that the Allies would launch limited attacks. The Reich Interior Ministry arranged a meeting for 31 May on what measures bureaucrats would take in case of an invasion.[66]

61. BA-MA N 247/66, Seeckt to Rantzau, 26 May 1919, fos. 164–65.
62. Meier-Welcker, *Seeckt*, 230–31.
63. *Adjutant im Preussischen Kriegsministerium Juni 1918 bis Oktober 1919. Aufzeichnungen des Hauptmanns Gustav Böhm*, ed. Heinz Hürten, Stuttgart, 1977, 151–52.
64. HStASt, M 77/1, Bü 642, RWM, Nr 1341/5.19 A 4, Berlin, 19 May 1919, signed Noske and Reinhardt; Baden, which would have been the first stop for the Allied armies, was not sent the decree.
65. HStASt, M 77/1, Bü 642, RWM, Nr 1341/5.19 A 4, Berlin, 19 May 1919.
66. BArch, R 43/1, 8, Reich Interior Ministry to states' governments and Prussian Ministries, 28 May 1919, fo. 12.

Not all the resistance would be passive. The Supreme Command decided to circulate a series of questions among local military command-ers to find out whether the civilian population would support a war if the terms were not moderated.[67] Yet even before the results of the survey Groener was trying to persuade his fellow officers that a war would be futile. At a meeting of Supreme Command officers on 19 and 20 May he rejected historical comparisons with Yorck and 1812. This was a refer-ence to the mutiny of Yorck, commander of the Prussian corps within the *grande armée*, in December 1812 when against Frederick William III's orders he repudiated the alliance with France and went over to the Russians. This act, at least in the historical myth surrounding it, sparked the popular uprising against Napoleonic hegemony in eastern Prussia. By denying the validity of the analogy Groener was attempting to restrict support for the plan first mooted by Reinhardt at the meeting on 14 May to resist the Entente from East Prussia. Instead of surrendering unity and preserving what many felt was the core of the German state, namely East Prussia, Groener pinned his hopes on the *Einheitsstaat* of the Reich.[68] On 27 May Scheidemann discovered the existence of the survey. At a cabinet meeting he demanded that the dissolution of the Supreme Command be speeded up. Reinhardt, perhaps hoping that the as yet unknown result of the survey would show popular support for resistance, argued that a rapid dissolution would damage the morale of the troops.[69] In fact Reinhardt was able to warn the Supreme Command about the cabinet's reaction through Colonel Kurt von Schleicher.[70] The dispute over the survey demonstrated the frayed civil-military relationship at a vital moment in the republic's history. Scheidemann had written to the Supreme Command, attacking the survey as 'an incursion into politics ... which runs directly counter to the policy of the Reich government.'[71] When the cabinet decided that Groener should come to Berlin to explain the survey, Reinhardt retorted that neither he nor Seeckt had been consulted about the military counter-proposals.[72] In terms of the relationship between Reinhardt and the civilian government, the debate over the Allies' peace terms was a difficult period, primarily because his ability to influence the broader field of foreign policy was limited.

Reinhardt's bottom line throughout May and June 1919 was that it was better to forsake the unity of the Reich, than to suffer the restrictions on sovereignty imposed by the peace terms, which he believed would morally weaken the German people. This attitude was prevalent in some sectors

67. Rakenius, *Groener*, 206–11.
68. *Zwischen Revolution und Kapp Putsch. Militär und Innepolitik 1918-1920*, ed. Heinz Hürten, Düsseldorf, 1977, 121–25.
69. *Kabinett Scheidemann*, 382.
70. Rakenius, *Groener*, 211–15.
71. Barch, R 43/I, 702, Scheidemann to the Supreme Command, 27 May 1919, fo. 18.
72. *Kabinett Scheidemann*, 397.

of German society, such as the military and nationalist circles, and led to plans for an East Prussian state.[73] Yet it is not clear at what stage he decided to advocate an open break with the Allies and the renewal of war. At a cabinet meeting on 4 June Erzberger and David clearly outlined the consequences of heroic gestures. Erzberger emphasised that the unity of the Reich had primacy over all other questions. Reinhardt's observations were vague, a simple statement that 'the will to resist is not there. There are enough men and materiel. In any case a war is pointless. A way not to sign the treaty must be found.'[74] He did not mention what the way to avoid signature would be, perhaps unwilling to test out the idea of forsaking Reich unity at the cabinet table.

Reinhardt was the most important supporter of the idea of an East Prussian state, but his connections with leading proponents of the plan such as Colonel Albrecht von Thaer of the Supreme Command and August Winnig of the SPD are not clear. Thaer was a close friend, but there is no correspondence between them on this issue. On 5 and 6 June there was a meeting hosted by the Prussian Interior Minister, Wolfgang Heine, on the question of an East Prussian state, and attended by Major von Willisen, Göhre, Batocki and Winnig. On the second day of the meeting Heine said that the Reich government supported the right of Prussia to defend itself against Polish attacks as long as the negotiations lasted. But he continued, 'The Reich government has refused to answer the question what would happen if a peace was signed that did not correspond to the wishes of the eastern provinces.'[75] Batocki reported he and Winnig had held with Reinhardt and Noske about the policy options if the peace terms were rejected. Unfortunately a memorandum of this discussion cannot be found. However Heine did conclude that 'in this case the resurrection of the German Reich must come from the east and therefore the east's primary consideration in any action it might take, must be to stay with the old Fatherland, to help in its reconstruction. Only in this way can I understand the plans and the ideas circulating in the east at the moment.'[76] The belief that the revival of the German state must come from the east reflected the Württemberger's views. In conjunction with Groener's record of Reinhardt's views it can therefore be assumed that he strongly supported the idea of an East Prussian state, albeit in a more guarded manner than some other generals.

He was well informed about the position of the south German states, Baden, Württemberg and Bavaria. Major Wolfgang Fleck, Reinhardt's chief of staff, had met Föhrenbach, the commander of 14th Army Corp

73. Hagen Schulze, 'Der Oststaat Plan 1919', *VfZ*, 18, 2, 1970, 123–63.
74. *Kabinett Scheidemann*, 419–20.
75. PA-AA, Deutsche Friedensdelegation, Versailles, R 22514, 'Besprechung vom 5. und 6. Juni im Ministerium des Innern.
76. Ibid.

in Baden, at Durlach near the border with Switzerland on 1 June. On 3 June Föhrenbach wrote to Reinhardt with a report on morale in Baden. The report did not make pleasant reading for Reinhardt. According to Föhrenbach, 'National viewpoints have retreated to the background. Many people are indifferent whether they are under German or French rule, as long as they get along well.'[77] The report concluded that Baden could easily leave the Reich and form part of a new *Rheinlandbund* (Rhineland League established by Napoleon) under protection from France. Reports such as these must have confirmed Reinhardt's views that the western and southern areas of Germany lacked the national pride which might sustain a revival.

The results of the Supreme Command's survey demonstrated that there was little popular support to take up arms once more, even if the terms were not moderated. Groener later used these results to justify his acceptance of the treaty. 'The west showed no interest in the east and likewise the east showed no interest in the west.'[78] Even before he knew the results of the survey Groener had opposed risking the break-up of the Reich. Unlike Reinhardt he was never an advocate of a *Volkskrieg*, so the survey merely confirmed his belief that the only option was acceptance. Reinhardt took a very different lesson from the state of public opinion. His hopes for a national regeneration based on vague but traditional German values were bound up with his view of the east, where the historical roots of the Prussian state lay.

These results were revealed on 10 June, and six days later the Allies presented an ultimatum to the German government. Colonel Ernst van den Bergh wrote 'We have five fateful days ahead of us.'[79] On 16 June, the day the Allies had handed their terms to the German peace delegation, Reinhardt attended the cabinet meeting, after which he asked Bergh to summon the leading officers in the *Reichswehr* to Weimar for a meeting early on 19 June with these officers, 'with whom the situation for a "Yes" and "No" should be talked through.'[80] According to Groener's account, Reinhardt had ordered the leading generals to come to Weimar, with a view to organising opposition to the treaty.[81]

On the afternoon of 18 June Reinhardt and Groener had a preliminary meeting. Reinhardt said that it was necessary to prepare measures in case of either a 'Yes', which he believed would lead to internal instability, or 'No', which would lead to an Allied invasion.[82] Groener replied that the

77. BArch, R 43/I, 8, Föhrenbach to Reinhardt, 3 June 1919.
78. BA-MA N42/12, Besprechung am 12. Juli 1919, fo. 132.
79. *Aus den Geburtsstunden der Weimarer Republik. Das Tagebuch des Obersten Ernst van den Bergh*, ed. Wolfram Wette, Düsseldorf, 1991, 94–95.
80. Ibid., 95.
81. Groener, *Lebenserinnerungen*, 500–502.
82. Horst Mühleisen, 'Annehmen oder Ablehnen? Das Kabinett Scheidemann, die Oberste Heeresleitung und der Vertrag von Versailles im Juni 1919', *VfZ*, 35, 3, 1987, 438–39.

principal guide must be the policy of the civilian government. The Supreme Command could not act successfully in opposition to the government. However he was prepared to defend Germany against Polish attacks. Reinhardt, on the other hand, made no direct mention of government policy, and how he believed the officer corps should react to it. Groener and Reinhardt had exchanged bastions of support over the Versailles issue. Whereas previously Groener had drawn his authority from his position within the Supreme Command, he now looked to the civilian government, while Reinhardt appealed directly to the officer corps, who were more susceptible to arguments based on notions of national honour. He argued that all independence movements in eastern Germany must be supported, which presumably meant the movement for the creation of an East Prussian state. The southern and western parts of Germany lacked national sentiment in Reinhardt's view. 'There are many different ways to hold together what is already together. In the west the peace will be workable, whereas in the east in my opinion it will be unworkable. There is the danger that the insipidness of the west and south will spoil the nationalist sensitivities of the nationalistic east. A breach between east and west will not be avoided, the breach will be huge. We can control the breach, give up the west, and create a strong east, which would include the area to the Elbe. The old Prussia will be the core of this Reich.'[83] In Reinhardt's terms, the republic faced a stark choice between the nationalist east or the west. His admiration for Prussia, and its state-building qualities led him to believe that a national revival based on the east was the best choice for Germany in June 1919. Groener ended the discussion with a sober assessment of Germany's position, which needed strong government to recover: 'We must pursue a steadfast internal policy, we do not have the means for foreign policy.'[84]

The following morning a larger group of over thirty generals and Noske met. The agenda for the meeting, which was clearly aimed at evaluating the prospects for military opposition to the Allies, had been prepared by Reinhardt. He wanted to know if the transport system could be maintained in working order, if the south and west of Germany could be evacuated without a fight, and what type of forces would be stationed behind the Elbe. He also wanted to know if the eastern border with Poland could be defended in case of an attack and what type of 'defensive operations' the Supreme Command would conduct. In case the peace was signed he wanted to know if the commanders believed that they could maintain civil order.[85] Reinhardt opened the discussion, and claimed that 'one should not conclude from these talks that a decision has already been made, it simply concerns the clarification of all the

---

83. Groener, *Lebenserinnerungen*, 502–503.
84. Mühleisen, 'Annehmen oder Ablehnen?', 440–42.
85. Ernst, 'Aus dem Nachlaß', 73.

military possibilities.'[86] Yet the tenor of the questions indicate that Reinhardt still hoped that the National Assembly would reject the terms, and that the Allied invasion would be resisted from eastern Germany. The aim of Reinhardt's hidden agenda raises the question of the nature of the meeting. Groener described the meeting as a 'council of war', and believed that a state would be created in the east with or without the government's approval.[87] It was probably a war council to the extent that it gave Reinhardt a forum in which he could argue the case for the rejection of the treaty and the feasibility, as he hoped, of resistance against the Allies. If Reinhardt managed to persuade the generals and Noske to follow this course, then he felt he could offer the government a strong alternative to signing the treaty. Yet there is no evidence of active links between Reinhardt and those plotting to create a state in East Prussia, and neither is there any evidence that he was planning a coup if the government accepted the terms. Rather the evidence leads to the conclusion that Reinhardt was hoping to establish a consensus in government circles against the terms and in favour of an East Prussian state.

The speeches of the generals demonstrated that a national consensus did not exist. General Fritz von Loßberg, who had worked with Reinhardt before the war, and was now commander of Army Command South, based around Silesia, reported that the working class in that area was becoming more nationalist. However the bulk of the rail workers were Poles, and there was also the danger of Sparticism. If forced to fight against an external foe, Loßberg believed that the *Einwohnerwehr* would be able to maintain internal order.[88] General Wilhelm Heye, the representative of Army Command North also believed that the 'If we want to assert our will militarily we have the means.'[89] However the reports from Möhl about Bavaria, Fortmüller about Saxony and Maercker about Leipzig were less hopeful. They expected trouble in some of the major cities, such as Erfurt and Nürnberg. As the generals continued to discuss the various matters on the agenda, any hopes of a miracle of the Weimar republic diminished. Groener estimated that resources for a defensive war would only last three months. Significantly Möhl, Renner, who was the Württemberg representative and Maercker all believed that if the terms were accepted, an outbreak of violence could be contained, while Loßberg feared that the troops would not evacuate the lands in eastern Germany.[90] The meeting underlined the division within the army between those based in the south and west and those based in the east. Even more significantly, Noske told the generals that the National Assembly would accept the terms of the treaty, and he stressed that there

86. Wette, *Aus den Geburtsstunden*, 97–98.
87. Groener, *Lebenserinnerungen*, 504.
88. Mühleisen, 'Annehmen oder Ablehnen?', 445–47
89. Ibid., 448.
90. Ibid., 448–60.

was no support for rejection and a subsequent war in the west.[91] The west would not suffer a catastrophe for the sake of the east, thus destroying the social and political pre-conditions for a *Volkskrieg*.

Reinhardt had three problems with his hopes for resistance. First, there was little support in the population as a whole or in the National Assembly for rejection and subsequent war. Second, Germany did not have sufficient materiel to wage a war. Finally, the west had everything to lose and nothing to gain from rejection, since it would bear the brunt of occupation. Nonetheless, Reinhardt continued to urge resistance in the name of 'the virtuous values' of the German people. He concluded by noting that 'we must form a different image of war, to the one to which we have become accustomed', which is an early indication that Reinhardt was thinking in terms of a *Volkskrieg*.[92] The meeting of the generals on 19 June led to no clear resolution, partly because the National Assembly intended to accept the terms with the exception of the war guilt and the extradition clauses. Reinhardt firmly believed that the Allies would not remove these clauses, and this may have hardened his attitude at the meeting.[93] Reinhardt attended three further meetings that day. In the afternoon he met with representatives from eastern Germany, who were less dedicated to the cause of an independent East Prussia, than had been assumed by many of the officers.[94] At a meeting of the states' representatives and later at the cabinet Reinhardt spoke against acceptance of the terms, although with no success.[95]

Two memoranda which he wrote around 19 June summarize his arguments against the treaty of Versailles. There were three elements to his argument. First, he did not trust the Allies, whose 'will, aimed before, during and after the war, at our planned diminution and suppression, a will which can only be broken by resistance, not through unilateral concessions.'[96] He argued that the hopes of the supporters of acceptance that the terms would be eased over the forthcoming years were misplaced. The experience of the ceasefire convinced him, 'that after a "Yes" we will have to disarm ourselves month after month, and make French despotism ever easier, more attractive and less dangerous for the French.'[97] Once the process of disarmament started Germany would never be able to recover its position owing to French dominance.

Second, he feared the impact an acceptance of the treaty would have on the troops. He predicted that the reduction of the army to 100,000

91. HStASt, M 660/034, Bü 17, Protokol der Sitzung in Weimar, 19 June 1919.
92. Ibid.
93. Ibid.; Groener, *Lebenserinnerungen*, 503.
94. BA-MA, N 18/4, Lebenserinnerungen des Generalobersts Heye. Teil II. Wie ich den Weltkrieg erlebte, 1914–1942, fos. 202–203; Schulze, 'Oststaat Plan', 153–54.
95. Ernst, 'Aus dem Nachlaß', 77.
96. Ibid., 77.
97. Ibid., 78.

men in a short space of time would cause mutinies in the *Reichswehr*. This was the clear implication of his argument that '"No" holds the military forces behind the government and allows it master the internal situation.'[98] The *Reichswehr* and other military forces had been central to the republic's successes against radical left-wing revolts. Yet the new regime faced a greater threat now from the Allies, and so this argument, which had been used successfully by the officer corps before, was greatly diminished in value. If the Allies invaded it was highly probable that within a few weeks there would not be any 'internal situation' worth mentioning.

Finally Reinhardt believed that rejection of the terms would lead to a moral regeneration of the German people. He summarized the morality of both sides:

> Let us look beyond these troubled weeks. None of us want to despair about the future of our people. The 'Yes' supporters do not want that, and they see their hope in the maintenance of our inner position, and in holding together the remaining German areas and avoiding enemy occupation. They take into account the poisonous seed of submitting voluntarily to a dishonourable treaty.
>
> Against this the 'No' supporters count on rebuilding on the basis of saved honour, on the staunch rejection of the slandering of a whole Volk, on loyalty towards our eastern Germans, our colonies, our two million dead heroes, who must be remembered today. They have given more for the rejection of such a peace, than now threatens us if we reject it.[99]

As a soldier, Reinhardt said, he had to advise rejection.[100] He was arguing from the perspective of military honour, which was deeply offended by certain terms, such as the extradition of officers for war crimes, and the guilt clause. He also believed that the German spirit would be poisoned, and this would have an adverse effect on a national revival. Despite the defeat in the First World War Reinhardt still entertained hopes about a recovery and was working for the next generation of Germans. The reaction of the present generation to the terms would be a guide to future generations: 'If we want to rear our youth nationalistically we have to give them teachers who themselves exemplify national deeds and behaviour. To fail nationally now and expect a national revival of our children is impossible.'[101]

Reinhardt's entreaties could not prevent the National Assembly from accepting the treaty on 22 June. Scheidemann, who had prophesised that the hand that signed the treaty would wither, resigned as Chancellor, and was replaced by another SPD member, Gustav Bauer, former activist in the Trade Union movement and friend of Ebert.[102] It was significant that

98. Ibid., 78.
99. Ibid., 80.
100. Hindenburg used a similar phrase in an open letter to the *Reichswehr*.
101. Ernst, 'Aus dem Nachlaß', 78.
102. Heinrich August Winkler, *Weimar, 1918-1933. Die Geschichte der ersten deutschen Demokratie*, Munich, 1993, 93-94.

Reinhardt also offered his resignation. For an officer whose prestige in the officer corps had been low since he accepted the post of Minister of War, association with the treaty of Versailles would have been deeply unwelcome from a political as well as from a personal point of view.[103] Van den Bergh, who spoke to Reinhardt on the evening of 21 June, when the resignation letter was drafted, was not convinced of the motives for Reinhardt's resignation, believing that it was an attempt to strengthen his image among the right-wing circles in the *Reichswehr*, while as a 'states-man he said silently that signing under protest and attempting to improve the whole thing was the right course.'[104] Although there is some truth in Bergh's assessment with regard to Reinhardt's reputation in right-wing circles, the Württemberger had invested too much effort in promoting the 'No!' cause for it to have been a purely cynical ploy.

In fact the terms of Versailles, which would be the foreign policy frame-work within which the young republic would have to restore Germany to its Great Power position, was, in Reinhardt's view, a fatal setback to the hopes for national recovery. The terms greatly hampered the 'military mission'. He wrote to Ebert that his main aim 'was to help strengthen the steadfastness of the broadest section of the *Volk* and to restore and anchor a measure of military capability in the populace through this, so that we could resist the dangerous efforts of eastern Bolshevism as well as the unlimited threats of the West.'[105] He doubted whether these tasks could be fulfilled under the terms of Versailles, and therefore he offered his resignation. Ebert rejected it immediately, a sign of faith in a general who so vehemently opposed the government's policy.

Ebert opened the way for Reinhardt to return to pragmatic co-opera-tion with the Republic. However Reinhardt made his opposition to the treaty public. In a speech to the Prussian State Assembly on 24 June he told the audience, 'that as Prussian Minister of War I fought to the last inch for the rejection of this peace.'[106] He criticised the treaty for under-mining the brotherhood of nations, an ideal which had always been close to German hearts! Having registered his opposition, he then called for 'calm and order', so that Germany could begin to recover. This could only be achieved 'through the merging of the army and the *Volk*.' Reinhardt was publicly proclaiming his military mission, which was founded on the ideal of co-operation between the *Volk* and the army. He concluded by praising 'the honourable German and the hard and powerful Prussian type.'[107] The task was to recognise the reality of the current situation. There was no other option but to carry out terms while striving for a 'real

103. Geheimes Staatsarchiv, 90a, Nr 6, B III, 2b, Bd 168, Prussian cabinet, 31 June 1919, fo. 14.
104. *Aus den Geburtsstunden*, 108.
105. BA-MA, N 86/15, Reinhardt to Ebert, 21 June 1919.
106. *Die Preußische Landesversammlung*, 1919, vol. 2, 2523.
107. Ibid., 2523–525.

peace'.[108] Despite rejecting the treaty, he accepted that the policy of fulfilment was the only political option for Germany in the short-term.

Reinhardt's reputation received a very temporary boost from his opposition to Versailles. *Das Militärwochenblatt*, previously one of Reinhardt's most persistent critics, was now certain 'that the current Minister of War has not sacrificed the old, tried and tested officers' character to the new era and in spite of all the contrary influences has striven to do what is humanly possible for the army for the good of the Fatherland.'[109] The rejection of his resignation had enabled Reinhardt to benefit from his opposition without incurring any loss of influence with either Noske or Ebert. Groener on the other hand was badly damaged by his realistic assessment of the situation, and he spent much of the summer, even after the dissolution of the Supreme Command and the announcement of his resignation, defending himself, and implicitly criticising Reinhardt. At a conference of leading Supreme Command officers he argued that Reinhardt's belief that Germany could be united again by an East Prussian state was far-fetched. He pointed to the dismemberment of Poland as a more likely historical example. Military defeat and economic collapse had only served to exacerbate particularist ideas within the Reich.[110] However it was Reinhardt's momentary strength and Groener's reward for his accurate assessment of Germany's position vis-à-vis the Allies, that together with the provisions of Versailles, allowed the Minister of War to dissolve the Supreme Command on 3 July.[111]

In the Prussian State Assembly Reinhardt had argued for a policy of fulfilment but this faced a number of crises in the second half of 1919 which directly impinged on the *Reichswehr*. The policy of fulfilment involved carrying out the terms of the treaty to prove Germany's good will and to demonstrate that the treaty was impossible to fulfil to the absolute letter. Not only did the reduction of the army to 100,000 men put stress on the morale of the *Reichswehr*, but Reinhardt also had to deal with the recalcitrant Iron Division, the arrival of the Inter-Allied Military Control Commission (IMCC), and the question of extradition.

German troops had arrived in the Baltic when the Allies under article 13 of the ceasefire agreement had demanded that German troops help the Latvian government under Karl Ulmanis against the Bolshevist Russian advance.[112] However as the German units, and especially the Iron Division, drove back the Bolshevist advance, the Allies began to fear that the German forces would re-establish German influence in the Baltic. They threatened the German government with sanctions, including a blockade on food imports if the troops did not return. When the troops

108. Ibid., 2523.
109. *Das Militärwochenblatt*, 26 June 1919, 2811–816.
110. BA-MA, N 42/12, Besprechung, 12 July 1919.
111. See Chapter 6.
112. Hagen Schulze, *Freikorps und Republik 1918-1920*, Boppard am Rhein, 1969, 125–201.

mutinied in August 1919, the government was caught between its inability to control its forces and the threats of the Allies. At first it replaced the commander, Rüdiger von der Goltz with General Magnus von Eberhardt, but to no avail. The cabinet dithered until 30 October. Reinhardt was caught between appeasing disobedient troops and exerting the authority of the government. In early October Stülpnagel had urged Reinhardt to support Goltz against the government's demands for his recall.[113] If Reinhardt did not act on this occasion, he pursued a more lenient line when it came to dealing with the returning troops. The cabinet decided to issue a final warning that if the troops had not returned by 11 November they would be treated as deserters and forfeit their German citizenship. Reinhardt pressed for a later deadline.[114] The evacuation only began on 25 November, partially due to transport problems, but also due to the negative attitude of the troops towards the government's authority. Yet the measures taken in cabinet were revoked by the *Reichswehrministerium* on 17 December.[115] The appeasement of mutineers set a precedent for the way in which the *Reichswehr* exercised its command. It preferred to cajole disobedient troops than take firm action against them. This eroded the authority of the senior officers, and more importantly the civilian authorities.

One of the principal fears of French officers in the 1920s was that Germany would evade the terms of Part V of the Versailles treaty.[116] To prevent this, the Allies set up the IMCC, which arrived in Germany on 15 September 1919.[117] The IMCC were dependent on the co-operation and honesty of the German officers. While pressure in terms of sanctions, or later a refusal to evacuate certain areas of western Germany could be used to force co-operation, the IMCC generally found the German officers obstructive. On 26 October Reinhardt issued instructions on dealing with Allied officers. While he ordered a policy of co-operation and the quick implementation of Allied demands in Germany's own interest, the tone of the order which advised against fraternization and reminded officers of outstanding issues, including extradition and the slow release of German prisoners of war, gave legitimacy to the obstructive behaviour of many officers.[118]

By January the head of the IMCC, General Niessel was complaining to Chancellor Bauer that many of his officers had been attacked or prevented

113. BA-MA N 5/18, Stülpnagel to Goltz, 5 October 1919, fo. 36.
114. *Das Kabinett Bauer, 21. Juni 1919 bis 27. März 1920*, ed. Anton Golecki, Boppard am Rhein, 1980, 334–35.
115. HStASt M 660/034, Bü 18, *Reichswehr-Fürsorgeblatt*, 17 December 1919.
116. MAE Serie Z, Sous-série Allemagne, 57, Foch to the President of the Peace Conference, 27 November 1919, fos. 128–30.
117. Michael Salewski, *Entwaffnung und Militärkontrolle in Deutschland 1919–1927*, Munich, 1967.
118. HStASt M 660/034, Bü 16, order dated 16 October 1919.

from carrying out their tasks.[119] Reinhardt travelled to East Prussia where many of the infractions had occurred and he recommended that trials take place in Berlin where they would be free of the pressures from local troops.[120] However this may well have been a cover-up. While some officers were dismissed from the service, two senior ones, Eberhardt and General Ludwig von Estorff were told that the trials and investigations were simply to appease the Allies. According to Bauer, they were a 'political necessity.'[121] When Reinhardt resigned as head of the Army Command in March 1920 the work of the IMCC was still in its infancy. However evasion and obstructiveness were already in evidence, produced by the natural antipathy of the German officers towards the idea of military control, but also endorsed by Reinhardt and even the cabinet.

Although the list of German officers to be extradited for war crimes trials was not presented until 3 February 1920, right-wing and military circles were aware of the impending demands. Even before the treaty had been signed Reinhardt feared that the question of extradition would lead to 'mistrust, posing and moral disintegration.'[122] In the autumn a Central Office for the Defence of Germans before Enemy Courts was established.[123] However it was not clear whether the extraditions would take place. Certainly these preparations indicate that the German government expected to have to give into Allied pressure, but there were others on the right who believed that the defendants would not get a fair trial and that the Allies were simply engaged in a propaganda exercise. On 24 June General Bernhard von Hülsen had drafted a plan in case of Allied demands, which involved the establishment of a military dictatorship under Noske. Notably he was ready to get rid of Groener immediately, whereas he would have retained Reinhardt as Minister of War.[124] This dubious accolade was probably due to Reinhardt's recently developed reputation as a staunch guardian of German honour. Wilhelm Reinhard, a *Freikorps* leader, organised one group which was prepared to hide alleged war criminals.[125] There were rumours, but no evidence, that Reinhardt met with Ludendorff and Falkenhayn on 8 January 1920 to organise resistance to the extraditions.[126]

119. BArch R 43 I/48, Aufzeichnung über die Unterredung zwischen dem Herrn Reichskanzler und dem General Niessel, 4 January 1920, fo. 191.
120. BArch R 43 I/48, memorandum on meeting of 15 January 1920, fos. 274–77.
121. BArch R 431/48, Bauer to Noske, 19 January 1920, fo. 267; HStASt M 660/034, Bü 18, Reinhardt to Eberhardt, 4 February 1920.
122. PA-AA, Deutsche Friedensdelegation, Pol 7a Band I, Winterfeldt to Surpeme Command, 27 May 1919.
123. BArch R 43 I/340, Noske to Bauer, 4 August 1919, fo. 31.
124. *Zwischen Revolution und Kapp Putsch*, 154–55.
125. Wilhelm Reinhard, *1918–19. Die Wehen der Republik*, Berlin, 1933, 117–18.
126. Horst Mühleisen, *Kurt Freiherr von Lersner. Diplomat im Umbruch der Zeiten, 1918-1920*, Marburg, 1984, 275–76.

On 3 February the Allies presented their list. The following day there was a meeting at the *Truppenamt* which was headed by Seeckt.[127] After this meeting Reinhardt issued what was effectively an information sheet, setting out the options open to those on the list. One could either surrender immediately, or else oppose the warrant on the basis that the Allies were both plaintiff and judge. A third option – a policy of wait and see – had the most appeal. Reinhardt assured his colleagues that any of the options would be an honourable course.[128] The following week he took a stronger line. The attitude of the government was now clearly one of refusal, so he felt more confident of his political basis. In a secret decree Reinhardt told fellow officers that he believed that the government would refuse the extradition of war criminals. This could mean war, but unlike the debate over the treaty of Versailles, Reinhardt argued that there was a greater unity of purpose between the government and the people. While he was certain that in the case of war an attack from Poland could be repelled, he recognised 'a substantial inferiority on our side, not just in terms of numbers but also in terms of weaponry.' Reinhardt implicitly ruled out the possibility of extradition when he argued that war could be forced on Germany by the Allies if the Reich refused to comply with the demands of the Allies. All that the *Reichswehr* could do was to remain prepared for war.[129] As in June 1919 Reinhardt was prepared to fight for what he saw as the moral dimension to a people's power. Reinhardt feared the Versailles treaty less because it weakened Germany by reducing its army to 100,000 men and banning offensive weapons, than because it threatened to destroy the cultivation of martial values by disgracing the deeds of the German army during the war and preventing a younger generation of Germans from experiencing the army through conscripted service.[130] However this time German was spared from choosing between conflict with the Allies and extradition when the Allies agreed to allow the trials to be held in Germany.

In November Rüdiger von der Goltz, erstwhile leader of the Iron Division, wrote to Reinhardt, arguing that France had achieved 'the eastern encirclement of Germany', and that the German government had no comprehension of the Baltic question.[131] Reinhardt's reply, which was written two months later, is an interesting insight into his conception of foreign policy after the treaty of Versailles. He believed events in the Baltic showed 'that France and England despite great differences on the path to the destruction of the German reputation are still united, and that

127. *Kabinett Bauer*, 595–96.
128. BA-MA N 247/70, Decree of *Reichswehrministerium, Heeresleitung*, 4 February 1920, fo. 4.
129. BA-MA N 86/16, Reinhardt, decree, 11 February 1920; see also Ernst, 'Aus dem Nachlaß', 97–98.
130. See the numerous references in *Wehrkraft und Wehrwille*, and Chapter 10 in this study.
131. HStASt, M 660/034, Bü 18, Goltz to Reinhardt, 4 November 1919.

United States is too weak in continental questions to prevent the French blows of oppression.'[132] Within this foreign policy context there were few options for Germany to regain her great power status through alliances. Reinhardt never mentioned Russia as a possible ally, not even during the period of co-operation with the Red Army during the 1920s. Therefore Germany would have to reassert itself through its own power, rather than through alliances. For Reinhardt national unity, in its broadest sense, was essential if Germany was to recover its position in Europe. However, he was pessimistic about the chances of Germans coming together in a second *Burgfrieden*:

> 'Already our comrades high and low, left and right are showing the insurmount-able German spirit of discord as strongly as the political parties. ... The old great Hohenzollerns prevented this falling apart with powerful constraints. Our situa-tion today presents is with the difficult task of voluntary integration in unitary action. I fear that the emergency must become far greater before we learn this. My actions and my life belong, alone, to combining forces for the Fatherland.'[133]

There are few letters or documents which convey so powerfully Rein-hardt's belief that the primary task of German politics after 1918 was the renewal of the state in preparation for the restoration of Germany's pre-1918 position in Europe.

At the same time as Reinhardt was arguing that Germany would have to recover on her own, Seeckt was developing his ideas for an alliance with the Soviet Union.[134] Both espoused the primacy of foreign policy, the restoration of order within Germany and its maintenance as a potential *Machtfaktor* in Europe but charted very different courses. Without an ally Germany could only recover by achieving internal unity and the militari-sation of society. It could not rely on the arms of an ally, and Reinhardt believed that even Seeckt's idea of a cadre army would be insufficient for German security. Reinhardt did not have to wrestle with questions about the ideological dimension of an alliance with Soviet Russia. At the same time as Seeckt was dismissing the importance of Bolshevism for German foreign policy, Reinhardt argued: 'The danger of Bolshevism is not to be dismissed or underestimated.'[135] Yet with the increasing fragmentation of German political life in late 1919 and early 1920, Seeckt's plan for an alliance with Soviet Russia looked more feasible than Reinhardt's vision of a militarized unified national community. Moreover Seeckt's vision of a professional, mobile force was more suited to the political conditions of Weimar Germany than Reinhardt's aim of a militarized nation.

132. HStASt, M 660/034, Bü 18, Reinhardt to Goltz, 2 January 1920; see also John Hiden, *The Baltic States and Weimar* Ostpolitik, Cambridge, 1987.
133. HStASt, M 660/034, Bü 18, Reinhardt to Goltz, 2 January 1920.
134. Manfred Zeidler, *Reichswehr und Rote Armee 1920–1933. Wege und Stationen einer ungewöhnlichen Zusammenarbeit*, Munich, 1993, 31–38.
135. BA-MA N 86/16, Reinhardt decree, 11 February 1920.

THE FORMATION OF THE
REICHSWEHRMINISTERIUM

*T*he signature of the treaty was a defeat for Reinhardt's policy of resistance. However the treaty enabled him to reduce the Supreme Command to the status of *Reichswehr* Command Post Kolberg and effectively to reduce the importance of Groener. This was part of the intertwined personal and bureaucratic rivalry which had characterized German military policy from December 1918. This process reached its zenith in the late summer of 1919 as the plans for the *Reichswehrministerium* (Reichswehr Ministry) were being drafted. Beyond these rivalries there was the important question of how to fit the command and administrative functions of the *Reichswehr* into the new constitution. The centralisation of the ministries had been the first stage but the second stage was overshadowed by the legacy of the General Staff in the *Kaiserreich* and its position outside the remit of parliamentary oversight. The debate about structures was an implicit criticism of the *Kaiserreich*'s deficits in this respect.[1] The political leaders of the Weimar government were adamant on the question of civilian primacy and the responsibility of the *Reichswehrminister* to the *Reichstag*. Yet the *Reichswehrminister* could have theoretical control of the ministry, but his actual control would be determined by the internal structures of the ministry, and even more so by his personal relationship with senior officers. Noske left the practical details to the officer corps.[2] Within the officer corps attitudes to the new internal structures were determined by the principle of 'where you sit is where you stand', but it was also the case that bureaucratic differences mirrored personal rivalries. In the final analysis the outcome would be determined by contingent factors, and

---

1. Markus Pöhlmann, 'Von Versailles nach Armageddon: Totalisierungserfahrung und Kriegserwartung in deutschen Militärzeitschriften', in *An der Schwelle zum Totalen Krieg. Die militärische Debatte über den Krieg der Zukunft 1919–1939*, ed. Stig Förster, Paderborn, 2002, 352–54.
2. Wolfram Wette, *Gustav Noske. Eine politische Biographie*, Düsseldorf, 1988, 361–68, 532–33

Reinhardt's view would prevail in this stage of the creation of the modern German army.

The development of policy on the internal structures of the *Reichswehrministerium* was shaped by the legacy of the *Kaiserreich*'s military institutions.[3] The *Kommandogewalt* was a key structure in the constitutional and political life of the *Kaiserreich*. The *Kaiser* exercised the *Kommandogewalt* without any restrictions from the *Reichstag*. The *Reichstag* could only exercise influence over military policy indirectly, through withholding money or trimming expenditure.[4] The Prussian Minister of War also made appearances in the *Reichstag* to explain policy and answer various questions, and therefore had to give a public account of military policy. However these parliamentary controls were weakened by a number of factors. A *Reichstag* that did not look favourably upon the government's budget could be dissolved, with the expectation that a pro-government majority would be returned at the ensuing election.[5] Further, the position of the Minister of War was weakened considerably in 1883 when Bismarck removed the General Staff from its control and placed it directly under the Kaiser. Dividing the generals did not necessarily help Bismarck control them. In the late 1880s he faced the same pressures for preventive war from Alfred von Waldersee as he had from Helmuth von Moltke in the 1870s. In the *Kaiserreich* personal power and influence, as much as structures, were the crucial determinants of the civil-military relationship. As we will see a similar argument can be made about the Weimar Republic. The result of the 1883 reforms split strategic planning from administration, which was inefficient, but it also meant that the *Reichstag* could not question the Minister of War on issues of strategic policy, for the simple reason that he was ignorant of the General Staff's business. In the same year the Military Cabinet took over responsibility for personnel issues from the Ministry of War.[6] This polycratic system was inefficient, and recognised as such by officers after 1918.

During the First World War the flaws of the system became apparent to both senior commanders and the *Reichstag*. The inadequacies of the government and the interference of the *Reichstag* were among the officers'

3. Thomas Nipperdey, *Deutsche Geschichte, 1866-1918. Machtstaat vor der Demokratie*, Munich, 1992, 201; David Blackbourn argues that the aftermath of the Zabern affair demontrated the weakness of the *Reichstag*, especially when 'the special place of the army was at stake', *The Fontana History of Germany. The Long Nineteenth Century*, London, 1997, 418.

4. For the interface between the *Reichstag* and the army, see Stig Förster, *Der doppelte Militarismus. Die deutsche Heeresrüstungspolitik zwischen Status-quo-Sicherung und Aggression, 1890-1913*, Stuttgart, 1985.

5. Ibid, 71-74.

6. Nipperdey, *Machtstaat*, 204-205.

favourite scapegoats for defeat in 1918.[7] The officers' critique of civilian understanding of warfare should not disguise the fact that many officers were thoroughly disillusioned by the performance of the *Kaiser* during the war.[8] Some recognised the virtues of the liberal form of civil-military relations which had made the western Allies such a formidable foe. As is the wont of the defeated, German officers looked, if not too obviously, at the models of military organisation offered in France and Britain.[9] Reinhardt warned officers not to forget the 'bad experiences' which the German army had had with the 'division of leadership into the General Staff, the Military Cabinet and the four War Ministries'. He concluded that while the bureaucracy of an army larger than the *Reichswehr* might need a further division of labour 'one person must oversee all, and from this overview, must decide on the ultimate course of action.'[10] Reinhardt's stress on decisionism, which emphasised the imperative of centralising the decision-making process in the interests of preserving the state during emergencies, was an element of the primacy of foreign policy. The reforms, therefore, were designed with the long-term recovery of Germany as a Great Power as well as the immediate constitutional needs.

Attempts to assert civilian control over the military were sporadic, reactions to incidents rather than forward thinking. It has already been pointed out that there was little opposition in either the cabinet or the National Assembly to the military's, and especially Reinhardt's, policies in the first half of 1919. While groups such as the soldiers' councils and the USPD had called for layers of control over officers, who might be natural opponents of the Republic, they were isolated and politically impotent. Given the discussions amongst the current ruling parties, notably the SPD, about unchecked military influence in civil society and politics in the *Kaiserreich*, it is surprising that more stringent efforts were not made to ensure civilian control over military policy after 1918.[11]

On 22 October 1918 Ebert had demanded that ministers, including the Minister of War and Chancellor, be made responsible to the *Reichstag*. A

7. Erich Ludendorff, *Kriegführung und Politik*, Berlin, 1932, 1; Ernst Wrisberg, *Der Weg zur Revolution*, Leipzig, 1921, 117–20; see Friedrich Freiherr Hiller von Gärtringen, '"Dolch-stoss"-Diskussion und "Dolchstoss-Legende" im wandel von vier Jahrzehnten', in *Geschichte und Gegenwartsbewußtsein*, Waldemar Besson, Friedrich Freiherr Hiller von Gärtringen, Göttingen, 1963, 123–60.

8. Bruno Thoß, 'Nationale Rechte, militärische Führung und Diktaturfrage in Deutschland, 1913–1923', *MgM*, 35, 1987, 35–60.

9. See for example the article by Curt Liebmann, 'Zur Frage der einheitlichen Kriegsleitung', *Wissen und Wehr*, 4, 1923, 197–220.

10. *Wehrkraft und Wehrwille*, 51.

11. On the pre-1918 debate, see: Werner Conze, Michael Geyer, 'Militarismus', in *Geschichtliche Grundbegriffe. Historische Lexikon zur politisch-sozialen Sprache in Deutschland*, 8 vols, Stuttgart, 1978 vol. 4, 1–42; Nicholas Stargardt, *The German Idea of Militarism. Radical and Socialist Critics, 1868–1914*, Cambridge, 1994; Geoff Eley, *From Unification to Nazism. Reinterpreting the German Past*, London, 1986, 85–109.

reform law was passed on 26 October. Since these ministers had to counter-sign orders issued by the Supreme Command, the military was more closely controlled by the *Reichstag*.[12] Hence one of the major aspects of the civil-military relationship in German politics had seemingly been resolved before the Revolution. This was, perhaps, complacent – the establishment of the Republic and the derivation of power from the will of the people, rather than the Kaiser, may have created the illusion that civilian control was a matter of course, as in other liberal democracies. But political realities do not automatically follow political theories, and Reinhardt and his fellow officers exerted the greatest influence over military policy in 1919, not the civilian cabinet.[13] There were other reasons – the need for order and the assertion of professional expertise which worked in the favour of the continued dominance of the officer corps in the narrow, but crucial, area of forming the institutional framework of the modern German army. By the time the SPD made serious criticisms of the *Reichswehr* the basic structures were in place.[14]

Over a matter of weeks the nature of civilian authority had changed from the *Kaiser*'s divine right to rule or traditional legitimacy to the sovereignty of the people. Despite continuities in personnel and attitudes the army had to operate in a completely different constitutional structure. This structure developed by informal practice and a series of formal decrees in the first half of 1919. Both General Heinrich Scheüch, on behalf of the Prussian Ministry of War, and Field Marshal Paul von Hindenburg, on behalf of the Supreme Command, subordinated the army to the newly established Council of People's Commissars.[15] The Council of People's Commissars also appointed a councillor (*Beigeordnete*) at both the Supreme Command headquarters and the Ministry of War, although Scheidemann saw the councillor's role as allaying the suspicions of his party colleagues, rather than as exercising control.[16] The decrees of 19 January 1919 were the first formal document that stated the nature of the relationship between the army and the civilian government. The decrees

12. *Zwischen Revolution und Kapp-Putsch. Militär und Innenpolitik 1918–1920*, ed. Heinz Hürten, Düsseldorf, 1977, xxvii–xxviii.

13. Christoph Gusy, *Die Weimarer Reichsverfassung*, Tübingen, 1997, 183–86.

14. Eckardt Opitz, 'Sozialdemokratie und Militarismus in der Weimarer Republik', in *Militär und Militarismus in der Weimarer Republik*, eds, Klaus-Jürgen Müller, Eckardt Opitz, Düsseldorf, 1978, 269–71, 275–81.

15. Ernst Heinrich Schmidt, *Heimatheer und Revolution 1918. Die militärische Gewalten im Heimatgebiet zwischen Oktoberreform und Novemberrevolution*, Stuttgart, 1981, 410; Gerhard Rakenius, *Wilhelm Groener als erster Generalquartiermeister. Die Politik der Obersten Heeresleitung*, Boppard am Rhein, 1977, 71–76; *Dokumente zur deutschen Verfassungsgeschichte. Dokumente der Novemberrevolution und der Weimarer Republik, 1918–1933*, 3 vols, ed. E. R. Huber, Stuttgart, 1966, vol. 3, 9.

16. Rakenius, *Groener*, 87–88; Wolfgang Elben, *Das Problem der Kontinuität in der deutschen Revolution. Die Politik der Staatssekretäre und der militärischen Führung von November 1918 bis Februar 1919*, Düsseldorf, 1966, 140–43.

turned the Ministry of War into the instrument of the Council of People's Commissars. For Reinhardt, the decrees meant that a split was avoided between the civilian government and the officer corps. Co-operation would be the basis for national revival.[17] The readiness of the army to accept the Council of People's Commissars as the legitimate government are evidence of the army's subordination to civilian authority.

Elections to the National Assembly were held in January 1919 and on 10 February the temporary constitution was passed. The decrees of 19 January had excluded the Supreme Command units from its terms, but according to the temporary constitution the President would appoint a government, to which Reich bureaucrats and the Supreme Command were subordinate.[18] The relationship of the army and civilian government was further copper-fastened by the law on the temporary *Reichswehr*. The President was the supreme commander of the *Reichswehr*, and commands were to be passed from the President to the *Reichswehrminister* who would countersign them and onto the Minister of War who was responsible for implementing them.[19] Reinhardt was responsible for the drafting of the law, but there is little information in the memorandum of 5 February on the formal constitutional relationship between the government and the army. This indicates that Reinhardt had fully accepted the subordination of the army to an elected President and government, but that he had not thought about the institutional framework of the army in this light. For him, military institutions were designed first and foremost to be efficient.[20] While the officers saw the President as a sort of *Ersatzkaiser*, the political environment in which the military acted had changed completely.[21] The constitutional framework established in February and March laid the basis for the *Reichswehr*'s position in the Weimar republic.[22]

Discussions on civil-military relations, even at the highest level, tended to focus on very specific issues, rather than on broader questions of civilian control of military institutions, as two examples will highlight. The first concerns an event in East Prussia. On 16 April there was a meeting in the Chancellery on the activities of the Supreme Command in the east its position vis-à-vis August Winnig, the Reich Commissar for the East.

---

17. *Der Zentralrat der deutschen sozialistischen Republik, 19.12.18–8.4.19. Vom ersten zum zweite Rätekongress*, Leiden, 1968, eds Eberhard Kolb, Reinhard Rürup, 441–3.
18. *Das Kabinett Scheidemann. 13. Februar bis 20. Juni 1919*, ed. Hagen Schulze, Boppard am Rhein, 1971, xxxv.
19. *Armeeverordnungsblatt*, nr 24, 1919.
20. BA-MA, N 86/16, 'Denkschrift über die Aufstellung der Reichswehr'.
21. Heinz Hürten, 'Reichswehr und Ausnahmezustand. Ein Beitrag zur Verfassungspolitik der Weimarer Republik in ihrem ersten Jahrfünft', *Rheinisch-Westfälische Akademie der Wissenschaften*, Düsseldorf, 1977.
22. Eckart Busch, *Der Oberbefehl. Seine rechtliche Struktur in Preußen und Deutschland seit 1848*, Boppard am Rhein, 1967, 49–52.

Reinhardt, Otto Braun, Philip Scheidemann, the Chancellor and Heinrich Albert, the secretary of the Chancellery, were all present, along with several officers as well as SPD deputies from the National Assembly.[23] The meeting gave the deputies a forum to present their complaints about the Supreme Command. In Danzig on 8 April the 17th Army Corps had occupied the train station to ensure safe passage of volunteers for border protection to the east. A general strike ensued in opposition to the occupation of the train station, and the military responded by declaring a state of emergency. Winnig described his relationship with the military up to this point as 'very good'. As soon as he heard of the events in Danzig he travelled there and was able to negotiate an end to both the strike and the state of emergency. However the commanding general changed the sense of Winnig's announcement in the local paper, the *Danziger Zeitung*, and implied that out of his own good will he had lifted the state of emergency, instead of being advised to do so by Winnig.[24] For Winnig, the ability to have the decisive say on any state of emergency in the east was essential in preserving the primacy of civilian control over the military. Reinhardt admitted that the complaints about officers and troops were justified, and suggested that a standing order should be issued, which would give Winnig and other commissars clearer instructions on dealing with a state of emergency. He also pointed out that the volunteers would be brought under the control of the *Reichswehr* and would take an oath to the government. Finally he wanted reports on any future incursions into politics by officers.[25]

Both the meeting and the efforts of Seeckt, the chief of staff of Army Command North, which was in charge of the offending 17th Army Corps, appeared to help resolve differences in the east. On 15 April Seeckt wrote to Winnig, informing him that he would be notified before any future declarations of states of emergency, or if this was impossible because of an urgent situation, he would be notified as soon as possible.[26] Later in April Reinhardt wrote to the Reich government, advising them that Army Command North should be left under the Supreme Command, especially since the transport of General Haller's Polish troops through Germany was about to take place. Reinhardt also said that he had contacted Winnig, who had agreed to the suggestions in the letter.[27] By June Reinhardt believed that Winnig and Army Command North were co-operating sufficiently smoothly on the basis of Seeckt's letter of 15 April.[28]

23. BArch, R 43, I/1844, Besprechung in der Reichskanzlei, 16 April 1919, fo. 22; *Kabinett Scheidemann*, 162–74.
24. Ibid., 165.
25. Ibid., 169–70.
26. BArch, R 43, I/1844, Abschrift of a letter from Seeckt to Winnig, dated 15 April 1919, fos. 44–5.
27. BArch, R 43, I/1844, Reinhardt, Göhre to Reichsministerium, April 1919, fo. 42.
28. BArch, R 43, I/1844, Reinhardt to Albert, 9 June 1919, fo. 57.

The meeting and the letters were elements of the informal political relationship between the military and the civilian government. Reinhardt was not trying to shield the Supreme Command from political control, and ultimately he supported the inclusion of the Supreme Command and the command structures of the army in the *Reichswehrministerium*. Rather Reinhardt's assessment of the situation in the first half of 1919 was based on the view that Germany was still at war, albeit unofficially. When the SPD deputies suggested greater powers for Winnig over the military than those set out in Seeckt's letter, officers argued that the Supreme Command was indispensable 'as long as the Reich finds itself in a wartime situation.'[29] While Reinhardt sought to fit the *Reichswehr* into the new political structures, his defence of the Supreme Command, which in many respects was an anachronism from the *Kaiserreich*, was based on short-term political calculations, which had little to do with the final constitutional position of the *Reichswehr*. He noted the benefits of leaving Hindenburg *in situ* which he felt would buttress the younger officers' sense of duty – a comment on the shaky loyalty of the officers to the new regime.[30] In the east Reinhardt's main concern was border protection and German proprietorship of as much territory as possible before the final peace settlement.

A second topic on the agenda at the meeting of 16 April was the rôle of the councillor (*Beigeordnete*), Paul Göhre, at the Ministry of War. Göhre, a member of the SPD since 1900, had volunteered for the army at the age of fifty in 1914. The institution of the councillor had been created in November 1918, so that the new government could oversee the activities of the ministers and bureaucrats who continued in office after the revolution.[31] Schöpflin was unimpressed by Göhre's performance, and demanded that 'in the Ministry of War a competent politician must be put beside the Minister of War.'[32] Reinhardt defended Göhre who had 'made a great effort and achieved much.'[33] In the context of the meeting, which was an airing of SPD unease with military policy, neither the criticisms nor Reinhardt's defence of Göhre is unexpected. The relationship between Reinhardt and Göhre was one of co-operation, although Reinhardt was definitely in control of policy. Reinhardt's personal relationships with SPD politicians does not fit into the paradigm of conflict, but of co-operation in order to "get the job done". Due to his unpopularity within the officer corps it was essential that he maintain good relations with political figures. Göhre had negotiated on Reinhardt's

29. BArch, R 43, 1/1844, memorandum of Reich Justice Ministry, 7 May 1919, fo. 51.
30. *Kabinett Scheidemann*, 53.
31. Elben, *Problem der Kontinuität*, 140–43, notes that Carl Giebel, councillor at the OHL, was swamped by tedious work and had no influence on OHL policy.
32. *Kabinett Scheidemann*, 172.
33. Ibid., 173.

behalf with the Central Council on the decrees of 19 January, a clear indication of the officer's trust in the SPD councillor. Göhre also defended the decrees in *Vorwärts*, although this article was prompted by a discussion of SPD deputies.[34] Göhre may well have been swamped by work, like his counterpart, Giebel, at the Supreme Command. From Reinhardt's point of view, Göhre's presence at the Ministry of War was extra political cover. On several occasions Reinhardt asked that Göhre be allowed to continue his work at the Ministry of War. In late March, Reinhardt and Noske told Scheidemann that 'Due to practical and political reasons the greatest value is placed on the further retention of the position of undersecretary of state and his advisors in the Ministry of War. The institution of the *Vertrauensleute* of the undersecretary has also proven useful, so that it would be beneficial to retain their services.'[35]

Göhre continued in the post until 1 May. At a cabinet meeting on 2 May Reinhardt argued that since two other SPD members were working on a private contract in the Ministry of War, there was no need appoint an SPD councillor, or secretary.[36] Why Reinhardt was so reluctant to fill the post is unknown, but the cabinet's relaxed attitude to the vacancy indicates that Reinhardt did not have any devious motives. It was only on 16 June that Albert Grzesinski, also a member of the SPD, was appointed to the post of political commissar in the Ministry of War.[37] Grzesinski later described himself as 'a thorn in the side of the military authorities', though there is no record of what activities this particular thorn got up to.[38] Instead he was put in charge of the *Abwickelungsstellen*, which were formed to demobilize the rump of the old army. His comment that his relationship with Reinhardt was based 'on mutual confidence' seems to be closer to the mark than any depiction of heroics against nasty reactionary officers. According to Grzesinski, 'Reinhard's (sic) appearance was not prepossessing, but he was a competent soldier and an upright man.'[39] Much of Reinhardt's influence and certainly his good standing with SPD cabinet members, which was vital in view of his fragile authority within the officer corps, was based on these qualities which appear repeatedly in assessments of his character. Informal and personal political relations were as important, indeed more important to civilian control of the military than the structures put in place.

34. BA-MA, N 86/16, Göhre's article in *Vorwärts*, 19 March 1919.
35. BArch, R 43 1/2293, Noske, Reinhardt to Scheidemann, no date, Berlin, Nr 1302/3.19 KM 2, fo. 8.
36. *Kabinett Scheidemann*, 257.
37. Ibid., 468.
38. Thomas Albrecht, *Für eine wehrhafte Demokratie. Albert Grzesinski und die preussische Politik in der Weimarer Republik*, Bonn, 1999, 99–119, especially, 109–19 does not provide a convincing picture of Grzesinski's efforts to 'democratise' the *Reichswehr*, despite an apparent recognition of the problem of a reactionary army.
39. Albert Grzesinski, *Inside Germany*, translated by Alexander Lipschitz, (New York, 1939) 81–86; the misspelling of Reinhardt's name is a common occurrence, and can lead to confusion with the *Freikorps* leader, Wilhelm Reinhard.

While Grzesinski was left to organise the demobilization of the final remnants of the imperial army and its bureaucracy, Reinhardt was preparing to begin the process of establishing the *Reichswehrministerium*.[40] The first stage had been the centralisation of the states' war ministries. One of the terms of the Versailles treaty was the prohibition of the General Staff, and its successor body, the Supreme Command. The challenge, which Reinhardt faced in the summer of 1919, was the establishment of a ministry, which combined the command functions, traditionally exercised by the General Staff, and the administrative functions, which had been the prerogative of the Ministry of War. For Reinhardt the issue was primarily one of military efficiency, by which he meant the creation of a position that would control both the functions of the military. There were other plans circulating throughout 1919 which challenged Reinhardt's dominant position in military policy. It is notable that these challenges came wholly from within the officer corps and that civilian politicians had little influence in the process. The political constellation represented a framework within which the Ministry would be set up, rather than a direct influence upon its internal structures.

In early February, General Martin von Oldershausen, a Saxon in the Supreme Command, produced a memorandum on the problem of how the General Staff would preserve its independence from the Ministry of War in the future constitution. He feared that the General Staff would be relegated to a department of the Ministry of War, 'a waste of Moltke's and Schlieffen's legacy.'[41] To avoid this outcome Oldershausen suggested that the states should retain their ministries. At Reich-level the army would be represented by a secretary of state, appointed by the President and advised by the General Staff and the head of the Admiralty. However, with the trend towards the centralisation of the German state, Oldershausen's plan had little chance. Its significance was its position as the first of many plans formulated by the Supreme Command, which aimed at preserving the independence of the General Staff from the Ministry of War.[42]

Groener, an exponent of the unitary state, fired the next series of shots across the bows of the Ministry of War. On 22 March at a meeting of senior Supreme Command officers on the deteriorating domestic situation, he presented his view of the structures of a future army ministry.[43] In contrast to Oldershausen, Groener accepted the principle of a united army, but beyond that there were clear differences between the Supreme

---

40. Hans Meier-Welcker, 'Die Stellung des Chefs der Heeresleitung in den Anfängen der Republik. Zur Entstehungsgeschichte des Reichswehrministeriums', *VfZ*, 4, 1956, 145–60.
41. Cited in Schmädeke, *Kommandogewalt*, 62–63.
42. Ibid., 62–65.
43. BA-MA, N 247/78, Abschrift of Groener's talk at the Supreme Command Headquarters, 22 March 1919.

Command's and Ministry of War's plans for the ministry. Groener was in favour of a Reich minister who would have a small staff, with most of the ministry's work (*Facharbeit*) being carried out by subordinate offices, whilst Reinhardt wanted the minister to have a larger staff, comparable to the Central Department in the Ministry of War.[44] A small staff would have reduced the minister's control of the day-to-day affairs of the ministry, but it also might have had the beneficial effect of preventing work overload and allowing the minister to concentrate on the general principles of military policy. Yet Groener's primary consideration was the preservation of the Supreme Command's position in military affairs. To achieve this he proposed not only that the control of the minister over *Facharbeit* would be reduced, but also that the General Staff would be in charge of 'education, leadership, and personnel preparation for war', and a *Reichskriegsamt* would be in charge of the material and technical preparations for war.[45] The Ministry of War argued 'that material and personnel preparation for war should not be separated.'[46] The basis for the Ministry's opposition to the division of labour proposed by Groener was Reinhardt's analysis of the flaws of the *Kaiserreich*'s system with its uncoordinated military bureaucracies. Efficiency was the key criterion for both the Supreme Command and the Ministry of War. Yet like so many other concepts, a definition of military efficiency was elusive, so that both groups tended to see their own power base as having special virtues.

At the meeting with liaison officers on 31 March Reinhardt compared the rights and duties of the *Reichswehrminister* and the President to those of the *Kaiser*.[47] Yet Reinhardt's comments had little reference to the refinements of a constitutional system that would guarantee the primacy of the civilian over the military. The fundamental principle, which guided his policy on the chain of command, was military efficiency. It was an axiom of German military thought that a clear chain of command was necessary for decisive action in war. Reinhardt believed that the form of the state, as either a monarchy or a republic, could not necessarily guarantee 'the more effective executive', but he argued that parliamentary democracies could avoid 'multiheadedness' (polycracy) in wartime by establishing a clear chain of command in times of peace.[48] Reinhardt accepted the form of the state, and then tried to fit the army into its constitutional structures in the most efficient manner.

Discussions on the structures of the *Reichswehrministerium* were put on hold until after the signature of the treaty of Versailles. The treaty of Versailles had prohibited the existence of the General Staff, and although

44. Ibid.
45. Ibid.
46. Ibid.
47. BA-MA, N 86/16, memorandum of meeting of Reinhardt with liaison officers on 31 March 1919.
48. *Wehrkraft und Wehrwille*, 85–86.

this clause was difficult to implement, because of the nature of planning and command in an army, it allowed Reinhardt to move against the Supreme Command. Reinhardt also used anger within the officer corps at Groener to diminish the Supreme Command. Reinhardt noted that senior officers, including General Walther von Lüttwitz, commander of *Reichswehr* Group I, and General Oskar von Watter, entertained a dim view of Groener.[49] Reinhardt was able to profit from his opposition to Versailles and pose as the defender of German honour.

On 3 July Reinhardt replaced the Supreme Command by the *Kommandostelle Kolberg* which would be responsible 'for the unitary implementation of border defence in the east, including changes on the basis of the peace treaty, evacuation of the Baltic and the welfare of the troops in the east.'[50] The Supreme Command still had considerable powers but it was now directly subordinate to the *Reichswehrministerium* and the Ministry of War. Groener was aware of the terms of the decree before its publication, and telephoned Reinhardt on the evening of 29 June. He accused Reinhardt of insulting him, and demanded the restoration of the 'unrestricted *Befehlsgewalt*'.[51] Reinhardt tried to assuage Groener's feelings. 'From the telephone conversation', he wrote, 'I gathered from your anger, which Your Excellency also underlined, that Your Excellency sees me as a personal opponent, something that I have felt with sadness for some time.'[52] Reinhardt appeared to believe that Versailles was the only issue which separated the two leading Württemberg officers. Their differences were deeper, touching on issues such as the rôle of General Staff officers in the *Reichswehr* and the form of the army ministry. Groener also harboured a distrust of Reinhardt, who, he believed, had sold his soul to the new regime in order to remain in high office. Finally Groener's and Reinhardt's paths went back to their youth in the Württemberg army and rumours that Reinhardt was a closet 'leftie'.[53] Ultimately there was little that Groener could do. He was isolated in the officer corps after he supported the acceptance of Versailles, and Reinhardt had chosen this moment to implement a reform of the chain of command. By rationalizing the command structures, Reinhardt was preparing for the formation of the *Reichswehrministerium*, and the fusion of the command and administrative functions of the army. The dissolution of the Supreme Command seemed to remove a major obstacle to Reinhardt's plans.[54] So while Groener had held meetings on the future of the German army, he had not realised that the centre of military policy

49. Ernst, 'Aus dem Nachlaß', 84.
50. *Armeeverordnungsblatt*, nr 63, 1919; HStASt, M 660/034, Bü 18, Entwurf der Auflösung der OHL, 2 July 1919.
51. Ernst, 'Aus dem Nachlaß', 85.
52. Ibid., 85–86.
53. See Chapter 2.
54. Ernst, 'Aus dem Nachlaß', 84–85.

making was not the Supreme Command headquarters, but Berlin where Reinhardt was the dominant officer. Groener's ambitions had been destroyed by his honest appraisal of Germany's situation in June. Although he did not resign immediately it was clear he would be unacceptable as a senior commander to many officers.

However a new challenge to Reinhardt's influence on military policy was emerging in the form of General Hans von Seeckt. He had also touted plans for the new army, and in February had sent a plan to both Reinhardt and Groener.[55] Seeckt had two positions of influence. First, he was the new head of the General Staff which was still home to many of the senior officers. The General Staff had a powerful corporate identity within the officer corps. Since the cabinet was leaving the formulation of military policy to the officers this gave Seeckt a stable base from which to challenge Reinhardt. Reinhardt may have been unaware of the challenge, or else he may have been trying to enlist Seeckt's aid, because in his draft of the decree that dissolved the Supreme Command he provided for Seeckt's appointment.[56] Certainly up to July there had been no visible indication of antagonism between Reinhardt and Seeckt. They had exchanged views on the formation of the *Reichswehr* and had been equally frustrated at the lack of consultation about military matters in the weeks before the signature of Versailles. However Seeckt and Groener had worked together in the first half of 1919 on border defence. Groener had also urged Seeckt to draft plans for the *Reichswehr*. If Reinhardt was trying to co-opt Seeckt to his project, it was a risky move which backfired.

From the outset Seeckt sought to build up an independent base within the future ministry. His decree of 6 July became a myth which undoubtedly consolidated his already burgeoning reputation within the officer corps: 'The form changes. The spirit remains the same, it is the spirit of silent, selfless fulfilment of duty in the service of the army. General Staff officers have no name.'[57] Even before this decree, Stülpnagel, alienated by Groener's acceptance of Versailles, had urged Seeckt to remain in the army in order to 'give the wretched shape of the new army a monarchically minded officer corps of the old type.'[58] He had restored a reference point which had been missing in the lives of many officers. Reinhardt had clearly failed to stamp such authority on the officers beyond his immediate circle of colleagues. The debate over the number of General Staff and front officers in the army that would take place in August 1919 was principally about political influence within the officer corps and the new ministry than about social justice or the relative merits of both types of

55. BA-MA, N 247/77, plan for the future army, 17 February 1919; Hans Meier-Welcker, *Seeckt*, Frankfurt, 1967, 203–206; since the *Reichswehr* committee dominated this area, Seeckt's plan was never implemented, or even fully considered by the Ministry of War.
56. HStASt M 660/034, Bü 18, Draft of decree, 2 July 1919.
57. BA-MA N 247/81, Aufruf an die Generalstabsoffiziere, 6 July 1919.
58. BA-MA N 247/80, Stülpnagel to Seeckt, 28 June 1919, fo. 2.

officer.[59] Where Seeckt used the General Staff as a base, Reinhardt sought to shore up his position by posing as the defender of the interests of front *and* General Staff officers.

The second position of Seeckt's influence was as chairman of the newly created committee on the organisation of the *Reichswehrministerium*, which should not be confused with the Preliminary Commission for the Organisation of the Peacetime Army. This committee was subordinate to Reinhardt as the Minister of War.[60] But in practice the committee was dominated by Seeckt's views on the internal structures of the ministry. He was appointed chairman on 5 July. The proximity of his appointment to these posts and the dissolution of the Supreme Command may be related. If Groener had lost the support of the officer corps, Reinhardt had not been the beneficiary. One historian argues that Seeckt was appointed because few general staff officers trusted Reinhardt to reorganise the army.[61] Seeckt's appointment was a blow for Reinhardt, not only because he had apparently lost control of the planning for the future ministry, but also because Seeckt had managed to exploit his support in the officer corps to be appointed by Noske and Ebert, on whom Reinhardt's influence depended. Now that the focus of the generals had turned away from the Supreme Command headquarters and towards Berlin Reinhardt's influence was threatened.

On 5 July there was an important meeting on the organisation of the *Reichswehrministerium*. Seeckt promised that at the next meeting of the committee he would present a plan, based on the 'collegiate system'.[62] On 9 July he drafted a memorandum on the structures for the *Reichswehrministerium*.[63] Seeckt accepted that the *Reichswehrminister* would be 'the actual personal head in all questions of command and administration.' He would be responsible to parliament and a member of the cabinet. Under the minister would be a *Heeresamt*, which would be made up of five officers, each head of a particular department within the ministry, and two secretaries, one for political matters, the other for military. Effectively the *Heeresamt* diminished ministerial control over the army. It appears as though an army council, composed of members of the *Heeresamt* and representatives of the states, was also to be represented in parliament and the cabinet by the political secretary, an idea which undermined the assumption that a minister should be responsible for the activities of his department. Another key element in Seeckt's plan was

59. Meier-Welcker, 'Die Stellung des Chefs der Heeresleitung', 153–54.
60. BKA, M Kr 14533, *Reichswehrministerium* to Bavarian Minister of War, 5 July 1919.
61. Meier-Welcker, *Seeckt*, 233–34; a report from the Württemberg military plenipotentiary in Berlin, Renner, claims the date of the appointment was 3 July, HStASt, E 130b, Bü 3728, Renner to the Württemberg Ministry of War, 3 July 1919.
62. GLAK, Abt. 233/12308, Baden military plenipotentiary to the *Staatenausschuß* to the Ministry of Military Affairs, 5 July 1919.
63. BA-MA, N 247/82, Gliederungsvorschläge für das Reichswehrministerium, 9 July 1919.

the establishment of a *Truppenamt* as a successor to the General Staff. Since Seeckt was head of the General Staff he would be in line for an appointment as head of the *Truppenamt*. The *Truppenamt* would be the principal of the five offices composing the *Heeresamt*. Once a week the *Heeresamt* would meet in the presence of either the head of the *Truppenamt* or the *Reichswehrminister*. Members of the *Heeresamt* could only meet the minister with the prior permission and in the presence of the head of the *Truppenamt* (see the diagram on the following page).[64]

Groener was now supporting Seeckt's plan[65] to the hilt. In a lecture to officers at Kolberg he expressed his hope that Seeckt would find ways to preserve the General Staff:

> The main thing which we must achieve is that the newly formed *Reichswehrministerium* completely carries the stamp of the General Staff; that the main departments of the General Staff are carried into the RWM; that on the other hand the Ministry of War will purely have the character of an administrative bureaucracy in the future…The departments of the Ministry of War will offer significant resistance to such a resolution.[66]

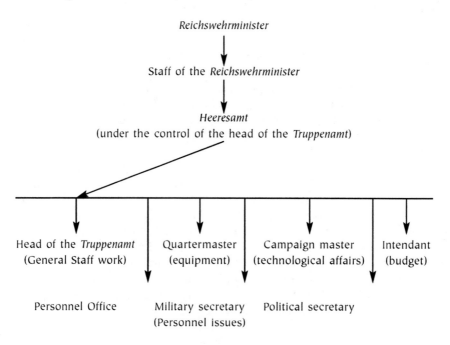

Figure 6.1 Seeckt's plan for the *Reichswehrministerium*

64. Ibid.
65. BA-MA, N 247/82, Gliederungsvorschläge für das Reichswehrministerium, July 1919; see the diagram on the following page.
66. BA-MA N 42/12, Groener, Die Frage der Erhaltung des Generalstabes, Besprechung, 12 July 1919, fo. 148.

Groener, whose ambitions seemed thwarted, consistently supported Seeckt. They were united by a common view of the virtues of the General Staff and a lack of respect for Reinhardt.

On 19 July Reinhardt and Noske issued further instructions to the committee. These offered two models: 'The general who deals with the education and training of troops is the superior of the leading generals or at least to have a position of pre-eminence, or else there will be one leading general over all areas of work.'[67] The first model would have secured the dominance of the general in charge of the General Staff, in other words Seeckt, over military policy. It was also similar to the plan which Seeckt had presented on 9 July. The second model was closer to Reinhardt's conception of an integrated administrative and command structure. It is not clear why Reinhardt, who was nominally the superior of the commission, did not take this opportunity to pursue his policy more aggressively. By offering alternatives he left the choice open to Seeckt. And there was little doubt what that choice would be. Seeckt presented the plan at a meeting of this committee on 21 July. The plan seemed to have been modified at this stage, possibly as a result of the complexities of the memorandum of 9 July. There was no mention of political secretaries, only a first secretary who would be an adviser to the *Reichswehrminister*. The head of the *Truppenamt* would still be effectively in charge of the *Heeresamt*. The proposals won the backing of the members of the committee, and the Württemberg envoy commented that 'the suggestion of General von Seeckt was nothing new; it has already been made in a similar form by General Gröner'.[68] Both Seeckt's draft memorandum and the plan presented on 21 July aimed to establish the *Truppenamt*, the successor to the General Staff, as the primary military office in the *Reichswehrministerium*. Seeckt's plans were effectively a continuation of Groener's, which had been first aired at the meeting of Supreme Command officers on 23 March, a meeting Seeckt attended. Now that the Supreme Command had an officer in a key position in Berlin, it was able to have a more direct influence on policy formulation.

The Bavarian representative, Kreß von Kressenstein, aired a counter-proposal at the meeting on 21 July which resembled the future structures of the *Reichswehrministerium* almost exactly: 'The Army Minister will be assigned a general as under-secretary of state for the army and an admiral for the marine. Apart from that the Minister will have at his disposal a personal staff, a central office and a press office.'[69] Although the relationship between Kressenstein and Reinhardt is not clear, it would

---

67. GLAK, Abt. 233/12308, 'Bildung des Reichswehrministeriums', 19 July 1919.
68. HStASt, M 10, Bd 6, Württemberg envoy's report on meeting of the *Vorkommission*, 22 July 1919.
69. HStASt M 660/046, Heft 28, minutes of meeting on 21 July 1919, taken by Waenker, the Baden military envoy to the Reich, fo. 94.

be too much of a coincidence for Kressenstein to have arrived at this plan independently.

It required a chance occurrence for the Kressenstein version to get approval. A week before the meeting of the committee Seeckt had fallen ill. For the next few months Seeckt was mostly confined to bed, and his views were represented by Colonel Otto Hasse and General Major von Berendt.[70] It appears as if the meeting on 21 July was one of his last public appearances, and his absence from the centre of policy-making meant yet another shift in the balance of power between the Ministry of War and the General Staff, between Reinhardt on the one hand, and Seeckt and Groener on the other. On 4 August Seeckt wrote to Noske and Reinhardt from his sickbed.[71] He criticised the instructions, which they had given to the committee on the formation of the *Reichswehrministerium*.[72] These instructions had apparently demanded a ministry which would be 'immediately functioning – therefore not a completely new creation with untried working methods', which could have meant that the Ministry of War would be simply transformed into the *Reichswehrministerium*, and that the general staff would be subordinate to the ministry. Reinhardt had already caused a stir when he told the Württemberg military envoy, Renner, in June that 'the Prussian Ministry of War should become the *Reichswehrministerium*'.[73] The evidence is circumstantial, but does indicate that Reinhardt exploited Seeckt's absence to extol the virtues of the Ministry of War, as Groener had feared in July.

On 15 August the Baden envoy was able to send the recommendations of the committee back to his government in Karlsruhe.[74] The *Reichswehrminister* was to exercise the *Kommandogewalt* with the President. Each major order would need their two signatures. Within the *Reichswehrministerium* there were a *Chef der Heeresleitung* and a head of the Admiralty, under whom there were a number of offices dealing with welfare, personnel, planning, and equipment. According to the report:

> the *Chef der Heeresleitung* and the head of the Admiralty represent the minister in the exercise of the *Kommandogewalt*…They head the offices and ensure their co-operation. They have no political responsibility. The heads of the offices have the right to represent their different opinions in the presence of their superior. The representative of the *Chef der Heeresleitung* is the head of the *Truppenamt* – in the case of the Admiralty, the general *Marineamt*.[75]

70. BA-MA, N 247/87, letter from Oberstleutnant Hasse, 19 July 1919; Meier-Welcker, *Seeckt*, 237.
71. BA-MA, N 247/87, Seeckt to Noske, Reinhardt, 4 August 1919.
72. These instructions could not be located, but they cannot have been the ones issued on 19 July.
73. HStASt, M 10/3, Renner to Württemberg Ministry of War, 16 June 1919.
74. GLAK, Abt. 233/12308, Bericht der Kommission zum Aufbau der künftigen Reichswehrministerium, enclosed in the report by the Baden envoy to the Baden cabinet, 15 August 1919.
75. Ibid.

The *Reichswehrminister* also had a staff of five adjutants to advise him on military policy. A *Heereskammer* would also be formed from the heads of the offices in the ministry and some retired generals to advise the minister on promotions. The increased importance of the public image of the army was indicated by the creation of a *Presseamt*. The *Truppenamt* was put in control of officer education and troop leadership, such as exercises and manoeuvres, while the *Waffenamt* was in charge of weapon procurement.[76]

Despite the absence of precise details on Reinhardt's role in drafting the organisation of the *Reichswehrministerium*, it is clear that he had the decisive influence. Seeckt mentioned a set of instructions sent by both Reinhardt and Noske to the committee that may have influenced Kressenstein. In a lecture on military leadership he said 'I created the position of the *Chef der Heeresleitung* on the basis of deep convictions formed in war and peace, and General von Seeckt, who along with General Gröner opposed the post, confirmed my thought by his record in this position.'[77] The position of the *Chef der Heeresleitung* was a key difference between the plan of the committee and that of Seeckt on 21 July. The *Chef der Heeresleitung*, unlike Seeckt's head of the *Truppenamt*, was unburdened by any particular planning duties. The position was designed to allow for the maximum co-ordination of military affairs, be they welfare, weaponry or strategic. Since the *Chef der Heeresleitung* also exercised, and therefore would presumably advise the minister and the President on the *Kommandogewalt*, he combined the administrative and the command functions in one person, a combination which Reinhardt believed would be more efficient than the separation of these duties, as had been the case in the *Kaiserreich*.

The suggestions of the committee were adopted (see the diagram on the following page). By order of President Ebert on 20 August 1919 the *Reichswehrministerium* was due to take over from the states' ministries on 1 October 1919.[78] There is no evidence of opposition from within the cabinet. This absence reinforces the argument that the civilian government had no alternatives to the officers' proposals. Despite the evidence by the summer of 1919 of increasing dissent within the military Noske and Ebert failed to tighten controls over the military. On the other hand, given the evolution of political control since the decrees of 19 January, this would have been a difficult policy change to execute. Within the *Reichswehrministerium* there were seven offices.[79] The *Chef der Heeresleitung* was the interface between the army and the *Reichswehrminister*. This dual

76. Ibid.
77. *Wehrkraft und Wehrwille*, 51.
78. Dokumente, ed., Huber, 171.
79. The composition of the *Reichswehrministerium* was published in the *Heeresverordnungs-blatt*, nr 29, 1919.

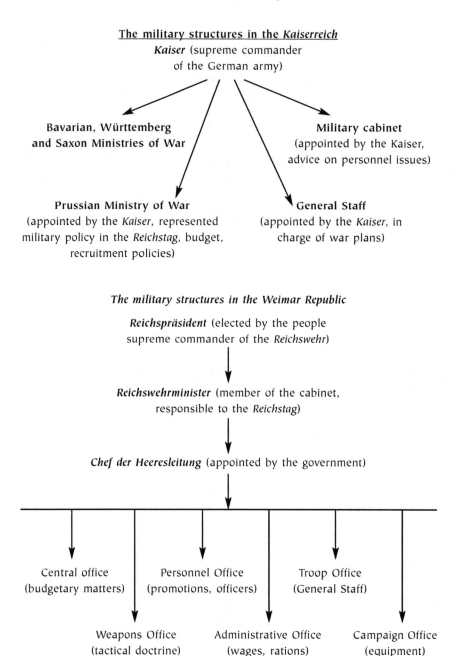

The military structures in the *Kaiserreich*

Kaiser (supreme commander
of the German army)

**Bavarian, Württemberg
and Saxon Ministries of War**

Military cabinet
(appointed by the Kaiser,
advice on personnel issues)

Prussian Ministry of War
(appointed by the *Kaiser*, represented
military policy in the *Reichstag*, budget,
recruitment policies)

General Staff
(appointed by the *Kaiser*, in
charge of war plans)

The military structures in the Weimar Republic

Reichspräsident (elected by the people
supreme commander of the *Reichswehr*)

Reichswehrminister (member of the cabinet,
responsible to the *Reichstag*)

Chef der Heeresleitung (appointed by the government)

Central office
(budgetary matters)

Personnel Office
(promotions, officers)

Troop Office
(General Staff)

Weapons Office
(tactical doctrine)

Administrative Office
(wages, rations)

Campaign Office
(equipment)

Figure 6.2 A comparison of military organisation in the *Kaiserreich* and the Weimar Republic

role of advising the minister and commanding the army was extremely powerful. The threads of military policy ran through the hands of the *Chef der Heeresleitung* and he could potentially obstruct as well as promote co-operation with the civilian authorities. The army would be tied into the constitutional and political framework through the *Reichswehrminister* who would be a cabinet member and the elected President. Yet ultimately the ties would be fastened or loosened by personal relationships. Where Seeckt wanted to shield the army from civilian eyes, Reinhardt believed a more open relationship would facilitate German military planning. Equally important was that Seeckt's position was based on his relations with officers, while Reinhardt was reliant on his good relations with the civilian government.

These opposing positions were crystallised at a meeting in July 1919 between Noske, Reinhardt and Seeckt in Weimar. Gustav Böhm, Reinhardt's adjutant and also present at the meeting, noted that Seeckt wanted to prevent parliamentary criticism of the army:

> As Noske said laughingly to him during the course of a conversation: 'So if I have understood you properly, you want to avoid parliamentary dirty work, and I should become your parliamentary punch bag', General von Seeckt answered, without changing the expression on his face, 'Yes'. He wants to keep the trust of the troops at all costs. The experiences of the Minister of War Reinhardt show how quickly one can lose that trust through parliamentary activity. However perhaps General von Seeckt was a bit too open. In any case it is not him, but Colonel Reinhardt who was appointed as head of the *Heeresamt*.[80]

Yet the position of *Chef der Heeresleitung* was so strong that it could be used to blunt parliamentary control of the army. Ultimately structures, although they might help, could not guarantee parliamentary control of the army. The personal relationship between the minister and the *Chef der Heeresleitung* was a fundamental aspect of the subordination of the military to the civilian government.

Noske and Reinhardt had established a good working relationship since January 1919, when both were appointed to the cabinet. Noske later described his meetings with Reinhardt: 'Often Reinhardt and I talked for hours whether such or such a measure would be possible, or whether its implementation could lead to great calamities. The result of such discussions was often a compromise, on which we were forced to agree. Reinhardt's honourable character meant that there was never any suspicion

---

80. *Adjutant im Preußischen Kriegsministerium Juni 1918 bis Oktober 1919. Aufzeichnungen des Hauptmanns Gustav Böhm*, eds Heinz Hürten, Georg Meyer, Stuttgart, 1977, 154–55. The entry in the diary was on 15 October, but the report seems accurate; it is also unclear whether Böhm is referring to Reinhardt's appointment as *Chef der Heeresleitung* and misnaming the post, or indicating that even under Seeckt's July plan, Reinhardt would still get the highest military post in the ministry.

of bad faith or lack of judgement.'[81] Fleck also noted the importance of trust in the working relationship between Reinhardt and the civilian authorities: 'Reinhardt's great service (to the republic) was, for the most part, that his loyalty prevented the Council of People's Commissars and the first Reich President from taking a radical course. He enjoyed such blind trust, and was so honourable in his advice that his every word was believed, and partly due to his personal will, the right path was taken.'[82] On the other hand he did not enjoy sufficient authority within the officer corps. As Fleck kindly put it: 'One must remember how difficult it was for the younger Reinhardt [inferior in rank] to impose himself on the older generals.'[83]

Indeed the day after Ebert had announced the creation of the *Reichswehrministerium*, on 21 August, Groener met Reinhardt, Hermann Müller, the Foreign Minister and Noske in Weimar to discuss the situation in the Baltic. After Reinhardt left the room, Groener questioned Noske about the position of *Chef der Heeresleitung*: 'In this question there is nothing more to be achieved. Reinhardt should just stay until next spring, then Seeckt can take his place.'[84] However Groener had not received any guarantee that Reinhardt was merely a stop-gap. Indeed it hardly seemed logical to leave Reinhardt in such a powerful position during the period when a new *Reichswehr* law had to be drafted to replace the temporary law of March 1919. As it turned Reinhardt was forced out in the spring, but Groener could not possibly have foreseen the development of events. His view of the *Reichswehrministerium* was a complete misreading of the rationale behind the post of *Chef der Heeresleitung*:

> The newly planned organisation of the *Reichswehrministerium* is too awkward and not logically constructed. Organisation, education and the use of troops are organically part of the duties of the *Truppenamt*. The *Waffenamt* should take over the technical tasks. The suggestion of the Minister of War makes work more difficult and means nothing other than the continuation of the divisions which have already existed for years between the Ministry of War and the General Staff.[85]

The protocol also mentioned a new line of attack against Reinhardt by urging the retention of members of the General Staff. Clearly, the establishment of the ministry had not ended the rivalry among the senior officers, but merely redirected it.

---

81. Gustav Noske, *Erlebtes aus Aufstieg und Niedergang einer Demokratie*, Offenbach am Main, 1947, 179.
82. Ernst, 'Aus dem Nachlaß', 94–95.
83. Ernst, 'Aus dem Nachlaß', 94.
84. BA-MA N 42/12, Protokoll über die Dienstreise des Generalleutnant Groener, 19–24 August 1919, fo. 194.
85. Ibid., fo. 194.

Seeckt, having been outmanoeuvred on the committee, now tried to strengthen his position by accommodating as many General Staff officers as possible within the *Reichswehrministerium*. His support of General Staff officers was not just a far-sighted judgement on their value in developing the *Reichswehr*, but it was also an effort to shore up his own prestige within the *Reichswehrministerium*. It is no accident that the attacks on the Personnel Office's and Reinhardt's policy on the retention of officers began at a stage when Seeckt had been outmanoeuvred on the establishment of the *Reichswehrministerium*. Certainly there were valid arguments in favour of the retention of General Staff officers.[86] Fears about the composition of the officer corps in the *Reichswehr* surfaced as early as March 1919 after a poorly worded circular from the Prussian Ministry of War, urging officers to consider the possibility of moving into civilian life.[87] On the other hand, little separated Reinhardt and Seeckt in their views of the merits of General Staff officers – personal interest was far more of a barrier to understanding on this issue.

Groener had already prepared the path by writing to Noske, a letter about which Seeckt knew. Groener urged Noske to retain as many General Staff officers as possible, but complained that he encountered the 'resistance of the Personnel Office [of the Ministry of War].' He stressed the moral debt owed to General Staff officers without whom Germany would have succumbed to Bolshevism, and he even went so far as to redefine the General Staff officer 'as the best front officer.'[88] Seeckt parroted exactly the same arguments to Noske on 30 August.[89] The previous day he had written to Reinhardt. Rejecting claims that the General Staff was unpopular, as socialist propaganda that the Personnel Office had adopted, and pointing to the Allied fear of the General Staff, Seeckt argued that the General Staff should have precedence over other groups in getting places in the new army.[90]

However the unpopularity of the General Staff, associated with the worst excesses of Wilhelmine militarism, was a problem. If they had once been demi-gods, the front officers were now the popular heroes. The difference between the front and General Staff officer, which Reinhardt as well as Seeckt denied, was an important division within the *Reichswehr*, and was played out in cultural representations of the heroic front officer and the leaden, bureaucratic desk general. Reinhardt, himself a General Staff officer, may have felt uncomfortable about Seeckt's demands. He assured Seeckt he shared his views and that the senior officers should think along the same lines about the 'maintenance of the roots of our

86. Corum, *The Roots of* Blitzkrieg. *Hans von Seeckt and German Military Reform*, Kansas, 1992, 34–35.
87. Ernst, 'Aus dem Nachlaß', 63.
88. BA-MA N 247/67, Groener to Noske, Kolberg, 24 August 1919, fos. 14–16.
89. BA-MA N 247/67 Seeckt to Noske, 30 August 1919, fo. 18.
90. Ernst, 'Aus dem Nachlaß', 91.

power.' Reinhardt considered that he had spent the war on the frontline. The idea of the front officer was a relative concept, particularly in this debate. Both Reinhardt and Seeckt tended to blur the clear institutional distinction between the General Staff and the ordinary army officer. Bearing this in mind, there are a number of reasons why Reinhardt, a general staff officer, supported the front officers and wounded. First, Reinhardt believed that society owed a debt to those who had risked their lives to defend the Fatherland whether those men remained in the army or not.[91] Second, Reinhardt seems to have admired the tales of heroism of people such as Walter Flex and the campaign waged by Paul Lettow-Vorbeck in Africa, whom he called the 'bravest of the brave'.[92] Third, Reinhardt's brother, Ernst, had lost an arm during the war, but was still an active officer, inspecting and training troops. His brother's experience may have been an example that a badly wounded man could still fulfil his soldierly duties.[93] Finally, Reinhardt hoped that by supporting the claims of the front officers he would build up a basis of loyalty within the army. Moreover it should be noted that Reinhardt's position was qualified by his acknowledgement that for a front officer to be preferred he would have to be as equally capable as his general staff counterpart. Certain posts were more suitable for general staff officers than for front officers and vice-versa.

Nonetheless the Supreme Command objected to what they saw as the policy of preferential treatment for front officers. On 23 March the Supreme Command wrote to Reinhardt to complain at the exodus of officers prompted by the letter of 7 March.[94] From July onwards Seeckt saw the General Staff as his power-base. At the end of August Seeckt wrote to Reinhardt, arguing that general staff officers should be retained in the *Reichswehr* in view of their service to the state during and after the war, and because they would bequeath the spirit of the imperial army to the *Reichswehr*.[95]

Reinhardt sent Seeckt's letter onto General von Braun, head of the Personnel Office and mentioned that he agreed with Seeckt's views on the performance of the General Staff.[96] Braun replied, arguing that he saw no fundamental difference between general staff and front officers. However general staff officers could not expect automatic entry to the *Reichswehr*,

---

91. *Verhandlungen der verfassungsgebenden Deutschen Nationalversammlung*, vol. 328, Berlin, 1920, 1728-729.
92. *Wehrkraft und Wehrwille*, 75; *Deutsche Allgemeine Zeitung*, 'Die Heimkehr der Kolonial-helden', 3 June 1919, 'Tapfersten der Tapferen'.
93. Wilhlem Kohlhaas, *Chronik der Stadt Stuttgart, 1918-1933*, Stuttgart, 1964, 14, 30-31; HStASt, M 77/1, Bü 85, memo on Württemberg *Ausbildungskommission*, of which Ernst Reinhardt was a member.
94. BA-MA, N 86/16, Supreme Command to Reinhardt, 23 March 1919.
95. BA-MA, N 247/84, Seeckt to Reinhardt, 29 August 1919.
96. Ernst, 'Aus dem Nachlaß', 91.

and it was necessary to consider 'the morale of further military circles, particularly those front officers, proved in war and revolution, who come to me daily with their worries.'[97] The main difficulty of assessing the outcome of this debate is the ambiguous difference between the front and the general staff officer. It was probably the case that while general staff officers dominated the *Reichswehrministerium*, and higher command positions, the front officers found a niche lower down the chain of command, commensurate with their experience of combat, as opposed to planning, in the First World War.[98] Seeckt had said as much at a meeting on 5 July on the future of the army: 'The personnel should be chosen from all groups of officers, the general staff, as well as the officers in the Ministry of War and front officers; from the last group people should be chosen who have fought the whole war, in order to retain their experience. From the best only the very best can be chosen; only the élite can join the new ministry.'[99] As in other instances the discourse of the debate centred on efficiency; as ever, the definition of efficiency was relative, determined by personal political interest.

The head of the Personnel Office was firmer. General von Braun pointed to the performance of front officers and leaders of troop units in the reconstruction of the army. The criteria for the selection of officers, which would hit General Staff officers, 'was not concerned with an alleged "caving in to supposed strands of a misinformed public", but rather with consideration of the justified mood of broad military circles, particularly those front officers, proven in war and revolution, who come to me daily with their worries about the future.'[100] Reinhardt supported this line. Perhaps realising that he had lost the respect of the General Staff officers, he believed that some support for front officers might compensate. This time Seeckt won. General Staff officers were obvious choices for most of the posts within the ministry which meant that Seeckt had powerful backing as head of the *Truppenamt*. By successfully appropriating the legacy of the General Staff Seeckt consolidated his prestige within the officer corps, and this would pay off after the Kapp Putsch when he was effectively chosen as the new *Chef der Heeresleitung* by General Staff officers in the absence of a functioning civilian government.

The efforts to undermine Reinhardt's position continued unabated. On 5 September Groener in a letter of resignation to Ebert, cited Reinhardt as one of the main factors behind his decision:

97. Ibid., 92.
98. The composition of the officer corps during the Weimar era is touched upon in Karl Demeter, *The German Officer Corps in State and Society, 1650–1945*, London, 1965, 47–52; Corum, *The Roots of* Blitzkrieg, 34–39.
99. GLAK, Abt. 233/12308, Baden's military plenipotentiary to the *Staatenausschuß* to Ministerium für militärische Angelegenheiten, 5 July 1919.
100. Ernst, 'Aus dem Nachlaß', 92.

You know very well that I have objections to the planned organisation of the *Reichswehrministerium*. Also, as I told you in my last visit to Weimar, I do not agree with the elevated position of Colonel Reinhardt and his powers. I would have preferred that the leading military figure in the ministry be General von Seeckt, with whom I share a military and personal outlook, and who is particularly able for this post and enjoys the trust of the army to a high degree.[101]

He mentioned that Reinhardt would only be the *Chef der Heeresleitung* until the spring, but that co-operation, even for this short period, was impossible. Such statements were designed to destroy the political support which Reinhardt had received since January from Ebert. He did not try to influence Noske in the same way, a sign of the strength of the Noske-Reinhardt axis. Groener paid close attention to the working relationship of Noske and Reinhardt, and believed that the former's dislike of day-to-day work allowed Reinhardt to dominate military policy making.[102]

Groener told Seeckt of his meetings with Ebert.[103] Seeckt wrote back to Groener, selflessly promising to work in the interests of the army and the General Staff. Seeckt saw the 'main danger in the unlimited insecurity and ignorance, into which the army has fallen due to the behaviour of the Prussian Ministry of War.'[104] The political infighting of the leading generals, Reinhardt, Seeckt and Groener had left a legacy of division in the officer corps that was a burden for the *Reichswehrministerium*. While Reinhardt had established a good working relationship with the civilian authorities, he had been unable to replicate this within the army. His prestige had suffered due to the January decrees and the subsequent struggles with Seeckt and Groener. Colonel Joachim von Stülpnagel, one of Reinhardt's harshest critics over the abolition of badges of rank, wrote to Colonel Wilhelm Heye in October, hoping 'for your co-operation with him (Seeckt) and for a strong leadership in the army, which Reinhardt, with the best will in the world, has not provided, and without which the officer corps will lose the rest of its unity and historical importance for the nation's future.'[105] These honestly expressed views meant that the value of Reinhardt's work remained obscured, a fact acknowledged by officers in the late 1920s and early 1930s. Heye who was close to Seeckt in 1919 later commented that Reinhardt was the 'first architect' of the *Reichswehr*. He also noted that Reinhardt, as well as Seeckt and Hindenburg, was an example 'who made the path easier for us officers.'[106] But in 1919 the doubts of senior officers about Reinhardt's ability made it

101. BA-MA N 42/12, Groener to Ebert, 5 September 1919, Kolberg, fos. 200–201.
102. BA-MA, N 247/88, Groener to Seeckt, 18 September 1919.
103. Ibid.
104. BA-MA, N 247/88, Seeckt to Groener, 24 September 1919.
105. BA-MA, N 5/18, Stülpnagel to Heye, 5 October 1919; Heye was the chief of staff at the *Truppenamt*.
106. BA-MA N 18/4, Lebenserinnerungen des Generaloberst Heye, Teil II, Wie ich den Weltkrieg erlebte, 1914–42, fos. 217, 224.

almost impossible for him to impose the authority on the army which was essential to the post of *Chef der Heeresleitung*.

Before the Kapp Putsch, Seeckt made one final attempt to restructure the ministry. In January 1920 he submitted a memorandum to Noske which proposed a fundamental reorganisation of the *Reichswehrminis-terium*. He argued that the ministry was suffering 'from the close intermeshing of two naturally different concepts: administration and command.'[107] According to his plan, the minister should appoint a general who had the trust of the army to the command position. The motive behind the plan is hard to discern. The minister would still be the commanding general's superior, and so presumably the *Reichstag* could still exercise an influence on the *Kommandogewalt*. Seeckt may well have been trying to outmanoeuvre Reinhardt, whom he had previously accused of introducing too much bureaucracy into the army, and in whose ability to command he had little faith. Seeckt's biographer, Hans Meier-Welcker, rules out political motives, though not personal ambition.[108] His failure to force any changes in the structures of the *Reichswehrministerium* indicates that Noske and Reinhardt were the dominant force within the ministry. Further this effort showed that Groener's belief that Reinhardt would be removed by the spring was erroneous. Had this been true, then it would not have made sense for Seeckt to press for change which would weaken a position into which he was about to step.

However he was able to bring about changes in the functions of the various offices in the ministry. On 8 November Seeckt wrote to Reinhardt to protest at the division of labour between the *Truppenamt* and the *Waffe-namt*. While the former appeared to be in charge of the General Staff and its education, the latter appeared to be in charge of working out training manuals for the cavalry and infantry.[109] Seeckt argued that it was neces-sary to combine tactical and formal education of officers to ensure a cohesive military doctrine. He proposed that the *Truppenamt* would prepare the *Vorschriften* (guidelines of military doctrine), and that both the *Truppenamt* and the *Waffenamt* would co-operate on officer education. Seeckt hoped to turn the *Truppenamt* into the primary office concerned with the development of military doctrine. This would ensure the unity of German military planning at the tactical level. Reinhardt agreed to Seeckt's suggestion. He recommended that the *Truppenamt* prepare the *Vorschriften* on the basis of the experiences in the First World War, whilst also taking account of the changed nature of the army.[110] The *Truppenamt*

---

107. Quoted in Meier-Welcker, 'Stellung des Chefs der Heeresleitung', 155–56.
108. Schmädeke, *Kommandogewalt*, 87–90; Meier-Welcker, 'Stellung des Chefs der Heeresleitung', 157.
109. BA-MA, N 86/16, Seeckt to Reinhardt, 8 November 1919; *Heeresverordnungsblatt*, nr 29, 1919.
110. BA-MA, N 86/16, Reinentwurf by Reinhardt, 12 November 1919.

was the motor of this process and altogether fifty-seven different committees and over five hundred officers would be involved.[111] Reinhardt had
little to do with the committees in the early 1920s, but this exchange of
ideas between Seeckt and Reinhardt was an example of how they could
have worked together with greater effect.

In fact progress was also made on the development of the *Reichswehr*
law, which was due to come into force in March 1920 to replace the
temporary law. On 28 February Noske was able to present a draft law to
the Reich Council.[112] Unfortunately from the remaining sources it is not
possible to tell who drafted the document. Nonetheless, the Weimar
agreement was enshrined in the draft law and many of the regulations of
31 March on service conditions were also included. The internal structure of the ministry with provision for a *Chef der Heeresleitung* and a similar
post for the navy was contained in the law. Although the law could not
be passed in March 1920, due to the Kapp Putsch, it was passed in
remarkably similar form the following year. Since Reinhardt had been the
central figure in negotiating the Weimar agreement, in issuing the regulations of 31 March and forming the internal structures of the
Reichswehrministerium, it is not an overstatement to conclude that the law
and the army it formed bore his stamp. The law had to be introduced in
March 1920 due to the treaty of Versailles and also because it was 'the
basis on which officers and troops would take up their place in the future
Reich army.'[113] However morale amongst officers and troops was plum-
meting by February 1920, and, allied to political discontent among senior
officers, it led to the Kapp Putsch.

The establishment of the *Reichswehrministerium* was based on two
important principles. First, it represented Reinhardt's ideal of a military
organisation, one which combined command and administrative functions. The military structures of the *Kaiserreich* had effectively been
dissolved – there were no longer any states' ministries nor an independent General Staff. Military policy-making was carried out by one cohesive
institution and there was no separate *Wehrverfassung* (military constitution) in the Weimar Republic, as had existed in the *Kaiserreich*. Second,
civilian control over the army was facilitated by the good relationship
between Reinhardt and the government – this was more important than
institutional and constitutional regulations. The significance of Reinhardt's appointment as *Chef der Heeresleitung* was his willingness to work
with the civilian government to fashion the most efficient military organisation possible. However Reinhardt as *Chef der Heeresleitung* also
presented a problem, namely his lack of prestige within the army. His
time as *Chef der Heeresleitung* did not last sufficiently long to be able to

111. Corum, *The Roots of* Blitzkrieg, 32–42.
112. BHStA, ML 1807, Entwurf des Reichswehrgesetzes, 28 February 1920.
113. BArch R 43 I/680, Reichswehrministerium, Chef der Heeresleitung to Chancellor Bauer,
12 February 1920, fo. 85.

judge whether he would have recovered from the personal attacks made by Groener, but Seeckt's January plan indicates that he was unwilling to continue working under Reinhardt for any lengthy period of time. The discordant relationship between the two men would have hampered the work of the *Reichswehrministerium*. Finally there was a danger that the power concentrated in the hands of the *Chef der Heeresleitung* could be abused by an officer less dedicated to working with the new regime than Reinhardt. Whereas Reinhardt – in 1919 at any rate – conceived of the post as an interface between the army and the government, Seeckt appeared to think of it as a shield with which he could blunt the interest of the *Reichstag* and public in military affairs. Ironically Seeckt took advantage of Reinhardt's creation for his own ends after his appointment in March 1920.

Chapter 7

THE KAPP PUTSCH AND THE FAILURE OF REINHARDT'S MILITARY POLICY

*T*he Kapp Putsch in March 1920 represents one of the major interruptions in the history of the Weimar republic. The Putsch is seen as a symbol of the weakness of the new regime, a weakness that was confirmed at the polls in June 1920 when the 'Weimar coalition' of the SPD, the Centre Party and the DDP lost their majority in the parliament, a majority which they never recovered during the rest of the period.[1] During the 1920s many of the protagonists wrote about their actions, and tried to justify the course of action adopted in early 1920. For example, Gustav Noske concluded a series of three articles on 2 April 1920, claiming that 'In its core part the army remained loyal and intact. My work was endangered and greatly disturbed by fools and criminals.'[2] However this demonisation of the protagonists in the Putsch is an inadequate portrayal of the problems that faced Reinhardt and Noske in late 1919 and early 1920. If Reinhardt had been appointed in January 1919 for his competence, the Putsch revealed the limits of that competence. Whereas he had managed to remain in position after the Versailles treaty, despite opposing the government's line, on this occasion when he was the sole senior military defender of the Republic, he resigned.

The difference was that the Putsch marked the failure of fifteen months of military policy. This is not to say that Reinhardt did not have any durable achievement. The *Reichswehr* bore his imprint. But the actual establishment of the army, hindered by the terms of Versailles, the pressures of rapid demobilization in an unstable economy and the financial

---

1. Heinz Hürten, *Der Kapp Putsch als Wende. Über Rahmenbedingungen der Weimarer Republik seit dem Frühjahr 1920*, Düsseldorf, 1989; Heinrich August Winkler, *Die Weimarer Republik, 1918-1933. Die Geschichte der ersten deutschen Demokratie*, Munich, 1993, 109-140.
2. BA-Koblenz, N 1046/9, *Vorwärts*, 2 April 1920. Noske's other articles in the same paper were dated 27 and 28 March 1920.

restrictions imposed on military policy, created pressures that culminated in the Kapp Putsch. If Reinhardt had been able to manipulate political and social circumstances to his benefit, or at least overcome some of the limits on military policy, he was increasingly constrained in late 1919. He was not necessarily doomed to fall in March 1920. The occurrence of the Putsch at that stage was largely due to contingent factors. But social disorientation and political disenchantment produced the conditions for the Putsch. The army of March 1920 was very different from the image Reinhardt and Pawelsz had put forward in February 1919. While a case can be made that Reinhardt was right to suggest armed opposition to the Putsch, and that it might have succeeded, it is significant that he could not persuade the officer corps to follow his lead nor the cabinet to order the army to oppose the Putsch. The erosion of morale and Reinhardt's efforts to counter this, as well as the drift from the policy of February 1919, provide the background to the Putsch.[3]

As part of the project to make the army a central element of German life, Reinhardt had called for a *Reichswehr* which included the different elements of society. However idealism gave way to practicality in 1919. Without conscription, joining the army was largely a matter of choice. And the men who had joined the *Freikorps* had already made a choice in favour of a military career. From the point of view of the state, which needed a stable army urgently, it made sense to look towards these groups. On 5 August 1919 the *Reichswehrministerium* issued general instructions to enlist 'the proven units of the *Grenzschutz Ost* [Eastern Border Defence] and proven units within Germany'. These were not to be diluted by other conscripts where possible.[4] By the end of September 1919 Reinhardt stressed that there were few places available in the *Reichswehr* and that preference should be given to the troops due to return from the Baltic.[5] By favouring volunteers from these *Freikorps* groups the *Reichswehr* increased its chances of recruiting a disproportionate number of anti-republican soldiers.

Recruitment did, however, take place. The Saxon *Reichswehr* instructed that the 'choice of the *Vertrauensmann* [who was present at the recruitment centre] is to be guided by whether the applicant supports the present government and is willing to serve in the *Reichswehr* in the interest of order and legality, independent of his political convictions.' The instructions went on to suggest that 'In many cases the chairmen of local party political groups will be able to give good advice on candidates, as well as the leading personalities in bourgeois, trade union and church circles This broad range will give the best information about applicants.

3. On the Kapp Putsch the most authoritative work remains Johannes Erger, *Der Kapp-Lüttwitz Putsch. Ein Beitrag zur deutschen Innenpolitik, 1919–1920*, (Düsseldorf, 1967).
4. BHStA Gesandschaft Berlin 1352, Reichswehrministerium, v. Kessel, 5 August 1919.
5. BA-MA RH 69/64, Abschrift, Reichswehrministerium, Reinhardt, 30 September 1919, fo. 40.

One-sided and biased judgements are to be avoided.'[6] The *Vertrauensleute* were supposed to be the guardians of the soldiers' welfare and also to keep an eye on any anti-republican activity amongst the officer corps, so their use in the recruitment process should, in theory, have led to counter-balance against the *Freikorps* recruits. However a report in October 1919, strangely entitled *Verbot jedweder Werbetätigkeit* (Ban on further recruitment), complained that the work of the *Vertrauensleute* was insufficient. It stressed that each member of the *Reichswehr* had the duty to recruit personally, by word of mouth.[7] This can only have reinforced the tendency to recruit anti-republican soldiers. If the *Reichswehr* recruited continually from the same groups, it would lose contact with broader German society. Reinhardt's vision was being undermined from below.

The reduction of the officer corps was used as an opportunity to purge the ranks of republican officers, although these were a small minority in the first place. The process began at the start of March when the Ministry of War issued a decree to officers which suggested that there would be an extremely limited number of places available in the new army and therefore 'the moment to choose a career' had arrived. As Reinhardt pointed out, disarmament was a certainty and there was also financial pressure to reduce the army. The army could not function as a welfare institution for officers when other groups of soldiers, such as the NCOs and the war wounded, had claims on scarce resources.[8] On 23 March Groener argued that the decree had led to the resignation of the best officers.[9] In fact this was probably far from the truth. Certainly none of the senior officers at General Staff level had resigned, and many officers had gone into volunteer units. However Groener's unwillingness to face the reality of imminent disarmament and the financial limits on military personnel policy was only partly motivated by his dislike of the Ministry of War and Reinhardt. It also signified a much deeper problem within the officer corps, namely its failure to come to terms with defeat and the onset of inflation. These were important restrictions on German military policy. By failing to consider them, the officers unjustly blamed republican politicians for shortcomings in military policy.

On 24 June Reinhardt issued a further proclamation. It reiterated the duty of the officer: 'we must put our personal doubts behind us, because the urgent duty of the hour to the Fatherland demands the maintenance of order and calm and the continuation of service.' The decree also allowed officers to resign with a guarantee that their welfare claims would

6. BA-MA RH 69/64, Organisationsplan (Werbung), Dresden, 18 September 1919, fos. 3–5.
7. BA-MA RH 69/64, Hauptwerbeamt, Dresden, to Reichswehr Brigades 12, 19, 25 October 1919, fo. 98.
8. BA-MA N 86/16, Abschrift, Besprechung mit den Verbindungsoffizieren, 31 March 1919.
9. BA-MA N 46/130, Besprechung, Kolberg, 23 March 1919.

not be affected.[10] Not surprisingly Reinhardt was accused of using the Versailles treaty and the shame paragraphs as a means of putting moral pressure on officers to resign. This would have the benefit of limiting the competition for places within the *Reichswehr* and hence splitting the officer corps.[11] Behind the question of honour and the reduction of the officer corps lay the issue of welfare and personal security.[12] The uncertain future, the dislocation in the personal lives of officers who had foreseen lifelong service to the Kaiser, eroded morale within the officer corps, and created conditions in which plots against the Republic could find sympathy.

While the reduction of the officer corps to the limits imposed by Versailles created social angst, it was a problem which was solved in a political fashion. The fate of the *Republikanischer Führerbund* is emblematic of the purge of the officer corps. Colin Roß, a member of the *Republikanischer Führerbund*, wrote in September 1919 that officers had distorted the character of the *Reichswehr*, 'which originally had been seen as a volunteer people's army', and imbued it 'with the reactionary spirit'.[13] The *Republikanischer Führerbund* pointed out that a loyal republican army needed to be staffed by officers with republican sympathies. The *Republikanischer Führerbund* documented a series of cases, where officers believed to be republican were given unimportant tasks or else forced out of the army.[14] Most officers were opponents of the *Republikanischer Führerbund*, and countered that it was a political organisation. In a speech designed to appease his critics within the SPD, who accused him of leniency towards reactionary officers, Noske said he would not allow groups of the *Republikanischer Führerbund* in the army![15] Opposed by both the civilian and military leadership of the Reich, it stood little chance of creating a republican officer corps. Perhaps a better argument against the claims of the *Republikanischer Führerbund* was that they had no members amongst the more senior officers, the ones whose expertise was needed to establish the *Reichswehr*.[16] Thus the reduction of the officer corps had a negative impact on Reinhardt's policy in two respects. First, it created discontent within the officer corps, something which was largely unavoidable. Second, the absolute failure to retain republican officers, even if they were few in number, meant that the officer corps was less prepared to

10. BA-MA N 86/16, Decree, issued by the Ministry of War, 24 June 1919.
11. BA-MA N 86/16, Decree, no date; it was clearly a response to complaints about the decree of 24 June.
12. BA-MA N 86/16, Bürkner to Reinhardt, Magdeburg, 26 July 1919.
13. Colin Roß, 'Republikanische Offiziere', 3 September 1919, in *Republikanerhetze in der Reichswehr*, ed. Republikanischer Führerbund, Döring, 1919, 31.
14. Ibid, 9–19.
15. *Vorwärts*, 29 September 1919; HStASt, M 365/6, Ernst van den Bergh to the *Republikanischer Führerbund*, 3 December 1919.
16. F. C. L. Carsten, *The Reichswehr and Politics, 1918 to 1933*, Oxford, 1966, 72–74.

make an unequivocal defence of the Republic against any Putsch from the right.

One of the further signs that the *Reichswehr* was a distorted version of the vision put forward in February was the programme of political education which it offered to the rank and file. From the perspective of the *Reichswehrministerium* it was a means of inoculating the troops against the seductions of communism. In May Noske and Reinhardt stressed the importance of the 'material and spiritual welfare' of the troops which had been shaken by defeat and revolution. Officers had to allay the 'disturbed, misled spirit.'[17] In early November Noske ordered:

> It is necessary to give the soldiers support in the political struggle for his soul, and above all to erect a dam against the subversive activities of those hostile to the state. Therefore it is necessary, without losing any time, to continue the civic education of the members of the *Reichswehr* and to create a core of intelligent and educated people who will counter the destructive propaganda amongst their comrades with skilful enlightenment.[18]

He ordered the establishment of schools in each command area. This appears to have built on previous structures which involved twelve-day courses for up to 200 participants.

Yet this laudable attempt to educate soldiers in the principles of the Republic was undermined by the content of the programme. At best it was anti-Bolshevist, but this could easily slip towards the rhetoric of the radical and conservative right. At worst it was the speeches of Adolf Hitler who served on these courses in late 1919 and early 1920.[19] The principle that the civic education courses were supposed to be non-party political was clearly not applicable if the politics of the party were 'right'. Major Prager of the Bavarian *Reichswehr*, who saw the army as a pillar of the state, argued that it was necessary to 'arouse a well-developed sense of responsibility and selflessness on the one hand, and the understanding for basic political ideas and national self-confidence.' While the content should be 'above party', it should also be scientific and *völkisch*.[20]

Social insecurity and ambivalence towards the Republic led to widespread demoralisation amongst the soldiers. At the end of November Stülpnagel, then commander of Infantry Regiment 19, collated the views of officers in his charge. Pay, high tax rates and inflation emerged as the causes of discontent.[21] While he asserted in January 1920 that the

17. *Zwischen Revolution und Kapp Putsch. Militär und Innenpolitik 1918–1920*, ed. Heinz Hürten, Düsseldorf, 1977, 112–13.
18. BKrA RWGrKdo 307, Circular, Noske, 6 November 1919.
19. Ian Kershaw, *Hitler. Hubris* (London, 2000), 153.
20. BKrA RWGrKdo 329, Major von Prager to Reichswehr Brigades 21, 23, 24, Munich, 13 June 1919.
21. BA-MA N 5/19, Stülpnagel, Reichswehr Brigade IR 19 to IR 19, Hannover, 29 November 1919, fo. 12.

situation was improving, he noted that robbery was increasing, which destroyed comradeship and that the attitude of soldiers to Germany was one of indifference: 'The majority are interested in questions of food and money.' He was confident that the troops would support the current government or one further to the right, but any lurch to the left would lead to mutiny. Stülpnagel's claim that the 'socialist dream is ship-wrecked', and that the mass of the people and the troops were ready to follow leaders who would maintain the 'old traditions' in the new era, indicated the fragile support of many within the army for the Republic.[22]

Of course, reports of discontent amongst troops could be exaggerated by commanders for political purposes. Lüttwitz, military leader of the Kapp Putsch, used such reports to try to prevent or delay the reduction of the *Reichswehr*. In a letter to senior military commanders, Noske, Rein-hardt and the chancellor, Gustav Bauer, he argued that the many of the soldiers to be released would fall into the clutches of 'Sparticist' groups. He claimed, 'Amongst the troops unease has taken hold, because the justified question: "When will I be thrown onto the streets?" is in every-one's head. Against this the leaders are powerless. It is clear, and has already been shown, that the inner value of the troops must suffer in such circumstances.'[23] He urged that the reduction of the army to 100,000 men be slowed down until conditions were more stable, both politically and economically. On 25 August Noske replied that the government would make efforts to slow the pace of disarmament.[24] The mixture of self-inter-est, fear of Bolshevism, and genuine regard for the fate of the troops, was present in Lüttwitz's demands.

Not all reports on morale were as negative as those of Lüttwitz and Stülpnagel. Days after the acceptance of the Versailles treaty, Oven, based in Breslau with Army Command South, assured Lüttwitz that the 'mood and behaviour of the troops are impeccable in every way.'[25] Another report from *Reichswehr* Brigade 12, based in Saxony, stated: 'The morale of the troops is definitely good. The troops are aware that the higher ranks and their officers are doing all that is possible to make life with the *Reichswehr* as comfortable as possible.'[26] There was not just one morale within the *Reichswehr*. Yet, even if it was only a significant minority who were disenchanted that would be sufficient to undermine the govern-ment's 'monopoly of legitimate violence'. Clearly many of the rank and file were in a volatile mood by the end of 1919. At the end of October

22. BA-MA N 5/19, Stülpnagel, IR 19, 4 January 1920, fos. 25–28; BA-MA N 280/106, Lagebericht Nr 20, 12 February 1920.
23. *Das Kabinett Bauer. 21. Juni 1919 bis 27. März 1920*, ed., Anton Golecki, Boppard am Rhein, 1980, 141–43.
24. Ibid., 143 (fn. 7).
25. BA-MA N 97/7, Oven to Lüttwitz, Breslau, 26 June 1919, fos. 16–17.
26. BA-MA RH 69/104, Reichswehr Brigade 12 to Wehrkreiskommando IV, 2 December 1919, fo. 67.

Franz Sperr, the Bavarian military envoy to the Reich, reported that morale was low owing to poor wages and uncertainty about the future. However he did not foresee any change 'until the final form of the 100,000 men army is implemented and the economic future of the soldier is secured.'[27] Could Reinhardt survive this transition period?

The Reich Finance Ministry under Matthias Erzberger, or rather the state of the German finances, was a further limitation on military policy in 1919. As Richard Bessel points out, the task of the German government after the war was to distribute poverty, not wealth. The tendency of the Finance Ministry to cut the government's expenditure reinforced the terms of Versailles. This is not to suggest that the army would have been reduced to 100,000 men, Versailles or no Versailles, but the army would have faced significant competition from other sources. The *Reichswehr* employed two general arguments in their attempt to win a bigger slice of the meagre cake. First, Germany owed a moral debt to men who had risked their life in war and during the revolution. The second argument deployed was that it was necessary to maintain as large an army as possible, right up to the date of demobilisation in order to prevent civil unrest. This was linked to the hope that the Allies might adopt a lenient approach, and allow the German army to retain 200,000 men. The irony of these arguments was that the expenditure on the army contributed, albeit in a small way, to the inflationary process after the war.[28] Inflation eroded the moral order of bourgeois Germany and contributed to the outbreak of civil unrest in 1923.

The budgetary demands of the army were made more complex by the uncertain pace of demobilization throughout 1919. Asking for 4,020 million Marks in February 1919, Reinhardt admitted: 'This sum is the result of a rough, indeed very rough, estimate, so that a guarantee for its reliability cannot be accepted. A somewhat more precise assessment of the budget needs will not be possible in the near future due to the extraordinarily difficult circumstances.'[29] By 17 March the amount had changed, to the lower sum of 3,927,822,000 Marks, due to a reassessment of the inflation rate.[30] Uncertainty was a hallmark of the military budget, although to ascribe it to the changing inflation rate would be unfair. Reinhardt also sowed a good deal of confusion about the timetable for demobilization, and he probably hoped that the army would benefit. The Finance Ministry was critical of what it saw as the sharp practice of the military. The sums were based 'on the most arbitrary assumptions'. The finances of the Reich demanded the 'utmost parsimony, which has

27. BKrA RWGrKdo 4, 135, Sperr to the Bavarian Foreign Ministry, 28 October 1919.
28. Bessel, *Germany*, especially chapters 3 and 4 on the demobilization of the army and economy; Gerald Feldmann, *The Great Disorder. Politics, Economics and Society in the German Inflation, 1914–1924*, Oxford, 1993, 188–208.
29. BArch R 2/50157, Reinhardt to the Treasury, 1 February 1919, fo. 83.
30. BArch R 2/50157, Reinhardt, Göhre to the Treasury, 17 March 1919, fo. 97.

been sadly lacking during the war.'[31] In the debate over Versailles the military issue had been relegated to the bottom of the list. Once again the primacy of the military in German politics was at stake. The changed political circumstances offered both opportunities and threats. The *Reichswehr* could always underline the maintenance of civil order, but the Finance Ministry tried to assert the primacy of fiscal rectitude.

Even after the acceptance of Versailles, which detailed the structures and size of the *Reichswehr*, disagreement continued. On 5 August the orders for the reduction of the army to 200,000 men were given, which was the first stage of fulfilling the terms.[32] Officers assumed that this process had to be completed by early March 1920. However now the pace of reduction became an issue. At a meeting of senior officials from both ministries, including Reinhardt, on 19 July the Finance Ministry complained of 'the enormous increase' in the demands of the *Reichswehr*, and demanded that the army be properly established by 1 October 1919. Reinhardt 'doubted that this would be possible. We still are at war and we must send units into domestic action unexpectedly. The revolution is not yet finished. Again and again a purging (*Bereinigung*) occurs. These cannot be predicted.' When the finance officials asked for a breakdown on the numbers of troops, Noske estimated that there were 400,000.[33] In fact there was no consensus about the number of troops in Germany, either within the old Imperial army, or the units destined for the *Reichswehr*. On 18 May 1919 the *Reichswehr* committee announced that the number of armed men in Germany had been reduced from 800,000 on 1 April to 415,000.[34] On 24 June 1919 the Bavarian military envoy to Berlin reported that there were 422,000 soldiers in *Reichswehr* units and 123,000 in old Imperial army units.[35] In November Foch warned the President of the Peace Conference that there were 430,000 armed men in Germany. Just before Christmas Reinhardt admitted that while there had been 300,000 armed men at the beginning of December, the reduction of the army would soon be completed, by 1 April.[36] In other words, demobilization either stalled after Versailles, or else the chaotic situation in Weimar Germany made it impossible to count the number of soldiers.

Relations between the two ministries deteriorated in the second half of 1919. The Finance Ministry tried to reassert the primacy of financial considerations over military ones. On 20 September Erzberger wrote:

31. BArch R 2/50157, Finance Ministry to Prussian Ministry of War, 9 May 1919, fo. 208.
32. HStASt M 1/4, Band 1710, Befehl für die Verminderung des Heeres auf 200.000 Köpfe, 5 August 1919, fo. 1.
33. BArch R 2/50157, Abschrift, Chefbesprechung beim Reichsfinanzministerium, Weimar, 19 July 1919, fo. 270.
34. BHStA Gesandtschaft Berlin 1351, Reichswehrausschuss, 18 May 1919.
35. BHStA Gesandschaft Berlin 1351, Bavarian Military envoy to the Ministry for Military Affairs, Berlin 24 June 1919.
36. MAE Serie Z, Sous-série Allemagne, 57, Foch to the President of the Peace Conference, 27 November 1919, fos. 128–30; Dutasta telegram, Berlin, 19 December 1919, fos. 171–72.

As highly as I hold the officer in his own right, the experiences of the war have shown, that in administrative questions he is too much inclined to allow the financial interest to take a back-seat to the military interest. Earlier that may have been tolerable. In the situation in which we now find ourselves, when military and economic interests are in competition, the financial situation of the Reich must be taken into consideration.[37]

A note by an official in the Reich Finance Ministry complained that the budgetary proposals were 'impenetrable to the Entente, the Reichstag and the finance officials.'[38] When Reinhardt asked for a meeting of senior officials and ministers to resolve the issue he was told that Erzberger was too busy to attend.[39]

The pressure exerted by the Reich Finance Ministry had an impact on the morale of the troops. At a *Chefsbesprechung* on 22 August the Finance Ministry sought to speed up the process of demobilization, and reach the 200,000 troop level as soon as possible. Yet Reinhardt, Noske and Pawelsz were able to get the Finance Ministry to agree to keeping an extra 50,000 'in order to counter domestic unrest.' Further they expressed the hope that the Allies would give their agreement to Germany retaining a 200,000 men army after March 1920. Therefore two budgets would be prepared – one for the 100,000 men army, and one for the 200,000 men army.[40] The unwarranted optimism of Reinhardt, and indeed of Seeckt before the Spa conference in June 1920, that the Allies would leave the *Reichswehr* as a 200,000 men force, only added to the uncertainty of the troops.

The Finance Ministry also tried to cut the wages of the soldiers. It planned to allocate 25 million Marks instead of 75 million for the *Kampfzulage* (fighting bonus). An important part of the income for the ordinary soldier came from the *Kampfzulage*, which amounted to 5 Marks per day. What originally had been a bonus was now an entrenched element of the income structure. Reinhardt warned against planned cuts:

It is clear that a decrease in the income of the soldier would equal a collapse of the *Reichswehr*. The wages of the workers are increasing steadily, while the payments to the soldier remain at the same level as before. When taking into account the costs of food which is now only worth 2.70 Marks per day, and the expenditure on clothes and accommodation, the recompense for the soldier is hardly higher than support for the unemployed.[41]

Since the *Reichswehr* was now dependent on volunteers, it had to compete in a labour market. The restrictions imposed by Versailles led to a stress on the quality of the individual soldier but this would be difficult to

37. BArch R 2/50158, Finance Ministry to Reichswehr Befehlsstelle Preußen, 20 September 1919, fos. 78–79.
38. BArch R 2/50158, note by Finance Ministry, fos. 98–99.
39. BArch R 2/50158, Reinhardt to the Finance Ministry, 20 September 1919, fo. 100.
40. BArch R 2/50158, Chefbesprechung, 22 August 1919, fo. 175.
41. BArch R 2/50158, Reinhardt to Finance Ministry, Berlin 13 October 1919, fos. 215–16.

achieve if decent terms were not offered. Reinhardt refused to take responsibility for the consequences of any reduction, which he believed would lead to

> great unhappiness, mass resignations and a worsening of the value of the *Reichswehr* which would make the influence of the revolutionary parties more attractive. The military administration cannot allow this in the current political climate. If the *Reichswehr* proves itself to be unreliable and falls into the hands of the government's opponents, then the continued existence of the government would be endangered.[42]

Reinhardt's use of vocabulary indicates that he expected that the communists would profit from the demoralization of the army. While Reinhardt cannot escape all responsibility for the teething problems of the *Reichswehr*, the constant pressure from the Finance Ministry made his task even harder.

In the *Reichstag* debate on the budget on 31 October Reinhardt reiterated these points about law and order, arguing that the 'satisfaction of justified desires of the troops' was not a financial sacrifice, but in actual fact a necessary investment. Stability, guaranteed by military power, was a pre-condition for economic revival. He was careful to stress what he saw as the martial values of the German character:

> During the work of the last months and of the whole year I have not been shaken in my belief that respect for the military and a love of the soldier's trade are the inalienable common property of the German national character, and can be found in all circles and parties, even if it is in different forms. I cannot allow it to be the privilege of single groups or individual parties.[43]

On the one hand this was an attempt to shore up the support of the SPD, whose members had become increasingly worried about the direction of the *Reichswehr*. It also reflected Reinhardt's belief that a German revival could only be based on a united national community, which embraced military values. If the military was central to this national revival, then the Finance Ministry would have to pay out.

Reinhardt undermined the Finance Ministry's control of budgetary policy by simply presenting bills for soldiers who were supposed to have been demobilized. As the *Reichswehrministerium* continued to delay in submitting a final proposal for the military budget, Erzberger demanded a draft based on the 100,000 men army, not on unfounded hopes in Allied benevolence. While Reinhardt had conflated the military and general interest in his *Reichstag* speech, Erzberger now argued 'that, while in case of any disagreements between the military and financial interests, it was natural that the commanders would accord the former primacy, this ran

---

42. Ibid., fo. 215.
43. *Verhandlungen der deutschen Nationalversammlung*, vol. 331, Berlin, 1920, 3620–621.

against the common good.'[44] On 22 December Reinhardt replied that the promised reduction in the size of the *Reichswehr* had not been carried out because of Allied demands, the domestic situation and the position on the eastern front. Therefore an army in excess of 200,000 soldiers would have to be retained until the end of March, which would require a supplementary budget. The Finance Ministry would simply have to foot the bill for this decision taken in the *Reichswehrministerium*.[45] Reinhardt pressed for an extra 170 million Marks. The Finance Ministry had little choice but to give in: 'I will adapt to the given circumstances, but ask that in order to reduce the mentioned difficulties of demobilization, the discharging should take place immediately.'[46] The refusal of the military to accept the primacy of fiscal rectitude contributed to the bloated budget of the government, and therefore to inflation. Reinhardt genuinely overestimated the threat from the left which had largely dissipated after the collapse of the Munich Soviet Republic. Even if Reinhardt did secure extra funds by a mixture of pleas and underhand practices, he did not restore certainty to the demoralized troops. Demobilization had to occur at some time. Putting it off may have increased the dangers by releasing a large number of troops into civil society at once.

Reinhardt did make efforts to help the soldier adjust to civil society by proposing welfare benefits for a transitional period, and trying to persuade government agencies to take on demobilized soldiers. If eking funds out of the Finance Ministry was one part of a strategy to maintain morale, then the development of social welfare policies was a second strand to this strategy. Fear of unemployment after demobilization was one of the factors contributing to demoralization among the troops. On the face of it this fear seems to have irrational. Unemployment was kept remarkably low in the immediate aftermath of the war, partly by replacing women workers with returning soldiers and partly by a policy of inflation which maintained economic productivity.[47] Yet traditional sources of employment in the state bureaucracy appeared blocked and it is also possible that some unions were boycotting volunteer soldiers whom they saw as strike-breakers.[48] Against the latter the government made a strong protest. Scheidemann predicted the collapse of the state if such boycotts were tolerated while Noske called for arrests of trade union leaders responsible for such actions.[49]

---

44. BArch R 2/50159, Erzberger to Noske, 9 December 1919, fos. 74–76.
45. BArch R 2/50159, Reinhardt to the Finance Ministry, 22 December 1919, fo. 105.
46. BArch R 2/50159, Finance Ministry to Reichswehr Ministry, 23 February 1920, fos. 127–28.
47. Richard Bessel, 'Unemployment and Demobilization in Germany after the First World War', in *The German Unemployed*, eds Richard Evans, Dick Geary, New York, 1987, 23–43.
48. BArch R 43 I/682, Deutscher Metallarbeiterverband to Scheidemann, 30 April 1919, fo. 27.
49. BArch R 43 I/682, Prussian Ministry of Justice to Scheidemann, 28 April 1919, fo. 28.

On other occasions trade unions helped soldiers who were looking for work. In May the Reich Labour Ministry reported that job agencies had been established in each of the rump units in the old army. These jobs agencies were headed by trade- union trained men, though the Labour Ministry assured the Ministry of War and other important military posts that politics was kept out of the job agencies.[50] They recommended that the *Generalkommandos* of the *Reichswehr* also set up these job agencies. *Vertrauensleute* were to talk to soldiers about the possibility of finding work, and were also to inform soldiers about aspects of the unemployment law. To monitor progress the *Vertrauensleute* were to send a weekly report on the number of soldiers making the transition to civilian employment.[51] Using the *Vertrauensleute* to improve the welfare of the soldiers was in the spirit of the institution. The Labour Ministry and the *Reichswehrministerium* aimed to try and get soldiers into employment.

The job agencies of the *Generalkommandos* were the forerunner for a more centralised agency, the *Reichswehrwirtschaftsausschuß*, mercifully known by the acronym, Rewa. Reinhardt informed Bauer on 6 September of the creation of the Rewa, 'as the central agency which is to deal with all questions of the accommodation of demobilized soldiers.'[52] It also had a second, although unstated aim, which was to preserve military units in the form of so-called work groups. Reinhardt had already sent information to the *Generalkommandos* and the trade unions on Rewa at the end of August.[53] The welfare aim of Rewa was to ease 'the transition to a new profession (*Beruf*)' through 'an effective employment exchange and job training'. He believed that a more centralised agency could match job demand and supply more effectively, which was possibly in reaction to the differing state of the labour market in the various regions of Germany. He also instituted the hopefully named *Arbeitsbeschaffungsstelle* (ABSt), which was to send information on local job markets to Rewa. *Vertrauensleute* were also to play a role in the new structures, as were trade unionists. Rewa demonstrated the seriousness with which Reinhardt and the Ministry of War approached the problem of integrating soldiers into civilian life. The Ministry of War had become accustomed to playing a more active role in economy and society in the First World War, and the creation of Rewa can be seen as an extension of this trend. The bureaucratic experience of war planning had swept away inhibitions about contending with market forces. The Reich Labour Ministry continued to help the *Reichswehr* by sending lists of jobs to the ABSt.

50. BArch, R 43/I, 692, Labour Ministry, circular memorandum, 2 May 1919, fos. 173–74.
51. BArch, R 43/I, 692, Reichsarbeitministerium, circular memorandum, 2 May 1919, fos. 173–74.
52. BArch, R 43/I, 692, Reinhardt to Bauer, 6 September 1919, Bl. 154; Rewa was officially established by Noske on 28 August 1919, BKA, Schützenbrigade 21, 79 (b), Reinhardt decree, 29 August 1919.
53. GLAK, Abt. 233/12441, Reinhardt decree, 23 August 1919.

A more detailed policy was outlined by Reinhardt in a decree on 29 August. One of the primary aims of Reinhardt's policy was to preserve morale in the *Reichswehr*, since '[T]he reliability of the remaining *Reichswehr* troops will essentially depend upon whether those who leave can be brought into the civilian economy in an orderly fashion.'[54] Once again he encouraged soldiers to join the *Sipo*, which would help Germany circumvent the aims of the treaty of Versailles. Soldiers were also given a 'loyalty bonus', which was designed to help the transition to civilian life by supporting the soldier while he was searching for work. Above all Reinhardt wanted to prevent soldiers from becoming a burden on welfare for the unemployed.[55] He had a strong work ethic, and he believed that 'arousing and polishing the willingness to work of people is the most important pre-condition for finding a job.'[56] When the army had originally started returning from the battlefields in December 1918, soldiers were supposed to go back to their old jobs. However, this was no longer possible, and Reinhardt instructed soldiers to go wherever there was work.

He saw two major job markets, in the mines and in agriculture. Reinhardt sought to combine his need to look after the troops leaving the *Reichswehr* and Germany's need to recover economically.[57] He proposed that soldiers form groups, which would look for work together. It was at this point that the policy moved from being one of welfare to an active attempt to evade the Versailles restrictions. These groups would elect a leader.[58] According to the proposal, '[T]he aim of the work group (*Arbeitsgruppe*) is to promote the economic development of the members through mutual comradeship and the connection of common matters of interest.'[59] The idea of forming a work group seems to have been prompted by rumours of attacks on individual soldiers in the work place. There were clearly more devious motives for forming soldiers' work groups. The structure of the groups was hardly distinguishable from that of a military unit. At the same time as Reinhardt tried to turn the army into a mirror of German society he sought to penetrate civil society with the military. East of the Elbe agrarian groups were setting up units of the *Einwohnerwehr*, which officers saw as a useful auxiliary force to the *Reichswehr*.[60] Groups of soldiers, ostensibly set up as work groups, could serve a similar function, while also escaping the terms of the treaty of Versailles. In fact,

54. BKA, Schützenbrigade 21, 79 (b), Reinhardt decree, 29 August 1919.
55. Ibid.
56. Ibid.
57. Ibid.
58. Ibid.
59. BKA, Schützenbrigade 21, 79 (b), Reinhardt decree, 29 August 1919, Anlage 2.
60. Jens Flemming, 'Die Bewaffnung des "Landvolkes". Ländliche Schützwehren und agrarische Konservatismus in der Anfangsphase der Weimarer Republik', *MgM*, 28, 2, 1979, 18–19.

the so-called Black *Reichswehr* groups, units armed illegally by the *Reich-swehr*, which were based in the countryside, resembled the structures outlined by Reinhardt, and may have originated from these instructions. The Black *Reichswehr* were later held responsible for terrorist attacks and posed a latent threat to the Republic throughout the 1920s.

Reinhardt adopted a different strategy for the demobilization of officers, partly because they were fewer. Traditionally officers and NCOs, after retiring from the army, had taken a post with the state administration. Reinhardt hoped to perpetuate this tradition in the new state. He feared the loss of the 'working potential and capabilities of the officer corps' if they were not given jobs. He suggested that older officers should be given preference for state posts while younger officers could go into the professions, presumably because this would lessen the long-term salary burden on the state and also propagate military values in broader social circles.[61] In June the Ministry of War sought to keep technical officers in state service, arguing that it was necessary to 'rescue these people who had served the state from personal ruin.'[62] Hence the arguments for providing demobilized soldiers and officers with job security ranged from the moral duty of the state to the issue of public order. However, at all levels of government there were few places for soldiers. The Bavarian Interior Ministry reported that the number of applicants per post was already very high.[63] There were other hard cases, such as bureaucrats who had lost their posts in Alsace-Lorraine.[64] The army had to compete for increasingly scarce resources which was in stark contrast to their privileged socio-political position before 1914.

This was unwittingly revealed by Reinhardt to the National Assembly when he spoke on the Officers Compensation Law on 18 August 1919. He argued that the *Reichswehr* was the 'main sufferer' of the Versailles treaty. Since the army had found it difficult to accept some parts of the Constitution, Reinhardt claimed that the Officers Compensation Law would be received as a sign that the new state had taken the soldiers to its heart.[65] In fact the cabinet had already watered down the 'far-reaching drafts' of the Ministry of War due to the financial situation.[66] During the debates in the National Assembly it was amended, unfavourably, for officers. Erzberger had proposed five years and three years compensation for

---

61. BArch R 43 I/692, Reinhardt, Göhre to Scheidemann, 17 April 1919, fo. 40.
62. BArch R 43 I/692, Circular from the Prussian Ministry of War, Nr 1181.6.19 A6, fo. 104.
63. BHStA ML 1729, Bavarian Interior Ministry to Ministry for Military Affairs, Munich, 22 April 1919.
64. BArch R 43 I/692, Reich Interior Ministry to the Prussian Ministry of War, Berlin 8 May 1919, fo. 49.
65. *Verhandlungen der deutschen Nationalversammlung*, vol. 329, 2559–561.
66. *Das Kabinett Bauer, 21. Juni 1919 bis 27. März 1920*, ed. Anton Golecki, Boppard am Rhein, 1980, 60.

married and unmarried officers respectively, but this was reduced to three and two years.[67] This seemed a generous aid to those officers, who had entered the army to pursue a professional military career and were prevented from doing so by Versailles. Reinhardt hoped that the law would offer sufficient security to officers and demonstrate the good-will of the state.

However one of the major organs of officer opinion, *Das Militär-wochenblatt*, asserted that the law was 'thoroughly depressing', and was 'further evidence that the socialist-clerical government has no heart for the officers, whom it should thank that there is no Bolshevist government at the helm in Germany today, not to mention the officers who served in the war.'[68] The rhetoric of moral obligation was mobilized. Considering the financial situation within Germany in 1919, and the plight of numerous other groups, ranging from the war wounded to widows, the Officer Compensation Law was a good deal. Inflated expectations and an inability to adjust to the impoverished state of the Reich finances led *Das Militärwochenblatt* to criticise the law. They only succeeded in further damaging the credibility of the Republic in the eyes of the officers without improving their material position.

In short, the scale of the social and political problems facing the *Reichswehr* in late 1919 made it a very fragile instrument. This was not a sufficient pre-condition for a Putsch. It was the political machinations of officers close to Lüttwitz, and Reinhardt's failure to take decisive countermeasures, which led to the Putsch. Aware of his own lack of support within the officer corps Reinhardt rarely tried to impose his authority on acts of disobedience within the *Reichswehr*. He preferred to cajole officers into line, a policy he followed right up until 12 March 1920.

Symbols were a constant source of friction in military policy in 1919.[69] The new German flag was black, red and gold, an echo of the flag of 1848. After the Constitution was passed by the National Assembly on 11 August, soldiers of the *Reichswehr* had to take their oath to the defence of the Reich and the elected government in front of the new flag.[70] Two officers, Colonel Lieutenant Hagen and Colonel Wilhelm Reinhard, refused to take this oath in front of the new flag.[71] Reinhardt replied that the issue was regulated by decree. The case of Wilhelm Reinhard became a *cause célèbre* in the autumn of 1919, when Philip Scheidemann, the former Chancellor, called for his removal from the army, while both Noske and Reinhardt defended him. A report in the *Vossische Zeitung* claimed that

---

67. *Verhandlungen der deutschen Nationalversammlung*, vol. 337, 346–49; vol. 338, 771–76.

68. *Das Militärwochenblatt*, 28 August 1919, 501–504.

69. Harold James, *A German Identity*, London, 1990, 121–25.

70. The text of the oath is contained in Georg Maercker's account, *Vom Kaiserheer zur Reichswehr. Ein Beitrag zur Geschichte der deutschen Revolution*, Leipzig, 1921, 223.

71. BA-MA, N 86/16, RWGrKdo 1 to Reinhardt, 24 August 1919; Fritz Ernst, 'Aus dem Nachlaß des Generals Walther Reinhardt', *Die Welt als Geschichte*, 18, 1958, 95–96.

Reinhardt was ready to strike a deal with his near-namesake, whereby Reinhard would leave the Berlin area, but remain in the *Reichswehr*.[72] Eventually Reinhard was forced out of the army, but the whole process confirmed that Noske and Reinhardt, left to their own devices, preferred a policy of cajoling soldiers into obedience than one of harsh discipline.[73]

Morale was also being sapped by a series of attacks on leading commanders and the institution of the *Reichswehr*. Some of these attacks were justified, such as the one in *Vorwärts*, flagged by the banner headline, 'A conspiracy in the Lüttwitz Corps'.[74] A memorandum by Major Schmolke of the Prussian Ministry of War demanded that the government publicly refute the allegations made in articles in *Vorwärts*. He argued that regular denunciations of officers in the press were undermining the relationship of trust between the troops and their officers.[75] While the officer corps had been the subject of press attacks before the war, these attacks by the leading organ of the SPD took place in a new context. Many identified the state with the SPD, and such attacks reinforced a belief among officers that the new regime was anti-military. While the SPD might have been more sensitive, the officer corps had failed to adjust to the culture of criticism of public institutions which is fundamental in a liberal democracy, especially when those criticisms happen to be founded on fact. Officers did not want a restoration of the monarchy but a more pro-military republic.

By the autumn of 1919 there is significant evidence that the level of morale was dropping and that the political attitudes fostered within the *Reichswehr* were antagonistic to the Republic. This situation was born out of the shock at the Versailles treaty and the limited material compensation that the state could offer soldiers. Further the state, or the parties which were associated with the Republic, appeared to be anti-*Reichswehr*. This meant that the officers were deprived of moral recompense, which had sustained morale in the *Kaiserreich*'s army where material reward had been virtually non-existent. Yet without political leadership, either from within or without the army, this mood of discontent may have fizzled out, or remained hidden, fleetingly revealed by minor acts of disobedience and criticism of the Republic. After all not every individual solider and officer was discontented. There was some way to travel before demoralization became open revolt. However since the summer a group of officers had been involved in planning a Putsch with Wolfgang Kapp, the former leader of the right-wing Fatherland Party, which had been the largest mass party in the last years of the war. The importance of the level of disaffection was that it prevented Reinhardt from acting decisively against these

---

72. BArch R 43 I/683, *Vossische Zeitung*, 6 January 1920, 'Oberst Reinhards Verabschiedung', fo. 3.
73. Wilhelm Reinhard, *1918–19. Die Wehen der Republik*, Berlin, 1933, 120–24.
74. BA-MA, N 42/15, *Vorwärts*, 24 June 1919, evening edition, fo. 37.
75. BA-MA, N 42/15, Major Schmolke, Entwurf, KM 5187/7.19 AMJ, fo. 39.

groups, since his authority within the army as a whole had been damaged.

One of Reinhardt's arguments against the acceptance of the treaty of Versailles was that it would put pressure on the nascent *Reichswehr*, due to the rapid reduction of the German military forces and the shame paragraphs. Indeed the origins of the Putsch can be located in the aftermath of the National Assembly's decision to accept the Allied terms. Although there were people calling for a dictatorship before June 1919, it was only then that anti-government groups in the *Reichswehr* began to come into contact with Wolfgang Kapp. He approached leading officers such as Colonel Wilhelm Heye. On 8 July General Erich Ludendorff met General Fritz von Below, recently dismissed from the *Reichswehr* for encouraging a revolt in the aftermath of the acceptance of the treaty of Versailles. Ludendorff's chief adviser during the First World War, Colonel Max Bauer, although no longer in the *Reichswehr*, was another senior military figure who was planning to overthrow the new state.[76] The question arises that, if such a large circle of officers and ex-officers were either approached or involved, how was it that Reinhardt and Noske failed to take action at an early stage to prevent the Putsch?

While Reinhardt's unwillingness to discipline wayward officers more stringently was partly due to his awareness of the volatile morale of the *Reichswehr*, it also stemmed from his lack of authority within the officer corps. Yet Seeckt and Reinhardt had a common interest in preventing a successful Putsch and the subsequent rise of Lüttwitz. Outside the *Reichswehrministerium* Lüttwitz was the most popular general in the army. The struggle between Reinhardt, Seeckt and Lüttwitz is one of the sub-plots of the Kapp Putsch. It is possible that Seeckt saw Lüttwitz as the more dangerous rival, despite Reinhardt's current ascendancy. First, Lüttwitz's popularity made him a future candidate for the post of head of the army command. Second, Seeckt's opposition to soldiers' involvement in politics is well documented. He was aware of Lüttwitz's connections with Kapp and believed that confrontation with the government would be counter-productive. Therefore Seeckt sought to shore up Reinhardt's position in order to prevent Lüttwitz from displacing both of them.

Seeckt warned Reinhardt as early as 3 October that Lüttwitz was involved in 'illicit political business'.[77] In an *Abschiedsgespräch* to officers on 29 March 1920 Reinhardt admitted, 'it had been known to us in the *Reichswehrministerium* for a long time that General von Lüttwitz, as champion of the idea, was urgently looking for a change in the composition of the government, and also in policy.' After a second report from Seeckt it appears as though Reinhardt met with Lüttwitz. Lüttwitz reaffirmed his oath to the constitution, and this satisfied Reinhardt. Lüttwitz's ability to

76. Erger, *Kapp-Lüttwitz Putsch*, 38–43.
77. Cited in Erger, *Kapp-Lüttwitz Putsch*, 58.

convince Reinhardt that he was not planning to launch a Putsch was essential, because it ensured that he remained commander of *Reichswehrgruppe I*, a position which gave him command of the troops in the Berlin area.[78] Reinhardt saved Lüttwitz from an early release because Noske, like Seeckt, had doubts about Lüttwitz's political views. Noske later commented that the decision not to remove Lüttwitz from his position 'was the one piece of Reinhardt's advice that proved fateful.'[79]

Reinhardt must have been aware that the antipathy of Lüttwitz was not merely directed at the Weimar coalition but also at him personally. According to Oldershausen, Lüttwitz had asked Reinhardt to resign. When this occurred is not clear, although since the letter was dated 11 December 1919, it could be assumed that it was on an occasion subsequent to Lüttwitz's reaffirmation of his oath.[80] Why Reinhardt failed to take action is not clear. In early July he had removed the very personal threat of Groener. Yet at that stage Groener's reputation within the officer corps had reached its nadir. Lüttwitz was a different proposition. If Seeckt had the ear of the *Reichswehrminister*, he would have been able to force the removal of Lüttwitz, and he also had sufficient authority within the officer corps to stamp out any opposition from Lüttwitz supporters. Could Seeckt and Reinhardt have combined against Lüttwitz? Certainly Seeckt was wary of the threat from Lüttwitz and he warned Reinhardt of it. Aware of his lack of authority and finding comfort in Lüttwitz's oath, Reinhardt failed to take action. The wages of naivety would be high.

By the beginning of 1920 many of the elements of a crisis were in place. There were numerous disenchanted troops. Officers believed that the state was becoming increasingly *militärfeindlich*. The Ehrhardt brigade, which was Lüttwitz's main source of military power for the Putsch, had arrived in the Berlin region, and in early 1920 it was housed in the barracks at Döberitz, about thirty kilometres from the centre of Berlin. The leader of this *Freikorps* brigade was Captain Hermann Ehrhardt, one of the more persistent intriguers and opponents of the Weimar republic. He had been approached by Kapp in July 1919, and joined Kapp's cover organisation, the *Nationale Vereinigung*.[81] However the planning for the Putsch itself was far from ready. Neither of the two right-wing parties, the *Deutsche Volkspartei* (DVP) or the *Deutsche National-Volkspartei* (DNVP) were prepared to support a Putsch at this stage. Kapp's power bases were almost exclusively in East Prussia and Bavaria.[82] Kapp was also sick

78. HStASt, M 660/034, Bü 24, Abschiedsrede des Herrn Generals Reinhardt am 29. März 1920.
79. Gustav Noske, *Erlebtes aus Aufstieg und Niedergang einer Demokratie*, Offenbach am Main, 1947, 179.
80. BA-MA N 247/87, Olderhausen to Seeckt, Berlin 11 December 1919, fo. 88.
81. Gabriele Krüger, *Die Ehrhardt Brigade*, Hamburg, 1971, 34–43.
82. Erger, *Kapp-Lüttwitz Putsch*, 94–96.

during January and February 1920.[83] This meant that the plotters were not properly prepared for the *dénouement* when it was suddenly foisted on them at the end of February.

The crisis was triggered by the Allies' demand, made by Lloyd George on 18 February, to reduce the *Reichswehr* to 200,000 men by 10 April, and to 100,000 by 10 July. On 29 February the *Reichswehrministerium* ordered the dissolution of the Ehrhardt and Loewenfeld brigades.[84] Also on 29 February, Reinhardt's wife, Luise died. Since 1918 Reinhardt had known how ill his wife was, but nonetheless, her death must have dominated his mind during the these days. He returned to Stuttgart where his three daughters lived. He was absent in every sense of the word from Berlin and its politics. Just outside Berlin, on 1 March there was a celebration at the Döberitz camp, and after a parade Lüttwitz spoke to the troops, 'I will not tolerate that one of my key units will be disbanded in such stormy times.'[85] The significance of Lüttwitz's speech is questionable, although at the parade Johannes Vögel, a pastor, gave 'a political speech, which urged us to strive with all our power to re-establish the German *Kaiserreich* and to let a new glory shine upon the German throne.'[86] Noske was unaware of this speech until 6 March. He complained 'that none of the men who were in the leading, or close to senior, positions, and who were aware of Lüttwitz's budding insubordination, informed me of anything.'[87] Yet many of those present, or who heard of it, may have believed that the speeches were merely parade ground rhetoric, the habitual but inconsequential threats against the new regime. Despite the monarchist speech by Vögel, restoring the Kaiser was not one of Lüttwitz's demands. It should also be remembered that the attitudes of the dominant figures in the officer corps and the cabinet were conditioned to perceive a threat from the left, and not from one of the forces of order, an attitude which led to constant misjudgement.

Even before Noske had heard of Lüttwitz's speech, he wrote to Bauer on 14 February in an attempt to slow down the reduction of the army. He sought to postpone the formation of the 200,000 men army until 10 April, the date which Lloyd George set four days later. Noske mentioned the 'ever increasing unrest' among the troops as the main reason for delaying the reduction.[88] However even after Noske and Reinhardt were made aware of the Lüttwitz speech, there was no mention of the possibility of a Putsch

83. BA-Koblenz, N 1150/26, Anklageschrift der Oberreichsanwalt gegen Jagow, Wagenheim, Leipzig, 11 July 1921, fo. 15.
84. *Kabinett Bauer*, 616–7.
85. Cited in Erger, *Kapp-Lüttwitz Putsch*, 115–16.
86. BA-Koblenz, N 1150/28, Verhandlung d. Masch-Maat Schwahn, Wilhelmshaven, 23 March 1920, fo. 15.
87. BA-Koblenz, N 1150/26, Anklageschrift der Oberreichsanwalt gegen Jagow, Wagenheim, Leipzig, 11 July 1921, fo. 294.
88. BArch R 43 I/680, Noske to Bauer, Nr 727.2.20 T 2, Berlin, 14 February 1920, fo. 86–87.

in discussions they held with other cabinet members about the reduction of the *Reichswehr*.[89] This was a serious misjudgement, because it meant that the cabinet was unprepared when the crisis came to a head in the early hours of 13 March. On the other hand, this rather casual approach to Lüttwitz's threats of a Putsch may indicate that Reinhardt and Noske felt that the crisis could be contained, and solved within the confines of the *Reichswehrministerium*. In the first week of March it appeared as though Lüttwitz's threats were empty. When Colonel Ahrens, the head of the *Sicherheitspolizei*, was told by two members of Lüttwitz's staff on 2 March of the plans for a Putsch, he doubted if the *Reichswehr* would support such a move.[90] At a meeting on 3 March Seeckt insisted that the dissolution of the brigades would go ahead, the first indication of his opposition to Lüttwitz during this crisis.[91] By the time Ahrens and another *Sipo* commander warned Lüttwitz against any revolt on 5 March, the general's ardour for the plot seemed to have cooled considerably.[92] Therefore senior officers in both the *Sipo* and the *Reichswehr* may have reasonably concluded that the crisis had passed, and that the dissolution of the brigades would pass without exceptional incident.

Nevertheless the impending dissolution of the brigades compelled Lüttwitz to take action. Meanwhile Reinhardt, mourning his wife's death, was unable to devote his full attention to the threat posed by Lüttwitz. First, he had to deal with the Erzberger libel case, in which his name had been mentioned. Matthias Erzberger, the Finance Minister, had brought a libel case against Karl Helferrich, a leading right-wing politician, and although Erzberger won his action, he was thoroughly discredited. The trial further contributed to the loss of the Weimar republic's legitimacy.[93] Reinhardt's main concern was not to become involved in the case because association with Erzberger, who had signed the ceasefire at Compiègne, would further diminish his reputation in the *Reichswehr*. On 3 March he was advised not to write to the press, because denial would merely arouse the suspicion of association.[94] This tactic appeared to work, and on 6 March the *Deutsche Zeitung* acknowledged that despite both being from Württemberg, Erzberger and Reinhardt had not known each other until they sat in the cabinet together. The article continued that this was understandable 'since General Reinhardt as a man of strict objectivity

89. On the cabinet discussions on the reduction of the *Reichswehr*, see the files in BArch R 43 I/680, fos. 86–97, 113–20.

90. BA-Koblenz, N 1150/26, Anklageschrift der Oberreichsanwalt gegen Jagow, Wagenheim, Leipzig, 11 July 1921, fo. 26.

91. BA-Koblenz, N 1150/26, Trotha evidence, dated 10 October 1921.

92. BA-Koblenz, N 1150/26, Anklageschrift der Oberreichsanwalt gegen Jagow, Wagenheim, Leipzig, 11 July 1921, fos. 28–29; on 4 March both the *Volkspartei* and the Nationalists refused to support the planned Putsch which was a further blow to Kapp's and Lüttwitz's plans, see Erger, *Kapp-Lüttwitz Putsch*, 117–18.

93. Winkler, *Weimarer Republik*, 117–18.

94. HStASt, M 660/034, Bü 24, Timann to Reinhardt, 3 March 1920.

would never have had the urge to have personal relations with a man as compromised as Mr Erzberger.'[95] Having preserved his good name, Reinhardt now had to undergo yet another emotionally-charged experience, the closure of the Cadet School at Lichterfelde. On 9 March a ceremony took place, at which Reinhardt delivered a speech. Reinhardt had been a cadet at Lichterfelde, and considering the rôle which cadets had played in German military history, the occasion must have served as another distraction from the pressing affair of Lüttwitz's opposition to the dissolution of the two brigades.[96]

On 7 March a meeting took place in the *Reichswehrministerium* at which Noske, Reinhardt and Lüttwitz were present. It appears to have been the first formal meeting on the dissolution of the brigades, and it is notable that it took place the day after Noske had heard of Lüttwitz's speech. In other words, Noske was sufficiently perturbed to meet Lüttwitz. Once again Lüttwitz argued that the order should be lifted. Reinhardt refused to make any concessions.[97] The sparse account of the meeting does not make clear whether Lüttwitz issued any threats against the government. It is probable he did not, because the following day Reinhardt went to Seeckt and 'sought him out, to stress the urgent necessity of the dissolution.'[98] This indicates that Reinhardt still believed that it was possible to keep Lüttwitz as the commander of *Reichswehrgruppe I*, while dissolving the brigades. Seeckt told Reinhardt that the details of the dissolution procedure had already been worked out with General Martin von Oldershausen, Lüttwitz's chief of staff, a further indication that despite Lüttwitz's vehement opposition few officers were prepared for a Putsch. Military preparations were not obvious. The Prussian State Commissar for Public Order met Lüttwitz on 6 March. A memorandum written after the Putsch commented: 'Since the State Commissar was unaware of any military preparations he had to surmise that he was listening to one of the general's frequent outbursts, which could be resolved through suitable negotiations without too much difficulty.'[99] On 8 March Ernst van den Bergh, Noske's adjutant, prepared a report which advised that the government should carry on as usual.[100] The assessment of the chances of a Putsch was cautious, revealing that both the police and the military expected that political violence was a tool of left-wing radicals, and not of embittered soldiers.

The assessment of the threat must have changed, because at a meeting on 9 March between Reinhardt, Seeckt and Admiral von Trotha, the head

95. *Deutsche Zeitung*, 6 March 1920.
96. HStASt, M 660/034, Bü 24, text of Reinhardt's speech on 9 March 1920.
97. BA-Koblenz, N 1150/26, Anklageschrift der Oberreichsanwalt gegen Jagow, Wagenheim, Leipzig, 11 July 1921, fo. 29–30.
98. Ibid., fo. 30.
99. BArch R 43 I/2305, Die Tätigkeit des Staatskommissars für die öffentliche Ordnung anlässlich des Staatsstreiches am 13. März 1920, fo. 49.
100. Erger, *Kapp-Lüttwitz Putsch*, 133–39.

of the navy, the possibility of removing the Ehrhardt brigade from Lüttwitz's command arose for the first time. The suggestion was made by Reinhardt and Seeckt, but Trotha rejected it. Since the brigades had started out as marine brigades, he had been in command of them in their initial stages. He believed that transferring the command back to him at this point would disrupt the process of dissolution.[101] Clearly Reinhardt and Seeckt expected considerably more trouble with the dissolution of the brigades than had been the case even the previous day. What made them change their mind is unclear. It is also significant that Seeckt and Reinhardt, who had clashed on many a previous occasion, had been co-operating closely on this issue. A common threat, Lüttwitz, had brought them together. The meeting on 9 March represents the first serious attempt to counter Lüttwitz, and yet it failed. Trotha was unwilling to take over command of the brigade, perhaps because he did not want to deal with this troublesome issue.

On 10 March a series of meetings took place which revealed the true extent of the crisis. Colonel von Gilsa, a senior officer in the *Reichswehrministerium*, met Ehrhardt to ask him about his intentions. Ehrhardt replied that he would obey an order by Lüttwitz to march on Berlin, unless Lüttwitz was explicitly removed from his position.[102] In the light of subsequent events it is doubtful if Ehrhardt was being fully truthful, but it is possible that if Lüttwitz had been dealt with more decisively, the military side of the revolt would have been unable to function, owing to the lack of a command structure. Certainly, if Lüttwitz had been arrested, then he would have been unable to give Ehrhardt the command to march on Berlin. On the same day Reinhardt and Seeckt, on the latter's request, returned to see Trotha. Both agreed that the Ehrhardt brigade had to be remove from Lüttwitz's command, and this time they ordered Trotha to take over the position. On this second visit, Trotha argued that the change of command would unsettle the Ehrhardt brigade, and that if there was a threat to the government, then defensive measures should be taken in Berlin.[103] However this time Reinhardt and Seeckt had the force of an order from Noske, who had been worried by reports from Gilsa about Ehrhardt' intentions, and so command of the brigade was transferred from Lüttwitz to Trotha, 'in order to carry out the dissolution as free of trouble as possible.'[104] Yet Trotha was an inappropriate choice for this post. Although he believed that a Putsch at this stage was inappropriate, he was not committed to the new regime, and would throw in his weight and that of the navy behind the Kapp government on 13 March.[105] On 10 March Gilsa

101. BA-Koblenz, N 1150/26, Trotha evidence, dated 10 October 1921, fo. 297.
102. BA-Koblenz, N 1150/28, Verhandlung von Erich von Gilsa, 10 March 1923, fos. 373–74.
103. BA-Koblenz, N 1150/27, Meldung des Admirals von Trotha, 27 March 1920, fo. 16.
104. BA-Koblenz, N 1150/28, Vernehmung von Walther Reinhardt, 26 February 1923, fo. 289.
105. Jost Dülffer, *Weimar, Hitler und die Marine. Reichspolitik und Flottenbau 1920–1939*, Düsseldorf, 1973, 32–34.

tried to get Trotha to talk to his new subordinate, Captain Ehrhardt, but the admiral refused 'because these attempts to get him to work on Ehrhardt went too far, as he had no power over Ehrhardt.'[106]

Lüttwitz's position was weakening. On 9 March he sent Ebert a list of demands, including new elections and the formation of a cabinet of *Fachminister* (expert ministers).[107] The following day Noske removed the two brigades from his command, and on 11 March, after consulting Reinhardt, Noske decided to send Lüttwitz on indefinite leave.[108] Thus slowly Noske and Reinhardt were dealing with threat presented by Lüttwitz. Yet each time Lüttwitz's power-base was weakened he was compelled to take more extreme action. His reaction to the dissolution of the brigades had triggered the crisis in the first place, and now he ordered Ehrhardt to prepare to march on Berlin.[109] To counter Lüttwitz, Reinhardt, Oldershausen, and another staff officer of *Reichswehrgruppe I*, Hammerstein, began to notify units that Lüttwitz was no longer their commander. Noske issued arrest warrants, but only captured two of the conspirators, Friedrich Grabowski, who was Jewish, and Karl Schnitzler.[110]In many respects 11 March was a lost day for the government, which failed to arrest the key conspirators, or persuade Ehrhardt not to support Lüttwitz. Trotha's assessment that he had little control over Ehrhardt's action, despite being his superior officer, was accurate. Neither putting the Ehrhardt brigade under Trotha's command, nor removing Lüttwitz from his post were successful in countering the preparations for the Putsch.

On 12 March more active steps for the defence of Berlin began to be taken. There were now two ways to prevent the Putsch – first, the government could send a representative to talk with Ehrhardt, and second, they could station *Reichswehr* and *Sipo* units in the government quarters in Berlin, and hope that the prospect of a battle would deter Ehrhardt from marching on the city. At 8.30 pm Reinhardt visited the new commander of *Reichswehrgruppe I*, General Lieutenant Burghard von Oven, who had commanded the units which defeated the *Räterepublik* in Munich in May 1919. Reinhardt wanted Oven to remind his troops of the oath they had taken to defend the elected government. However Oven 'at this opportunity talked about the internal state of his troops, and explained that the officers would do their duty, but the majority of soldiers would not shoot on other *Reichswehr* soldiers.'[111] As Otto Hahn, adjutant to Noske, noted:

106. BA-Koblenz, N 1150/26, Anklageschrift der Oberreichsanwalt gegen Jagow, Wagenheim, Leipzig, 11 July 1921, fo. 32.
107. Although Lüttwitz has often been seen as a representative of the 'restorationists' within the officer corps, his demands never included the re-establishment of the monarchy.
108. BA-Koblenz, N 1150/26, Anklageschrift der Oberreichsanwalt gegen Jagow, Wagenheim, Leipzig, 11 July 1921, fo. 31–34.
109. Ibid., fo. 37.
110. Erger, *Kapp-Lüttwitz Putsch*, 123–26.
111. HStASt, M 660/034, Bü 24, Bericht über die Besprechungen und Verhandlungen in der Nacht vom 12. bis 13. März und am 13. März morgens.

'What was always feared happened: the *Reichswehr* and the *Sipo* would only act reliably against attacks from the left; as soon as it came to acting against right-wing radical circles a conflict of conscience arose which degenerated into open support or at least neutrality.' However the *Sipo*, as Hahn himself later admitted, may have been more reliable than the *Reichswehr*.[112] Reinhardt continued to prepare for a military defence of the government quarters, a policy with which Noske agreed. At 10.00 pm Reinhardt told Colonel von Thaysen, second in command of the *Sipo*, 'that violent action by the Marine-Brigade must be opposed by force.'[113] Despite the reservations of many officers about a battle in the streets of Berlin against the Ehrhardt brigade, it appears as though they would have followed orders to fire. Oven, as has been noted, believed that the officers would be willing to their duty, and he also ordered Thaysen to resist the Putsch.[114]

The other means of foiling the Putsch was a mission to the Döberitz camp to try to persuade Ehrhardt not to carry out Lüttwitz's order to march on Berlin. Early that evening Noske, Reinhardt and Trotha met.[115] Noske wanted to travel to Döberitz, but Reinhardt felt it would be too dangerous, and volunteered for the mission instead. However Trotha pointed out that Reinhardt's presence at Döberitz would be counter-productive, 'because he was the most hated man in the brigade', a further indication of Reinhardt's lack of prestige in the *Reichswehr*.[116] Trotha drove out to the camp with his adjutant, Captain Wilhelm Canaris, and once again he told Ehrhardt that a Putsch would be futile.[117] Trotha also looked for any signs that the brigade was preparing for an imminent march on Berlin. However he found the camp 'the picture of complete peacefulness', although he later argued that this was no guarantee of inaction because the brigade could mobilize in a very short period of time.[118] Canaris confirmed that 'the camp gave the Admiral and me the impression of calm.'[119]

---

112. HStASt M 660/014, Heft 14, memorandum by Otto Hahn, 'Meine Erlebnisse beim innerpolitischen Umsturz im März', 7 April 1920, fo. 2.
113. HStASt, M 660/034, Bü 24, Bericht über die Besprechungen und Verhandlungen in der Nacht vom 12. bis 13. März und am 13. März morgens.
114. BA-Koblenz, N 1150/26, Anklageschrift der Oberreichsanwalt gegen Jagow, Wagenheim, Leipzig, 11 July 1921, fo. 42.
115. Reinhardt's memorandum on the events of 12/13 March 1920, which was written immediately after the Putsch, implies that Trotha had already gone to Döberitz. However his 1923 statement, and other witnesses, confirm that he was present at the meeting. The reason for the omission in his memorandum is not clear, but may have been caused by embarrassment at his lack of authority.
116. BA-Koblenz, N 1150/26, Anklageschrift der Oberreichsanwalt gegen Jagow, Wagenheim, Leipzig, 11 July 1921, fo. 44.
117. BA-Koblenz, N 1150/27, Meldung d. Admirals von Trotha, 26 March 1920, fo. 14.
118. Ibid., fo. 17.
119. BA-Koblenz, N 1150/28, Meldung von Wilhlem Canaris, 7 March 1923, fos. 328–29.

How hard Trotha tried to dissuade Ehrhardt from his course of action is unknown, but it has been suggested that if Noske had gone to Döberitz, events might have turned out differently. Alex Schmalix, a former republican naval officer, later commented:

> I believe that in the Kapp Putsch Noske made the mistake of sending Admiral von Trotha to the Brigade at Döberitz. If he had gone himself, he would have underwent the risk of arrest but he would most likely have been successful. At Döberitz his appearance would have made a powerful impression on the troops, because some NCOs were already refusing orders.[120]

That night as news reached the *Reichswehrministerium* that the Ehrhardt brigade had begun its march, Oven and Oldershausen travelled towards Döberitz to try for the final time to dissuade Ehrhardt from continuing with the Putsch.

All attempts to dissuade Ehrhardt had proved fruitless, and now the question of defending the capital by military force came to the fore. At 1.00 am on 13 March, Noske asked Reinhardt to come to a meeting at the *Reichswehrministerium*, where Seeckt, Trotha, Hammerstein and other leading officers had gathered to discuss the situation. Hammerstein reported that Ehrhardt had told Oven to present demands to the government, and would negotiate on the basis of these demands. Noske opposed the idea of negotiations, as did Reinhardt, who 'stressed likewise that negotiations could not take place with rebellious troops.'[121] However Seeckt advised that they should await the return of Oldershausen and Oven. This was the first sign that the Reinhardt-Seeckt front, which had opposed Lüttwitz over the previous week, had broken down. Whereas Reinhardt was unwilling to countenance anything less than obedience, Seeckt sought a settlement. About half an hour into the meeting Oven brought back the demands, which included the replacement of both Noske and Reinhardt, the creation of a cabinet of *Fachminister*, and an amnesty for all those involved in the Putsch. Oldershausen's comment, 'he had never seen such marvellous soldiers', can only have added weight to the arguments of those who wanted a negotiated settlement rather than an active and bloody defence of the government quarters.[122] Even Noske admitted 'that there was no doubt that purely militarily these two units were of a higher value than any of a series of other battalions and regiments that were at my disposal at that time.'[123] Yet despite

120. BArch, R 43 I/2728, Alex Schmalix, *Gerechtigkeit für Kapitän Ehrhardt*, Leipzig, 1923, 19, fo. 48.
121. HStASt, M 660/034, Bü 24, Bericht über die Besprechungen und Verhandlungen in der Nacht vom 12. bis 13. März und am 13. März morgens.
122. HStASt, M 660/034, Bü 24, Bericht über die Besprechungen und Verhandlungen in der Nacht vom 12. bis 13. März und am 13. März morgens; BA-Koblenz, N 1150/26, Anklageschrift der Oberreichsanwalt gegen Jagow, Wagenheim, Leipzig, 11 July 1921, fos. 48-50.
123. BA-Koblenz, N 1150/26, Noske evidence, dated 10 October 1921, fo. 321.

this assessment Noske, Reinhardt and Gilsa continued to argue in favour of armed resistance. Oven and Oldershausen, according to Reinhardt's memorandum, repeated 'that *Reichswehr* troops never shoot on other *Reichswehr* troops.'[124] Seeckt and Hammerstein argued that a split in the army had to be avoided, in the expectation that the *Reichswehr* would be used to put down radical left-wing revolts.

The question remains as to why Reinhardt now advocated a policy of resistance while Seeckt backed down. The moment of crisis changed the political constellation and the assessments of both men. Personal ambition continued to play a role. The Putsch meant that the end of Reinhardt's career, and on one level his policy of resistance can be seen as an attempt to save his own position. Simply put, he had nothing to lose. Seeckt did, and he must have concluded that his adherence to the Reinhardt policy would only discredit him as well as destroying the army. This leads into the second changed dynamic in this moment of crisis. In Seeckt's view the unity of the *Reichswehr* had primacy over all other considerations. In domestic policy it would be needed against an expected radical left-wing uprising, whilst in foreign policy it provided the basis for Germany's emergence as a *bündnisfähig* power, capable of forming alliances. Seeckt continually asserted the primacy of the professional army. Reinhardt never believed that a small army such as the *Reichswehr* could lead to Germany's recovery of her Great Power position. He argued that only in close conjunction with the populace could a small army be an effective instrument for domestic order and foreign policy. Therefore the dramatic change in Reinhardt's and Seeckt's views in the early hours of 13 March was related to the character of the *Reichswehr*, as well as to their personal rivalry. Reinhardt chose a *Katastrophenpolitik* for the army, in order to preserve the army's credibility with the people, while Seeckt was willing sacrifice this to preserve the professional integrity and unity of the *Reichswehr*.

The decision on whether to oppose the Ehrhardt brigade was not taken by the generals but by a hastily convened cabinet meeting, at which all the officers, save for Reinhardt and Gilsa, were excluded. The meeting took place in the Chancellery at 5.00 a.m. At the meeting two questions were discussed, namely whether the government should resist Ehrhardt, and if not, whether they should stay in Berlin.[125] It was decided not to resist, and Reinhardt was the only significant figure who spoke in favour of defending Berlin. Albert, the secretary of state to the chancellor, commented: 'The unanimous view of the generals, who with the exception of General Reinhardt spoke against military resistance, was

---

124. HStASt, M 660/034, Bü 24, Bericht über die Besprechungen und Verhandlungen in der Nacht vom 12. bis 13. März und am 13. März morgens.
125. BA-Koblenz, N 1150/27, Bericht des Staatssekretärs in d. Reichskanzlei, Albert, 10 June 1920, fos. 175–76.

decisive.'[126]The government made a judgement on the basis of the generals' recommendations. The generals did not refuse to defend Berlin, and in Reinhardt, the government had a competent general who was willing to risk a street battle. By making its judgement wholly on the basis of the views of generals like Oven and Seeckt, the cabinet abdicated its political responsibility by failing to take other factors into account, such as the consequences of a humiliating retreat away from Berlin. Following the decision not to resist the march of Ehrhardt's brigade on Berlin, Reinhardt resigned as head of the army command.

The possibility that armed resistance, or the spectre of armed resistance, might have thwarted the Putsch has never been seriously examined by historians. Erger argued that the leaders of the *Sipo* force of 9,000 had already let Ehrhardt know through Pabst that it would not resist the brigade.[127] However there is circumstantial evidence that Reinhardt's arguments to defend Berlin were not as quixotic as the judgements of Oldershausen and Seeckt might lead one to believe. First, the cabinet did have qualified officers who were willing to resist the Ehrhardt brigade. Reinhardt had been a front general in the First World War, and so was no stranger to combat. Thaysen, who was in charge of the heavily armed *Sipo* units, was also prepared to resist, because 'it was against his military honour to allow himself to be overrun.' Admittedly Thaysen gave this statement after the failure of the Putsch, but the evidence regarding the attitude of the *Sipo* does not conclusively point to their unwillingness to oppose Ehrhardt.[128] Together the *Sipo* and *Reichswehr* units stationed in Berlin constituted a significant military force. There were 3,000 *Reichswehr* soldiers alone in the city and a *Sipo* force of 9,000.[129] This military force may also have acted as a deterrent to Ehrhardt. He was a determined officer, but he was also confronted by the same dilemma as officers in Berlin. Would he risk a street battle, and could he be certain that his own troops would fire on *Reichswehr* colleagues? It is significant that when Oldershausen went to Ehrhardt in the early hours of 13 March, he told him to expect resistance in Berlin. At this stage Oldershausen may have been trying to call Ehrhardt's bluff. Ehrhardt did not expect to face resistance, but he did agree to wait at 7.00 a.m. at the *Siegessäule*, which at that stage was near the *Reichstag* building, and almost a kilometre away from government buildings in Wilhelmsstraße. Thus at 7.00 a.m. he expected to have an answer to his demands, but the fact that he agreed to wait before occupying government quarters, marked a deviation from

126. Ibid., fo. 176.
127. Erger, *Kapp-Lüttwitz Putsch*, 117, 134–35.
128. BA-Koblenz, N 1150/26, Anklageschrift der Oberreichsanwalt gegen Jagow, Wagenheim, Leipzig, 11 July 1921, fo. 50.
129. HStASt M660/014, Heft 27, memorandum by Otto Hahn, 'Meine Erlebnisse beim innerpolitischen Umstürz im März', 7 Arpil 1920, fo. 4.

the original order from Lüttwitz, and a softening of Ehrhardt's resolve, caused in all probability by the spectre of a street battle.[130]

Second, as Schmalix noted, there were a number of men in the Ehrhardt brigade who were refusing to follow orders to march against the elected government. The evidence gathered from the troops involved in the Putsch is inconclusive, but it does suggest that their morale and determination had been overestimated by officers such as Oldershausen and Oven. For example, Corporal Alwin Wischmeyer, told state lawyers that he had been fooled into thinking that the brigade was going on an exercise.[131] Sergeant Alex Schwend realised that the plans for an exercise were a pretext for a revolt. His superior officers were aware that he would be loyal to the government, so they put him under arrest for five days.[132] Naturally there were many soldiers who were only too happy to help overthrow a government which they felt had betrayed them. Captain Karl von Killinger listed a series of issues, including the evacuation of the Baltic, the Erzberger libel trial and the attacks by left-wing papers, which prompted him to participate in the Putsch.[133] The three different responses of Ehrhardt's troops that have been outlined here, namely rejection, ignorance, or commitment to the Putsch, demonstrate that the brigade was less cohesive than has generally been thought. This lack of cohesion might have been exploited if the government had decided to oppose the march on Berlin. Ultimately Reinhardt's advice was not followed, and the counter-factual argument suggested here was never tested.

Instead the government fled Berlin, first for Dresden and then onto Stuttgart. On 15 March the trade unions called for a general strike, which along with the unco-operative attitude of the bureaucracy and certain parts of the *Reichswehr*, would convince Kapp that his Putsch was doomed. Reinhardt remained in Berlin. On the morning of 13 March he went to see General von Hülsen at Potsdam to try to prevent him from joining the Putschists, but failed.[134] When he returned to his service flat, a soldier from the newly formed Kapp government came to arrest him. Reinhardt resisted arrest, and demanded that a general 'of his party' come to explain the situation. 'After some time I received a message from my adjutant that the Kapp government apologised to me, and demanded only that

130. BArch, R 43 I/2728, Der Oberreichsanwalt, Anklageschrift gegen Ehrhardt, Leipzig 5 May 1923, fos. 93–95.
131. BA-Koblenz, N 1150/28, Verhandlung des Gefreiten Alwin Wischmeyer, Wilhelmshafen, 23 March 1920, fos. 9–13.
132. BA-Koblenz, N 1150/28, evidence of Sergeant Alex Schwend, Wilhelmshafen. 26 March 1920, fos. 23–24.
133. BA-Koblenz, N 1150/28, evidence of Captian Karl von Killinger, Dresden, 4 January 1921, fos. 66–72.
134. HStASt, M 660/034, Bü 24, Bericht über die Besprechungen und Verhandlungen in der Nacht vom 12. bis 13. März und am 13. März morgens.

I would not undertake any action against them. In response I explicitly reserved my freedom of action.'[135] Reinhardt talked to some cabinet ministers who had remained behind, most notably with Eugen Schiffer on both 16 and 17 March.[136] Within a few days it was clear that the Kapp Putsch would be unsuccessful. A combination of the general strike, called by the socialist trade unions, and the refusal of most of the state bureaucracy to co-operate with the Kapp government, rendered it impotent. On 17 March a deputation of officers went to meet Lüttwitz at the chancellery, and demanded that he resign, a demand which he refused. On their way out the officers met Reinhardt and General von der Lippe, who were on a similar mission, agreeing 'that the condition of the Berlin troops urgently demanded that Lüttwitz step down immediately.'[137] Reinhardt, according to another account, was one of several soldiers along with Generals von der Lippe and von Hülsen, who urged Schiffer to bring a demand for Lüttwitz's resignation to the *Reichswehrministerium*.[138]

On 17 March Seeckt began to position himself to take over as the head of army command when the Putsch collapsed. Reinhardt had resigned his post on 13 March. Schiffer was charged by Ebert to make a choice between Reinhardt and Seeckt for the position. Schiffer contacted Bauer, one of Lüttwitz's closest associates to see whom Lüttwitz would accept as a successor. He rejected Seeckt, Reinhardt and even Groener, but later relented and accepted Seeckt.[139] That Lüttwitz was even consulted may have been an attempt by Schiffer to end the Putsch without a struggle. Schiffer rang Seeckt, and asked him 'if he would stay in his current position under Reinhardt. He rejected this brusquely, and explained that he would not work with Reinhardt, even if the latter was subordinated to him. This explanation struck me all the more, since Reinhardt had told me that he was ready to serve the Fatherland and the army under Seeckt.'[140] Now that Lüttwitz had been removed as a factor in the bureaucratic struggle for control of military policy, Seeckt turned on his temporary ally, Reinhardt. Seeckt's abrupt behaviour, and his refusal to have anything to do with Albert, the state secretary to the Chancellor, meant that Schiffer found it difficult to appoint him. However, the die was heavily loaded in Seeckt's favour because a group of officers had agreed that he should become the next head of army command.[141]

135. BA-Koblenz, N 1150/28, Vernehmung von Walther Reinhardt, 26 February 1923, fo. 290–91.

136. Ernst, 'Aus dem Nachlaß', 99–100.

137. BA-Koblenz, N 1150/26, Anklageschrift der Oberreichsanwalt gegen Jagow, Wagenheim, Leipzig, 11 July 1921, fo. 161, although the details of what Reinhardt said to Lüttwitz are unknown.

138. BArch R 3001/22130, Schiffer to Untersuchungsangerichter der Reichsgericht, April 1920, fo. 46.

139. BA-Koblenz, N 1191/I/5, diary entry, dated 17 March 1920, fo. 10.

140. Ibid., fo. 10.

141. Erger, *Kapp-Lüttwitz Putsch*, 284–85.

The manner of Seeckt's appointment was yet another example of how easily the officer corps were able to control the decision-making process of military policy. Although the cabinet asked Reinhardt to return to his post as head of army command on 18 March, he spoke to Seeckt, 'who retained the command.'[142] Seeckt's appointment was not welcomed, and as he left Schiffer's office on 17 March, one SPD deputy shouted at him, 'I don't trust that donkey.'[143] Noske's position was also made untenable by the Putsch. On 18 March the trade-union leader, Carl Legien, called for his resignation. Support within the SPD for Noske also dissolved, and Ebert realised that no SPD deputy would take over the sensitive position as *Reichswehrminister*.[144] Many believed that it was time for a general to take over as the *Reichswehrminister*. Ironically Reinhardt's name surfaced in connection with the post. At a meeting of the SPD party on 23 March Trimborn asked, 'For the post of war minister is there not a good general, like Reinhardt?' Noske replied, 'No, Reinhardt stands and falls with me.'[145] If Reinhardt had lost credibility within the officer corps, he still retained, and perhaps had enhanced, his reputation as a loyal servant of the republic by his actions during the Kapp Putsch. Yet it is significant that there was no way in which Reinhardt could continue as head of the army despite the support of many civilian politicians. Instead it was Seeckt who held the most important card in March 1920, support amongst the officer corps. Reinhardt's position in the *Reichswehrministerium* had been shored up by Noske and Ebert. One of the crutches, Noske, fell away. The Noske-Reinhardt axis, which had been at the centre of military policy formation for fifteen months, was replaced by the partnership between the new *Reichswehrminister*, Württemberg Democratic party deputy, Otto Gessler, and Hans von Seeckt.[146]

On 25 March Reinhardt submitted his resignation to Ebert, who ratified the decision of Schiffer to appoint Seeckt as head of the army on 17 March.[147] He recognised that many of his achievements were made possible by co-operation with Noske: 'With very different basic political ideals, we were united in the belief that an army, expertly led and formed, morally upright, withdrawn from party conflict but loyal to the constitution, was a vital necessity for the German *Volk*, because without one, internal order could not be not be maintained, our right to self-determination could not be guaranteed and our borders could not be protected. With eyes fixed on this goal, I, hand in hand with *Reichswehrminister*

142. Ernst, 'Aus dem Nachlaß', 100.
143. BA-Koblenz, N 1191/1/5, diary entry, dated 17 March 1920, fo. 10.
144. Wolfram Wette, *Gustav Noske. Eine politische Biographie*, Düsseldorf, 1989, 659–66.
145. *Kabinett Bauer*, 757.
146. For a recent and more positive interpretation of Gessler's role, see Heiner Möllers, *Reichswehrminister Otto Gessler. Eine Studie zu "unpolitischer" Militärpolitik in der Weimarer Republik*, Frankfurt, 1998.
147. Ernst, 'Aus dem Nachlaß', 105–106.

Noske, took up and pressed forward restlessly with the arduous work of construction from January 1919.'[148] For Reinhardt the failure to complete the tasks of reorganising the German army after the First World War was a bitter blow. Within a month he had lost both his wife and his job. At his leaving speech on 29 March, which Seeckt did not attend, he admitted 'The experiences of the night of 12 March were shattering for me, for me they were more bitter than those of November 1918.'[149] He was highly critical of the misadventures, lies and rumours, which he felt had destroyed many careers.

The history of the Kapp Putsch underlines several features of the limits of Reinhardt's influence over military policy. First, the treaty of Versailles constrained policy options. Second, within the officer corps Reinhardt lacked authority. His approach to recalcitrant officers was lenient, and he was unable to impose his will on Lüttwitz. Third, his position was dependent on the support he received from the civilian government. In the antechamber of power in the early hours of 13 March, his judgement did not carry as much weight as those of Oven, Seeckt and Oldershausen. In June 1919 during the debate on the treaty of Versailles Groener dominated Reinhardt, and Noske accepted his view that Germany could not resist the Allies. In March 1920 the cabinet also accepted the assessment of the other officers. In two of the most fundamental political decisions taken in the early years of the Weimar republic, Reinhardt's opinion was heard, but not accepted. March 1920 marked the end of his 'political' career, but it would also be the beginning of the revival of Reinhardt's reputation within the officer corps.

For the immediate future of the *Reichswehr* it also marked a victory for Seeckt's conception of a professional army. The outcome of personal rivalries had important political consequences. In March 1920 Reinhardt had proposed what amounted to a *Katastrophenpolitik* for the army, in order to save its reputation with the people. Reinhardt saw the army as an integral part of society. Seeckt, on the other hand, argued that the preservation of the *Reichswehr* should have primacy. Both policies were conceived with the future in mind. For Reinhardt this meant the regeneration of Germany through a close partnership of the military and the people. For Seeckt it meant the preservation of the army to suppress the expected communist rising, and then the creation of a *bündnisfähig* Germany which would renew its traditional alliance with Russia, albeit Bolshevist Russia. They represented two different paths to Germany's re-establishment as a Great Power. From March 1920 until 1923 Seeckt's vision would dominate German military policy.

---

148. Ibid., 105.
149. HStASt, M 660/034, Bü 24, Abschiedsrede des Herrn Generals Reinhardt am 29. März 1920.

Chapter 8

REINHARDT AND MILITARY POLITICS IN THE 1920S

*I*n the early hours of 13 March 1920 Reinhardt appeared to consolidate his reputation as the republican general when he exhorted the cabinet to defend Berlin militarily. The Putsch led to Reinhardt's resignation, but he served in the *Reichswehr* until 1927. He remained involved in military affairs until his death in 1930. By the time he retired at the end of 1927 he had forfeited his pro-republican reputation within the liberal and left-wing press. In April 1927 the *Schwäbische Tagwacht*, a SPD paper, characterised Reinhardt as an officer motivated by career ambitions who turned to the Republic in 1919, and then as commander of *Wehrkreis V* built up the *Reichswehr* as a 'state within the state. He regained the trust of the reactionaries step-by-step through practical acts while he only had loyal phrases for the constitution.'[1] This was not an isolated criticism. By 1930 a series of incidents had alienated many republicans from Reinhardt from his role in the 1923 crisis to his criticism of the SPD's and DDP's military policy in 1927.

However, Reinhardt had not changed direction in a desperate attempt to ingratiate himself with the right and haul himself out of the headquarters of *Wehrkreis V* in Stuttgart. Instead the principles of promoting military values in society and of restoring Germany as a Great Power, which had guided his policies in 1919, continued to inform his actions in the 1920s. First and foremost he was a militarist, and it was a consequence of this which led him to favour right-wing parties in 1923, and attack what he saw as the anti-military stance of the DDP and SPD in 1927. The divergence in aims between the SPD and Reinhardt, which had been masked by the potential for necessary reforms in 1919, now came out into the open. If Reinhardt's career in the 1920s can be seen as a natural continuation of his activities in the German revolution, then it

---

1. *Schwäbische Tagwacht*, 1 April 1927, 'Revolutionäre Reichswehr. Der loyale General Reinhardt'.

shows that the possibilities for long-term cooperation between the SPD and the 'republican' general were distinctly limited. Reinhardt had accepted the Republic in 1918 as the best option for Germany. As the Republic failed to restore German military power, Reinhardt became increasingly disenchanted. In December 1926 Schleicher called on the *Reichswehr* to accept the Republic but also to adapt it to their own aims. This is what Reinhardt tried to achieve in the 1920s. The question which Reinhardt would never live to see answered was whether there was an alternative to the Republic if it did not fulfil the officers' aims.

After the collapse of the Kapp Putsch, the Weimar state faced a challenge from the radical left, particularly in the Ruhr. The weakness of the government was demonstrated by its reliance on *Freikorps* to defeat left-wing armed groups in the Ruhr.[2] Recognising the lack of reliable military power, and aware that political tensions would rise in the period before the June elections, the government decided to establish an experimental brigade which would be stationed in the Döberitz camp, thirty kilometres outside Berlin. Otto Gessler, the new *Reichswehrminister*, appointed Reinhardt as commander of this brigade which became known as the *Lehrbrigade Döberitz*.[3] The government, worried about further putsches and political violence, was determined to defend the capital. Reinhardt, in his inaugural order to the brigade, commented: 'We have been ordered here to be readily available through our proximity [to Berlin] and to become more effective through combined weapons practice. By achieving this the brigade, which is directly under the head of army command, should form an especially strong support for the constitutional power of the Reich.'[4] In the event the brigade became a training unit.[5] It was dissolved in August 1920 after the elections passed off peacefully. Nonetheless it did provide a feeling of security for the government in the difficult period after the Kapp Putsch.[6]

Since the *Lehrbrigade Döberitz* was only a temporary unit, Reinhardt had already been assigned his next post, as commander of *Wehrkreis V*, which was composed of Württemberg, Baden, Hessen and Thuringia. It is significant that Wilhelm Blos, the state president of Württemberg, suggested Reinhardt's name for the post. Just as his appointment as commander of the *Lehrbrigade* reflected the trust many politicians accorded to Reinhardt, so did his appointment as commander of *Wehrkreis V*.[7] Reinhardt was now removed from the centre of military policy formation, and the nature of

2. Hagen Schulze, *Freikorps und Republik, 1918-1920*, Boppard am Rhein, 1969, 304–18.
3. Otto Gessler, *Reichswehr in der Weimarer Zeit*, Stuttgart, 1958, 145.
4. HStASt, M 660/034, Bü 25, 6 May 1920, Lehrbrigade, Ia, Nr. 36, Brigadebefehl 1.
5. HStASt, M 660/034, Bü 25, Reinhardt lecture, 7 June 1920, Manneszucht im Heere.
6. For instance see the report of the French chargé d'affaires to the French Foreign Minister, Millerand on 30 April 1920, in *Documents diplomatiques français*, ed. Stefan Martens, vol. 1, Bonn, Berlin, 1999, 566.
7. HStASt, M 660/034, Bü 26, RWM, PA, Nr. 3501/5.20, 28 May 1920.

his work changed accordingly. In a letter to Noske in 1921 he commented: 'It is a characteristic of our impoverished military situation that one must travel around the land like a wandering teacher, in order to get to know one's few battalions well. Luckily they are at least good, as is the whole of today's *Reichswehr*, and we can be happy for each other that this is the modest harvest of our work.'[8] One of Reinhardt's main concerns during these years was the morale of the troops and officers, and he sought to improve their living conditions, pay and general welfare. For example, he wrote to the *Personalamt*, warning that the reduced chances for promotion would have a negative impact on morale.[9] His concern for troops' welfare had been an influential factor in his policy during his time in Berlin, and a feature of his leadership style that won him respect from the troops. Richard Scheringer, one of the officers convicted at the Ulm trial in 1930 for spreading Nazi propaganda within the *Reichswehr*, noted Reinhardt was 'especially highly regarded in the 5th Division. In the 5th Division one found his picture in the soldiers' quarters above their beds.'[10]

Although the years between March 1920 and early 1923 were more peaceful than the first seventeen months of the Weimar Republic's existence, there were still moments of internal unrest. In March 1921 a failed rising by the KPD led to the death of sixty people.[11] During the strike, 5th Division sent a small number of troops to back up the police. Reinhardt portrayed the revolt alternatively as a crime and as the work of Russian Bolshevists. He explicitly distanced 'the socialist German workers' from any blame.[12] Reinhardt believed that the primary political identification of the working class was with the German nation, rather than with some form of international socialism. The ideal of the 1914 *Burgfrieden* was a fundamental aspect of his politics. Another of his hopes was that the German people would place their trust in the *Reichswehr*. He felt that the actions of the *Reichswehr* soldiers in 1921 'have justified the trust which the German *Volk* have placed in you.'[13]

Reinhardt was aware that in the unstable political conditions of the early 1920s the *Reichswehr* could be called upon to suppress internal unrest at any time. Internal stability was a key pre-condition of a successful foreign policy, and had not yet been achieved in Germany. Towards

---

8. Gustav Noske, *Erlebtes aus Aufstieg und Niedergang einer Demokratie*, Offenbach am Main, 1947, 212.
9. HStASt, M 660/034, Bü 27, Reinhardt to *Personalamt*, November 1920, fo. 1.
10. Richard Scheringer, *Das große Los unter Soldaten, Bauern und Rebellen*, Hamburg, 1959, 182.
11. Heinrich August Winkler, *Weimar, 1918-1933. Die Geschichte der ersten deutschen Demokratie*, Munich, 1993, 150–53.
12. HStASt, M 660/034, Bü 26, Reinhardt to the 5. Division, Abt. Ia, Nr. 620, Stuttgart, 28 March 1921.
13. HStASt, M 660/034, Bü 27, Reinhardt to the 5. Division, Abt. Ic, Nr. 1012, Stuttgart, April 1921.

the end of 1920 Reinhardt worked on guidelines for his officers on the use of troops in cases of internal unrest, summarized in the document 'Suppression of internal unrest'.[14] In Reinhardt's view a suitable response to internal disorder was based on a detailed knowledge of the relevant decrees and orders, and 'a great level of political understanding on the part of the leader.' The use of soldiers was clearly a last resort, and it was up to the civilian powers to keep order. He stressed that the *Reichswehr* was not to get involved in situations without first having received a request for aid from the civilian authorities. In his view the *Reichswehr* was 'the servant of the state, and of the people of the state. They must avoid any appearance of acting on their own account or of getting involved for an economic or political social group.'

Yet as Prussian Minister of War Reinhardt had defended the record of troops used against the Sparticist revolt in Berlin, and the *Räterepublik* in Munich. When the National Assembly deputy Seger claimed that the army was an enemy of the people, Reinhardt replied: 'The deputy has characterised the army as being against the people. The army is there for the people even if in these times it must also act against the people.'[15] The experiences of the *Reichswehr* as the *ultimo ratio* of the civilian authorities demonstrated the difficulties of appearing to be even-handed with all groups in society. Reinhardt was hardly involved in the suppression of revolts in 1919, and therefore the crisis of the Weimar state in 1923, and the subsequent use of the army during the state of emergency, provides a good example of how Reinhardt put the theory of intervention laid out in the document 'Suppression of internal unrest' into practice – and failed in his declared aim of being even-handed.[16] He feared the extreme left more than the extreme right, partly because it was stronger in central Germany, and partly because he agreed with the rhetoric of aggressive national strength espoused by the right.

On 9 January 1923 Germany was declared in default on reparations payments. Two days later the French and Belgian armies occupied the Ruhr.[17] Reinhardt hated the French, whom he described as 'this *Volk* of deep immorality'.[18] He warned his troops that venereal disease was due to the fact that German troops had spent years fighting within France, a country with 'low moral and hygienic conditions', as well as the presence

---

14. HStASt, M 660/034, Bü 27, the document was entitled. 'Die Mitwirkung der Reichswehrtruppen bei der Unterdrückung innerer Unruhen', Wehrkreis V, Abt. Ia/Ic, Nr 1001, 1 January 1921.

15. *Verhandlungen der verfassunggebenden Nationalversammlung*, vol. 328, 1733.

16. One of the major problems in judging Reinhardt's motives in 1923 is the almost complete lack of information on the period in his *Nachlaß*.

17. For the background, see Marshall Lee, Wolfgang Michalka, *German Foreign Policy, 1917–1933. Continuity or Break?*, Leamington Spa, 1987, 44–46; Peter Krüger, *Die Aussenpolitik der Republik von Weimar*, Darmstadt, 1985, 193–206.

18. HStASt, M 660/034, Bü 22, Reinhardt to Ebert, 3 February 1921.

of the French army of occupation in western Germany.[19] A series of articles written for a German-Brazilian paper, *Die Serra Post*, probably by Reinhardt, laid Germany's current economic misery at the feet of the Allies, 'our blood-suckers and oppressors.'[20] He feared that Germany lacked the unity for the struggle with France. Economic pressure was driving the different groups in society apart. With the internal structures crumbling, it was clear 'that there can be no strong front against external pressure.'[21] Yet it was the idea of a united front against foreign oppression that was the guide to his policy in 1923 as he sought to impose law and order, and maintain the Reich as a factor in the European system. Unlike June 1919 he was in no position to drive a *Katastrophenpolitik* in the face of foreign occupation.

Momentarily Germans forgot the deep divisions afflicting their society, and the spirit of 1914 returned.[22] However as the French occupation continued, German national solidarity collapsed.[23] On 8 August printers went on strike in defiance of the orders of the *Allgemeine Deutsche Gewerkschaftsbund* (ADGB) trade union. Wilhelm Cuno, the chancellor since late 1922, resigned, and was replaced by Gustav Stresemann of the DVP, who had recently affirmed his support for parliamentary democracy.[24] Stresemann hoped that foreign pressure might encourage the French to negotiate, but a meeting on 19 September between the British Prime Minister, Stanley Baldwin and the French president, Raymond Poincaré, led Stresemann to conclude that Germany could expect no favours. On 26 September he announced an end to the policy of passive resistance. Almost immediately, Bavaria declared a state of emergency, and the following day the Reich responded, using Article 48 of the Weimar Constitution.[25] Under the terms of the state of emergency declared by Ebert on 27 September, power over the civil administration was transferred to the *Reichswehrminister*.[26] Gessler, the *Reichswehrminister*, could delegate these powers to the military commanders in the *Wehrkreise*. This meant that Reinhardt had executive powers in four states – Württemberg, Baden, Hessen and Thuringia. The *Reichswehr* had been placed in a position of power over civil society, albeit for a maximum period of six months.

19. HStASt M 660/034, Bü 27, Reinhardt, Blomberg decree, 'Bekämpfung der Geschlechtskrankheiten', 18 January 1922, fos. 41–42.
20. HStASt M 660/034, Bü 30, *Die Serra Post*, 23 February 1923, based on a letter written in November 1922.
21. HStASt M 660/034, Bü 30, *Die Serra Post*, 2 March 1923, based on a letter written on 7 January 1923.
22. Gunther Mai, '"Verteidigungskrieg" und "Volksgemeinschaft". Staatliche Selbstbehauptung, nationale Solidarität und soziale Befreiung in Deutschland in der Zeit des Ersten Weltkrieges, (1900-1925), in *Der erste Weltkrieg. Wirkung, Wahrnehmung, Analyse*, ed. Wolfgang Michalka, Munich, 1994, 592–94.
23. Conan Fischer, *The Ruhr Crisis, 1923-1924*, Oxford, 2003, 192–98.
24. Jonathan Wright, *Gustav Stresemann. Weimar's Greatest Statesman*, Oxford, 2002, 212–59.
25. Winkler, *Weimar*, 203–11.
26. BArch, R 43 I/2702, Reichstag, Nr. 6202, Berlin, 27 September 1923, fo. 157.

The principal aim of the *Reichswehr* in 1923 was to hold the Reich together, so as to provide a basis on which the government could negotiate with the French.[27] Reinhardt gave expression to the primacy of foreign policy in a letter to the SPD Thuringian president (officially chairman of the cabinet), August Frölich. He hoped that both men could co-operate so that 'the German *Volk* will be guaranteed a period of civil peace.'[28] It was necessary for Germans to overcome internal strife and look towards the enemy on the Rhine. Reinhardt's view of the Franco-German conflict was highly confrontational. Only by coming together could the German people give the government the platform 'to carry through the coming reckoning with France.'[29]

The initial indications from *Wehrkreis V* were that the delegation of executive powers to Reinhardt was an unnecessary measure. The Württemberg state president, Hieber, wrote to Ebert on the evening of 27 September, objecting to the state of emergency. He claimed that Reinhardt would be overburdened, and possibly distracted by unrest elsewhere in the unwieldy geographical spread of *Wehrkreis V*. He asked for executive powers for Württemberg.[30] Two days later Stresemann replied to Hieber's complaints, arguing that only the concentration of power in the hands of military commanders guaranteed the unity and speed of response which the present crisis warranted.[31]

Adam Remmele, of the SPD and Baden president, had more specific objections to Reinhardt's powers. According to the treaty of Versailles most of Baden lay within a demilitarized zone. He feared that the French would occupy part of Baden, claiming that Reinhardt's military command in Baden represented a threat to French security. Remmele was also sceptical about the *Reichswehr*'s commitment to even-handedness. At the end of June the Baden government complained that Nazis were being recruited for the *Reichswehr*.[32] In mid-September a Lieutenant Colonel Kirchstein had been arrested in Donaueschingen, a small town in south Baden, where he was delivering weapons to *völkisch* groups.[33] Over a month later Reinhardt, who had been on a tour of inspection, suggested 'to put the affair to one side, as cause for complaint in the event in question has not

27. *Das Krisenjahr 1923. Militär und Innenpolitik, 1922–24*, eds Erich Matthias, Hans Meier-Welcker, Düsseldorf, 1980, 334.
28. Ibid., Reinhardt to Frölich, letter dated 29 September 1923, 83.
29. Ibid., 84.
30. BArch, R 43 I/2702, Hieber to Ebert, Stuttgart, Nr. 6152, 27 September 1923, fos. 174–5.
31. BArch, R 43 I/2702, Stresemann to Hieber, Berlin, Nr. 10775, 29 September 1923, fos. 178–9.
32. GLAK, Abt. 233/12550, Baden cabinet to the Reichswehrministerium, Nr. 10543, Karlsruhe, 30 June 1923.
33. BArch, R 43 I/2702, Remmele to Ebert, Stresemann, Karlsruhe, 29 September 1923, fos. 198–200.

occurred for some time.'[34] The dismissal of the Baden government's complaints cannot have helped to build up a relationship of trust between the government and the *Wehrkreis* command in Stuttgart. Reinhardt did not pay the same attention to political relationships as he had in Berlin. This was a particular problem, because the Baden and Thuringian governments were both dominated by the SPD, which, at a regional level, had a much greater distrust of the *Reichswehr* than the SPD politicians in Berlin. Consequently, it was in Baden and most of all Thuringia that Reinhardt had the greatest difficulty in 1923.[35]

Three main factors made Thuringia a flashpoint for political conflict in 1923.[36] First, the elections in 1921 had returned a minority USPD/SPD coalition which was supported by the KPD. The precarious political balance in Thuringia shifted towards the right in local elections in 1922, but this did not stop the coalition government from continuing with policies which alienated the middle classes. The government was accused of giving the KPD preferential treatment, when its disregard for a marching ban went unpunished. By the summer of 1923 politics in Thuringia had been polarised between right and left.[37] Second, this polarisation was accentuated by the political currents in neighbouring Bavaria, particularly in the northern part of that state, in Coburg.[38] In November 1923 it was estimated that there were between 12,000 and 15,000 members of radical right groups camped in Coburg, ready for a march on Berlin. However to get to Berlin, they would have had to pass through Thuringia, which would undoubtedly have led to serious clashes with organised radical left-wing groups there.[39]

Furthermore, the *Reichswehr* had a third problem of its own making, namely it lacked influence in Thuringia. It had only a few garrisons, and it lacked the wholehearted support of the Frölich government. As in the case of Baden, it was a case of socialists' initial mistrust being confirmed by the cavalier attitude of the *Reichswehr*. The Thuringian government complained that an officer from *Wehrkreis* V had arrested a French

34. GLAK, Abt. 233/12550, Reinhardt to Remmele, Stuttgart, Ic Nr. 3931, 1 August 1923.
35. The state president of Hesse, Ülrich, also objected to Reinhardt's powers, BArch R 43 I/2702, Ülrich to Stresemann, 28 September 1923, fo. 159.
36. On the history of Thuringia in Weimar Germany, see Beate Häupel, *Die Gründung des Landes Thüringen. Staatsbildung und Reformpolitik, 1918-1923*, Weimar, Cologne, Vienna, 1995; Friedrich Facius, *Politische Geschichte in der Neuzeit. Geschichte Thüringens*, vol. 5, Cologne, 1978, 456–64.
37. For a contemporary account see Georg Witzmann, *Thüringen von 1918-1933. Erinnerungen eines Politikers*, Meisenheim, 1958, 55–62; Häupel, *Staatsbildung und Reformpolitik*, 128-36, 156–58; Helga Matthiesen, 'Das Gothaer Bürgertum und der Nationalsozialismus', in *Nationalsozialismus in Thüringen*, eds Detlev Heiden, Gunther Mai, Weimar, 1995, 99–108..
38. Donald R. Tracey, 'Der Aufstieg der NSDAP bis 1930', in *Nationalsozialismus in Thüringen*, eds Detlev Heiden, Gunther Mai, Weimar, 1995, 51–52.
39. BHStA, MA 104 381, Verbal note, Bavarian Foreign Ministry, 15 November 1923.

deserter from the army of occupation on Thuringian territory, without permission, and therefore had violated the state's rights.[40] Seeckt, who was dragged into the affair, wrote to the Chancellor in July, asking him to inform the Thuringian government 'that my time is too precious for me to be in the position of concerning myself with such touchiness and sensitivities.'[41] Seeckt was justified to a certain extent, but his manner of expression lacked diplomacy, and contributed to the impression that the *Reichswehr* was unresponsive to civilian fears. Why Reinhardt, who had more time for these matters than Seeckt, did not take the time to cultivate his relations with the civilian government in Thuringia as well as Baden is unclear. It may be simply that neither state had many units, and hence he spent little time there, whereas he had been born in Stuttgart and knew Württemberg extremely well. He also proved reluctant to send a liaison officer to the Thuringian government.[42] Relations were soon exacerbated by disputes over public order and personnel changes in local administration.

Despite the tense relations between the *Reichswehr* and the Thuringian government, the latter issued an appeal to the people on 27 September 1923, which supported the declaration of the state of emergency, 'so that the necessary measures for the restoration of public order and security can be taken.'[43] The following day Reinhardt ordered the Thuringian government to ban public demonstrations. 'Measures are to be taken immediately against each action, which demands a general strike or a civil war.'[44] The procedure employed during the state of emergency meant that Reinhardt issued decrees to the various state governments, and these were then passed on through the normal chain of bureaucracy. This was supposed to ensure that the civil administration suffered the minimum disruption. However the Thuringian government reworded Reinhardt's decree. The rewording banned public demonstrations which were anti-republican, but it also singled out *Deutscher Tag* parades which appeared to demonstrate bias against the right.[45] Nonetheless, since the decree also banned calls for general strikes, the quintessential tool of trade-union and left-wing political pressure, Reinhardt overreacted to the specific mention of *Deutscher Tag* parades as being anti-republican. On 3 October he wrote to Frölich, stressing that all gatherings were anti-republican 'which made it their aim to change the legal foundations on which today's constitution is based.'[46] He mentioned supporters of the 'councils' as a threat to

40. BArch R 43 I/2314, Thuringian cabinet to Cuno, 11 May 1923, Bl. 53–55.
41. BArch R 43 I/2314, Seeckt, RWM to the Chancellor, Berlin, 14 July 1923, Bl. 97.
42. BArch, R 43 I/2314, Reinhardt to Frölich, Ic 4096, Stuttgart, 29 September 1923.
43. BArch R 43 I/2314, Aufruf an die Thüringische Bevölkerung!, 27 September 1923, fo. 221.
44. *Das Krisenjahr 1923*, 81.
45. BArch R 43 I/2314, Thuringian cabinet, 30 September 1923, fo. 221–22.
46. *Das Krisenjahr 1923*, 84–85.

the state. The assessment of the principal threat to the state showed the gulf between the *Reichswehr* and the left-wing parties, and was an issue which would eventually force the SPD out of Stresemann's cabinet. The early dispute between Reinhardt and the Thuringian government also demonstrated how difficult it was to create a broad centre in a political environment as polarised as Thuringia.

Reinhardt's guidelines for military action during periods of internal unrest had underlined the importance that the *Reichswehr* was not to be seen to favour one group over another. By acting under the orders from the government he hoped to avoid involvement in politics. Instead Reinhardt was quickly sucked into the political maelstrom of Thuringia. In his decree to the Thuringian government on 28 September he ordered that the civil administration would remain untouched, in other words that the *Reichswehr* would not impose personnel changes on the local bureaucracy. When the Thuringian government passed on the decree, it instructed the appropriate local police to enforce the orders. However in Eisenach, where normally the municipal police were in charge, it was decided to give these powers to the Landkreisdirektor, Hörschelmann. The Stadtdirektor, Dr Janson, was facing prosecution, and this was the reason for the change in the administrative change of command. The Janson case was emblematic of the conflicts in areas of authority and attitudes between Reinhardt and the Thuringian government.[47] The municipal authorities in Eisenach complained to Reinhardt, who considered that the change constituted a violation of the order that the bureaucratic personnel were to stay in place. Reinhardt was concerned about events in Eisenach because it was a garrison city for the *Reichswehr*, and he felt 'that in the present serious times the leaders of a parish should not simply be changed without pressing need.'[48] Clearly Reinhardt did not consider imminent criminal charges as sufficient cause to remove someone from office. By defending Janson, he compromised his political neutrality, although because of the issues of public order and the importance of Eisenach, he may have felt that he had little choice but to intervene in the affair.

On 5 October, a day after Reinhardt's letter in support of Janson, the *Zweckverband der Arbeitgeber für Eisenach und Umgebung* wrote to him. According to them, the replacement of Janson by Hörschelmann would lead to further disorders. They praised Janson's past record, and claimed that the charges against him were groundless.[49] This letter was followed by one on 8 October from the *Verband der Mitteldeutschen Industrie*. They

47. BArch R 43 I/2314, Thuringian cabinet, 30 September 1923, fo. 221–22.
48. BArch R 43 I/2314, Reinhardt to the Thuringian cabinet, 4 October 1923, WK V, Abt. Ic/IIi Nr 2330, Stuttgart, fo. 225.
49. BArch, R 43 I/2314, Zweckverband der Arbeitgeber für Eisenach und Umgebung to Reinhardt, 5 October 1923, fo. 227.

feared that Hörschelmann's control of the local police in conjunction with the expected entry of the KPD into government with the SPD would lead to a collapse of order in Eisenach. It would provide a model for other cities and areas where left-wing groups wished to take control. They asked Reinhardt to help prevent this unconstitutional behaviour, and to take measures 'in the interest of the maintenance of public order, peace and security.'[50] The industrialists' fears that the KPD would enter government were confirmed by the formation of a KPD/SPD coalition on 17 October. This both increased and solidified the polarization of Thuringian politics.[51]

On the same day the new government was formed Frölich wrote to Reinhardt. He rejected the *Wehrkreis* commander's right to interfere in the Janson case. Moreover, now that the KPD had entered government and sworn an oath to the constitution their demonstrations could not be banned, because according to Frölich they had metamorphosed into a constitutional party. Finally, Frölich argued that it was unfair to ban strikes when the employers refused to raise the workers' wages. The workers would strike unless Reinhardt intervened to promote better employment practices.[52] The letter reflected the change of government, and it led to a more serious confrontation between Reinhardt and the Thuringian government. On 18 October Reinhardt simply reinstated Janson, and even if the prosecution was successful, which Reinhardt doubted, the Thuringian government would have to consult him before removing Janson.[53] Whether or not this policy of confrontation would end with the *Reichswehr* marching into Thuringia depended on whether public order deteriorated further. The two major threats to public order were the formation and activities of radical left-wing groups, called 'hundreds' or a march to Berlin by the Bavarian radical right.

Ministerialdirektor Brill got the impression from a meeting at *Wehrkreis* headquarters in Stuttgart on 5 October that Reinhardt was intent on intervening in Thuringia.[54] When discussing potential areas of conflict Brill noted that '[it] was very characteristic that the states' representatives repeatedly used the expressions "communist fire-brand" and "communist nest", without contradiction from the *Wehrkreis* commanders.'[55] Reinhardt refused to discuss the threat posed by National Socialist groups in

50. BArch, R 43 1/2314, Verband der Mitteldeustchen Industrie to Reinhardt, Weimar, 8 October 1923, fo. 139–41.
51. Häupel, *Staatsbildung und Reformpolitik*, 165–68.
52. BArch, R 43 1/2314, Frölich to Reinhardt, I 7544, 17 October 1923, 230–31.
53. BArch, R 43 1/2314, Reinhardt, WK V, III Ec Nr 4238, Stuttgart, 18 October 1923, Entscheidung anläßlich der Beschwerden betr. die teilweise Dienstenthebung des Oberbürgermeisters Janson, fo. 231.
54. BArch, R 43 1/2314, Bericht über die Lage am 5. Oktober 1923 im Wehrkreiskommando V stattgefundene Besprechung über die Handhabung des Ausnahmezustands, fo. 225.
55. Ibid., fo. 226.

Thuringia. After the meeting Brill spoke to Blomberg about co-operation between the police and the *Reichswehr*. Blomberg told him that the unrest caused by national socialists in southern Thuringia was a matter for the local police. Brill found this remark interesting, because it indicated that the *Reichswehr* did not want to find itself in a confrontational situation with the radical right. At the end of the meeting Reinhardt told reporters from the regional papers 'that he considered it his task as holder of plenipotentiary power in *Wehrkreis V* to create a sort of internal civil peace as a basis for the conduct of foreign policy by the Reich government.'[56] On the other hand Brill believed 'that the use of the *Reichswehr* during the state of emergency is mostly directed against the left.'[57]

The difference between Reinhardt's conception of his own task, and the motives attributed to him by his critics, requires careful consideration. Seeckt's adviser, Hasse, feared Reinhardt was trying to exploit the state of emergency to win the favour of the right by suppressing the 'hundreds'.[58] This confuses cause and consequence. Reinhardt did not openly sympathise with the radical right, as his ban of the SA showed. However he was sympathetic to their nationalist rhetoric. He saw communist groups with their internationalist rhetoric as a far greater threat to Germany than the radical right. During the state of emergency his assessment of the threat to the state led him to listen to complaints and fears about armed left-wing groups, complaints which inevitably came from sections of the middle class. When he began to apply the same criticisms to the DDP and SPD after 1923, the consequences were to undermine the original political basis of the Republic in order to shift it towards the promilitary parties of the right.

The 'hundreds' were the left's poor cousins of the paramilitary groups on the right of the political spectrum. In February Frölich had called on the working class to arm themselves in the same manner as the radical right had.[59] What made the 'hundreds' so exceptionally dangerous in the eyes of many in 1923 was that they were dominated by the KPD, which was widely believed to have violent revolutionary plans. When the KPD entered the Thuringian government in October 1923 the 'hundreds' began to participate more openly in public life.[60] This was an open challenge to Reinhardt's authority. On 6 October 1923 he had banned paramilitary groups, such as the 'hundreds' and the SA.[61] The Thuringian government, at that stage the SPD, was negotiating with the KPD, and so Reinhardt's

56. Ibid., fo. 226.
57. Ibid., fo. 226.
58. *Akten der Reichskanzlei. Die Kabinette Stresemann*, 2 volumes, eds Karl Dietrich Erdmann, Martin Vogt, Boppard am Rhein, 1978, vol. 2, 1196.
59. BArch, R 43 I/2314, Reich Ministry of the Interior to the Chancellor, Berlin, Nr. VII 7313, 1 December 1923, fos. 217–19
60. Ibid., fos. 217–19
61. *Das Krisenjahr, 1923*, 88-89.

order was only passed on 15 October, and then a loophole was created so as to allow the continued existence of the 'hundreds'.[62] The *Truppenamt* analysis commented: 'But this ban [by Reinhardt] remained ineffective, because the Thuringian government only issued it on 15 [October], and the influence of the *Reichswehr* in Thuringia, where they had virtually no garrisons, was not brought to bear.'[63]

The malfunctioning of the chain of command between Reinhardt and the Thuringian government, coupled with grave concerns over the security situation in central Germany, brought the active intervention of the *Reichswehr* nearer. The Reich Interior Ministry, which believed that *Reichswehr* intervention in Thuringia was essential, sent information on the 'hundreds' to Gessler.[64] However a series of reports from the police chief, Hermann Müller-Brandenburg, stressed that the police were in full control of the situation. They had disarmed several gangs of 'hundreds', including one group at an arms factory at Zella-Mehlis.[65] A report compiled by the *Reichszentrale für Heimatdienst* in early November noted that both bourgeois and working-class groups were fearful of the train of events in Bavaria, which could lead to a civil war in central Germany. The report compared the calm to that before a storm. Arguing that unrest was more likely to be caused by economic factors, than by political ones, it urged the Reich government to ensure that people were able to earn enough to buy basic necessities.[66]

Since the formation of the coalition government, relations between Reinhardt and Frölich and his colleagues had worsened. Reinhardt had heard rumours that Karl Korsch, the Minister for Justice, had made an inflammatory speech about the *Reichswehr* on 18 October, threatening to crush it under the feet of a thousand workers.[67] Korsch rejected the accusations, and claimed he saw the *Reichswehr* as an ally.[68] Whether true or not, the rumour was an indictment of the mistrust which plagued Reinhardt's relationship with the Thuringian government. Frölich wrote to Stresemann on 15 October, asking for the state of emergency to be lifted. He argued that Reinhardt had undermined republican strength in Thuringia by his measures. In Frölich's view he favoured right-wing groups, hence his order that all requests for 'Fatherland feasts' (*Vaterlandsfeste*) should be directed personally to him. The ban on leaflets had

62. BArch, R 43 I/2314, Thuringian Interior Ministry, III E Ib 1524 II, Weimar, 15 October 1923, fo. 277.
63. *Das Krisenjahr, 1923*, 340.
64. BArch, R 43 I/2314, Reich Ministry of the Interior to the Chancellor, Berlin, Nr. VII 7313, 1 December 1923, fos. 217–19.
65. BArch, R 43 I/2314, reports of Müller-Brandenburg to the Thuringian Interior Ministry, 27/28 October 1923, fos. 153–54.
66. BArch, R 43 I/2314, Reichszentrale für Heimatdienst, 7 November 1923, fos. 176–78.
67. BArch, R 43 I/2314, Reinhardt to Thuringian cabinet, 22 October 1923, Stuttgart, II Nr 8/23 pers., fo. 233.
68. BArch, R 43 I/2314, Korsch memorandum on speech, fo. 233.

been counter-productive.[69] By writing to Stresemann, Frölich was trying to undermine the Reich government's support for Reinhardt. The complaint must have been passed on to Reinhardt, because on 2 November he wrote a long letter to Gessler, which justified his actions during the state of emergency. He claimed that the Thuringian government had continually distorted the decrees he issued, had favoured the radical left, and had made illegal changes in the bureaucracy. Restrictions on press freedom were designed to maintain public order: 'With the best will in the world I cannot believe that the distribution of pamphlets, which stir up the masses in unconscionable ways, can contribute to the political understanding of the parties and their voters in this time of high political tension.'[70] Reinhardt equated economic and political demands, and therefore he interpreted calls for a general strike as calls for an uprising. The consequence of this was that he sided with the middle classes in Thuringia: 'In conclusion I would like to add that complaints about general security reach me daily from the bourgeois section of the Thuringian population. In my view, the form of the Thuringian government is such that it is not in a position to master this uncertainty.'[71] Reinhardt's letter was a clear step on the way towards *Reichswehr* intervention in Thuringia.

The *Reichswehr* had already taken action in Saxony after the KPD had joined the Zeigner SPD government.[72] Stresemann hoped that Zeigner would resign and so spare himself a confrontation with the *Reichswehr*. On 29 October, after Zeigner refused to resign, Ebert gave the cabinet the power to appoint a civilian commissar, Karl Rudolf Heinze of the DVP. This was a *Reichsexekution* against the Zeigner government, meaning the federal government had removed the state's government since it posed a threat to the Republic. On 30 October Alfred Wellisch, also a SPD member of the Saxon *Landtag*, formed a minority government.[73] Reinhardt supported the *Reichsexekution* against the Saxon government, 'in whose ranks outspoken opponents of our state have found a place.'[74] In an open letter to the troops Reinhardt referred to events in Bavaria. He believed that officers in Munich and Berlin were motivated by 'lofty feelings for the greatness of the German Reich'. He urged them to resolve their internal differences, and turn to their attention to the foreign enemy, France. Since 5th Division was made up of units from different states, Reinhardt believed they had a special appreciation of German unity. This was

69. GLAK, Abt. 233/12484, Frölich to Stresemann, Th I 7456/23, 15 October 1923.

70. *Das Krisenjahr 1923*, 107.

71. Ibid., 109–10.

72. David Pryce, 'The *Reichswehr* and Saxony, 1923: the decision to intervene', *CEH*, 10, 1, 1977, 112–47.

73. Heinrich August Winkler, *Von der Revolution zur Stabilisierung. Arbeiter und Arbeitsbewegung in der Weimarer Republik, 1918 bis 1924*, Berlin, Bonn, 1984, 657–60.

74. HStASt, M 660/034, Bü 27, 5. Division, 30 October 1923, Nachrichten für die Truppen.

underlined by the experiences that smaller west German states had had with French occupations in the past. He declared his loyalty to Seeckt: 'We stand shoulder to shoulder beside the head of army command, who, with an overview of the whole situation, will lead Germany's development towards the point which all of want to see, we who desire our Fatherland to be free and great; and we hope to find our Bavarian comrades by our side in this imperative and disciplined integration into the whole.'[75] He concluded his letter with a reference to the rising political temperature in Thuringia.

Written at a vital juncture during the state of emergency, between the *Reichsexekution* in Saxony and the Hitler Putsch in Munich, the letter gives significant clues to Reinhardt's thinking. He had labelled the Saxon government as an enemy of the state, whereas he believed that the Bavarian government were well-meaning, but misguided. The nationalist rhetoric emerging from Bavaria would have appealed to Reinhardt for whom the unity of the Reich was of supreme importance. Ultimately the primary issue in his political landscape was a reckoning with France, and national strength and unity were pre-requisites for a successful struggle. Nationalist rhetoric stressed these ideas, whereas left-wing rhetoric emphasised the class struggle, which appeared to weaken the nation. On this reading, Reinhardt's instinctive favouring of the right's political cause should not be attributed to class bias, nor can he be seen as some sort of capitalists' tool. Instead his actions were motivated by a desire to maintain German unity, and by his belief that only a strong Germany could defy France.

The Thuringian government was aware of the parallels with Saxony. On 30 October Brill met Major Curze, Reinhardt's liaison officer in Thuringia. He was due to return to Stuttgart the following day, a journey which Brill believed presaged *Reichswehr* intervention. To forestall any decision Brill told Curze that the five hundred Prussian *Schützpolizei* were to be stationed in Thuringia. Curze was doubtful, and he argued that the local authorities seemed to have little idea about the true extent of the 'hundreds' influence. He claimed that weapons were still being distributed from the factory at Zella-Mehlis. He concluded that '[Action] must be taken here, and without delay, so that one group of political fools does not precipitate the whole populace into misfortune.'[76] Curze told Reinhardt that the suppression of the 'hundreds' had not been complete. Reinhardt had agreed that the stationing of an extra five hundred *Schützpolizei* would help the security situation, but he also ordered *Reichswehr* units in Thuringia to increase their public presence. Although Curze represented this move as an effort to maintain public order, it could also

75. Ibid.
76. BArch, R 43 I/2314, memorandum of Ministerialdirektor Brill, fos. 235–36; it is dated 30 October 1923, but also contains details about Curze's activities in Stuttgart, which suggests that it maight have been updated from day to day.

be interpreted as a prelude to moving further *Reichswehr* units into Thuringia.[77] Brill then began to organise a police swoop against para-military groups, including the 'hundreds' as well as groups on the radical right. This was due to start on 5 November.[78]

Reinhardt may not have been aware of Brill's plans, but on 5 November he ordered 3rd Cavalry Division under General Lieutenant Hasse to move into Thuringia, where he had command over the police. In a letter to the Thuringian government, he accused them of failing to counter the threat posed by the 'hundreds'. Many of these groups had simply changed their names to '*Republikanische Notwehr*'. He had received pleas from many quarters to take action, and these could no longer be ignored: 'This condition is intolerable for a great part of the populace and will have the most drastic consequences, while the restriction of production and trade threatens, and further the oppressed sectors of the populace look for illegal support, which to some extent already appears to have happened.'[79] There are strong similarities between this note and the letter which Reinhardt wrote to Gessler. Reinhardt made no mention of the escalating tensions in Bavaria. As he saw it, the situation in Thuringia was entirely due to indigenous factors. The political environment was polarized, and the formation of a KPD/SPD coalition government could only serve to heighten those tensions. This was exacerbated by the apparent inability of the Thuringian government to suppress the 'hundreds'. While objectively the threat from the 'hundreds' was minimal compared to that from Bavaria, Reinhardt was open to the subjective opinions of the Thuringian middle classes. Thus when the *Reichswehr* intervened in Thuringia, it benefited the middle classes. Reinhardt's instructions that the *Reichswehr* must not benefit one social group over another were shown to be inadequate in the polarized political situation in Thuringia. The maintenance of order was not simply a policing issue, but a political issue.

By 8 November the *Reichswehr* had occupied the square in front of the *Fürstenhaus*, where both the *Landtag* and the Ministry of the Interior were located.[80] Like Reinhardt, Hasse stressed the calls from sectors of the populace for *Reichswehr* intervention.[81] Between 5 and 13 November Hasse discovered twenty 'hundreds' in various parts of Thuringia. This meant that there were approximately two thousand armed men in Thuringia, not a large figure in the context of paramilitary power in Germany in the 1920s, but a considerable number for a state as small as Thuringia. It

77. Ibid., fo. 236.
78. Ibid., fos. 236–37.
79. BArch, R 43 I/2314, Reinhardt to the Thuringian cabinet, Stuttgart, 5 November 1923, fo. 234.
80. BArch, R 43 I/2314, report by Thuringian Press Office, 'Weimar mit Reichswehr besetzt', 8 November 1923, fo. 237.
81. BArch, R 43 I/2314, Hasse, 'Aufruf an die Bevölkerung', fo. 237.

also suggests that the police had not been as thorough as the civilian authorities would have liked to think.[82] However many of the measures taken by the *Reichswehr* during their occupation of Thuringia appear to have been unreasonable. Karl Volkmer, a resident of Frankenhausen, submitted a report to the Thuringian government on 29 November. On 22 November the town had been occupied by troops from the Reiter-regiment 16, who then proceeded to arrest people indiscriminately, and even attack onlooking children. In his words: 'Each passer-by, who in the eyes of the soldiers could be a foreigner (Jews were singled out), was arrested without any obvious reason, and the same went for any inhabitant as soon as he uttered an unguarded word, so that some eighty arrests, of which only twelve were upheld, took place.'[83] The President of the *Landtag* also complained that the privileges of parliamentary deputies had been violated by arrests and house searches.[84] Hasse's strong policing methods eventually led Ebert to reprimand him.[85]

Reinhardt's rôle in Thuringian politics came to an end on 15 November when Seeckt decided to hand over full executive powers in that state to Hasse. The reason behind this decision is unclear. Seeckt's dislike of Reinhardt may have played a rôle. He could also have been worried that Reinhardt had political motives in Thuringia. On 19 November Reinhardt complained about the transfer of his powers in Thuringia to Hasse. Otto Hasse, a close adviser to Seeckt, believed that 'Reinhardt felt piqued, because he could no longer rehabilitate himself in right-wing circles by taking action against the left.'[86] Although Reinhardt's interventions benefited the right of the political spectrum, there is no evidence that personal political motives were behind his actions in 1923. In fact Reinhardt's record was coming under increasing criticism within military circles. On 6 November Frölich met Gessler. The former claimed that Reinhardt was exaggerating the danger posed by the 'hundreds'. Although Gessler supported Reinhardt, Kurt von Schleicher and Hasse urged the minister to write to Reinhardt, ordering him to keep in close contact with the Thuringian government.[87] Three days later, Münzel, the Thuringian plenipotentiary to the *Reichsrat*, told Schleicher that Reinhardt and Hasse were passing reams of information to Seeckt on the 'hundreds', information which should, but was not, given to Frölich.[88] On 12 November

---

82. BArch, R 43 I/2314, Hasse, Denkschrift, Ic, Nr 2426, Weimar, December 1923, fos. 260–7.
83. BArch, R 43 I/2314, Abschrift, Karl Volkmer to the the Thuringian cabinet, 29 November 1923, fos. 210–11.
84. BArch, R 43 I/2314, Präsident des Landtags, Leber to Stresemann, Weimar, 23 November 1923, fos. 192–93.
85. *Das Krisenjahr 1923*, 261–62.
86. *Kabinette Stresemann*, II 96.
87. BArch, R 43 I/2314, Sollmann Denkschrift, on meeting in Berlin, 6 November 1923, fo. 234.
88. BArch, R 43 I/2314, Münzel to Frölich, 10 November 1923, fo. 277.

Münzel reported that Schleicher was angry at the way Weimar was occupied on 8 November, just two days after Gessler had promised Frölich closer co-operation with the *Reichswehr*. Schleicher told the plenipotentiary that Reinhardt would be ordered to stay in close contact with the Thuringian government.[89] On 13 November Münzel met Gessler, and presumably emphasised that Reinhardt was not co-operating with the government.[90] Because Reinhardt was based in Stuttgart and had to deal with four state governments, it was difficult for him to keep abreast of all developments. Evidently Thuringia was a priority, but it was also the state that he knew least well within his *Wehrkreis*. Therefore it made sense to transfer Reinhardt's powers to Hasse, who had been in charge of *Reichswehr* operations in Thuringia. Hasse, as has been noted, did not prove to be a more conciliatory commander than Reinhardt.

The sources on the state of emergency in Baden and Württemberg illustrate some of the other issues confronting Reinhardt in 1923. Remmele feared that the French would use Reinhardt's powers over Baden as an excuse to occupy more German territory.[91] Although genuine, fear of French occupation could also be used as a tactical tool. In a note to the Reich Ministry of the Interior, the Baden government complained that Reinhardt had imposed a ban on demonstrations, despite the fact that demonstrations in Baden over the previous few months had passed off peacefully. According to the note the ban could not be policed properly because there were too few ordinary policemen in Baden. This shortfall could not be made good by drafting in the *Sipo* (*Sicherheitspolizei* – armed security police), 'because I [Remmele] know how to judge the mentality of our French neighbours from old experiences.'[92] Baden fears of the French were genuine, but also convenient, since it allowed the government to keep the *Reichswehr* at arm's length.

On 1 October Blomberg wrote to the Baden and Hessen governments, noting that the treaty of Versailles had not foreseen a situation like the current one. Under Article 43 of the treaty no troops were allowed in the demilitarized area, so therefore Reinhardt would have to exercise his authority through the local police.[93] In Baden, where the political temperature was relatively low, the use of local police by Reinhardt was probably sufficient to control the situation. Nonetheless the Baden government still pressed for exemption from Reinhardt's military commands. On 5 October the Baden railway director, Funk, was told by a French officer, Captain Caillault, that the French were worried by the possible establishment of

---

89. BArch, R 43 I/2314, Münzel to the Reichspräsident, 12 November 1923, fo. 277.
90. BArch, R 43 I/2314, Münzel to Frölich, 13 November, Berlin, fo. 278.
91. See above, pp. 174–75 which refer to Remmele's fears.
92. GLAK, Abt. 233/12484, Baden Interior Ministry to the Reich Interior Ministry, Nr 94230, 3 October 1923.
93. GLAK, Abt. 233/12484, Blomberg to Baden, Hessen cabinets, WK V, Abt. Ic, Nr 4105, Stuttgart, 1 October 1923.

a dictatorship in Germany under the guise of the state of emergency.[94] This message, along with other indications of possible French aggression were relayed to Stresemann.[95] However the problem was resolved in the manner suggested by Blomberg. On 11 October, Niesser, the Baden envoy to the Reich, wrote in his political report: 'The military commander in Stuttgart has been instructed to send his instructions and wishes to the Baden state government, and to the appropriate civilian bodies, so that the *Sicherheitspolizei* receive their orders from the same posts as before.'[96]

The Baden paper, *Der Volksfreund*, was critical of Reinhardt's handling of demonstrations. Since the different governments in *Wehrkreis V* had different policies on 'Fatherland Festivals', Reinhardt decided that all applications for such parades would be made directly to him, thus eliminating discrepancies between the states. This naturally incurred suspicion: 'The prerogatives of the military commander are so conceived that they should contribute to securing peace, not that they should cause unease amongst the people. And that is what is happening with this decree.'[97] Even though Reinhardt's decree on 6 October banned both the SA and 'hundreds' throughout *Wehrkreis V*, it was left-wing groups that bore the brunt of the *Reichswehr*'s policing. This was partly due to orders from Seeckt. On 20 November he banned the KPD's youth organisation for spreading sedition in the army.[98] While this led to raids on KPD offices and the confiscation of documents, the Württemberg branch of the *Vereinigte Vaterländische Verbände*, the Nazi-led grouping of right-wing paramilitaries, was left untouched. They were able to continue to hold meetings, and according to one report to the Reich Commissar for Public Order, had been drafted into the so-called *Hilfpolizei*, auxiliary police units which had been created for the duration of the crisis.[99]

Whereas Reinhardt's actions in Thuringia had led to a civil-military crisis and the fall of the government, the very different political conditions of Württemberg ensured smooth, if biased, co-operation. Communist groups had been identified as the main threat by the Württemberg government, even before the state of emergency.[100] At a meeting with Reinhardt on 29 October Bolz complained that the *Reichswehr* had done little to curb the growth of communism 'which is leading to the

94. GLAK, Abt. 233/12484, Aktennotiz, Baden Ministry of the Interior, 8 October 1923.
95. GLAK, Abt. 233/12484, Remmele to Stresemann, Nr 96690, Karlsruhe, 10 October 1923.
96. GLAK, Abt. 233/12484, Niesser to Remmele, Politische Bericht, Nr 41, 11 October 1923.
97. GLAK, Abt. 233/12484, *Der Volksfreund*, Karlsruhe, 12 October 1923.
98. GLAK, Abt. 233/12484, Chef der Heeresleitung, Nr 590/23 T 1.III, Berlin, 20 November 1923.
99. BArch, R 1507/67150, 233, Abschrift zu RKO, Nr 9211/23, fos. 20–22.
100. See some of the reports form the Württemberg Police President, in HStASt E 151/03/698. In the same file the letter from State President Hieber to Ebert, 14 August 1923, justifies the declaration of a local state of emergency due to the KPD threat.

terrorisation of the people.' He urged Reinhardt to take tougher measures, including the use of special courts (*Ausnahmegericht*).[101] Reinhardt's knowledge of conditions in Württemberg and the presence of a sympathetic government meant that this state was one of the more peaceful areas in Germany in 1923. Maintaining law and order was dependent on the social and political context, and not simply on the strength of the *Reichswehr*.

The state of emergency was lifted at the end of February 1924. Reinhardt wrote a letter to the state governments in *Wehrkreis V*, thanking them for their help in what he called 'the work of making our German Fatherland healthy again.'[102] The state of emergency in 1923 marked a significant stage in the relations between the *Reichswehr* and the republic. The differing treatment of right-wing Bavaria and left-wing Saxony and Thuringia appeared to confirm that the *Reichswehr* was less than committed to the principle of '*Überparteilichkeit*' (being above party). The events of 1923 presented Reinhardt with very different challenges to those he had faced in 1919 when he had managed for the most part to avoid association with the suppression of the radical left in Berlin and Munich. What conclusions can be drawn? First, his relations with the various governments within his *Wehrkreis* depended both on their political orientation, and on his personal relationships with them and his knowledge of the state. Second, his hopes that the *Reichswehr* could act in an even-handed manner when called upon by the civilian authorities to keep order proved illusory. In a state as polarised as Thuringia, where the preservation of public order were subjects of intense political debate, there was little chance that Reinhardt could act in a neutral way. Nonetheless, he did not help his own cause by ignoring the legitimate fears of left-wing groups about events in Bavaria. Third, the *Reichswehr* was more than a police force. Officers had a wide conception of 'public order'. In Reinhardt's view, the state had to maintain social cohesion by intervening in economic and social affairs. Intervention would promote national unity, a key element of the primacy of foreign policy.

The state of emergency also revealed a shift in Reinhardt's political views away from left-wing political parties and towards the right which he believed would offer a better political basis for the restoration of Germany as a Great Power. Did the Republic offer a basis for a foreign policy directed towards this goal? In the immediate term his principal concern was to hold Germany together, so that the state could begin negotiations with France. Disunity and separatism would only serve the French goal of weakening the German state. The internal political corollary of this was that Reinhardt, and other officers, were sympathetic to

101. HStASt E 151/03/698, Abschrift, 'Massnahmen gegen inneren Unruhen', 3 November 1923.
102. *Das Krisenjahr 1923*, 315.

the nationalist rhetoric which the radical right as well as the moderate right espoused. Officers genuinely believed that the threat from the KPD was much greater than that from the right. Reinhardt was not avowedly anti-republican and his actions in overthrowing the KPD-SPD coalition in Thuringia can be construed as a defence of the Republic. The events of 1923 show that the *Reichswehr* was in favour of the Republic, in favour of a nationalistic republic. The problem was that if the Republic failed to 'go the German way', to paraphrase Seeckt, then the army might undermine it. Reinhardt's relations with the Republic from 1923 until his death were determined by his subjective analysis of the progress of the state and society towards what he saw as the national mission of militarisation and liberation from the Versailles system.

The *Reichswehr* had favoured the right in 1923 because they seemed to share a similar political vocabulary. The restrictions on military power, and in particular the prohibition of conscription, led officers to fear that martial values which they associated with Germany's greatness, were losing ground in the Republic. Military festivals became a visual means to promote the *Reichswehr* and its desire for a militarised society. However such spectacles, which often centred around the meeting of an old imperial regiment, were criticised by democratic and socialist politicians who saw in the pageantry a threat to the Republic. Commemorative politics, which touched on issues such as the flag and the memory of the war and the *Kaiserreich*, became a point of conflict between the military and those parties most closely associated with the Republic, the DDP and the SPD.

At the end of 1924 Reinhardt crossed swords with the DDP deputy from Baden, Ludwig Haas. Haas objected to the use of the imperial flag at a military religious service in August 1924, an event incidentally which Reinhardt, having lost his religious faith in the war, did not attend. However he argued that the republican colours, black, red and gold, had only been introduced in the first place as a concession to tempt Austria to unite, and as a sop to the USPD. Now that the former was no longer a possibility and the latter no longer a political force, Reinhardt felt that the parties in the centre of German politics, the Catholic Centre, the DDP and the DVP, should lead a campaign to re-institute the more popular imperial colours.[103] Haas upbraided the general for his lack of political sensitivity. Rather than promoting military values and a sense of social unity, such incidents 'made the creation of understanding relations between the *Reichswehr* and the republican sectors of society, especially the Social Democrats, more difficult.' Like Reinhardt he recognised that working-class support was fundamental to the recreation of German military power.[104] There was however a major difference. Where Haas wanted a republican military, Reinhardt wanted a militarised Republic. The transmission of

103. HStASt M 660/034, Bü 22, Reinhardt to Haas, 11 October 1924.
104. HStASt M 660/034, Bü 22, Haas to Reinhardt, 1 November 1924.

values went in the opposite directions. This exchange probably reflects Reinhardt's frustration at the lack of progress on the revision of the military clauses of Versailles and the allegedly low prestige of military values in Weimar society. This did not damage Reinhardt's career – at the end of 1924 Reinhardt was promoted to commander of *Reichswehrgruppen-kommando II*, which was based in Kassel and in charge of the army units in western and southern Germany.

There was one last chance for Reinhardt to return to the highest echelons of the *Reichswehr*. During the autumn manoeuvres of 1926, for which he earned considerable praise, rumours began to circulate that the son of the Crown Prince had attended the manoeuvres of a conservative regiment. Seeckt, who had forfeited the trust of Gessler and Hindenburg, was forced to resign.[105] Reinhardt ascribed Seeckt's fall not so much to the actual scandal but to the personal confrontation between Gessler and Seeckt, as well as the latter's intolerant attitude to his fellow officers.[106] Reinhardt emerged as a candidate, although as he recognised 'it became a matter of who would have the decisive word.'[107] However there were a number of problems. First, the new *Chef der Heeresleitung* would need the support of Ebert's successor as President, Field Marshal Paul von Hindenburg. Memories of Reinhardt's role in 1919 were an important obstacle. Moreover Reinhardt's record in the First World War came in for a withering examination. The *Bergische-Märkische Zeitung* argued that his post-war career was due to 'his political skills', since the defeat of 7th Army in July 1918 was his responsibility.[108]

In the end General Wilhelm Heye, the 'good uncle' as he was known, was chosen to succeed Seeckt. Reinhardt took it in good grace, but the fact that he was passed over signalled that he was yesterday's man. In a letter congratulating Heye, he wrote: 'At an earlier time when the post of the *Chef der Heeresleitung* came under attack and there was the possibility of General von Seeckt's resignation, I explained to the *Reichswehrminister*, that I would regret such an event, but would ask that the successor be chosen from the younger generals.' He concluded: 'I see my further service as only a stage of transition.'[109] However before he retired he would make one final serious intervention in military politics with an article in January 1927.

Seeckt's resignation was only one of several issues, which shook the *Reichswehr* in 1926, and it is in the context of these, and the fall of the third Marx government in December 1926, that Reinhardt's article of 10 January 1927 and the debate surrounding it, must be understood. Briefly

105. F. C. L. Carsten, *The Reichswehr and politics, 1918-1933*, Oxford, 1966, 245–50.
106. Reinhardt's memorandum on Seeckt's resignation, in Fritz Ernst, 'Aus dem Nachlaß', 116–17.
107. Ibid., 117.
108. *Bergische-Märkische Zeitung*, 9 October 1926.
109. HStASt M 660/034, Bü 31, Reinhardt to Heye, Cassel, 18 October 1926.

the article alleged that the SPD's and DDP's anti-military, pacifist tendencies were discouraging their voters from applying to join the *Reichswehr*.[110] In November the leader of the *Jungdeutscher Orden*, Arthur Mahraun, revealed the plans which General Watter had developed in 1923 to sabotage the French occupation of the Ruhr. These would have led to high civilian casualties, and Gessler made a strong statement in the *Reichstag* distancing the *Reichswehr* from such plans, even though Watter had left the army in 1921.[111] However the right-wing *Deutsche Zeitung* ran an article which defended the general's sense of responsibility to the nation and the ideals of sacrifice.[112] Public opinion seemed to be on Gessler's side, but the officer corps was probably less enamoured with the disparaging remarks about a former colleague. Further it exposed how little support there was in the country for any sort of *Volkskrieg*. This may not have been on the immediate agenda, but the project of militarizing society must have seemed further away than ever.

There were two more serious threats. Paul Löbe, SPD deputy and President of the *Reichstag*, had proposed to change the system of recruitment, which allowed officers effectively to pick and choose recruits, a system which seemed to be biased against socialist applicants.[113] Löbe wanted to introduce a recruitment board which would be overseen by the *Reichstag* in order to ensure a fair process. This, argued officers, would lead to the politicisation of recruitment and the army. The second challenge to the *Reichswehr* came from Philipp Scheidemann, who in a *Reichstag* speech in December 1926 spoke of the links between the Red Army and the *Reichswehr* at a sensitive time in negotiations for the withdrawal of the Inter-Allied Military Control Commission.[114] Although the *Manchester Guardian* had already revealed these links, Scheidemann's speech brought the issue into the domestic political sphere. What made the situation even more dangerous for the *Reichswehr* was that the third Marx cabinet, composed of the DDP, DVP and Centre Party, had collapsed. The new government could either include the SPD or the nationalist DNVP. The period between the third and fourth Marx governments is central to the political history of the *Reichswehr* as it sought to protect its position in the face of public ire and governmental change.[115] That it succeeded was in no small way due to the machinations of Schleicher.

110. *Deutsche Allgemeine Zeitung*, 'Der Heeresersatz', 8 January 1927.
111. *Berliner Tageblatt*, 25 November 1926.
112. *Deutsche Zeitung*, 25 November 1926.
113. A report conducted by the *Reichswehr* in late 1926 to counter accusations of bias showed that 32% of soldiers had working-class backgrounds; BA-MA RH 12-1/ v. 12, 'Übersicht über Herkunft und Familienstand der Soldaten des Reichsheeres und den Beruf ihrer Väter', 20 October 1926.
114. Carsten, *Reichswehr and politics*, 255–56.
115. Josef Becker, 'Zur Politik der Wehrmachtabteilung in der Regierungskrise 1926/7: zwei Dokumente aus dem Nachlaß Schleicher', *VfZ*, 14, 1966, 69–78.

His activities behind the scenes have been well detailed by Becker. However it is possible to surmise that he was also the instigator of Reinhardt's article as part of a carefully orchestrated campaign to counter left-wing attacks on the army. The text of the article was known by Gessler before its publication.[116] Correspondence which related to the post-publication debate ran through Schleicher's hands.[117] Reinhardt was also the most suitable figure within the officer corps to conduct a public attack on the SPD and DDP. Reinhardt's – admittedly declining – reputation for objectivity might disarm those who saw pro-military statements as being purely reactionary. Further Reinhardt's career in the military had clearly come to an end. Overlooked in favour of Heye, he had become expendable. He could risk public controversy. Of course it is possible that Reinhardt simply wrote the piece himself, since it certainly expressed fervent convictions. Given that it was published in the *Deutsche Allgemeine Zeitung*, a leading conservative national paper, and that Schleicher was trying to shift the balance of political power to the right, Reinhardt's contribution was part of a larger strategy.

In his article of 8 January 1927 Reinhardt defended the current process of recruitment, which guaranteed the best choice of candidates because the officer knew local people and conditions. The most important qualities were 'a sense of comradeship, bravery and a willingness to fight.' Party political allegiances should not enter the equation unless the candidate belonged to party 'fanatically' opposed to the state. This was a standard argument, but Reinhardt concluded by attacking the 'firm faith in "No more war"' and the lack of support in the DDP and SPD, the parties of Gessler and Noske, for 'national military strength (*nationalen Wehrhaftigkeit*)'. The lack of soldiers from the liberal, democratic and socialist milieu was the result of the parties' consistently negative attitude to the *Reichswehr*. It was not the ordinary workers, but their political representatives with whom Reinhardt found fault.[118] The article shifted responsibility for flaws in the recruitment process from reactionary officers to pacifistic politicians.

The range of reactions was predictable. A meeting of the DDP saw it as another 'intolerable' example of 'generals getting mixed up in politics'.[119] The SPD paper in Württemberg revelled in the national exposure of Reinhardt as a 'reactionary', which had been clear to all in the region 'during his years in Stuttgart.' It asserted that Reinhardt now saw the army as an instrument of political reaction, or a war of liberation.[120] The

116. BA-MA N 42/42, Gessler to Theodor Wolff, 19 January 1927, fo. 39.
117. BA-MA N 42/42, see the exchange of letters between Haas and Reinhardt, fos. 43–45.
118. *Deutsche Allgemeine Zeitung*, 'Der Heeresersatz', 8 January 1927.
119. *Linksliberalismus in der Weimarer Republik. Die Führungsgremien der Deutschen Demokratischen Partei und der Deutschen Staatspartei*, eds L. Albertin, K. Wegner, Düsseldorf, 1980, 422.
120. *Schwäbischer Tagwacht*, 'Der Reichswehrersatz', 11 January 1927.

latter point was taken up by the liberal *Frankfurter Zeitung*: 'Does Reinhardt not understand that for a peaceful Republic there can be no greater danger than to be protected by people who take war lightly, who press for adventures?'[121] There was a larger issue at stake than simply recruitment, namely whether the Weimar Republic would be a peaceful or belligerent state. While Germany was in no position to pursue an aggressive military *Machtpolitik* in 1927, theories of *Volkskrieg* had been gaining ground within the officer corps.[122] Moreover the continued existence of paramilitary groups pointed to a more aggressive and violent form of nationalism, which was given a voice by writers like Ernst Jünger. Reinhardt feared the growth of pacifism, but republican circles recognised the increasing popularity of military forms in civilian life.[123] If German society was militarized, then it called into question the values, and hence the existence, of the Republic. The motivation behind Reinhardt's article was not to overthrow the Republic, but to change it in favour of the *Reichswehr* agenda. Nonetheless, the consequence of these attacks on parties who failed to promote the militarization of society was to undermine the Republic. If the Republic did not adopt the *Reichswehr*'s agenda, then a new state would have to be established.

In the summer of 1927, aged fifty-five, Reinhardt decided to retire from the army.[124] He did not explain his reasons, but the official line was that he had retired to make space for the promotion of younger officers.[125] Reinhardt had raised the slow process of promotion on occasion.[126] Once Heye had been chosen as head of Army Command, it was clear that Reinhardt was marking time in the army. His plans for the so-called Reinhardt course, which is the subject of the next chapter, may have been in their embryonic stage, and he probably thought that he could do more for the *Reichswehr* by retiring, and turning to teaching and writing, than by preventing the promotion of younger officers. His leaving speech drew on the ideals of sacrifice and the memory of the war dead: '[The picture presented to me today] will remind me of the fallen, and I want to remember them today. Because without blood sacrifice there will be no future. The greatest wealth (*höchste Güter*) can only be gained and maintained with the greatest commitment, freedom can only be paid for with blood.

---

121. *Frankfurter Zeitung*, 'General Reinhardt über die Heeresersatzfrage', 9 January 1927.
122. Wilhelm Deist, 'Die Reichswehr und der Krieg der Zukunft', *MgM*, 34, 1, 1989, 81–92.
123. Wolfram Wette, 'Von Kellogg bis Hitler (1928–1933). Die öffentliche Meinung zwischen Kriegsächtung und Kriegsverherrlichung', in *Pazifismus in der Weimarer Republik*, eds Wolfram Wette, Kurt Holl, Paderborn, 1981, 149–72; Bernd Weisbrod, 'Violence and Sacrifice: Imagining the Nation in Weimar Germany', in *The Third Reich Between Vision and Reality. New Perspectives on German History, 1918-1945*, ed. Hans Mommsen, Oxford, 2001, 5–19.
124. HStASt M 600/034, Bü 31, Reichswehrministerium to Reinhardt, 8 August 1927.
125. See the collection of articles in HStASt M 660/034, Bü 31.
126. HStASt M 660/034, Bü 32, Reinhardt memorandum, 'Beförderungsverhältnisse im Reichsheere', probably 1926–27.

The fallen remind us to complete their work.'[127] Only in June 1919 during the debate over the treaty of Versailles had he spoken in such terms but the sacred sense of mission, with which the liberation of Germany from Versailles was bound, had remained a central motivation in his career.

There was one final episode in his life which revealed the waning of that missionary zeal. At the end of 1928 *Die Welt am Abend* claimed it had exposed a second German army, which was being secretly trained by Reinhardt.[128] This allegedly explained why Reinhardt had taken early retirement.[129] According to *Die Welt am Abend* Reinhardt had established a central organisation which could call upon 'a great number of nationalist paramilitaries'. Apparently Reinhardt's nemesis from the Kapp Putsch, Captain Hermann Ehrhardt, now a right-wing terrorist, had put Reinhardt in touch with Hitler. This was probably the most unlikely aspect of the rumour, and there is no evidence that Reinhardt was involved in such a project.[130] The Prussian police had trailed Ehrhardt for the best part of a decade, and Reinhardt did not appear once in their files.[131] Finally, it is difficult to believe that Hitler would be willing to surrender so much control to the *Reichswehr*. On 3 December 1928, in response to rumours about SA participation in *Reichswehr* exercises in Hessen, Hitler banned any National Socialist from colluding with the state: 'The national socialist has no reason to lift a finger for today's state which has no comprehension of our sense of honour and which can only perpetuate the misfortune of our people.'[132]

Reinhardt's name did appear after his death in August 1930 in connection with the Ulm trial of three young officers who had spread Nazi propaganda in their barracks. Richard Scheringer, one of the officers on trial and later a convert to communism, had mentioned that he had visited Reinhardt.[133] General Ludwig Beck, who was the superior officer, dismissed the idea that Reinhardt had any plans for the overthrow of the Republic. He did mention that he had spoken to Reinhardt about morale within the army just before the latter's death. Reinhardt was 'deeply worried about the *Reichswehr*'s zest (*Schwung*) to keep the spirit of a man alive who would serve for twelve years.'[134] In this context Scheringer's

127. HStASt M 660/034, Bü 31, Abschiedsansprache, 12 January 1928.

128. *Die Welt am Abend*, '"Reinhardts Volksarmee", und wieder Schwarze Reichswehr', 17 December 1928.

129. This detail was added by *Die Rote Fahne*, 'Neue Enthüllungen über Reinhardt', 10 January 1929.

130. The files of the *Reichskommissar für öffentliche Ordnung*, which contained the above articles, did not have any evidence, BArch R 1507/67104, nr 64.

131. Geheimes Staatsarchiv, Dahlem, Rep 77, Titel 4043, Nr 189 (Preußisches Ministerium des Innerns, Abteilung VI, Inhalt Ehrhardt 1923–1932).

132. *Hitler. Reden Schriften Anordnungen. Februar 1925 bis Januar 1933*, eds Bärbel Busik, Klaus Lankheit, vol. 3/1, Juli 1928 – Februar 1929, Munich 1994, 294–96.

133. Peter Bucher, *Der Reichswehrprozeß. Der Hochverrat der Ulmer Reichswehroffiziere 1929/30*, Boppard am Rhein, 1967, 283.

134. Ibid., 225.

account of his meeting with Reinhardt in Lichterfelde in December 1929 is significant. Scheringer believed that he needed the support of a respected general to give credibility to the nascent Nazi movement within the army and he revealed his plans to Reinhardt whom he had known as commander of *Wehrkreis V*. Reinhardt did not want to get involved: 'I am too old, too exhausted, I really cannot do it.' He also objected on practical grounds, first because there was no mass movement at that time, and second because it was impossible to start a mass movement from within the *Reichswehr*. However he did acknowledge Scheringer's idealism and promised not to reveal the young officer's plans.[135]

The encounters with Beck and Scheringer reveal a man who was not only ageing prematurely, but also resigned, disappointed with a state and a society which, he felt, had not fully accepted the *Reichswehr*. It was for this reason that he admired Scheringer's youthful idealism even though it was clearly hostile towards the Republic. The failure of the Republic to militarize German society and pursue a more aggressive and successful revision of the military clauses of the Versailles treaty, in other words to fulfil the subjective tests of a state that had been set by officers, had diminished Reinhardt's support for the Republic. Yet as he pointed out there was no alternative. He died before the Nazis established themselves but it is not too difficult to believe that had Reinhardt lived he would have seen in them, like many others, the saviours of Germany, the movement which would fulfil the mission for which two million German soldiers had died in the war.

135. Richard Scheringer, *Das große Los unter Soldaten, Bauern und Rebellen*, Flemburg, 1959, 183–84.

Chapter 9

THE *REINHARDTSKURSE* AND REINHARDT'S MILITARY THOUGHT

Reinhardt's major legacy to German military history was the establishment of the *Reichswehr* in 1919. However he also was an important representative of the theories of the militarization of society and *Volkskrieg*. These were, respectively, the pre-condition and means of the restoration of Germany as a Great Power. This marked him out from Seeckt, the advocate of limited warfare and a professional army, and Groener who accepted the possibility of a limited war in an interdependent international system. If total war never occurred, it existed as a concept in interwar Germany. Officers such as Reinhardt and Joachim von Stülpnagel were two significant representatives. They advocated the absolute conflation of the military and national interest. State and society were to be organised for military conflict, and the ability of the state to wage war lent it legitimacy. The political constellations of Weimar Germany never allowed for the implementation of the doctrine. If one reads Reinhardt's military thought, and bears in mind the political foundations of the Republic, then it becomes clear that the logic of Reinhardt's thought was anti-republican, despite his own assertions to the contrary. The militarized version of the primacy of foreign policy led the *Reichswehr* to reject the Republic as a solution to the problem of liberating Germany from Versailles. But in the late 1920s when Reinhardt was putting his thoughts down on paper, there was no alternative to the Republic. Theory did not lead inexorably to action, and pragmatism outweighed radicalism in his career with the significant exception of Versailles. Whether or not his military thought would have led him to destabilize the Republic in the 1930s is a counter-factual proposition to which we can return later.

His military thought can be best examined through the lectures he gave to young officers attending the *Reinhardtskurse*. Between his retirement from the *Reichswehr* at the end of 1927 and his death in August 1930, the *Reinhardtskurse* became the main focus of his life. The origins of the course are not clear.[1] In 1947 Gessler wrote a letter to Rudolf Pechel, editor of *Deutsche Rundschau*, claiming that 'the so-called *Reinhardtskurse* was set up by me, and Groener tried to dismantle it due to his personal animosity towards General Reinhardt. Heye was opposed to this.'[2] This would suggest that the course had been set up in late 1927, before Gessler's resignation as *Reichswehrminister* and Reinhardt's from the army. However it is unlikely that Groener opposed the idea and content of the courses, no matter what his personal feelings for Reinhardt were. Groener was an advocate of a broad education for young officers.[3] Much of the criticism of the *Reichswehr* military training programme argues that it had a narrow focus on tactics and operations, and Reinhardt hoped to correct this imbalance.[4]

Reinhardt was highly regarded by his pupils. Hermann Teske, a general staff officer in the *Wehrmacht*, claimed that Reinhardt could stand shoulder to shoulder with military thinkers such as Clausewitz, Gneisenau and Schlieffen, amongst others. He stressed the quality of their thinking: 'They were not simply military writers, who were transmitting their experiences to the world, but rather experts, who raised their experiences and knowledge through systematic thought about the core of the issue and brilliant inspiration to a level of prophetic wisdom.'[5] Although Teske may have vastly overestimated Reinhardt's influence and wisdom, his writings warrant serious investigation.

In fact, it was significant that the course took place at all. For example, in the French army there was little debate on developments in military affairs in the inter-war years. The opinions of radical military thinkers were often ignored.[6] Therefore the fact that Reinhardt had an important forum in which he could express his views on military affairs demonstrates the relative openness of the *Reichswehr*. What is even more interesting is that the *Reinhardtskurse* were connected to the *Hochschule für Politik*, an institution set up and populated by figures such as Theodor Heuss, liberal political scientist and future president of the Federal

---

1. The source material relating to the course concentrates on the content of the lectures, rather than administrative matters.
2. Otto Gessler, *Reichswehrpolitik in der Weimarer Zeit*, Stuttgart, 1958, 509–510.
3. Detlef Bald, 'Zur Reform der Generalstabsausbildung in der Weimarer Republik: Die Reinhardt-Kurse', in *Militärische Verantwortung in Staat und Gesellschaft. 175 General-stabsausbildung in Deutschland*, ed. Detlef Bald, Koblenz, 1986, 116.
4. David N. Spires, *Image and Reality. The Making of the German Officer, 1921–1933*, West-port, London, 1984, 115–17; Dennis E. Showalter, 'Past and Future: The Military Crisis of the Weimar Republic', *War & Society*, 14, 1, 1996, 60–62, 66.
5. Hermann Teske, *Die silbernen Spiegel. Generalstabsdienst unter der Lupe*, Heidelberg, 1952, 13–14.
6. Williamson Murray, 'Armored Warfare: The British, French and German Experiences', in *Military Innovation in the Interwar Period*, eds Alan Millett, Williamson Murray, Cambridge, 1996, 32–34.

Republic, and Otto Suhr, a trade union leader.[7] Reinhardt encouraged his pupils to take a broad view of military affairs.

The *Reinhardtskurse* were a more comprehensive project than the lectures that Reinhardt gave. Attendance at Heuss's lectures on politics indicate that the officers' experiences were not simply confined to the study of Reinhardt's ideas. When Reinhardt felt that he was not in a position to lecture on a certain topic, he invited other speakers. For example, Josef Koeth, the former head of the War Raw Materials Office, delivered a lecture on his experiences during the war.[8] On another occasion Reinhardt took his charges to the Krupp factory in Essen to hear lectures from scientists working there.[9] Altogether he planned to give nine or ten lectures, which would take place in the winter term of 1928/9.[10] The lectures would provide a useful counterpart to practical experience: 'the practice is not contradictory to study, but rather is engaged in continuous intercourse with it. Only by thinking about the nature and connection of wartime events, does one succeed in mastering them, and only through practice can one find the opportunity to test these connections.'[11] His approach to the study of military affairs was to examine military history so as to gain an insight into the nature of warfare. His lectures focused on three areas, namely the formation of a militarily capable state, the preparation of society for war, and the nature of war. After Reinhardt's death in 1930 the course continued until 1933 and has been seen as a pre-cursor in some respects to the *Wehrmacht-Akademie*.[12]

For Reinhardt, and indeed all officers, the primary aim of any German government after 1918 was the revision of the treaty of Versailles. His policies as Prussian Minister of War and then as head of the army command sought to strengthen Germany to achieve this essential foreign policy goal. His military thought was thus based on the primacy of foreign

---

7. Theodor Heuss, *Soldatentum in unserer Zeit*, Tübingen, 1959, 26–28; id, *Erinnerungen, 1905–1933*, Tübingen, 1963, 267; on Heuss's career before 1933, see Jürgen Heß's study, *Theodor Heuss vor 1933. Ein Beitrag zur Geschichte des demokratischen Denkens in Deutschland*, Stuttgart, 1973.

8. HStASt, M 660/034, Bü 39, 'Die Elemente der Wehrhaftigkeit', 5; *Walther Reinhardt. Wehrkraft und Wehrwille. Aus seinem Nachlaß mit einer Lebensbeschreibung*, ed. Ernst Reinhardt, Berlin, 1932, 88.

9. Historisches Archiv Krupp, WA 48/121, itinerary for the visit of Reinhardt, 20 September 1929. I would like to thank Professor Hortmut Pogge von Strandmann for bringing this source to my attention.

10. HStASt, M 660/034, Bü 39, note on lecture list.

11. HStASt, M 660/034, Bü 38, 'Über Art und Wert wissenschaftlicher Arbeit für ältere Soldaten', fo. 1.

12. Hansgeorg Model, *Der deutsche Generalstabsoffizier. Seine Auswahl und Ausbildung in Reichswehr, Wehrmacht und Bundeswehr*, Frankfurt, 1968, 60–63, 105; see also Bald 'Die Reinhardt-Kurse', 118–21; *Tradition und Reform im militärischen Bildungswesen. Von der preussischen Allgemeinen Kriegsschule zur Führungsakademie der Bundeswehr. Eine Dokumentation 1810–1985*, eds Detlef Bald, Gerhild Bald-Gerlich, Eduard Ambros, Baden-Baden, 1985, 164–68.

policy. Reinhardt expected that Germany would achieve military equality with the other European powers. As early as January 1919, he told a colleague that he expected that Germany would be rearmed with the most modern weapons by 1935.[13] He urged the *'wehrhafte Mann'* (militarily proficient/capable man[14]) to demand, 'that foreign policy fights for the removal of the unjust and one-sided mutilation of our military sovereignty.'[15] At another point he argued that 'peace in the form of tolerating injustice, subjugation and slavery can never be pleasant; it can only be seen as a period in which all forces are gathered for the restoration of justice and freedom.'[16] The revision of the treaty of Versailles remained a fixed goal in his considerations. The institutions of state and society, in Reinhardt's argument, were subordinated to this political aim, which could be achieved through either military force or negotiation.

There was a tradition of military renewal in German history on which Reinhardt could draw, and which gave him and many other Germans hope that they would recover from defeat. The history of Prussia's recovery from the defeat at Jena to final victory over Napoleon in 1815 had been recycled many times over the century that divided 1806 and 1918.[17] Reinhardt wrote: 'After we have experienced a catastrophe, it is useful to read about how a clever young officer thought about the catastrophe of his army and nation.'[18] He went on to praise the triumvirate of reformers, Gneisenau, Scharnhorst and Clausewitz for their 'insight, clarity and honourable seriousness.'[19] Reinhardt recognised that warfare had changed significantly during the previous century, and he looked more towards the spirit of the Prussian reformers for inspiration, rather than to copy the exact pattern of recovery from the commission on army reform to victory over Napoleon. It was the fact that the defeats at Jena and Auerstadt had not resulted in the permanent decline of Prussia that engendered feelings of optimism that the subjugation of Germany by the treaty of Versailles would only be temporary.

The agent of recovery would be the state, which drew its power from the *Volk*. Reinhardt defined the state as 'the form of bringing the power of the people together for certain purposes.'[20] He drew on the work of

---

13. *Albrecht von Thaer. Generalstabsdienst an der Front und in der OHL. Aus Briefen und Tagebuchaufzeichnungen 1915–1919*, ed. Siegfried Kaehler, Göttingen, 1958, 283.
14. There is no adequate English translation of the phrase *wehrhafter Mann*, which denotes a person who is militarily capable, i.e. can use weapons, has skills that would be useful in war. To avoid further awkward translations, I have left the phrase *wehrhafter Mann* in the main body of the text.
15. *Wehrkraft und Wehrwille*, 107.
16. Ibid., 77.
17. Michael Jeismann, *Das Vaterland der Feinde. Studien zum nationalen Feindbegriff und Selbstverständnis in Deutschland und Frankreich 1792–1918*, Stuttgart, 1992.
18. *Wehrkraft und Wehrwille*, 117–18.
19. Ibid., 119.
20. Ibid., 79.

Machiavelli, and consequently his analysis of the state and its rôle in military affairs was couched in terms of *Realpolitik*.[21] In Reinhardt's view the military functions of the state were essential to its existence. Quoting Machiavelli, he argued that 'the organs of the state are maintained through the care of the spirit which formed them.'[22] The spirit which informed the formation of the modern German state was a military one, and it was Reinhardt's aim to help maintain awareness of military affairs in the Weimar republic. If the state was formed by military means, it was also held together by the reciprocal duty of the state to defend its citizens, and of the citizens to defend the state.[23]

In common with other prominent German thinkers such as the historian Otto Hintze, Reinhardt's analysis of the formation and duty of states, and of citizens reflected his belief in the primacy of foreign policy.[24] This is especially evident in his analysis of the development of the German state. In his view, England, France and Spain had all developed as states in the middle ages because they were forced to expand their military forces by the 'life-threatening struggle for existence'. On the other hand the Holy Roman Empire 'continually removed itself from the efficiency of the state structures [of the western European states]'.[25] Instead of centralising the state in order to exploit its military potential, the Emperor had been forced to beg for money from the estates. This led to 'a weak federal army.'[26] He put the relationship between the state's struggle for existence, warfare and centralisation at the core of his critique of the historical development of the state. Reinhardt related the emergence of the modern German state to the establishment of the North German Confederation in 1867, when the king of Prussia became the overall commander of the federal German armies.[27]

From this historical analysis Reinhardt drew a number of lessons, which could be applied to the state in times of peace: 'If one accepts that the concentration of many elements for the use of force is a core element of war, then one will realise without difficulty, that this concentration through the centralisation of the state in peacetime will be of military value.'[28] Reinhardt admired the newly centralised power of the Reich government in the Weimar Republic in matters such as finance and taxation. His position on the centralisation of the state was similar to

21. Ibid., 79, 84.
22. 'Der Geburtstag der Reichswehr', by Reinhardt, *Deutsche Allgemeine Zeitung*, 6 March 1929.
23. *Wehrkraft und Wehrwille*, 79.
24. Otto Hintze, 'Military Organisation and the Organisation of the State', in *The Historical Essays of Otto Hintze*, ed. Felix Gilbert, New York, Oxford, 1975, 180–218.
25. *Wehrkraft und Wehrwille*, 81.
26. Ibid., 82.
27. Ibid., 83.
28. Ibid., 84.

Groener's. Both men saw the centralised state as a pre-condition for the recovery of Germany's great power status.[29] Reinhardt believed in a model of bureaucratic power that radiated out from the centre. As an expert on French affairs, he would have been familiar with the bureaucratic systems introduced after the revolution, and in particular by Napoleon. While he admired the way in which the French had fought for Paris in 1914, he was also wary that the aims of centralisation could be easily forgotten. He stressed, 'the formation of a central point should not be pursued for its own sake, but rather the central point always remains a function of the totality, and the totality in this case is the preservation of the *Volk* in war.'[30] The centre was not to be equated with the whole in Reinhardt's vision of the state.

A centralised state was necessary for war because it would allow for effective administration and decision-making. Because of the speed of events in war and the need to take political advantage of military victories, it was widely believed that the head of the state should control both military and civilian administration. Yet whether the state should have a monarchical or republican form of government was regarded as irrelevant by Reinhardt. The historical record gave no indication 'that either one of the two forms of state of itself had boosted military capacity.'[31] On an emotional level, Reinhardt was a convinced monarchist, and after 1918 he had remained in contact with members of the Württemberg royal family with whom he had worked before 1914.[32] From his professional point of view, he believed that the form of the state was less important, than whether the state could form an effective executive power in time of war. It was against this standard which the Republic was measured. In terms of military and financial structure Reinhardt was confident that the Republic had made considerable progress.[33]

Like other officers he sought a strong leader. He believed that such a leader would emerge only from a culture which promoted military values. In other words the actual form of the state was less important in this respect than the ethos: 'The great personality always knew how to assert himself, or the manly military will of the ruling classes either created a militarily efficient organisation of the state, or in an emergency would use force to push aside a weak organisation, and under their guidance make the state suitable for the care and utilisation of the military capacity.'[34] Nonetheless it was best to make preparations for war in peacetime so Reinhardt argued that the state should establish 'a particular head'

29. Johannes Hürter, *Wilhelm Groener. Reichswehrminister am Ende der Weimarer Republik*, Munich, 1993, 26–29.
30. *Wehrkraft und Wehrwille*, 85.
31. Ibid., 85.
32. See for example the series of letters, HStASt, M 660/034, Bü 22.
33. See the chapter on centralisation.
34. *Wehrkraft und Wehrwille*, 85–86.

(*Spitzenbildung*). He chose the French committee of national defence as an example of how a democratic state could adequately prepare for war. The establishment of such a body 'should remove the question of "statesman and army leader" and create a clear relationship.'[35]

This formula sought to avoid the question of the relationship between the Feldherr and the statesman. He trusted that in time of war the right leader would be found:

> It is good, if in this agency [*Spitzenbildung*] the state's aim of self-preservation is given its rightful place in the administration in peace-time. The demands of national defence require, even in peace-time, a higher and unifying attention; but in war fate will not invalidate the secret commanding power of the person-ality, and no matter how the roles of the highest leadership may be distributed, monarch, president, chancellor, minister or head of the army command, the strongest will decide, and the destiny of the *Volk* will be determined by his capability or lack of it.[36]

To a certain extent Reinhardt was placing his faith in the emergence of a charismatic leader. The notions of the charismatic leader could take different forms in Germany in the first half of the twentieth century. For Kurt Hesse, the radical military thinker, the charismatic leader's origins were shrouded in mystery, and the mystery became part of his power.[37] For Max Weber, the sociologist, the charismatic leader would emerge through a party hierarchy or the military. Weber saw a structured ascent to power, whereas Hesse had a more messianic vision. Indeed part of the functions of institutions, such as political parties and Parliament, was to choose the best leader.[38] By advocating rational structures of government, Reinhardt followed the Weberian model, although the themes of fate and a warrior class or personality echoed Hesse's writings.

The charismatic leader combined civilian government with control of the military. Reinhardt and many other officers admired the charismatic leadership of Napoleon and Frederick the Great because they fused civil and military power, and avoided the debilitating clashes that had char-acterised German politics in the First World War. Reinhardt demanded:

> In peacetime the leading statesman must also be a military politician, in wartime commander of the army, which we understand not simply as leader of the army, but as leader of the war effort. And we know well from history that the leader of the army must become the statesman in war, or else to the detriment of the *Volk* neither statesman nor leader of the army grasp the reins to master the war politically, which then leads to defeat.[39]

35. Ibid., 86.
36. Ibid., 86.
37. Hesse, *Feldherr Psychologos*; Wilhelm Deist, 'Die Reichswehr und der Krieg der Zukunft', *MgM*, 34, 1, 1989, 82–83.
38. *Weber. Political writings*, eds Peter Lassmann, Ronald Speirs, Cambridge, 1994, 313, 336–53.
39. *Wehrkraft und Wehrwille*, 126.

For Reinhardt the principal concern was that one person should provide decisive leadership in war. The possibility that this person could be a general underlines the primacy of military necessity in Reinhardt's thought.

The liberal theory of civil-military relations has interpreted Clausewitz as according primacy to civilian political control.[40] Reinhardt's writings on the subject of the civil-military relationship drew heavily from *On War*. Arguing that the *Feldherr* needed an in-depth knowledge of foreign policy, he quoted Book I of *On War*, 'Conduct of war and politics coincide, and the leader of the army becomes the statesman.'[41] Clausewitz argued that war was an instrument of politics.[42] It is important to remember that Clausewitz did not give primacy to civilian government, but rather to the political aspects of waging war. Ideally, he hoped that the statesman and soldier would be 'combined in one person'. If this were not the case, then a war cabinet should be formed, including the supreme military commander, 'so that the cabinet can share in the major aspects of his activities.'[43] Reinhardt interpreted Clausewitz as giving primacy to political over purely military considerations. This did not, however, mean that the leading influence in policy formation in wartime could not be the supreme commander. In the *Spitzenbildung*, advocated by Reinhardt, which bears some resemblance to the Clausewitzian war cabinet, the 'strongest' would seize the reins of leadership.

Reinhardt's appraisal of Hindenburg's role as supreme commander emphasises the possibility that the *Feldherr* could become the statesman:

> Political points of view, for the supreme commander of subordinate importance, came into the foreground of decisions. Hindenburg saw his new task as the unerring adherence to and support of the military idea of subjugation, which Ludendorff powerfully advocated, while Falkenhayn had deserted it and turned to a strategy of exhaustion. ... We recognise here [in Hindenburg's person] an inner conflict, which lies at the core of the highest military leadership. The soldier, who must be in any *Feldherr*, struggles with the universal comprehension of military leadership, which also includes politics, both of which complement each other. It was a wonderful turn of fate, that Hindenburg, whose soul tended towards the soldierly in this struggle, was called upon to exchange his career as a *Feldherr* with that of the statesman.[44]

Although modern research would not agree that Hindenburg fused his rôles as soldier and politician successfully, Reinhardt believed that Hindenburg's dominance of German politics from his appointment as head of the Supreme Command, was an improvement on the lack of co-ordination that

40. Peter Paret, *Clausewitz and the state*, Oxford, 1976.
41. *Wehrkraft und Wehrwille*, 39.
42. Carl von Clausewitz, *On War*, eds Michael Howard and Peter Paret, London, 1993 edn, 731–7.
43. Ibid., 735.
44. HStASt, M 660/034, Bü 48, 'Hindenburg unser Feldherr', fos. 5–6.

had afflicted the war effort for the first two years.[45] In relation to the debate on the invasion of Belgium, Reinhardt wrote: 'Looking back on the war we sorely missed this co-operation between statesman and army leader, which is already necessary at the stage of the war-plan.'[46] In his thought it is important to differentiate between the organisation of the state for war, and the prosecution of war. The structures of the state were formed in line with the principles of military efficiency. This enabled the statesman to wage war more effectively. In short, the militarized configuration of the state was subordinated to the statesman who would make the final decision on policy.

The foreign policy aims of the state could be achieved by peaceful as well as by violent means. However even if the path of peaceful negotiations was chosen, a certain degree of military strength was necessary to support those negotiations: 'The strengthening of the military will is not only a pre-condition of future national defence, it is also the best, indeed the indispensable support for all peaceful negotiations, which aim at winning back our lost security and self-determination.'[47] Although Reinhardt's advocacy of foreign policy backed by military strength ran contrary to the primacy of economics in Weimar's foreign policy[48], his doctrine did not lead inexorably towards war. Reinhardt called war 'the last resort', and therefore it was wise to prepare the state for such an eventuality. War, if necessary, was a means to an end, not a perpetual condition:

> The final aim of every war is a peace. Therefore love of peace and the qualities of the warrior are in no way incompatible. Conducting a war only makes sense, if the aggressor lives in the hope that the war will lead to a better situation than the current one, or if the defender believes that without a war, the current situation will worsen.[49]

The decision for or against war would be made on political grounds, not military ones. Reinhardt differentiated between military capability and intention to use it.

Nonetheless Reinhardt was making an implicit criticism of the conditions of Weimar foreign policy which patently lacked the military backing for its goals. Stresemann's own aims of territorial revision could not have

45. Peter Graf Kielmannsegg, *Deutschland und der erste Weltkrieg*, Frankfurt, 1968, 661–3.
46. *Wehrkraft und Wehrwille*, 170.
47. Ibid., 78.
48. Peter Krüger, *Die Aussenpolitik der Republik von Weimar*, Darmstadt, 1985, puts forward the thesis of the primacy of economic power in German foreign policy until 1930; other studies have underlined the importance of leading businessmen in Weimar foreign policy, Hartmut Pogge von Strandmann, 'Grossindustrie und Rapallopolitik. Deutsch-Sowjetische Handelsbeziehungen in der Weimarer Republik', *HZ*, 222, 2, 1976, 265–341; Karl Heinrich Pohl, *Weimars Wirtschaft und die Außenpolitik der Republik 1924–1926. Vom Dawes-Plan zum Eisenpakt*, Düsseldorf, 1979.
49. *Wehrkraft und Wehrwille*, 73–74.

been fulfilled without sufficient military power to defeat Poland, which the *Reichswehr* did not possess. Even if Stresemann achieved important revisions of the treaty, his multilateral style of foreign policy could be nothing more than a stop-gap as far as officers like Reinhardt were concerned, who ultimately sought a return to traditional German *Machtpolitik*. This was both a means of restoring Germany as a Great Power, and a definition of how a Great Power should conduct itself in the international system.

As well as advocating the construction of the state according to military needs, he believed that society should be prepared for war. For example, he argued, 'It is not a question of what sort of army the state puts in the field, but also how suitable the state is, in the form of its structures, to release and harness the military capacity of the *Volk*.'[50] For Reinhardt the *Volk* existed before the state. The *Volk* would come together in the form of a state to achieve certain goals, such as 'the preservation of individual existence', and national defence. The close relationship between *Volk* and *Staat* was evident in his definition of war as 'the use of force by a *Volk* or state or a similar community, in order to compel an opponent, also using force, to fulfil our will.'[51] While Reinhardt acknowledged his debt to Clausewitz for this definition, he was also aware of the changed nature of warfare since the first half of the nineteenth century.[52] In the age of modern industrial warfare, Reinhardt recognised 'the inner bonds of struggle and life between the homeland and army.'[53] The mobilization of society, of the *Volk* for war was necessary due to total war, which was analysed in "ideal type" terms.[54] In the struggle for existence between nations, Reinhardt argued that nobody's individual military capacity could be disregarded.

The doctrine of total war which Reinhardt advocated was close to the ideas put forward by Colonel Joachim von Stülpnagel, head of the Army Department in the *Truppenamt* between 1923 and 1926. Reinhardt was aware of Stülpnagel's work on the modern *Volkskrieg*.[55] His plans for opposition to the Versailles treaty involved what amounted to a *Volkskrieg*. After the occupation of the Ruhr in 1923 by the French and Belgian armies, more attention was paid to the idea of a *Volkskrieg*. The occupation had led officers like Stülpnagel to two conclusions. First, Seeckt's

50. Ibid., 79–80.
51. HStASt, M 660/034, Bü 39, 'Die Elemente der Wehrhaftigkeit', fos. 2–3.
52. On the transition to modern *Volkskriege* see Moltke. *Vom Kabinettskrieg zum Volkskrieg. Eine Werkauswahl*, ed. Stig Förster, Bonn, 1992, 241–42.
53. HStASt, M 660/034, Bü 38, 'Rüstung und Landesfestigung', fos. 9–10.
54. *Great War, Total War. Mobilisation and Combat on the Western Front, 1914–1918*, eds Roger Chickering, Stig Förster, Cambridge, 2000; *An der Schwelle zum totalen Krieg. Die militärische Debatte über den Krieg der Zukunft 1919–1939*, ed. Stig Förster, Paderborn, 2002; *The Shadows of Total War. Europe, East Asia and the United States, 1919–1939*, eds, Roger Chickering, Stig Förster, Cambridge, 2003.
55. BA-MA, N 5/20, Reinhardt to Stülpnagel, 12 April 1925, fo. 85.

faith in a highly trained mobile, but small army, seemed misplaced. The cadre had not materialised. Second, the populace – according to proponents of *Volkskrieg* – were willing to fight the occupiers, albeit with limited means.[56] The mobilization of society for military ends was adopted by German military planners as the solution to the inadequacies of a 100,000 men army. In a lecture in May 1924 Stülpnagel commented: 'So compared with earlier eras the *Volkskrieg* gains great significance in the German conduct of war in the future...Without its implementation [as a policy] wars in the future do not appear possible.'[57] While Stülpnagel concentrated on the operational dimensions, Reinhardt developed the concept, by examining the preparation of society for such a war. One of the characteristics of war planning in the First World War had been the complete lack of preparation for a long struggle, which meant that measures had been introduced haphazardly.

The origins of the 'people's war', '*Volk im Waffen*', and the '*levée en masse*' are to be found in the wars of the French revolution. One of the most striking arguments in Reinhardt's analysis of total warfare has direct echoes of the decree of 23 August 1793, issued by the Committee for Public Safety which called on all French citizens, young and old, men and women, to defend *la patrie*.[58] Reinhardt argued 'that every male and female out of infancy has a certain amount of military capacity.'[59] His ideas had democratic and totalizing implications. Reinhardt sought to maximize the nation's military capacity by exploiting each citizen's military potential. He approached the issue of war and modern society as a social engineer. On the use of women in wartime, he wrote:

> With the full use of military capable men, the use of women at the front is not necessitated by the force of numbers; also in the service branches behind the front there is no mass of places free for women. But it remains a possibility to withdraw men and insert women, not due to lack of numbers, but following a considered plan. From the standpoint of effectiveness it will be right where women do better work, from the standpoint of maintaining the *Volk* it will be just as good, if a surplus of women can be prevented, or if such a surplus can be reduced. In this case it must be remembered that the use of women without being separated from men is always doubtful, and this limits the use of women.[60]

The exact nature of the tasks which Reinhardt believed women could carry out was not clear. Nonetheless his willingness to use women in the theatre of operations cut across traditional concepts of gender roles. He

56. Deist, 'Der Krieg der Zukunft', 85–86; Michael Geyer, *Aufrüstung oder Sicherheit. Die Reichswehr in der Krise der Machtpolitik 1924–1936*, Wiesbaden, 1980, 19–27.
57. BA-MA, N 5/20, Stülpnagel lecture, May 1924, fo. 29.
58. T. C. W. Blanning, *The French Revolutionary Wars*, London, 1996, 100–01; D. M. G Sutherland, *France, 1789–1815. Revolution and Counterrevolution*, London, 1985, 201.
59. *Wehrkraft und Wehrwille*, 63.
60. Ibid., 64.

was also prepared to use women in the factories, where they could release men for service at the front. In this case Reinhardt simply suggested 'a legal compulsory war service duty for women.'[61] He envisaged these measures as temporary, lasting the duration of the war.

Defeat in the First World War had been commonly attributed by many officers to the collapse of the home front. Their analysis took two forms. On one hand there was the 'stab-in-the-back' thesis which argued that the morale of the home front had been sapped by a motley crew of Sparticists, Jews, and other undesirable types. On the other hand it was argued that the home front had simply collapsed after the deprivations of war. Reinhardt adopted the second position, one devoid of the emotions of hate and distrust which characterised the myth of the 'stab-in-the-back'. He was aware of the need to hold society together in time of war, and it was within this context that he saw a role for the elderly, whom he defined as sixty and older. Reinhardt told his pupils:

> The background to every war, which springs from moral forces, is the preservation of the Fatherland, its greatness, its future, its transmission [from one generation to the next]. The homeland is embodied in our parents, our children and our wives. If we put the elderly in the home army after the young men have gone, we rob the children of their teachers, the women of their mentors; so we completely lose the values of the homeland, for which the war is waged. Then finally the heart of the *Volk* will collapse from weakness, while the limbs have become far too big.[62]

Reinhardt had found a rôle in wartime for all groups in society. What made Reinhardt's vision of society in war unusual was its inclusive nature. He did not discriminate against any social groups. He was part of a tradition from Clausewitz and the Prussian reformers to Groener in the War Office, which saw the common people as allies of the state, rather than as a threat to the ruling élites.[63] Traditionally service in war and citizenship had been closely linked. Max Jähns, a nineteenth-century military historian whose work Reinhardt admired, argued that 'today the concepts of "man", "citizen", and "warrior" are the one and the same; because they are no more unfree men.'[64] Jähns's view of the emancipated citizen soldier was Hegelian, in that the individual found his freedom through the state.[65] Jähns and others traced the development of citizenship to the

---

61. Ibid., 64; on the experiences of women during the First World War, see Ute Daniel, *The War from Within. German Working Class Women in the First World War*, New York, Oxford, 1997.

62. *Wehrkraft und Wehrwille*, 64–65.

63. *Carl von Clausewitz. Historical and Political Writings*, ed. Peter Paret, Princeton, 1992, 313–28; Wilhelm Deist, *Militär, Staat und Gesellschaft. Studien zur preußisch-deutschen Militärgeschichte*, Munich, 1991, 83–102; Gerald D. Feldman, *Army, Industry and Labor in Germany, 1914–1918*, London, 1992 edn, details Groener's wartime activities.

64. Max Jähns, *Heeresverfassung und Völkerleben. Eine Umschau*, Berlin, 1885, 400–401.

65. See for example, Georg Hegel, *The Philosophy of History*, translated by J. Sibree, New York, 1991, 39.

war of liberation in 1813, when men won their right to become citizens by taking up arms against the French armies.[66] While the idea that all Germans were citizens was widely touted, social reality was lagging behind. If the thesis that military service was a fundamental mark of citizenship is accepted, then it becomes clear that certain social groups were discriminated against. Reinhardt knew that according to the 1913 army bill only 55 percent of the annual cohort were actually conscripted. In the *Kaiserreich* recruitment was biased against the working class, because the Prussian Ministry of War feared that working class conscripts, socialised in trade unions and the SPD, would destabilise the army.[67] Another group which faced particular discrimination was the Jews.[68] The discrimination in the army reflected the social divisions of the *Kaiserreich*.

The conservatism of the Prussian Ministry of War, which saw the army's rôle as the maintenance of social order within Germany, led to disputes with the General Staff.[69] The latter body, and the one in which Reinhardt worked before 1914, was far more concerned about the need to win a war, possibly on two fronts, than with potential social unrest in Germany.[70] Reinhardt continued to represent this tradition in the Weimar Republic. Although the *Reichswehr* had been used on numerous occasions to suppress internal unrest, he believed that its primary function was an instrument to restore Germany's great power status in Europe. As was noted in an earlier chapter, Reinhardt's main goal during the crisis of the state in 1923 was to restore domestic stability, so as to create a viable basis for negotiations with France.[71] He believed that internal divisions were a distraction and weakened the state. In his view, all energy should be harnessed towards the foreign policy goal. To deny the ability of groups like the working class and the Jews to contribute to this goal would be to waste their 'military potential'. By recognising the contribution which these groups could make to a war effort, Reinhardt recognised them as full citizens, not just in a legal but also in a social sense. In a climate of increasing anti-Semitism, Jewish groups also resorted to similar utilitarian arguments about their place in German society.[72]

---

66. Jähns, *Heeresverfassung*, 397–401; *Geschichtliche Grundbegriffe. Historisches Lexikon zur politisch-sozialen Sprache in Deutschland*, 8 volumes, eds Otto Brunner, Werner Conze, Reinhart Koselleck, Stuttgart, 1972, vol. 1, 709–10.
67. Stig Förster, *Das doppelte Militarismus. Die deutsche Heeresrüstungspolitik zwischen Status quo Sicherung und Aggression 1890-1913*, Stuttgart, 1985, 20–21.
68. Werner Angress, 'Prussia's Army and the Jewish Reserve Officer Controversy before World War I', *Leo Baeck Institute Yearbook*, 17, 1972, 19–42.
69. David Herrmann, *The Arming of Europe and the Making of the First World War*, Princeton, 1996, 184–91.
70. This is one of the major themes in Förster's *Militarismus*.
71. See chapter 8.
72. Arnold Paucker, *Der jüdische Abwehrkampf gegen Antisemitismus und Nationalsozialismus in den letzten Jahren der Weimarer Republik*, Hamburg, 1989, 34, 140, 240–42.

His advocacy of full rights for Jews was exceptional in the German officer corps.[73] However his views were informed more by military necessity than by liberal sentiment.[74] He did not embrace a liberal view of universal human rights, and he was prone to making racist comments about the French, Poles and troops of African origin who served in European armies, criticising their 'lowly moral and hygienic standards.'[75] As far as Germany was concerned he argued that anti-Semites, rather than Jews, were responsible for creating artificial social divisions. He interpreted the Dreyfus case, when a French Jewish officer had been wrongly convicted of espionage, as a conflict between clerical and free-thinking officers for the soul of the Third Republic's army. The affair was only resolved when nationalist officers from both camps came together to focus on the defence of the nation.[76] Reinhardt's argument was clear – the Weimar republic, born out of defeat like the Third Republic, could not afford to be distracted by internal divisions. True nationalists would focus on the external, rather than a mythical internal enemy.

In a letter to his former comrades in the *Lehrbrigade Döberitz* he made a comprehensive statement on the position of Jews in Germany:

> In the interest of internal peace I want to make my position on the Jews clear. Those who damage the German Fatherland, or even only view it with equivocation, must be fought, but those who, as German Jews, feel and fight with us, must be recognised and valued. The spirit of Mammon, the lust for profit, deserves contempt, and we must reject it in Jews and Christians, above all we cannot allow ourselves to become slaves of money and therefore of Jews through pleasure-seeking. This defensive form of anti-Semitism is to be praised, it is confirmed not in hatred for Jews, but in self-discipline. The much criticised power of the so-called Jewry, which in reality is the power of money, will be broken if morality and love of the Fatherland is valued more highly in society than comfortable furs, clothes and cars.[77]

73. Werner Jochmann, 'Die Ausbreitung des Antisemitismus', in *Deutsches Judentum im Krieg und Revolution*, ed. Werner Mosse, Tübingen, 1971, 422; Anthony Kauders, 'Legally Citizens: Jewish Exclusion from the Weimar Polity', in *Jüdisches Leben in der Weimarer Republik*, eds Wolfgang Benz, Arnold Paucker, Peter Pulzer, London, Tübingen, 1998, 159–72.

74. Bald argues that Reinhardt was part of a liberal tradition of German military reformers, 'Die Reinhardt-Kurse', 115–17.

75. He blamed the Poles and the French occupying armies after the First World War for the spread of sexually transmitted diseases in Germany, HStASt, M 660/034, Bü 27, 'Bekämpfung der Geschlechtskrankheiten', 18 January 1922, signed Reinhardt, Blomberg; see also his comment on African troops at the cabinet meeting on 21 March 1919, *Akten der Reichskanzlei. Das Kabinett Scheidemann 13. Februar bis 20. Juni 1919*, ed. Hagen Schulze, Boppard am Rhein, 1971, 76; Sally Marks, 'Black Watch on the Rhine: A Study in Propaganda, Prejudice and Prurience', *European Studies Review*, 13, 3, 1983, 297–334; Reiner Pommerin, "Sterilisierung der Rheinlandbastarde". *Das Schicksal einer farbigen Minderheit*, Düsseldorf, 1979.

76. HStASt, M 660/034, Bü 38, 'Die staatliche Wehrmacht', fo. 9–10.

77. HStASt, M 660/034, Bü 25, Reinhardt, 'An meine Kameraden von der Lehrbrigade', Easter 1921, Stuttgart.

Although Reinhardt expressed some stereotypical anti-Semitic ideas, such as the association of money and Jewish power, the tenor of this letter and other statements he made on the issue of Jews in German society indicate that he was not anti-Semitic. Rather he saw anti-Semitism as a substantial threat to the cohesion of German society.

It is possible to see Reinhardt's stance towards Jews, women, the working class and the elderly, as an attempt to construct an inclusive German nation – but one motivated by military necessity. He spoke of 'a *Volksgemeinschaft* of the militarily willing', and from his discussions of the relationship of the individual and their *Wehrkraft*, it is clear that he did not automatically exclude any social groups.[78] German politics in the first half of the twentieth century was characterised by an attempt to define the nation or the *Volksgemeinschaft*.[79] Often these attempts were automatically exclusive, by establishing criteria of race, class or gender as a requirement for admission into an idealised community. It is not surprising that the most inclusive conceptions of the *Volksgemeinschaft* came in August 1914 and January 1923. At these moments Germans focused on the external enemy. However these moments of national unity passed, and even dissolved into bitter recrimination. Reinhardt's continued adherence to an inclusive ideal of the *Volksgemeinschaft* was a result of his constant awareness that Germany must be unified if her great power status was to be restored. What Reinhardt demanded of Germans was 'patriotism' (*Vaterlandsliebe*), and 'morality', feelings which could motivate the miner in the Ruhr as easily as an East Prussian landowner. Therefore people were not automatically excluded by criteria of class, race or gender from Reinhardt's idea of the German nation. He considered these identities to be secondary to German identity. In Reinhardt's view it was possible to choose to be a German nationalist.

His vision of German society remained only potentially inclusive. Indeed the corollary of Reinhardt's democratic and inclusive society was that he expected all citizens to be inspired by the same set of beliefs. This model of the democratic polity was widespread in the Weimar republic, and was neither liberal nor consitutional.[80] Carl Schmitt, the legal theorist, wrote: 'Democracy requires ... first homogeneity, and second – if the need arises – elimination or eradication.'[81] Schmitt wrote this before the National Socialists began to exclude Jews from civil society and then to

78. *Wehrkraft und Wehrwille*, 107.
79. Gunther Mai, '"Verteidigungskrieg" und "Volksgemeinschaft". Staatliche Selbstbehauptung, nationale Solidarität und soziale Befreiung in Deutschland in der Zeit des Ersten Weltkrieges, (1900–1925), in *Der erste Weltkrieg. Wirkung, Wahrnehmung, Analyse*, ed. Wolfgang Michalka, Munich, 1994, pp. 583–602; Manfred Messerschmidt, 'The *Wehrmacht* and the Volksgemeinschaft', *JCH*, 18, 4, 1983, 719–44.
80. Axel Schildt, *Militärdiktatur mit Massenbasis? Die Querfrontkonzpetion der Reichswehrführung um General von Schleicher am Ende der Weimarer Republik*, Frankfurt, 1981, 46, 102–109.
81. Carl Schmitt, *The Crisis of Parliamentary Democracy*, translated by Ellen Kennedy, Cambridge, MA, 1985, 9.

murder them, and it would be misleading to impute an 'intentionalist' logic to Reinhardt's thought. However it is clear that Reinhardt had no rôle for those who did not share his belief that the primary task of German politics after the First World War was the reversal of the treaty of Versailles. Those who, he believed, detracted from this task, such as rabid anti-Semites and profiteers, internationalists and pacifists, including many in the SPD and DDP, were not included in his vision of German society. Brought to its logical conclusion Reinhardt's vision of the *Volksgemeinschaft* was in no way compatible with the Republic or any form of liberal democracy.[82] However during the 1920s Reinhardt and the *Reichswehr* recognised that the forceful imposition of their ideology on German society would fail, and instead used the liberal value of free speech to promote their vision.

Although recent research has shown that pacifism declined in the late 1920s Reinhardt believed it was a growing problem in German society.[83] As has been noted it was a major point of contention with the SPD and Democratic party in his 1927 article. Reinhardt differentiated between the pacifist who was prepared to use force in self-defence, and the pure pacifist, whom he characterised as 'a man, to whom every war appears worse than the most rotten peace.'[84] Reinhardt argued that the treaty of Versailles was a despicable peace and was prepared to fight a war, if necessary and feasible, in order to reverse the post-war settlement. It would not be possible for Germany to wage a war against the Allied powers, if its society was riddled with pacifism, as Reinhardt believed. He cited the election of Walter von Molo as president of the German *Dichter-Akademie* as a sign of an increasingly pacifistic society, because Molo had praised Erich Maria Remarque's *Im Westen nicht Neues*.[85] He saw himself in a long line of soldiers who had warned the civilian populace against the dream of permanent peace: 'At all times it was the task of the true leaders of the *Volk* to pit themselves against a purely pacifist spirit, to promote military capability, and not to let the honour and meaning of being a warrior be maligned.'[86]

As well as denigrating the virtues of pacifists, Reinhardt also sought to promote a militaristic spirit in German society. The treaty of Versailles had destroyed Germany's organised military capacity. To make good this deficit Reinhardt urged each German to concern himself with military affairs and to strengthen his '*Wehrwille*' (military will):

82. Kurt Sontheimer, *Antidemokratischen Denken in der Weimarer Republik. Die politischen Ideen des deutschen Nationalismus zwischen 1918 und 1933*, Munich, 1964, 97.
83. See the collection of essays, *Pazifismus in der Weimarer Republik*, eds Kurt Holl, Wolfram Wette, Paderborn, 1981.
84. *Wehrkraft und Wehrwille*, 74.
85. Ibid., 75.
86. Ibid., 75.

There is no doubt, that the promotion of military will has been made more difficult by the Versailles Diktat, that apart from the small standing army, all state or private corporate military activity in Germany is forbidden. No agency, no school, no association can concern itself with military affairs or have contact with the *Reichswehr*. This is all well-known to Germans, but unfortunately only very few are aware that the treaty of Versailles does not take any German's personal right, to look comprehensively at military affairs, and to get oneself mentally and physically into the best possible military condition.[87]

Although the treaty of Versailles had banned military activities in Germany by any organisation other than the *Reichswehr*, officers were aware of the military potential represented by the *Kriegervereine*.[88]

Reinhardt estimated that there were two and a half million former soldiers in 27,000 associations. While on the one hand Reinhardt praised groups like the *Stahlhelm* and *Jungdeutscher Orden* for maintaining the German military will, on the other hand he feared that this will could never be properly exploited because there were too many different groups.[89] Political rivalries within Germany meant that a military planner could never be certain of the condition of the paramilitary groups. Neither was he impressed by the *Reichsbanner*, the paramilitary association backed primarily by the SPD, but also by the Centre and Democratic parties.[90] He argued, 'it is only of low value for the effective promotion of the military will. At least this spirit (of militarism) outweighs the [*Banner's*] competing spirit of pacifism which objects to wartime service.'[91] He believed that the *Reichsbanner*, like the SPD and the Democratic party, was split between pro- and anti-military wings.[92] Reinhardt concluded 'that the military will of the *Volk* has not been extinguished, but due to the lack of conscription and insufficient capabilities of the *Wehrbünde*, it is in no way currently strong enough for German vital interests measured against the strength of pacifism, which objects to service in war.'[93]

In what almost amounted to a negation of the spirit of the *Volksgemeinschaft*, Reinhardt stressed the rôle of the individual: 'The militarily capable man is the cornerstone of national defence because he is the carrier of the manly and holy will, which opposes enslavement, which

87. Ibid., 78.
88. See Volker Berghahn, *Der Stahlhelm. Bund der Frontsoldaten*, Düsseldorf, 1966; James Diehl, *Paramilitary Politics in Weimar Germany*, Bloomington, London, 1977.
89. HStASt, M 660/034, Bü 39, 'Die Elemente der Wehrhaftigkeit', fos. 25–27; Hans Mommsen, 'Militär und zivile Militarisierung in Deutschland, 1914–1938', in *Militär und Gesellschaft im 19. und 20. Jahrhundert*, ed., Ute Frevert, Stuttgart, 1997, 268.
90. Karl Rohe, *Das Reichsbanner Schwarz Rot Gold. Ein Beitrag zur Geschichte und Struktur der politischen Kampfverbände zur Zeit der Weimarer Republik*, Düsseldorf, 1966.
91. HStASt, M 660/034, Bü 39, 'Die Elemente der Wehrhaftigkeit', fo. 25.
92. Rohe, *Reichsbanner*, 169–83, charts the uneasy relationship between the *Banner* and the *Reichswehr*.
93. HStASt, M 660/034, Bü 39, 'Die Elemente der Wehrhaftigkeit', fo. 29.

seeks freedom.'[94] His focus on the individual was a means of circumventing the spirit of the treaty of Versailles. He was searching for an effective military doctrine within the narrow confines of the treaty terms. Reinhardt recommended that the individual should prepare himself for the day of reckoning. According to Reinhardt the *wehrhafte Mann* would read the histories of the rise and fall of great nations. He would not be distracted by the siren songs of eternal peace, but would sharpen his 'military will' by examining the 'military efforts of neighbouring peoples.' Having prepared himself mentally, the next stage involved hiking through border areas, climbing mountains and swimming in rivers. Wide exploration would allow the *wehrhafte Mann* to exploit the natural defences of the countryside. His abilities would extend to a knowledge of Morse code, radios and the use of motor vehicles. 'He will enter the kingdom of technology, and will gain the ability to forge weapons for his needs through service to the god Hephestos.'[95] He also needed to study the workings of the financial world, because the state's credit would be vital in prosecuting a successful war.[96] Evidently nobody could hope to master all these tasks, so the ideal of the renaissance *wehrhafte Mann* was a fantasy. Presumably Reinhardt hoped that each individual would tailor the tasks to his abilities, providing Germany with a massive reservoir of manpower.

Apart from the list of instructions for the *wehrhafte Mann*, he had a number of more practical suggestions, which would help maintain the German military will. In 1924 Reinhardt was invited by Lieutenant Colonel Bircher to the '*Eidgenössisches Schützfest*', a shooting competition, at Aarau in Switzerland.[97] It was common for *Reichswehr* officers to travel to other countries in order to examine other military developments.[98] The trip to Aarau made a significant impression on Reinhardt. He quoted approvingly from the booklet on the festival: 'Only military capability (*Wehrhaftigkeit*) can guarantee the inviolability of our homeland. To strengthen this military capability by awakening interest in shooting competitions is one of the primary aims of the great Fatherland organisation.'[99] Reinhardt was eager to promote shooting as a sport because of its close relation to military activities. His support of *Wehrsport*, military sports, was a tradition which dated back to Turnvater Jahn, who organised athletic clubs with a view to circumventing Napoleon's restrictions on Prussia's military capacity. Sporting activity was not simply designed

---

94. *Wehrkraft und Wehrwille*, 109.
95. Hephestos was a Greek god of craftsmen. He was also lame and had been cast off Mount Olympus by his mother. Whether Reinhardt saw any analogies with Germany's position in the late 1920s is unclear.
96. Ibid., 105–106.
97. HStASt, M 660/034, Bü 27, Schießplan for the Eidgenössisches Schützenfest, 18 July to 5 August 1924.
98. Geyer, *Aufrüstung oder Sicherheit*, 148-65.
99. *Wehrkraft und Wehrwille*, 71.

to improve the physical health of the individual, but also to develop his will: 'Whether sport also inspires the will, is in my view an open question, which remains to be decided in the future. The purely physical side to sport hardly achieves it at all, but the competitive spirit it fosters leads in this direction.'[100]

This mass of individuals was of no use without organisation: 'if a lot of militarily capable men have trained themselves, and made themselves ready, their most heroic efforts will fail, if their formation as a whole is not expertly deployed.'[101] Reinhardt, like all other officers, was determined that the *Reichswehr* would retain its primacy of organising military force. Therefore the professionalism of the *Reichswehr* guaranteed its continued monopoly of the 'state power', even in Reinhardt's idealised society where individuals would were to train for war. He concluded: 'Our *Reichswehr* carries the full weight of responsibility as the guardian of the art of war and the only bearer of the military will of the whole German people, to whom they present this will as an example in pure, selfless and purposeful form.'[102]

The *Reichswehr* could only encourage martial values in the civilian population if it had the necessary prestige. Reinhardt admired the social elevation of the officer by the Hohenzollern monarchs, because as the backbone of the army, a prestigious officer corps would encourage national military pride. In a state or nation where the ruling class transmitted military values from one generation to the next, 'one can raise armies from the earth, as once happened in Rome or Gaul or the German lands.'[103] In the context of the Weimar Republic, he believed 'the aim is to establish the soldiering class as the most suitable model for the mid-level state and local bureaucrats, and to join it [the soldiering class] closely to the body of the *Volk* in this social role.'[104] Reinhardt advocated interaction with civil society, rather than isolation from it, as a means of increasing awareness of military affairs. The prestige of the *Reichswehr* was inextricably bound with its 'vocational ideal', which was the defence of the Fatherland:

> The old 'With God for King and Fatherland' was a short, clear and vocational belief of great power. I can only think with sadness that it is lost to us. But we cannot honestly escape the recognition that the preservation of the German *Volk* cannot be bound up with the monarchy and is not a consequence of belief in God, in other words that we must defend our *Volk* and Fatherland against the foreign enemy...Therefore it remains the service to the Fatherland [that matters], and it corresponds to this when today we profess 'Deutschland über alles'.[105]

100. Ibid., 70.
101. Ibid., 107.
102. Ibid., 78.
103. HStASt, M 660/034, Bü 38, 'Die staatliche Wehrmacht', fo. 6.
104. Ibid., fo. 14.
105. Ibid., fo. 8.

Reinhardt advocated a growing militarisation of Weimar society, not simply to increase the prestige of the military, but ultimately as a means of defending that society.

A third element of Germany's military organisation was the 'Land'. Reinhardt argued that even an army like the small *Reichswehr* 'will no longer be separated from the land, *Volk* and state as before, but will form a common body with nerves, arteries and all its feeding processes.'[106] He drew on Friedrich Ratzel's works on political geography, and the historical works of Albert von Hoffmann. The *Volk* was intimately related to its *Staatsboden* (state's territory). Reinhardt's concept of 'Land' added to German military capacity in a number of ways. First, it was a source of raw material. He accepted that Germany could never achieve full autarky, but argued that the war had demonstrated the importance of exploiting raw materials. He defined the most important areas as 'value areas' (*Wertgebiete*), which were 'main lines of traffic that crossed each other, areas of high industrial development with sources of raw material or great manufacturing plants or both, then the so-called bread-baskets, and finally a core area of particularly faithful, militarized and healthy people.'[107] Reinhardt, although aware of the importance of industrial and food production to a war effort, failed to indicate how Germany's potential could be maximized. He had no personal experience of these issues, having spent the war at the front, in contrast to an officer like Groener, who had headed the War Office in the Prussian *Kriegsministerium*.

Second, Reinhardt believed that the military strength of any nation was related to its population. He disagreed with the Malthusian theory that 'shortage of space' (*Raumnot*) would militate against a growing population. This problem could be overcome by expanding the state's territory. He had little sympathy for the rights of certain nations to a certain territory:

Nobody has succeeded in proving that the distribution of land is of Godly origin; where we sit, others have sat before us and the possession of today's land of our fathers is the result of the power of these ancestors, who had once fought for and developed it. A *Volk* which has an excess of man-power has no less right to existence than some old possessor. The value that lives within the *Volk* will be decisive. It is a beautiful thought to create the conditions for population growth by developing one's own land, and is well worth the noble toil; but the creation of new land for the people of higher value at the expense of the less valuable people is an ancient natural law. The standard is at first peaceful competition, the *pénétration pacifique*, the last resort is war. The move to expand will always be in the direction of the weakest resistance, therefore it will seek to fulfil goals firstly in colonial activity; it was well for the peoples of Europe when they knew how to alleviate their tensions in this way. But woe is the *Volk* which wearily foregoes this competition! The moment will come when it will fall victim to those who did not want to surrender their children to such a sacrifice.[108]

106. HStASt, M 660/034, Bü 38,'Rüstung und Landesfestigung', fo. 10.
107. *Wehrkraft und Wehrwille*, 88-89.
108. *Wehrkraft und Wehrwille*, 69.

Reinhardt was following the tradition established by Ratzel, who advocated that the primary goal of policy should be to guarantee 'the growing *Volk* the necessary land.'[109] This strand of thought represented an uncompromising form of *Realpolitik*. Reinhardt probably did not recognise the irony of dismissing the right of indigenous people, while at other times claiming that territories, including Alsace, should be returned to Germany, because they were 'an ancient German possession of the Allemans.'[110] Ultimately his primary concern was with the German *Volk*. While he did not distinguish between more and less valuable members of society within Germany, he divided the international community into higher and lower peoples.

Finally, his primary interest in military geography was the rôle of the landscape in operations. The landscape was both strategically and tactically important, and could be used to maximize the potential of the *wehrhafter Mann*. He argued that modern weapons, such as gas and airpower, would be insufficient to remove a determined defender 'out of the ruins of large houses'. He continued: 'The limitless exploitation of material superiority will be limited in rugged landscape. On the other hand the wealth of useful, brave men and the skill in the use of small fire-arms including the light cannon will be fully realised in such an atmosphere.'[111] While Reinhardt was hopeful that the landscape could be tactically beneficial to a militia-style German army, he was less confident that Germany's current borders offered natural strategic defensive points.[112] French occupation of the Rhineland and the loss of Alsace and Lorraine significantly increased the strategic vulnerability of Germany.

In Reinhardt's thought the political leadership would choose the means to restore Germany's position in Europe, a task that he assumed to be the primary goal of German politics after 1918. As a professional soldier it was his role to prepare for the next war. For Reinhardt, war was a struggle for existence between nations: 'The nature of war is the struggle of wills involving the use of violence against an enemy, force being the violence exercised not by individuals but by large human communities.'[113] For a person who had commanded a regiment at Verdun, he had a romantic vision of warfare. For example, he claimed that:

> [the commanding general] does not stand among the masses [of soldiers], but above the masses; for him the mass is nothing other than the sword which he wields in a duel with his opponent. For him there is no longer obedience or

109. Quoted in Franz Ebeling, *Geopolitik. Karl Haushofer und seine Raumwissenschaft 1919–1945*, I Berlin, 1994, 47–48.

110. HStASt, M 660/034, Bü 36, Reinhardt article, 'Unparteiische Geschichtsschreibung', *Das Militärwochenblatt*, 1926, 874–75.

111. *Wehrkraft und Wehrwille*, 93.

112. Ibid., 98.

113. Ibid., 62.

comradeship, neither as supports nor as duties, he must have the virtues of the soldier in self-discipline, and in the love and care for his army, as the true knight feels for his horse.[114]

The imagery of the sword, the horse and the knight were echoes of a chivalrous notion of warfare. The continued existence of these types of notions after the First World War may seem paradoxical. However, despite the industrialisation of warfare, there were still time-honoured ideals of honour, duty and obedience to which soldiers professed to adhere. The persistence of the idea of two commanders duelling with their armies imparted a more benign image of warfare, than that put forward by veterans like the painter, Otto Dix, or the author, Erich Maria Remarque. Reinhardt admitted that Remarque's account had elements of truth, but argued that it missed the positive aspects of the war experience conveyed in the literature of Walter Flex and Ernst Jünger, two frontline soldiers.[115] Chivalric notions could also serve a more sinister agenda – the reduction of the masses to mere swords was a brutal dehumanization of the *Volk* and perhaps, in its own way, a necessary pre-condition for the conduct of modern war.

The nature of the next war was open to question, and was a major subject of contention amongst officers in the *Reichswehrministerium*. Reinhardt admitted that the current military capability of the *Reichswehr* was limited: 'In our present condition we cannot defend our country against a great power. At the moment we have to resort to the defensive philosophy of somewhere like Switzerland or Belgium or Holland.'[116] This assessment was remarkably similar to the sober memoranda drawn up by Groener on the possibility of using the *Reichswehr* in international conflict.[117] While accepting that the training of troops was an important element in military performance, Reinhardt stressed that numbers were important: 'Those people who think one can have too many soldiers are wrong.'[118] He also noted that the *Reichswehr* did not have tanks or an air force. The First World War had demonstrated the importance of modern weaponry. Within these limited means Reinhardt set three military targets. First, the *Reichswehr* would be strong enough to resist attacks from Germany's smaller neighbours. Second, the *Reichswehr* should be sufficiently strong to force Germany's larger neighbours, (presumably France and Poland) to think twice before launching an attack. Third, in a general war the *Reichswehr* would make Germany 'attractive to allies' (*bündnisfähig*).[119]

114. Ibid., 53.
115. Ibid., 75; Raimund Neuß, *Anmerkungen zu Walter Flex. Die "Ideen von 1914" in der deutschen Literatur: ein Fallbeispie*, Schornfeld, 1992; Ernst Jünger, *Sämtliche Werke. Essays I. Betrachtungen zur Zeit*, 'Der Kampf als inneres Erlebnis', Stuttgart, 1980.
116. *Wehrkraft und Wehrwille*, 100.
117. Hürter, *Groener*, 91–95.
118. *Wehrkraft und Wehrwille*, 167–68.
119. Ibid., 100.

These aims were akin to those set out by Groener in a 1928 memo-randum, which argued that the *Reichswehr* was a purely defensive instrument.[120] The subtle, but important difference was that Reinhardt hoped that the *Reichswehr* would help Germany to attract allies, whereas Groener believed it was too weak to achieve even that goal. The implication of this difference is that Reinhardt may have welcomed a general war in Europe as an opportunity to attach Germany to the victors. Within the framework of a victorious alliance Germany could revise the treaty of Versailles. Geyer argues that the *Reichswehr*'s foreign policy sought to keep European tensions simmering, so that if Germany's international position improved it would be able to take advantage of latent conflicts. Reinhardt, although he never pointed to any specific tensions in Europe nor mentioned any possible allies, implied that even with the weak *Reichswehr* he was prepared to seek diplomatic advantage in a general European war. Groener was more cautious, and looked to German economic strength as a tool of foreign policy, which was evidence of his broad conception of the means of diplomacy. Ultimately, however, the difference between Reinhardt and Groener was one of degree, rather than nature. Both stressed that that current capability of the *Reichswehr* meant a defensive strategy, but Reinhardt was more of an opportunist in looking at the possibilities offered by an alliance.

Reinhardt had relatively moderate aims, at least for the weakened *Reichswehr*, and they were couched in defensive terms. The real problem for Germany was if a large neighbouring state attacked. In this case Rein-hardt followed Stülpnagel's ideas on a *Volkskrieg*.[121] It was at this point that Reinhardt's *wehrhafter Mann* would become a substantial part of the national defence: 'When one cannot prevent the invasion of a great power, but can make it difficult and more or less costly, the national defence demands not just one great resistance, but thousands of small pockets of resistance.'[122] He advocated a programme of passive resistance in the conquered areas, while the small *Reichswehr* and the *wehrhafte Männer* would slow down the advance of the enemy, using the landscape and sabotaging transport lines, amongst other things. Propaganda would also be vital to discredit the invaders, and diplomacy would lead to help from friendly neighbouring powers. This form of *Volkskrieg* was designed to fulfil the *Reichswehr*'s task of defending Germany. He concluded: 'The result of such a national defence is not certain; it depends to a large extent on the general world situation, the moral and financial support of benevolent neutrals, or the co-operation of allies, in short on political relations of all types, in which such a resistance can be framed by the

120. Geyer, *Aufrüstung*, 201–205.
121. BA-MA, N 5/20, Stülpnagel lecture on the war of the future, 29–35.
122. *Wehrkraft und Wehrwille*, 103–104.

art of the statesman.'[123] Popular resistance to the invader, both passive and active, was essentially a means to delay the invasion and to maintain the will of the conquered territories to resist, while German statesmen sought help from the international community. Whether this represented a realistic strategy is open to question. Exercises between 1927 and 1929 had shown the clear limitations of this form of *Volkskrieg*, and it was not clear that any state was in a position to offer aid to Germany, surrounded as it was by France and Poland.[124]

Reinhardt's strategy was not only dependent on the will of the people to resist, but also on the operational and tactical ability of the *Reichswehr*. He was caught between the task of discussing the current capabilities of the *Reichswehr* and outlining general theoretical guidelines. For example, although Germany was in no position to wage an offensive war, he adhered to the belief in the moral advantage of the offensive.[125] This dichotomy between current capability and doctrine reflected a central problem of the *Reichswehr* – it saw itself as a temporary institution, the basis for an expanded army. Therefore officers were not only engaged in planning for short-term contingencies, but also in developing doctrines suitable for a larger army.[126]

His tactical ideas were suitable for a large army, rather than for the *Reichswehr*. Believing that the offensive was preferable to the defensive, he stressed the importance of the 'decisive battle'. To achieve victory, it was necessary to form a 'focus', concentrate fire on this point, and pierce the enemy lines.[127] A wide range of weapons were involved in his battle scheme, including infantry, tanks, long-range artillery and gas. Although not an expert in weapons technology, he recognised its significance in modern warfare.[128] Fire-power was the key to battle-field success in Reinhardt's view. In the last year of the war he had been responsible for drawing up many of the artillery plans for the 7th Army. However the impact of artillery in the First World War had been limited by its immobility. Reinhardt argued that 'the invention and use of the tank is a natural and necessary reaction to machine-gun fire, which pins down troops.'[129] In his view the most significant characteristic of tanks and airplanes was mobility. He saw the possibilities offered by integrating these weapons with new means of communication: 'If one adds to the new means of military transport the wireless communications, one has the elements

123. Ibid., 104.
124. Geyer, *Aufrüstung*, 192–95.
125. *Wehrkraft und Wehrwille*, 146–48.
126. Williamson Murray, 'Strategic Bombing: The British, American and German Experience, 1918-1941', in Murray, Millett, eds, *Military Innovation*, 128.
127. HStASt, M 660/034, Bü 38, 'Gliederung und Ausbildung der Wehrmacht', fo. 5.
128. HStASt, M 660/034, Bü 26, Fritz Haber to Reinhardt, 8 January 1921; his attendance at a Haber lecture is just one example of his interest in weapon development.
129. *Wehrkraft und Wehrwille*, 129.

that have given today's form of warfare a new form, which was only hinted at in the world war.'[130] Reinhardt came close to describing the doctrine of *Blitzkrieg*.[131] However he did not develop his ideas any further. For example, although he saw an air force as an independent part of any military force, he did not discuss how air and tank power would be integrated in battle.

In terms of strategy, mobility rather than fire-power was the key factor. He argued: 'The expenditure of force through forward movement only takes its toil in strategies which are concerned with long-distance movements. In comparison to earlier wars large spaces are easier to cover today. Connections of increasing length exhausts increasing amounts of energy, and this exhaustion should be taken into account only in judging a strategic offensive.'[132] Reinhardt pointed to armies, such as the Mongols and Spanish in South America, which had managed to overcome the problems of vast spaces through their mobility. To maximize strategic mobility required organisation: 'Had Napoleon's strategy of 1812 started with the organisation of a mobile army, rather than his plan of campaign, he might have become ruler of the area, which his heavy and demanding west European divisions could not master.'[133] Reinhardt did not outline a programme to modernise the German army, nor did he give any indication that he knew about training links with the Red Army, which aimed to develop German knowledge of tanks and air power. His support for the modernisation of the *Reichswehr* was strong, but vague on details. An army 'with the most modern weapons' was an aspiration, while the IMCC remained in Germany until 1927.[134] Even after that date German military capacity remained severely limited by the treaty terms, so that theoretical discussions could not yet be translated into planning.

In short, the *Reinhardtskurse* covered almost every relevant aspect of military affairs. It is in the nature of the professional soldier to plan for the worst-case scenario. Reinhardt's military thought was based on his experiences and analysis of the First World War, the military situation of the Weimar Republic and a his reading of history. Essentially, he advocated the restructuring of the state and society, so that Germany would be able to meet the challenges of total war. Within that context, his suggestions appear rational. From a professional point of view, he offered a theoretical solution to the problem of maximizing German military potential. State and society would be militarized, so that if and when the time for war came, Germany would be ready. It was a condition of being

130. HStASt, M 660/034, Bü 38, 'Rüstung und Landesbefestigung', fo. 8.
131. James Corum, *The Roots of* Blitzkrieg. *Hans von Seeckt and German Military Reform*, Kansas, 1992; William J. Fanning, 'The origins of the term "*Blitzkrieg*": another view', *Journal of Military History*, 61, 1997, 283–302.
132. *Wehrkraft und Wehrwille*, 150–51.
133. Ibid., 161.
134. Kaehler, ed., *Thaer. Tagebuchaufzeichnungen*, 283.

perpetually ready for the worst-case scenario. He combined a number of strands of German military thought in the inter-war period. Like Groener, he advocated a centralised state with a strong executive, and sought the support of the whole populace for the *Reichswehr*. Both men also stressed the defensive nature of the *Reichswehr*'s tasks, in contrast to some of the more aggressive designs of generals like Werner von Blomberg, who had been Reinhardt's chief of staff. Reinhardt was also influenced by Stülpnagel's ideas on *Volkskrieg* in contrast to Groener who believed that such a war would be futile and wasteful. He embraced Seeckt's tactical emphasis on mobility, but was careful not to let tactics overwhelm his military thought.

If theory were to guide practice, Reinhardt's military and political thought would have driven him away from the Republic, had he lived beyond 1930. His programme could never have been carried out in the conditions of the Weimar Republic, even if there had there been a right-wing majority. The fundamental values of the Weimar Republic's constitution, which stressed individual rights, freedom of expression and the rule of law, were all obstacles to the total militarization of society. Although he had developed an inclusive vision of society, it was a society which demanded subservience and an acceptance of militaristic values. While it could be argued that all liberal democracies restrict human rights when under foreign threat, they do so in order to protect the state and return to those rights as soon as the threat has passed. Reinhardt's vision of society was based on radically different premises, the perpetual readiness for war, justified by the constant existential threat to the *Volk*. 1919 saw a pragmatic Reinhardt work successfully with the institutions of a liberal democracy. The *Reinhardtskurse* saw an idealistic Reinhardt, whose aims were incompatible with the existence of the Republic. Yet during his own lifetime there was no realistic alternative to the Republic, and he co-operated with it, taking advantage of its changing political constellations to promote the re-establishment of German military power.

Chapter 10

CONCLUSIONS

*I*n late 1929 Ernst Reinhardt noted the deterioration in his brother's health. In early May 1930 after a visit to some friends in Stuttgart, Reinhardt fell seriously ill, and he returned to his home in Berlin where he lived out his remaining days, dying on 8 August 1930.[1] He was buried at the Prague cemetery in Stuttgart on 12 August 1930. The following day the *Stuttgarter Neues Tagesblatt* reported the funeral under the title 'At the graveside of the founder of the *Reichswehr*'.[2] His primary goals were the revival of German military power and the reversal of the result of the First World War, goals that he shared with most officers. Yet only a handful enjoyed the opportunity to influence policy and politics in a significant way – Groener, Seeckt, Schleicher, Stülpnagel, Heye and Blomberg were arguably the others, with the first three the most prominent. Reinhardt differed from them because he combined an acute sense of what was politically possible with a radical utopian militaristic outlook, which, if implemented, would have been the negation of politics as the art of the possible.

Since the militarisation of society was a process, pragmatic co-operation with the Republic was not necessarily contradictory. Reinhardt's experiences in the Weimar Republic demonstrated that it was possible for senior officers to adapt to the new political situation in Germany, and to achieve important goals. He was able to work within the liberal democratic framework established in November 1918. His appointment as the last Prussian Minister of War was partly due to the reluctance of others to take the post, but once he started work, he co-operated with the leading politicians of the day, in particular with Gustav Noske, the *Reichswehrminister*, and Friedrich Ebert, the President. Much of the historiography on the rôle of the military in the German revolution

---

1. *Walther Reinhardt. Wehrkraft und Wehrwille. Aus seinem Nachlaß mit einer Lebensbeschreibung*, ed. Ernst Reinhardt, Berlin, 1932, 25.
2. *Stuttgarter Neues Tagesblatt*, 13 August 1930, 'Am Grabe des Schöpfers der Reichswehr'.

stresses the so-called Ebert-Groener pact. However this has meant that the significant contribution of what might be called the Ebert-Noske-Reinhardt axis has been minimised. In fact, many of the permanent achievements in military policy in 1919 were the result of the close collaboration of the two SPD politicians and Reinhardt. Reinhardt was the driving force behind the centralisation of the war ministries, his ideas on the *Reichswehrministerium* were translated into reality and he shaped the terms for serving in the *Reichswehr*. It has been argued that Reinhardt's achievements in these areas were due primarily to the political support that he received from the Council of People's Commissars, and later from the first Weimar coalition government. Reinhardt was able to use the norms of cabinet government to achieve his goals of establishing the most rational military organisation possible under the terms of the treaty of Versailles. While his opinions during the debate on the treaty of Versailles and the Kapp Putsch carried little weight, his advice on organisational military policy was often accepted, because he was an military expert, and perhaps more importantly because he was trusted.

Yet despite his reputation as a trusted supporter of the republic, which was enhanced by his record during the Kapp Putsch in March 1920, he was never emotionally committed to the new regime. He was a *Vernunftrepublikaner*. He admitted that he was a monarchist at heart before his appointment as Prussian Minister of War. In November 1924 after a *Reichswehr* ceremony involving the old imperial flag, Ludwig Haas, the Democratic party deputy, wrote to Reinhardt, regretting such incidents, 'because the creation of sympathetic relations between the *Reichswehr* and the republican social groups, in particular the Social Democrats, is made more difficult.'[3] Haas recognised that Reinhardt was not engaged in conspiring against the state, but he hinted at the problem which the so-called *Vernunft-republikaner* created for the regime; their lack of genuine sympathy meant that they were insensitive to the symbolism of many of their acts and contributed to the delegitimization of the Republic. Reinhardt's support for the Weimar Republic was of a very practical nature, such as his co-operation with Ebert and Noske in 1919, and his strong opposition to the Kapp Putsch. Yet he never wholeheartedly embraced the Republic. In his lectures he argued that from a military perspective it did not matter whether a state was monarchical or republican, it only had to be efficient at mobilizing its resources for war.

The strongest claim one could make about his political orientation is that he was a German nationalist. His prime concern was the revival of Germany as a great power, a concern which he voiced as early as January 1919 to his friend, Colonel Albrecht von Thaer. After the collapse of the *Kaiserreich* Reinhardt saw the Republic as offering the best hope for the recovery of German power. This was a very practical choice, and reflects

3. HStASt, M 660/034, Bü 22, Haas to Reinhardt, Berlin, 1 November 1924.

his belief in the primacy of foreign policy. Reinhardt focused on the re-establishment of German power as the ultimate goal, even at stages of great internal unrest, such as in 1919 and 1923. His nationalism was more inclusive than other forms of German nationalism which made racialist or class-based criteria essential to membership of the *Volksgemeinschaft*. In Reinhardt's opinion the primary identity of Germans was their nation, not their racial or class group. He argued that these created divisions which distracted from the task of renewing German power. Reinhardt was genuinely imbued with the *Burgfrieden* spirit of August 1914, and it is significant that when the French occupied German territory in 1923 he appealed to the state governments to help him create 'a sort of *Burgfrieden*.' Reinhardt's awareness of potential threats to Germany, real and imagined, forged an inclusive style of nationalism. Yet the realisation of Reinhardt's militarized *Volksgemeinschaft* could only occur under an authoritarian regime.

If Reinhardt displayed a degree of ideological flexibility, this was related to the practical business of being a soldier. Thus the second context in which he must be located is that of a professional officer in the modern era. The concept of modernity includes the ideas of industrialisation and rationalization, trends which affected the way war was fought, and hence the professional planning of the officer corps in peace time. One of the characteristics of Reinhardt's policies in 1919 was the rationalization of military structures at all levels. Hence he centralised the states' war ministries in the *Reichswehrministerium*, and he combined the planning and administrative aspects of military organisation in the new ministry, which rid the German military organisation of the awkward split between the Prussian Ministry of War and the General Staff. His arguments against the soldiers' councils were couched in terms of military efficiency, as were his arguments in favour of *Vertrauensleute*. While it can be argued that one officer's military efficiency was another's inefficiency, the process by which Reinhardt arrived at a policy was scientific in the traditions of German military planning. His ideas were derived from a wide knowledge of military history, coupled with his own experiences. Reinhardt can therefore be seen as an example of a professional officer, whose knowledge and application of it legitimized his influence over government military policy in 1919.

Industrialised warfare was one of modernity's children. The task of the professional officer in the modern era was to prepare to fight such a war. This involved both the rationalization of military organisations, and also the preparation of state and society for war. Reinhardt advocated state structures which would be appropriate in times of war. Hence he saw the centralised military organisation of the *Reichswehrministerium* as an ideal preparation for war, as was the strong position of the elected president in the Weimar republic. To overcome the disadvantages of a small army, he argued that individuals should become 'militarily capable.' This mass of individuals could then be mobilized and organised in wartime by the *Reichswehr*. While Reinhardt was aware of the implications of modern weaponry, he was more comfortable with ideas of mass mobilization, and the dual use of government structures for addressing the needs of society in times of war and peace. Reinhardt's military and political thought is illustrative of the dangers Weber saw in bureaucracies which 'possess an inherent drive to extend their control of societal affairs within their sphere of activity ever further, eventually taking virtually everything into their group in order to eliminate any sources of irrational or unpredictable social contact.'[4] Yet it is important to distinguish between Reinhardt's thoughts on military affairs and the implementation of those thoughts. While his ideas on the rationalization of military structures were translated into reality, his ideas on mass mobilization were not.

Peter Hayes described Schleicher, leading general and the last Chancellor before Hitler, as a 'bundle of atavistic impulses and rational assessments of contemporary facts, always balancing, always trimming, [he] personified the schizophrenia of Weimar's political and social establishment.'[5] Reinhardt was also caught between the logic of his ideas and the logic of politics, which dictated pragmatism. But he differed in one important respect from Schleicher. The latter was intimately involved in the creation and destruction of cabinets. He sought to fashion political constellations, which were conducive to the *Reichswehr*'s policies. Reinhardt never engaged in politics at this level. He took advantage of political situations, but he was reactive, rather than pro-active, with the exception of the Versailles debate which turned out to be a doomed effort. He cooperated with the Republic because there was no other option, but his pragmatism would have led him to support a better option. Reinhardt, more than any other general, stands out as the embodiment of the civil-military relationship between the *Reichswehr* and the Republic, and the way in which it was governed by political opportunism and military ideology.

4. Wolfgang Mommsen, *The Political and Social Theory of Max Weber*, Cambridge, 1989, 114.
5. Peter Hayes, '"A question mark with epaulettes"? Kurt von Schleicher and Weimar politics', *JMH*, 52, 1, 1980, 65.

BIBLIOGRAPHY

Archival Sources

Bayerisches Hauptstaatsarchiv (BHStA)
Ministerium des Äußern, 104 380, 104 381
Ministerium des Innern, 71538
Ministerium für Land- und Forstwirtschaft, 1729, 1807
Bayerische Gesandschaft nach Berlin, 1007, 1351, 1352
Bayerisches Kriegsarchiv (BKA)
Schützenbrigade 21, Band 19, 34, 79 (b), 200, 209, 210, 265, 281, 300
Reichswehrgruppenkommando IV, Band 58, 135, 307, 329, 712
Bundesarchiv, Koblenz (BA-K)
Nachlaß Eduard David, N 1027
Nachlaß Otto Gessler, N 1032
Nachlaß Matthias Erzberger, N 1097
Nachlaß Walther Luetgebrune, N 1150
Nachlaß Eugen Schiffer, N 1191
Bundesarchiv, Lichterfelde (BArch)
Akten der Reichskanzlei: R 43/1 8, 48, 49, 117, 164, 340, 384, 609, 613, 680,
    682, 683, 684, 685, 686, 692, 693, 700, 701, 702, 705, 1796, 1844, 1863,
    2265, 2293, 2305, 2314, 2703, 2708, 2728.
Reichskommissar für öffentlichen Ordnung: R 1507/1019c, R1507/1079, R
    1507/67104 nr 46, R 1507/67145 nr 213, R 1507/67150 nr 233, R
    1507/67151 nr 234
Bundesarchiv-Militärarchiv (BA-MA)
Nachlaß Joachim von Stülpnagel, N 5
Nachlaß Artur Hauffe, N 11
Nachlaß Wilhelm Heye, N 18
Nachlaß Heinrich Scheüch, N 23
Nachlaß Kurt von Schleicher, N 42
Nachlaß Wilhelm Groener, N 46
Nachlaß Walther Reinhardt, N 86
Nachlaß Otto von Below, N 87
Nachlaß Hans von Seeckt, N 247
RW 1/13 Denkschrift des Reichswehrausschusses
RW 1/15 Besprechung in Kolberg, Ansprache Groener

MSg. 1/269, Ergänzung der Verordnung vom 19. Januar 1919
Armeeoberkommando 7: PH 5 II, 481, 482
Armeeverordnungsblatt, PHD 1/1918
Heeresverordnungsblatt, RHD 1, Band 1, 1919
Friedrich Ebert Stiftung, Archiv der SPD
Nachlaß Carl Severing
Nachlaß Gustav Noske
Generallandesarchiv, Karlsruhe (GLAK)
Staatsministerium, Abteilung 233: 4286, 12116, 12241, 12242, 12245, 12295,
    12298, 12300, 12301, 12304, 12308, 12315, 12325, 12341, 12342, 12352,
    12363, 12379, 12451, 12458, 12484, 12550, 12569, 25928, 34854
Hauptstaatsarchiv, Stuttgart (HStASt)
Nachlaß Walther Reinhardt, M 660/034
Staatsministerium: E 130 b, Büschel 218, 3724, 3725, 3727, 3728, 3729, 3730,
    3731, 3733, 3736
Military files: M 1/3, Band 519, 536, 537, 683
 M 1/4, Band 993, 1007, 1014, 1168, 1612, 1613, 1642, 1710, 1712,
 1713, 1714
 M 10, Band 1, 3, 6
 M 33/2, Büschel 55, 217, 245, 298, 393
 M 77/1, Büschel 81, 82, 83, 84, 85 642
 M 365, Band 2, 3, 4, 5, 6, 7, 8, 9
 M 430/1, Büschel 2155
Historisches Archiv Krupp
WA 48/121, Besuchsprotokoll General Reinhardt
Ministère des affaires étrangères, Paris
MAE Série Z, Sous-série Allemagne
Politisches Archiv, Auswärtiges Amt (PA-AA)
Files from the series *Weltkrieg*
Files from the series *Friedensdelegation*
Preußisches Geheimes Staatsarchiv, Dahlem
Preußisches Kabinett, 1919: 90 a, Nr 6, B III, Band 168
Vereinigung Graf Schlieffen: Rep 77, Titel 4043, Nr 400
Preußisches Ministerium des Innern: Rep 77, Titel 4043, Nr 189

Printed primary source material

Albertin, L. and Wegener, K., eds, *Linksliberalismus in der Weimarer Republik. Die
    Führungsgremien der Deutschen Demokratischen Partei und der Deutschen
    Staatspartei.* Düsseldorf, 1980.
Akten zur deutschen auswärtigen Politik. November 1918 bis Mai 1919. Serie A:
    1918-1925, volume 1, edited by John P. Fox, Peter Grupp, Pierre Jardin.
    Göttingen, 1982.
Becker, Josef, 'Zur Politik der Wehrmachtabteilung in der Regierungskrise
    1926/7: zwei Dokumente aus dem Nachlaß Schleichers', *VfZ*, vol. 14
    (1966): 69–78.

Boldt, Bärbel, Boldt, Werner, Maock, Ute, Nickel, Gunther, Siems, Renke, and Wagner, Frank, eds, *Carl von Ossietzky. Sämtliche Schriften*. Vols 3–7, Oldenbourg, 1994.

Busik, Bärbel, and Lankheit, Klaus, eds, *Hitler. Reden, Schriften, Anordnungen. Februar 1925 bis Januar 1933*. Vol. III/1, Juli 1928 – Februar 1929, Munich, 1994.

Clausewitz, Carl von, *On war*, eds, Michael Howard, and Peter Paret. London, 1993.

Demobilmachungsplan für das deutsche Heer. Berlin, 1918.

Epkenhans, Michael, '"Wir als deutsches Volk sind doch nicht klein zu kriegen." Aus den Tagebüchern des Fregattenkapitäns Bogistav von Selchow', 1918/19, *MgM*, vol. 55, no. 1 (1996): 165–224.

Erdmann, Karl Dietrich, Vogt, Martin, eds, *Die Kabinette Stresemann*. 2 vols, Boppard am Rhein, 1976.

Ernst, Fritz, 'Aus dem Nachlaß des Generals Walther Reinhardt, *Die Welt als Geschichte*, vol. 18 (1958): 39–121.

Förster, Stig, ed., *Moltke. Vom Kabinettskrieg zum Volkskrieg. Eine Werkauswahl*. Bonn, 1992.

Gessler, Otto, *Reichswehrpolitik in der Weimarer Zeit*. Stuttgart, 1958.

Golecki, Anton, ed., *Das Kabinett Bauer. 21. Juni 1919 bis 27. März 1920*. Boppard am Rhein, 1980.

Goltz, Rüdiger von der, *Meine Sendung im Finnland und im Baltikum*. Leipzig, 1920.

Groener, Wilhelm, *Lebenserinnerungen. Jugend, Generalstab, Weltkrieg*. Göttingen, 1957.

Grzesinski, Albert, *Inside Germany*, translated by Alexander Lipschitz. New York, 1939.

Heilfron, Eduard, ed., *Die deutsche Nationalversammlung im Jahre 1919 in ihrer Arbeit für den Aufbau des neuen Volkstaates*. 6 vols, Berlin, 1919–1920.

Hesse, Kurt, *Der Feldherr Psychologos. Ein Suchen nach dem Führer der deutschen Zukunft*. Berlin, 1922.

Heuss, Theodor, *Soldatentum in unserer Zeit*. Tübingen, 1959.

———— *Erinnerungen 1905–1933*. 4th edn Tübingen, 1963.

Huber, Ernst, ed., *Dokumente der Novemberrevolution und der Weimarer Republik 1918-1933*. Stuttgart, 1966.

Hürten, Heinz, 'Heeresverfassung und Länderrecht. Württemberg in den Auseinandersetzungen der Weimarer Nationalversammlung um die Bildung einer einheitlichen Reichswehr', *MgM*, vol. 23, no. 1 (1978): 147–82.

———— ed., *Zwischen Revolution und Kapp Putsch. Militär und Innenpolitik, 1918-1920*. Düsseldorf, 1977.

———— and Meyer, Georg, eds, *Adjutant im preußischen Kriegsministerium Juni 1918 bis Oktober 1919. Aufzeichnungen des Hauptmannes Gustav Böhm*. Stuttgart, 1977.

Jähns, Max, *Heeresverfassung und Völkerleben. Eine Umschau*. Berlin, 1885.

Jünger, Ernst, *Sämtliche Werke. Essays. Betrachtungen zur Zeit*. Zweite Abteilung, Stuttgart, 1980.

Kaehler, Siegfried, ed., *General Major Albrecht von Thaer. Generalstabsdienst an der Front und in der Obersten Heeresleitung. Aus Briefen und Tagebuchaufzeichnungen 1915–1919*. Göttingen, 1957.

Kolb, Eberhard and Rürup, Reinhard, eds, *Der Zentralrat der deutschen Sozialistischen Republik 19.1.18–8.4.19. Vom ersten zum zweiten Rätekongreß*. Leiden, 1968.

Loßberg, Fritz von, *Meine Tätigkeit im Weltkriege 1914–1918*. Berlin, 1939.

Ludendorff, Erich, *Meine Kriegserinnerungen 1914–1918*. Berlin, 1919.

_____ *Kriegführung und Politik*. Berlin, 1922.

Maercker, Georg, *Vom Kaiserheer zur Reichswehr. Ein Beitrag zur Gecshichte der deutschen Revolution*. Leipzig, 1921.

Martens, Stefan, ed., *Documents diplomatiques français. 9 janvier – 30 juin 1920. Französische Diplomatenberichte aus Deutschland*. Volume 1. Bonn, 1992.

Matthias, Erich and Meier-Welcker, Hans, eds, *Das Krisenjahr 1923. Militär und Innenpolitik 1922–1924*. Düsseldorf, 1980.

Miller, Susanne, ed., *Die Regierung der Volksbeauftragten*. 2 vols, Düsseldorf, 1969.

Mühleisen, Horst, 'Annehmen oder Ablehnen? Das Kabinett Scheidemann, die Oberste Heeresleitung und der Vertrag von Versailles im Juni 1919', *VfZ*, vol. 35, no. 4, (1987): 419–81.

Noske, Gustav, *Von Kiel bis Kapp. Zur Geschichte der deutschen Revolution*. Berlin, 1920.

_____ *Erlebtes aus Aufstieg und Niedergang einer Demokratie*. Offenbach am Main, 1947.

Paret, Peter, ed., *Carl von Clausewitz. Historical and Political Writings*. Princeton, 1992.

Phelps, Reginald, 'Aus den Groener-Dokumenten', *Deutsche Rundschau*, vol. 76 (1950).

Preuß, Hugo, *Staat, Recht und Freiheit. Aus 40 Jahren deutscher Politik und Geschichte*. Hildesheim, 1964.

Reinhard, Wilhelm, *Die Wehen der Republik, 1918–19*. Berlin, 1933.

Reinhardt, Ernst, ed., *Walther Reinhardt, Wehrkraft und Wehrwille. Aus seinem Nachlaß mit einer Lebensbeschreibung*. Berlin, 1933.

Reinhardt, Walther and Admiral Zenker, *Wehrwille und Wehrgedanke in Deutschlands Jugend. Zwei Vorträge auf der Freusberger Schulungswoche 1929*. Berlin, 1930.

Republikanischer Führerbund, ed., *Republikanerhetze in der Reichswehr*, 1919.

Scheringer, Richard, *Das große Los unter Soldaten, Bauern und Rebellen*. Hamburg, 1959.

Schmalix, Alex, *Gerechtigkeit für Kapitän Ehrhardt*. Leipzig, 1923.

Schmitt, Carl, *The Crisis of Parliamentary Democracy*, translated by Ellen Kennedy. Cambridge, MA, 1985.

Schulze, Hagen, ed., *Das Kabinett Scheidemann. 13. Februar bis 20. Juni 1919*. Boppard am Rhein, 1971.

Schustereit, Hartmut, 'Unpolitisch-überparteilich-Staatstreue. Wehrfragen aus der Sicht der Deutschen Demokratischen Partei 1919–1930', *MgM*, vol. 15, (1974): 131–72.

Sitzungsberichte der verfassungsgebenden preußischen Landesversammlung, Tagung 1919–21, vols 1–3. Berlin, 1919–1920.

Teske, Hermann, *Der silberne Spiegel. Generalstabsdienst unter der Lupe*. Heidelberg, 1952.

Treue, Wolfgang, ed., *Deutsche Parteiprogramme, 1861–1954*. Göttingen, 1954.

Verhandlungen der verfassungsgebenden deutschen Nationalversammlung, vols 326, 328, 329, 331, Berlin, 1919–1920.

Vogt, Martin, ed., *Kabinett Müller I. März–Juni 1920*. Boppard am Rhein, 1971.

Wette, Wolfram, ed., *Aus den Geburtsstunden der Weimarer Republik. Das Tagebuch des Obersten Ernst van den Bergh*. Düsseldorf, 1991.

Witzmann, Georg, *Thüringen von 1918–1933. Erinnerungen eines Politikers*. Meisenheim am Glan, 1958.

Wrisberg, Ernst, *Der Weg zur Revolution*. Leipzig, 1921.

Secondary literature

Albrecht, Thomas, *Für eine wehrhafte Demokratie. Albert Grzesinski und die preussische Politik in der Weimarer Republik*. Bonn, 1999.

Angress, Werner, 'Das deutsche Militär und die Juden im Ersten Weltkrieg', *MgM*, vol. 19 (1976): 77–146.

_____ 'Prussia's Army and the Jewish Reserve Officer Controversy before World War I', *LBIYB*, vol. 17 (1972): 19–42.

Bald, Detlef, 'Zur Reform der Generalstabsausbildung in der Weimarer Republik: die Reinhardt-Kurse', in Detlef Bald, ed., *Militärische Verantwortung in Staat und Gesellschaft. 175 Jahre Generalstabsausbildung in Deutschland*. Koblenz, 1986.

_____ *Der deutsche Offizier. Sozial- und Bildungsgeschichte des deutschen Offizierkorps im 20. Jahrhundert*. Munich, 1982.

_____ *Der deutsche Generalstab 1859–1939. Reform und Restauration in Ausbildung und Bildung*. Munich, 1977.

_____ and Bald-Gerlich, Gerhild, Ambros, Eduard, eds, *Tradition und Reform im militärischen Bildungswesen. Von der preussischen Allgemeinen Kriegsschule zur Führungsakademie der Bundeswehr. Eine Dokumentation 1810–1985*. Baden-Baden, 1985.

Bénoist-Méchin, Jean, *Histoire de l'armée allemande*. 2 vols, Paris, 1936.

Benz, Wolfgang, *Süddeutschland in der Weimarer Republik. Ein Beitrag zur deutschen Innenpolitik 1918–1923*. Berlin, 1970

_____ and Paucker, Arnold, eds, *Jüdisches Leben in der Weimarer Republik*. London, Tübingen, 1998.

Berghahn, Volker, *Militarism. The History of an International Debate*. Leamington Spa, 1981.

_____ *Der Stahlhelm. Bund der Frontsoldaten 1918-1935*. Düsseldorf, 1966.

Bessel, Richard, *Germany after the First World War*. Oxford, 1993.

_____ 'Unemployment and Demobilisation in Germany after the First World War', in R. J. Evans and Dick Geary (eds), *The German Unemployed*. New York, 1987.

Blackbourn, David, *The Fontana History of Germany. The Long Nineteenth Century*. London, 1997.

_____ 'The German Bourgeosie: An Introduction', in David Blackbourn, Richard Evans, eds, *The German bourgeoisie*. London, 1991.

Blanning, T. C. W., *The French Revolutionary Wars, 1787–1802*. London, 1996.

Boemeke, Manfred, Feldman, Gerald and Glaser, Elisabeth, eds, *Treaty of Versailles. A Reassessment after 75 years*. Cambridge, 1998.

_____ Chickering, Roger and Förster, Stig, eds, *Anticipating Total War. The German and American experience, 1871–1914*. Cambridge, 1999.

Bracher, Karl Dietrich, *Die Auflösung der Weimarer Republik. Eine Studie der Machtverfalls in einer Demokratie*. Düsseldorf, 1984.

Brandt, Peter and Groh, Dieter, *"Vaterlandslose Gesellen". Sozialdemokratie und Nation 1860–1990*. Munich, 1992.

Brunner, Otto, Conze, Werner, and Kosselleck, Reinhardt, eds, *Geschichtliche Grundbegriffe. Historisches Lexikon zur politisch-sozialen Sprache in Deutschland*. 8 vols, Stuttgart, 1975.

Bruns, B., ed., *Württemberg unter der Regierung König Wilhelms II*. Stuttgart, 1916.

Bucholz, Arden, *Moltke, Schlieffen and Prussian War Planning*. New York, 1991.

Bucher, Peter, *Der Reichswehrprozeß. Der Hochverrat der Ulmer Reichswehr-offiziere 1929–1930*. Boppard am Rhein, 1967.

Burleigh, Michael, *Germany Turns Eastward. A Study of Ostforschung in the Third Reich*. Cambridge, 1988.

Busch, Eckart, *Der Oberbefehl. Seine rechtliche Struktur in Preußen und Deutschland seit 1848*. Boppard am Rhein, 1967.

Butenschön, Rainer and Spoo, Eckart, eds, *Wozu muss einer der Bluthund sein? Der Mehrheitssozialdemokrat Gustav Noske und der deutsche Militarismus des 20. Jahrhunderts*. Heilbronn, 1997.

Caplan, Jane, *Government Without Administration. State and Civil Service in Weimar and Nazi Germany*. Oxford, 1988.

Caro, Kurt and Oehme, Walter, *Schleichers Aufstieg. Ein Beitrag zur Geschichte der Gegenrevolution*. Berlin, 1933.

Carsten, Francis, *The Reichswehr and Politics, 1918-1933*. Oxford, 1966.

Chickering, Roger and Förster, Stig, eds, *The Shadows of Total War. Europe, East Asia, and the United States, 1919–1939*. Cambridge, 2003.

_____ and Förster, Stig, eds, *Great War, Total War. Mobilization and Combat on the Western Front, 1914–1918*. Cambridge, 2000.

_____ and Förster, Stig, 'Introduction', in Chickering, Förster, eds, *The Shadows of Total War. Europe, East Asia, and the United States, 1919–1939*. Cambridge, 2003.

_____ 'Total war: the use and abuse of a concept', in Boemeke, Chickering, Förster, eds, *Anticipating Total War. The German and American experience, 1871–1914*. Cambridge, 1999.

Clemente, Steven, *For King and Kaiser. The Making of the Prussian Army Officer, 1860–1914*. New York, 1992.

Cocks, Geoffrey and Jarausch, Konrad, eds, *German Professions, 1800–1950*. Oxford, 1990.

Corum, James, *The Roots of* Blitzkrieg. *Hans von Seeckt and German Military Reform*. Kansas, 1992.

Craig, Gordon, *The Politics of the Prussian Army, 1640–1945*, New York, 1964.

_____ *Germany, 1866–1945*. Oxford, 1978.

Daniel, Ute, *The War from Within. German Working Class Women in the First World War*. New York, Oxford, 1997.

Deist, Wilhelm, *Militär, Staat und Gesellschaft. Studien zur preußisch-deutschen Militärgeschichte.* Munich, 1991.

———— *The Wehrmacht and German Rearmament.* London, 1986.

———— 'Die Reichswehr und der Krieg der Zukunft', *MgM*, vol. 34, no. 1 (1989): 81–92.

———— 'Verdeckter Militärstreik im Kriegsjahr 1918?', in Wette, ed., *Der Krieg des kleinen Mannes. Eine Militärgeschichte von unten.* Munich, 1992.

Demeter, Karl, *The German Officer Corps in Society and State, 1650–1945,* translated by Angus Malcolm, London, 1965.

Diehl, James, *Paramilitary Politics in Weimar Germany.* Bloomington, 1977.

Dülffer, Jost, *Weimar, Hitler und die Marine. Reichspolitik und Flottenbau 1920–1939.* Düsseldorf, 1973.

Ebeling, Frank, *Geopolitik. Karl Haushofer und seine Raumwissenschaft 1919–1945.* Berlin, 1994.

Elben, Wolfgang, *Das Problem der Kontinuität in der deutschen Revolution. Die Politik der Staatssekretäre und der militärischen Führung von November 1918 bis Februar 1919.* Düsseldorf, 1966.

Eley, Geoff, *From Unification to Nazism. Reinterpreting the German past.* London, 1986.

Erdmann, Karl Dietrich, 'Die Geschichte der Weimarer Republik als Problem der Wissenschaft', *VfZ*, vol. 3 (1955): 1–19.

Erger, Johannes, *Der Kapp-Lüttwitz Putsch. Ein Beitrag zur deutschen Innenpolitik 1919–1920.* Düsseldorf, 1967.

Ernst, Fritz, 'Walther Reinhardt, (1872–1930)', *Zeitschrift für württembergische Landesgeschichte,* (1957): 331–64.

Euler, Friedrich Wilhelm, 'Die deutsche Generalität und Admiralität bis 1918', in Hoffmann, ed., *Das deutsche Offizierkorps 1860–1960.* Boppard am Rhein, 1980.

Facius, Friedrich, *Politische Geschichte in der Neuzeit. Geschichte Thüringens,* vol. 5, Cologne, 1978.

Fanning, William J., 'The Origins of the Term *Blitzkrieg*: Another View', *Journal of Military History,* vol. 61 (1997): 283–303.

Feldmann, Gerald, *Army, Industry and Labor in Germany, 1914–1918.* Providence, 1992 edn.

———— *The Great Disorder. Politics, Economics and Society in the German Inflation, 1914–1924.* New York, Oxford, 1993.

Ferguson, Niall, 'Public Finance and National Security: The Domestic Origins of the First World War Revisited', *Past and Present,* no. 142 (1994): 141–68.

Fischer, Conan, *The Ruhr Crisis, 1923–1924.* Oxford, 2003.

Fischer, Fritz, *From Kaiserreich to Third Reich. Elements of Continuity in German History, 1871–1945.* London, 1986.

Fischer, Joachim, 'Das württembergische Offizierkorps 1866–1918', in Hoffmann, ed., *Das deutsche Offizierkorps 1860–1960.* Boppard am Rhein, 1980.

Flemming, Jens, 'Die Bewaffnung des "Landvolks": ländliche Schutzwehren und agrarischer Konservatismus in der Anfangsphase der Weimarer Republik', *MgM*, vol. 26, no. 2 (1979): 7–36.

Frevert, Ute, ed., *Militär und Gesellschaft im 19. und 20. Jahrhundert.* Stuttgart, 1997.

_____ *Die kasernierte Nation. Militärdienst und Zivilgesellschaft in Deutschland.* Munich, 2001.

Förster, Stig, *Der doppelte Militarismus. Die deutsche Heeresrüstungspolitik zwischen Status-Quo-Sicherung und Aggression 1890-1913.* Stuttgart, 1985.

_____ 'Der deutsche Generalstab und die Illusionen des kurzen Krieges, 1871-1914. Metakritik eines Mythos', *MgM*, vol. 40, no. 1 (1995): 61-95.

_____ ed., *An der Schwelle zum Totalen Krieg. Die militärische Debatte über den Krieg der Zukunft 1919-1939.* Paderborn, 2002.

Gärtringen, Friedrich Hiller von, '"Dolchstoss"-Diskussion und "Dolchstoss-Legende" im Wandel von vier Jahrzehnten', in Waldemar Besson, Friedrich Freiherr Hiller von Gärtringen, eds, *Geschichte und Gegenwartsbewußtsein.* Göttingen, 1963.

Gall, Lothar, *Bismarck. The White Revolutionary.* 2 vols, London, 1986.

Geyer, Michael, *Aufrüstung oder Sicherheit. Die Reichswehr in der Krise der Machtpolitik 1924-36.* Wiesbaden, 1980.

_____ 'Die Wehrmacht der deutschen Republik ist die Reichswehr. Bemerkungen zur neueren Literatur', *MgM*, vol. 13, (1973): 152-99.

_____ 'Insurrectionary Warfare: The German Debate about a *levée en masse* in October 1918', *JMH*, vol. 73, no. 4 (2001): 459-527.

_____ 'The Past as Future: The German Officer Corps as Profession', in Cocks, Jarausch, eds, *German Professions, 1800-1950.* Oxford, 1990.

_____ 'Der zur Organisation erhobene Burgfrieden' in Müller, Opitz, eds, *Militär.*

_____ 'The Militarization of Europe, 1914-1945', in Gillis, ed., *The Militarization of the Western World.* New Brunswick, 1989.

Gilbert, Felix, ed., *The Historical Essays of Otto Hintze.* New York, Oxford, 1975.

Gillis, John, ed., *The Militarization of the Western World.* New Brunswick, 1989.

Gordon, Harold, *The Reichswehr and the German Republic, 1919-1926.* Princeton, 1957.

Grupp, Peter, *Deutsche Außenpolitik im Schatten von Versailles 1918-1920. Zur Politik des Auswärtigen Amts vom Ende des Ersten Weltkrieges und der Novemberrevolution bis zum Inkrafttreten des Versailler Vertrags.* Paderborn, 1988.

Guske, Claus, *Das politische Denken des Generals von Seeckt. Ein Beitrag zur Diskussion des Verhaltnisses Seeckt-Reichswehr-Republik.* Hamburg, Lübeck, 1971.

Gusy, Christoph, *Die Weimarer Reichsverfassung.* Tübingen, 1997.

Guth, Ekkehart, *Der Loyalitätskonflikt des deutschen Offizierkorps in der Revolution 1918-1920.* Frankfurt, 1983.

Hansen, Ernst Willi, 'Zum "Militärisch-Industriellen-Komplex" in der Weimarer Republik', in Müller, Opitz, eds, *Militär und Militarismus in der Weimarer Republik.* Düsseldorf, 1978.

_____ 'The military and the military-political breakdown in Germany 1918 and France 1940', in Müller, ed., *The military in politics and society in France and Germany in the twentieth century.* Oxford, 1995.

Hayes, Peter, ' "A Question Mark With Epaulettes" ? Kurt von Schleicher and Weimar Politics', *JMH*, vol. 52, no. 1 (1980): 35-65.

Häupel, Beate, *Die Gründung des Landes Thüringen. Staatsbildung und Reformpolitik 1918-1923.* Weimar, 1995.

Heiden, Detlef and Mai, Gunther, eds, *Nationalsozialismus in Thüringen*. Weimar, 1995.

Hennig, Diethard, *Johannes Hoffmann. Sozialdemokrat und Bayerischer Ministerpräsident*. Munich, 1990.

Herrmann, David, *The Arming of Europe and the Making of the First World War*. Princeton, 1996.

Herwig, Holger, *The First World War. Germany and Austria-Hungary, 1914–1918*. London, 1997.

Heß, Jürgen, *Theodor Heuss vor 1933. Ein Beitrag zur Geschichte des demokratischen Denkens in Deutschland*. Stuttgart, 1973.

_____ 'Das ganze Deutschland soll es sein'. *Demokratischer Nationalismus in der Weimarer Republik am Beispiel der Deutschen Demokratischen Partei*. Stuttgart, 1978.

Hewitson, Mark, *National Identity and Political Thought in Germany. Wilhelmine Depictions of the French Third Republic, 1890–1914*. Oxford, 2000.

Hiden, John, *The Baltics and Weimar Ostpolitik*. Cambridge, 1987.

Hoffmann, Hans Hubert, ed., *Das deutsche Offizierkorps 1860–1960*. Boppard am Rhein, 1980.

Holl, Kurt, Wette, Wolfram, eds, *Pazifismus in der Weimarer Republik*. Paderborn, 1981.

Horne, John, ed., *State, Society and Mobilization in Europe during the First World War*. Cambridge, 1997.

_____ Kramer, Alan, *German Atrocities, 1914. A History of Denial*. New Haven, 2001.

Hürten, Heinz, 'Der Kapp Putsch als Wende. Über Rahmenbedingungen der Weimarer Republik seit dem Frühjahr 1920', *Rheinisch–Westfälische Akademie der Wissenschaften*. Düsseldorf, 1989.

_____ Weimarer Republik in ihrem ersten Jahrfünft, *Rheinisch–Westfälische Akademie der Wissenschaften*. Düsseldorf, 1977.

Hürter, Johannes, *Wilhelm Groener. Reichswehrminister am Ende der Weimarer Republik*. Munich, 1993.

_____ ' "Vor lauter Taktik schlapp" ? Die Personalunion von Wehr- und Innenministerium im Zweiten Kabinett Brüning', *MgM*, vol. 57, no. 2 (1998): 465–81.

James, Harold, *A German Identity, 1770–1990*. London, 1990.

Jeismann, Michael, *Das Vaterland der Feinde. Studien zum nationalen Feindbegriff und Selbstverständnis in Deutschland und Frankreich 1792–1918*. Stuttgart, 1982.

Jochmann, Werner, 'Die Ausbreitung des Antisemitismus', in Mosse, ed., *Deutsches Judentum in Krieg und Revolution, 1916–1923*. Tübingen, 1971.

Kauders, Anthony, 'Legally Citizens: Jewish Exclusion from the Weimar Polity', in Benz, Paucker, eds, *Jüdisches Leben in der Weimarer Republik*. London, Tübingen, 1998.

Keylor, William, 'Versailles and International Diplomacy', in Boemeke, Feldman, Glaser, eds, *Treaty of Versailles. A Reassessment after 75 years*. Cambridge, 1998.

Kielmannsegg, Peter Graf, *Deutschland und der erste Weltkrieg*. Frankfurt, 1968.

Klein, Fritz, 'Between Compiègne and Versailles: The Germans on the Way from a Misunderstood Defeat to an Unwanted Peace', in Boemeke, Feldman, Glaser, eds, *Treaty of Versailles. A Reassessment after 75 Years*. Cambridge, 1998.

Kluge, Ülrich, *Soldatenräte und Revolution. Studien zur Militärpolitik in Deutschland 1918/19*. Göttingen, 1975.

Koch, H. W., *Der deutsche Bürgerkrieg. Eine Geschichte der deutschen und österreichischen Freikorps 1918-1923*. Frankfurt, 1978.

Kocka, Jürgen, *Klassengesellschaft im Krieg. Deutsche Sozialgeschichte 1914-1918*, 2nd edn. Göttingen, 1978.

_____ 'The European Pattern and the German Case' in Kocka, Mitchell, eds, *Bourgeois society in nineteenth century Europe*. Oxford, 1993.

_____ and Mitchell, Allan, eds, *Bourgeois society in nineteenth century Europe*. Oxford, 1993.

Koistenen, Paul, 'Towards a warfare state: militarization in America during the period of the World Wars', in Gillis, ed., *The Militarization of the Western World*. New Brunswick, 1989.

Kolb, Eberhard, *Die Arbeiterräte in der deutschen Innenpolitik 1918-1919*. Frankfurt, 1978.

_____ *The Weimar Republic*. London, 1988.

_____ Pyta, Wolfram, 'Die Notstandsplanung unter den Regierungen Papen und Schleicher', in Winkler, ed., *Die deutsche Staatskrise 1930-1933. Handlungsspielräume und Alternativen*. Munich, 1992.

Kohlhaas, Wilhelm, *Chronik der Stadt Stuttgart 1918-1933*. Stuttgart, 1964.

Krüger, Gabriele, *Die Brigade Ehrhardt*. Hamburg, 1971.

Krüger, Peter, *Deutschland und die Reparationen 1918/9. Die Genesis des Reparationsproblems in Deutschland zwischen Waffenstillstand und Friedensschluß*. Stuttgart, 1973.

_____ *Die Aussenpolitik der Republik von Weimar*. Darmstadt, 1985.

Kruse, Wolfgang, 'Krieg und Klassenheer. Zur Revolutionierung der deutschen Armee im ersten Weltkrieg', *GG*, vol. 22 (1996): 530-61.

Lassmann, Peter and Speirs, Ronald, eds, *Weber. Political Writings*. Cambridge, 1994.

Lee, Marshall and Michalka, Wolfgang, *German Foreign Policy, 1917-1933. Continuity or Break?* Leamington Spa, 1987.

Löbel, Uwe, 'Neue Forschungsmöglichkeiten zur preußisch-deutschen Heeresgeschichte', *MgM*, vol. 51, no. 1 (1992): 143-49.

Lösche, Peter, *Der Bolschewismus im Urteil der deutschen Sozialdemokratie, 1903-1920*. Berlin, 1967.

Lütgemeier-Davin, Reinhold, 'Basismobilisierung gegen den Krieg. Die "Nie-wieder-Krieg" Bewegung in der Weimarer Republik', in Holl, Wette, eds, *Pazifismus in der Weimarer Republik*. Paderborn, 1981.

Mai, Gunther, ' "Verteidgungskrieg" und "Volkgemeinschaft". Stattliche Selbstbehauotung, nationale Sicherheit und soziale Befreiung in Deutschland in der Zeit des Ersten Weltkrieges', in Michalka, ed., *Der erste Weltkrieg. Wirkung, Wahrnehmung, Analyse*. Munich 1994.

Marks, Sally, 'Black Watch on the Rhine: A Study in Propaganda, Prejudice and Prurience', *European Studies Review*, vol. 13, no. 3 (1983): 297-334.

Matthiesen, Helga, 'Die Gothaer Bürgertum und der Nationalsozialismus', in Heiden, Mai, eds, Heiden, Detlef and Mai, Gunther, eds, *Nationalsozialismus in Thüringen*. Weimar, 1995.

Matthews, William Carl, 'The Economic Origins of the Noskepolitik', *CEH*, vol. 27, no. 1 (1994): 65–86.

Matuschka, Edgar Graf von, and Wohlfeil, Rainer, *Reichswehr und Republik, 1918–1933*. Frankfurt, 1970.

Meier-Welcker, Hans, 'Die Stellung des Chefs der Heeresleitung in den Anfängen der Republik. Zur Entstehungsgeschichte des Reichswehrministeriums', *VfZ*, vol. 4 (1956): 145–60.

_____ *Seeckt*. Frankfurt, 1967.

_____ 'Der Weg zum Offizier im Reichsheer der Weimarer Republik', *MgM*, vol. 19, no. 1 (1976): 147–80.

Messerschmidt, Manfred, 'The *Wehrmacht* and the Volksgemeinschaft', *JCH*, 18, 4 (1983): 719–44.

Michalka, Wolfgang, ed., *Der erste Weltkrieg. Wirkung, Wahrnehmung, Analyse*. Munich 1994.

Millett, Alan, Murray, Williamson, eds, *Military Innovation in the Interwar Period*. Cambridge, 1996.

Mitchell, Allan, *Revolution in Bavaria, 1918-1919. The Eisner Regime and the Soviet Republic*. Princeton, 1965.

Model, Hansgeorg, *Der deutsche Generalstabsoffizier. Seine Auswahl und Ausbildung in Reichswehr, Wehrmacht und Bundeswehr*. Frankfurt, 1968.

Möllers, Heiner, *Reichswehrminister Otto Gessler. Eine Studie zu "unpolitische" Militärpolitik in der Weimarer Republik*. Frankfurt, 1998.

Mombauer, Annika, *Helmuth von Moltke and the Origins of the First World War*. Cambridge, 2001.

Mommsen, Hans, 'Militär und zivile Militarisierung in Deutschland 1914–1938', in Frevert, ed., *Militär und Gesellschaft im 19. und 20. Jahrhundert*. Stuttgart, 1997.

Mommsen, Wolfgang, *Imperial Germany, 1867–1918. Politics, Culture and Society in an Authoritarian State*, translated by Richard Deveson. London, 1995.

Moncure, John, *Forging the King's Sword. Military Education between Tradition and Modernisation – the Case of the Royal Prussian Cadet Corps, 1871-1918*. New York, 1993.

Mosse, Werner, ed., *Deutsches Judentum in Krieg und Revolution, 1916–1923*. Tübingen, 1971.

Muhleisen, Horst, *Kurt Freiherr von Lersner. Diplomat im Umbruch der Zeiten 1918-1920. Eine Biographie*. Marburg, 1984.

Müller, Christian, 'Anmerkungen zur Entwicklung von Kriegsbild und operativ-strategischem Szenario im preußisch-deutschen Heer vor dem Ersten Weltkrieg', *MgM*, vol. 57, no. 2 (1998): 385–442.

Müller, Klaus-Jürgen and Opitz, Eckart, eds, *Militär und Militarismus in der Weimarer Republik*. Düsseldorf, 1978.

_____ ed., *The Military in Politics and Society in France and Germany in the Twentieth Century*. Oxford, 1995.

_____ 'The Military and Diplomacy in France and Germany in the Inter-war Period', in Müller, ed., *The Military in Politics and Society in France and Germany in the Twentieth Century*. Oxford, 1995.

Mulligan, William, 'Restoring Trust Within the *Reichswehr*: The Case of the *Vertrauensleute*', *War & Society*, vol. 20, no. 2 (2002): 71-90.

_____ 'Civil-Military Relations in the Early Weimar Republic', *HJ*, vol. 45, no. 4 (2002): 819-41.

_____ 'The *Reichswehr*, the Republic and the Primacy of Foreign Policy', *German History*, vol. 21, no. 3 (2003): 275-91: special issue *The Primacy of Foreign Policy in German History*, eds, William Mulligan, Brendan Simms.

Murray, Williamson, 'Strategic Bombing: the British, American and German Experience, 1918-1941', in Millett, Murray, eds, *Military Innovation in the Interwar Period*. Cambridge, 1996.

Neuß, Raimund, *Anmerkungen zu Walter Flex. Die "Idee von 1914" in der deutschen Literatur: ein Fallbeispiel*. Schonfeld, 1992.

Nipperdey, Thomas, *Deutsche Geschichte 1866-1918. Machtstaat vor der Demokratie*, vol. 2. Munich, 1992.

Opitz, Eckart, 'Sozialdemokratie und Militarimus in der Weimarer Republik', in Müller, Opitz, eds, *Militär*.

Orlow, Dietrich, *Weimar Prussia, 1918-1925. The Unlikely Rock of Democracy*. Pittsburgh, 1985.

Otto, Helmut, 'Der Bestand Kriegsgeschichtliche Forschungsanstalt des Heeres im Bundesarchiv', *MgM*, vol 51, no. 2 (1992): 429-41.

Paret, Peter, *Clausewitz and the State*. Oxford, 1976.

_____ ed., *Makers of Modern Strategy. From Machiavelli to the Nuclear Age*. Princeton, 1986.

Paucker, Arnold, *Der jüdische Abwehrkampf gegen Antisemitismus und Nationalsozialismus in den letzten Jahren der Weimarer Republik*, 3rd edn. Hamburg, 1989.

Peukert, Detlev, *The Weimar Republic. The Crisis of Classical Modernity*, translated by Richard Deveson. London, 1991.

Pogge von Strandmann, Hartmut, 'Grossindustrie und Rapallopolitik. Deutsch-Sowjetische Handelsbeziehungen in der Weimarer Republik', *HZ*, vol. 222, no. 2 (1976): 265-341.

Pöhlmann, Markus, *Kriegsgeschichte und Geschichtspolitik: der Erste Weltkrieg. Die amtliche Militärgeschichtsschreibung 1914-1956*. Paderborn, 2002.

_____ 'Von Versailles nach Armageddon: Totalisierungserfahrung und Kriegserwartung in deutschen Militärzeitschriften', in Förster, ed., *An der Schwelle*.

Pommerin, Reiner, *"Sterilisierung der Rheinlandbastarde". Das Schicksal einer farbigen Minderheit*. Düsseldorf, 1979.

Pryce, David, 'The *Reichswehr* and Saxony, 1923: The Decision to Intervene', *CEH*, vol. 10, no. 1 (1977): 112-47.

Pyta, Wolfram, 'Konstitutionelle Demokratie statt monarchische Restauration. Die verfassungspolitische Konzeption Schleichers in der Weimarer Staatskrise', *VfZ*, vol. 47, no. 3 (1999): 417-41.

_____ 'Vorbereitungen für den militärischen Ausnahmezustand unter Papen/Schleicher', *MgM*, vol. 51, no. 2 (1992): 385-428.

Rakenius, Gerhard, *Wilhelm Groener als erster Generalquartiermeister. Die Politik der Obersten Heeresleitung*. Boppard am Rhein, 1977.

Rau, Friedrich, *Personalpolitik in der Reichswehr (200 000 Mann)*. Ph.D. thesis, University of Munich, 1970.

Reichsarchiv, *Der Weltkrieg 1914 bis 1918*, 16 vols. Berlin, 1925–44.

Reimer, K., *Rheinlandfrage und Rheinlandbewegung (1918-1933)*. Frankfurt, 1979.

Rohe, Karl, *Das Reichsbanner Schwarz-Rot-Gold. Ein Beitrag zur Geschichte und Struktur der politischen Kampfverbände zur Zeit der Weimarer Republik*. Düsseldorf, 1966.

Rürup, Reinhard, 'Demokratische Revolution und "dritter Weg": die deutsche Revolution von 1918/19 in der neueren wissenschaftlichen Diskussion', GG, vol. 9 (1983): 278–301.

_____ 'Friedrich Ebert und das Problem der Handlungsspielräume in der deutschen Revolution, 1918/19', in Rudolf König, Hartmut Soell and Hermann Weber, eds, *Friedrich Ebert und seine Zeit. Bilanz und Perspektive der Forschung*. Munich, 1990.

Salewski, Michael, *Entwaffnung und Militärkontrolle in Deutschland 1919-1927*. Munich, 1967.

_____ 'Reichswehr, Staat und Republik', *Geshichtswissenschaft und Unterricht*, no. 5 (1980): 271–88.

Samuels, Martin, *Doctrine and Dogma. German and British Infantry Tactics in the First World War*. New York, London, 1992.

Schattkowsky, Ralph, 'Separation in the Eastern Provinces of the German Reich at the End of the First World War', JCH, vol. 29 (1994): 305–24.

Schildt, Axel, *Militärdiktatur mit Massenbasis? Die Querfrontkonzpetion der Reichswehrführung um General von Schleicher am Ende der Weimarer Republik*. Frankfurt, 1981.

Schmädeke, Jürgen, *Militärische Kommandogewalt und parlamentarische Kontrolle. Zum Problem der Verantwortlichkeit des Reichswehrministers in der Weimarer Republik*. Lübeck, Hamburg, 1966.

Schmidt, Ernst-Heinrich, *Heimatheer und Revolution 1918. Die militärische Gewalte im Heimatgebiet zwischen Oktoberreform und Novemberrevolution*. Stuttgart, 1981.

Schneider, Werner, *Die Deutsche Demokratische Partei in der Weimarer Republik*. Munich, 1978.

Schulz, Gerhard, *Zwischen Krieg und Diktatur. Verfassungspolitik und Reichsreform in der Weimarer Republik*, 2 vols. Berlin, 1987.

Schulze, Hagen, *Freikorps und Republik 1918-1920*. Boppard am Rhein, 1969.

_____ 'Der Oststaat Plan 1919', VfZ, vol. 18, no. 2 (1970): 123–63.

Schwabe, Klaus, *Woodrow Wilson, Revolutionary Germany and Peacemaking, 1918-1919. Missionary Diplomacy and the Realities of Power*, translated by Rita and Robert Kimber. Chapel Hill, 1985.

_____ 'Germany's Peace Aims and International Constraints', in Boemeke, Feldman, Glaser, eds, *Versailles*.

Showalter, Denis, 'Past and Future: The Military Crisis of the Weimar Republic', *War & Society*, vol. 14, no. 1 (1996), 49–72.

_____ 'Plans, Weapons, Doctrines. The Strategic Culture of Interwar Europe', in Chickering, Förster, eds, *Shadows*.

Simms, Brendan, 'The Return of the Primacy of Foreign Policy' *German History*, vol. 21, no. 3 (2003): 275–91: special issue *The primacy of foreign policy in German history*, eds, William Mulligan, Brendan Simms.

Sontheimer, Kurt, *Antidemokratisches Denken in der Weimarer Republik. Die politischen Ideen des deutschen Nationalismus 1918-1933*, 2nd edn, Munich, 1964.

Spires, David, *Image and Reality. The Making of the German Officer, 1921-1933*. Westport, 1984.

Stargardt, Nicholas, *The German Idea of Militarism. Radical and Socialist Critics, 1866-1914*. Cambridge, 1994.

Strachan, Hew, 'War and Society in the 1920s and 1930s', in Chickering, Förster, eds, *Shadows*.

_____ 'From Cabinet War to Total War: The Perspective of Military Strategy, 1861-1918', in Chickering, Förster, eds, *Great War, Total War*.

Sutherland, D. M. G., *France, 1789-1815. Revolution and Counterrevolution*. London, 1985.

Thoß, Bruno, 'Nationale Recht, militärische Führung und Diktaturfrage in Deutschland 1913-1923', *MgM*, 49, no. 2 (1987): 27-76.

Tracey, Donald, 'Der Aufstieg der NSDAP bis 1930', in Heiden, Mai, eds, *Nationalsozialismus*.

Turner, Henry Ashby, 'Continuity in German Foreign Policy? The case of Stresemann', *International History Review*, vol. 1, no. 4 (1979).

Venohr, Wolfgang, *Ludendorff. Legende und Wirklichkeit*. Berlin, Frankfurt, 1993.

Verhey, Jeffrey, *The Spirit of 1914. Militarism, Myth and Mobilization in Germany*. Cambridge, 2000.

Voss, Heinfried, *Das neue Haus der Reichswehr. Militärische Sozialisation im politischen und militärischen Übergang*. St Katherinen, 1992.

Weisbrod, Bernd, 'Violence and Sacrifice: Imagining the Nation in Weimar Germany', in Hans Mommsen, ed., *The Third Reich Between Vision and Reality. New perspectives on German history, 1918-1945*. Oxford, 2001.

Wette, Wolfram, *Gustav Noske. Eine politische Biographie*. Düsseldorf, 1988.

_____ 'Von Kellogg bis Hitler (1928-1933). Die öffentliche Meinung zwischen Kriegsächtung und Kriegsverherrlichung', in Holl, Wette (eds), *Pazifismus*.

_____ ed., *Der Krieg des kleinen Mannes. Eine Militärgeschichte von unten*. Munich, 1992.

_____ 'Militärgeschichte von unten', in Wette, ed., *Krieg des kleinen Mannes*.

Winkler, Heinrich August, *Von der Revolution zur Stabilisierung. Arbeiter und Arbeiterbewegung in der Weimarer Republik, 1918-1924*. Berlin, 1984.

_____ 'Die Revolution von 1918/19 und das Problem der Kontinuität in der deutschen Geschichte', *HZ*, 250 (1990), 303-19.

_____ *Weimar 1918-1933. Die Geschichte der ersten deutschen Demokratie*. Munich, 1993.

_____ ed., *Die deutsche Staatskrise 1930-1933. Handlungsspielräume und Alternativen*. Munich, 1992.

Wheeler-Bennett, John, *The Nemesis of Power. The German Army in Politics, 1918-1945*. London, 1961.

Wright, Jonathan, *Gustav Stresemann. Weimar's Greatest Statesman*. Oxford, 2002.

Zeidler, Manfred, *Reichswehr und Rote Armee 1920–1933. Wege und Stationen einer ungewöhnlichen Zusammenarbeit*. Munich, 1993.

Zimmermann, Wilhelm, *Die Wehrpolitik der Zentrumpartei in der Weimarer Republik*. Frankfurt, 1994.

INDEX